The Disaffected

EARLY AMERICAN STUDIES

Series editors:
Daniel K. Richter, Kathleen M. Brown,
Max Cavitch, and David Waldstreicher

Exploring neglected aspects of our colonial, revolutionary, and early national history and culture, Early American Studies reinterprets familiar themes and events in fresh ways. Interdisciplinary in character, and with a special emphasis on the period from about 1600 to 1850, the series is published in partnership with the McNeil Center for Early American Studies.

A complete list of books in the series
is available from the publisher.

The
DISAFFECTED

Britain's Occupation of Philadelphia
During the American Revolution

Aaron Sullivan

PENN

UNIVERSITY OF PENNSYLVANIA PRESS

PHILADELPHIA

Publication of this volume was aided by the
C. Dallett Hemphill Publication Fund.

Copyright © 2019 University of Pennsylvania Press

All rights reserved. Except for brief quotations used
for purposes of review or scholarly citation, none of this
book may be reproduced in any form by any means without
written permission from the publisher.

Published by
University of Pennsylvania Press
Philadelphia, Pennsylvania 19104-4112
www.upenn.edu/pennpress

Printed in the United States of America
on acid-free paper

1 3 5 7 9 10 8 6 4 2

Library of Congress Cataloging-in-Publication Data

Names: Sullivan, Aaron, author.
Title: The disaffected: Britain's occupation of Philadelphia during the American Revolution / Aaron Sullivan.
Other titles: Early American studies.
Description: 1st edition. | Philadelphia: University of Pennsylvania Press, [2019] | Series: Early American studies | Includes bibliographical references and index.
Identifiers: LCCN 2018045832 | ISBN 9780812251265 (hardcover)
Subjects: LCSH: Philadelphia (Pa.)—History—Revolution, 1775–1783. | Philadelphia (Pa.)—History—Revolution, 1775–1783—Conscientious objectors. | Philadelphia Campaign, 1777–1778. | United States—History—Revolution, 1775–1783—Social aspects. | United States—Politics and government—1775–1783.
Classification: LCC E263.P4 S85 2019 | DDC 974.8/1103—dc23
LC record available at https://lccn.loc.gov/2018045832

CONTENTS

Introduction	1
Chapter 1. Consent	19
INTERLUDE. The Brothers Allen	45
Chapter 2. Invasion	50
INTERLUDE. The Road to Virginia	76
Chapter 3. Siege	83
INTERLUDE. Crossing the Lines	119
Chapter 4. Occupation	124
INTERLUDE. Elizabeth Drinker Goes to Washington	165
Chapter 5. Evacuation	172
INTERLUDE. Change and Continuity	193
Chapter 6. Aftermath	199
Epilogue	223
Notes	231

Bibliography 271

Index 285

Acknowledgments 295

INTRODUCTION

> No one can simultaneously serve two masters who are opposed to each other. Anyone who adheres to one party will be hated and persecuted by the other. Anyone who tries to remain neutral and keep on terms with neither or both parties will be oppressed and harassed by both sides when the controversy is pushed so far that proposals of peace are rejected and the matter is to be decided by resort to arms.
> —Henry Melchoir Muhlenberg, November 24, 1777

Elizabeth and Henry Drinker of Philadelphia were no friends of the American Revolution. Yet neither were they its enemies. They neither took up arms against the Revolutionaries nor raised regiments of Loyalists; they were not outspoken champions of King George III or Parliament, nor did they conspire to overthrow the independent governments of Pennsylvania and the United States. A merchant family, the Drinkers were Quakers and pacifists; they shunned commitments to either side in the struggle and strove to pass through the storm of war uninvolved and unscathed. They failed. In 1777 the war came to Philadelphia when the city was taken and occupied by the British army. Elizabeth faced that army, in the streets and in her own home, alone, because before the British came for Philadelphia, the American Revolution came for Henry Drinker.

They arrived on September 2, while it was still morning, and moved systematically through the city and suburbs of Philadelphia. Agents of Pennsylvania's new Supreme Executive Council, they carried with them a long list containing the names of prominent men who, very soon, would be surprised to learn that they had been declared enemies of the state. Those on the list were to be arrested or detained, their papers and effects searched and seized. In a reversal of standard practice, it was hoped that the searches would provide evidence to retroactively justify the arrests. Surprise was essential; the council's agents, some two dozen men led by David Rittenhouse and Colonel William Bradford, divided themselves into smaller groups to reach their targets more speedily and directed their first moves with care. An early priority was John Hunt, a Quaker merchant who lived in Germantown, some five miles from the city, and so might successfully escape if word of the arrests reached him before the council's deputies. Leaders and record keepers, those like John Pemberton and Samuel Emlen, were also among the first to be confronted, lest they attempt to hide or destroy the evidence which, it was hoped, would vindicate the day's actions.

Some of the targets went peacefully, submitting quietly to the alleged authority of the Supreme Executive Council and those sent to carry out its orders. Others took this moment to pledge their allegiance to the Revolutionary governments and swore to keep themselves under house arrest until summoned or released by order of the council. If they were also, in the eyes of the council, "men of reputation" and promised to never again speak or write anything "inimical" to the new regime, they were allowed to remain free, though their property was still subject to search and their papers liable to be seized. Few on the list, however, felt such complete loyalty (or humility) toward the newly created, highly contested, and as yet untried independent governments of the United States. The council's men soon met resistance, though not the kind one often associates with Revolutionary wars; after all, most of the men on the list were pacifists.

Three of the council's deputies came to arrest John Pemberton and search his papers. Pemberton, a Quaker merchant in his fifties, explained that he had never done anything harmful to his country and that, indeed, his well-known religious beliefs forbade any violent or treasonous acts. Appealing to their sense of justice, he pointed out that he had been accused of no crime, that no judge had issued a warrant for his arrest, and that the council had sent them to carry out an act of oppression. The deputies squirmed and confessed "that it was very disagreeable to them to execute such orders" but that the decision was not theirs to make, prompting Pemberton's wife to remind them that Pilate had similarly attempted to excuse his involvement in Christ's crucifixion. When the council's men attempted to take Pemberton by force, he wrapped his old hands around his sturdy wooden chair and refused to be moved. In the end, a band of soldiers were called in to bodily lift the elderly Quaker, carry him out the door, and escort him to confinement in the Masonic lodge. The deputies later returned to search the house and, since Pemberton would not voluntarily surrender the keys, smashed their way into his locked desk. They came away with minutes from Quaker meetings, several documents regarding the manumission of slaves, and no evidence whatsoever that Pemberton was a threat to the country.

Pemberton was not alone in protesting the legality of the council's actions. More than one target on the list demanded to see a formal warrant for their arrest and scoffed at the suggestion that orders from the Supreme Executive Council were a sufficient substitute. Some, like Thomas Fisher, nonetheless eventually yielded to their demands, preferring to go quietly rather than have their homes invaded by soldiers. Others, like John Hunt, flatly refused to obey what they considered illegal orders. Like Pemberton, Hunt would not be moved unless physically forced out. The council's agents had no choice but to return the following day with more manpower; contrary to their concerns, Hunt made no attempt to flee.

It was shortly before noon when Colonel Bradford and two of his deputies came to the home of Henry and Elizabeth Drinker at 110 North Front Street. It was an impressive residence, two stories with a forty-foot front along one of Philadelphia's major thoroughfares, financed by Henry's success as shipper and importer in the firm James & Drinker. From the upstairs windows the Drinkers could watch the ships docking along the Delaware, their livelihood in motion. Behind the house, reaching back along Drinker's Alley, was the garden. Though crowded by stables, outhouse, and well, the garden was spacious enough to offer what Elizabeth called "room enough in the City, and such elegant room"; in the spring flowering trees draped the space in red and white blossoms and in the summer they offered the family blessed shade without the stifling stillness that came from being indoors.

That day, however, the Drinker home was a place of sickness. The youngest son, named after his father, had been severely ill for two weeks past. "Our dear little Henry," as Elizabeth called him, was plagued constantly by fevers, worms infested his stool and vomit, and he was at times too weak to even sit up without assistance. The eight-year-old's health consumed his mother's attention; Elizabeth and Henry had already lost three children.

Little Henry's father was also unwell. Feeling unfit to leave and attend religious services, the elder Henry remained home and, late in the morning, settled in the front parlor to attempt some paperwork. He was there when the council's men came for him. Like so many others, the Drinkers protested the arrest. Yet Henry's poor condition, combined perhaps with the severe illness of his son, spared him from being taken that day. Seeing that he would be physically unable to flee even if he desired to, the men left the Drinkers to ponder their fate throughout the night. As Elizabeth recorded in her diary, they returned at nine the next morning "and took my Henry to the [Masonic] lodge—in an illegal, unprecedented manner."

In the days that followed, Henry Drinker and the other prisoners would repeatedly petition the new government of Pennsylvania, the Continental Congress, and the courts, demanding to know why the nation that had declared liberty an inalienable right had arrested and imprisoned them. From the council and Congress they received only silence. After two weeks of imprisonment, the chief justice of Pennsylvania issued a writ of habeas corpus, demanding that the men either be charged with a crime or else released; the Revolutionary soldiers guarding them ignored the order. Two days later, the members of the Supreme Executive Council formally granted themselves the authority to imprison anyone who they suspected, for any reason, of attempting to subvert their position; the authority was granted retroactively, thus legitimizing the earlier arrests. Furthermore, in an open break with centuries of legal tradition, the government declared that such imprisonment was immune from any interference or challenge by any judicial authority, including writs of habeas corpus. Finally, the council explicitly declared itself "fully and absolutely indemnified" against any legal or civil actions brought against them with respect to such arrests.[1] Shortly thereafter the prisoners were ordered out of the state altogether, exiled to live in Virginia. There they would remain, unable to tend to their families, friends, or businesses even as Philadelphia, their home, became the epicenter of a revolutionary war. Of the twenty men banished to Virginia, two would never return, dying in exile. None of them would ever be charged with a crime or given a trial.[2]

What danger did Henry Drinker and his fellows represent? They were not threats to the American cause, at least not in the traditional sense. They had not taken up arms against the new nation, nor were they ever likely to do so. Some, it's true, were Loyalists at heart and others had been criticized for not supporting independence with sufficient vigor, but it's surprising that such offenses of opinion would warrant banishment without trial. Though the US Constitution and its amendments were yet to be written, Pennsylvania's own constitution, adopted in 1776, declared that the people had the right "to hold themselves, their houses, papers, and possessions free from search and seizure," "to freedom of speech, and of writing, and publishing their sentiments," and to "a speedy public trial, by an impartial jury of the country." What would make a new nation, dedicated to the ideals of liberty, abandon such principles in order to arrest and exile these men? And why did this act of tyranny take place in the summer of 1777, two years after the War for Independence began?

The pages that follow attempt to answer both those questions, and others, by exploring the great crisis that befell the Delaware Valley in the midst of the Revolution: the British occupation of Philadelphia. This is a story about what happened when the redcoats came to Pennsylvania, about the terrible and sometimes tyrannical steps the Patriots took to secure the loyalty of the people, about the military occupation of America's first capital, about the Continental siege led by George Washington's army, and about the many Americans who consequently found themselves caught between the lines, both literally and figuratively. It is a story that questions old assumptions about American loyalties, explores the darker facets of the Patriots' ideology, and challenges traditional narratives of when and how the Revolution was won. It rests on the premise that the most revealing moments for a people, a movement, or a revolution are those of transition and insecurity; that desperate times lead to measures which are not only desperate but that serve to expose the true hearts of leaders and governments.

The occupation of Philadelphia was neither unprecedented nor incomparable; all of America's largest ports, Boston, New York, Newport, Philadelphia, Charleston, and Savannah were at some point occupied by the British military. Though the Revolution was different in each colony and changed as the war progressed, it was nonetheless bound together over space and time by common leaders, goals, and beliefs. Yet, though it speaks to the meaning of the Revolution across the colonies and across the years, my story is still primarily of a specific people, a peculiar time, and a particular place. Each merits individual introduction before we begin.

A Persecuted People

This book is less about the lives and thoughts of individual persons than about the existence and experiences of an entire group of people: a people who were pursued, pressured, and at times persecuted, not because they chose the wrong side in the Revolution, but because they tried *not* to choose a side at all. Through their varied, sometimes conflicting, perspectives we can see how the British occupation and the ever-shifting nature of the Revolution affected the people of the Delaware Valley.

Perhaps no single individual is better suited to represent the story of the occupation than Elizabeth Sandwith Drinker. On the eve of the occupation the Patriots took her husband from her; she would spend the months that followed trying to get him back. As the occupation unfolded she petitioned the generals of Great Britain and America, and even shared dinner with George Washington himself. She would see her friends divided, as some embraced and others fled the coming of King George's army. Her home would be subject to an occupation all its own when the British forced residents to make room for soldiers in their own houses. The officer who slept at the Drinker residence would disrupt her life, arouse the suspicions of her exiled husband, protect her from the depravations of his own army, and in time become her friend. The fate of American independence rarely seemed important to Elizabeth one way or the other, and she did her best to avoid taking sides in the dispute. Foremost in her mind was the security and well-being of her family, her home, and her neighbors.

Elizabeth Drinker was neither a Patriot nor a Loyalist. She was one of the many Americans who stood apart from and outside those two warring camps. It is these people who are truly the central character of this book; it is their story that needs to be told. There has never been a shortage of historical works on the lives of American Revolutionaries; the victorious Patriots began writing them almost at once. More recently, Revolutionary historians have looked across the lines to seriously consider the experiences of the American Loyalists.[3] Yet it would be a mistake to imagine that these categories encompassed all Americans or all American political sentiment, for both presume *some* strongly felt allegiance to one side or the other, some *meaningful* affection for the empire or independence. In the pages that follow, I would like us to consider the large and ever-shifting mass of people who were not strongly aligned with either side, a people that historians often still struggle to describe, that the British misunderstood, and that the Revolutionaries themselves preferred to overlook.[4]

Some of these people, like the Drinkers, were pacifists, but many more became or remained disengaged from the Revolutionary conflict as a matter of pragmatism, not principle. They have been called "the great middle group of Americans . . . who were dubious, afraid, uncertain, indecisive, many of whom felt that there was nothing at stake that could justify involving themselves and their families in extreme hazard and suffering."[5] Persistently disinterested in or opposed to involvement with imperial politics and committed to separate goals, they quietly pursued their own livelihoods to the best of their ability amid the turmoil, helping or hurting either side more incidentally than intentionally, and hoping to come through the Revolutionary storm with as little harm and as much profit as possible, whichever side eventually proved triumphant. They would yield, but not rally to, whoever held power over them. When no party clearly held the reins of authority, they looked to their own interests by whatever means were available. Both the Revolutionaries and the British referred to this diverse group as "the disaffected," perceiving correctly that their defining feature was less *loyalty to* than a *lack of support or affection for* either party in the dispute. If we assume that all Americans must be classified as either "Patriots" or "Loyalists," we risk mischaracterizing these people as fickle, opportunistic, apathetic, or even treasonous. But if we can recognize them as the disaffected, a people without any strong political attachments to betray, their actions might yet appear to be rational and consistent.[6]

Disaffection existed in a variety of forms and arose from numerous causes. Among Americans who were aware of and engaged with colonial politics, a group that expanded rapidly in the third quarter of the eighteenth century, there was nearly universal disapproval of the new taxes and regulations imposed by Britain in the 1760s and early 1770s. Differences of opinion existed as to the severity of the threat and the proper colonial response to it, but in general Americans of various stripes began to look across the Atlantic with a more wary and less trusting gaze. The colonists' long-standing attachment to the British monarch, already strained, was stretched to the breaking point by the harsh imperial crackdown on Massachusetts following the Boston Tea Party and by the bloodshed at Lexington. Horrified by this seemingly unabashed imposition of tyranny, many Americans were pushed into an ill-defined and loosely connected resistance. Throughout the colonies they assembled into committees; in Philadelphia they convened a Continental Congress; in New England they formed an army.[7]

Yet as the resistance to parliamentary overreach expanded in unanticipated ways after 1774, an increasingly large number of Americans found it unpalatable, particularly once the goal of securing the British constitutional liberties of American subjects was subsumed by the pursuit of independence. Driven by negative personal experiences with radical Revolutionaries, economic conflicts with the Revolutionary program, political and ideological disagreements with the ever-evolving Revolutionary agenda, attempts to preserve or undermine social and economic hierarchies, or some combination of these, they distanced themselves from the movement. In the end, some would conclude that the opposition was no more desirable, or just as terrible, as their oppressive monarch. "I love the cause of liberty," wrote James Allen in 1776, "but cannot heartily join in the prosecution of measures totally foreign to the original plan of Resistance."[8] Rather than pushing men and women *back* toward a greater affection for the empire, such pressures pushed them *out*, away from both loyalism and rebellion, and *down*, into a seclusion and silence that came naturally to those who could find no cause to rally around. Though much of his family embraced the Loyalist cause and sought protection from the British military, Allen retreated to his country home where he and his acquaintances endeavored to "banish Politics" from their lives and conversations.[9]

Disaffected individuals may be among the most difficult Revolutionary figures to discover. Some, like many Quakers, explicitly and defiantly made their disaffection known, but others took a more pragmatic approach. It was in their interest to present themselves as agreeable, if not avid, supporters of whatever party was in power. Outside of personal correspondence and journals, they rarely risked political remarks that might garner the ire of whatever force then dominated their region. Even within such private writings, those who were most disengaged from the ongoing political struggle were, by definition, least likely to spend their time commenting on it. Quiet acquiescence was often the surest path through the storm. Thus, it is when that path was closed to them or when the tides of power turned, and they were forced to adapt their strategies to pacify a new ruling authority, that we can most clearly see through the protective web of compliance such individuals spun about themselves. Such was the case during the British occupation of Philadelphia.

A Peculiar Time

In 1815, John Adams famously wrote to Thomas Jefferson that the American War for Independence "was no part of the Revolution; it was only an effect and consequence of it." The real Revolution, Adams claimed, "was in the minds of the people" and it took place "in the course of fifteen years before a drop of blood was shed at Lexington."[10] It should not surprise us that Adams, ever the statesman but never a soldier, should downplay the importance of the war in his account of the Revolution, or that, three decades after that conflict ended, he began to imagine that "the minds of the people" were all united behind his Revolutionary cause before the *bodies* of the people were made to bleed and die for it on the battlefield. Yet no careful investigation of the period can long sustain that hopeful narrative.

The fifteen years between the succession of George III in 1760 and the shot fired at Lexington in 1775 did, indeed, lead many Americans to change their minds about the nature of government and liberty in dramatic, revolutionary, ways. But their minds continued to change as fighting broke out in New England and spread south across the continent. As others have noted, war changes society; the act of fighting on the battlefield affects who and what a soldier is willing to fight for, the process of governing a nation in wartime changes the nature of government, and old allegiances tried by fire sometimes crack and give rise to new loyalties.[11]

The story of the occupation of Philadelphia takes place in the midst of war and it is a story of people and societies changing the way they perceive and interact with the Revolutionary world. Over the course of the occupation men of great ideals would come to sacrifice those lofty virtues, sometimes for victory, sometimes for peace; common men and women, Loyalist and Patriot alike, would lose heart and forsake their allegiances, sometimes in the face of defeat but just as often upon their side achieving success; still others would radicalize and expand their visions, transforming a struggle to preserve old freedoms into an attempt to create a new, unprecedented political order.

It is in times like these, in the midst of war, that we are most likely to recognize the disaffected and the ways in which they changed the Revolution. It was during the war that Revolutionary authorities were most likely to embrace desperate measures in the quest to secure their legitimacy and control. Mounting demands for increasingly explicit expressions of consent for the Revolutionary cause and active involvement in the struggle could separate the committed Patriots from those who were merely hoping to be left alone. The movement and proximity of military forces could also reveal hitherto hidden dissent and disaffection by stripping the ruling authority of its monopoly on coercive force. Though in some instances the coming of the British army sparked a new level of Revolutionary fervor in the hearts of the colonists, in others the arrival of imperial forces suddenly sapped the Patriots of their strength and manpower as those who were less than fully committed, or served only because they feared retribution from the Revolutionary authorities, took the opportunity to abandon the cause and return home.

The war also created situations in which observers from starkly divergent political perspectives, Loyalist and Patriot civilians, British and Continental officers, were all attempting to determine and describe the loyalties of the same regions and populations. Though few individuals would have straightforwardly declared themselves disaffected from the conflict, the combined testimony of these multiple observers reveals the extent of disinterest and disengagement that often emerged between the lines. That both sides simultaneously denounced the same populations for their apathy, enmity, selfishness, and refusal to participate is a strong indicator that the people in question were neither the Loyalists the Revolutionaries accused them of being nor the rebels the British took them for, but rather a category unto themselves, wearied by and withdrawn from the imperial conflict.

Finding the disaffected in the war years also highlights some important and often overlooked consequences of Revolutionary ideology. Leading Patriots subscribed to a republican conception of politics which envisioned the nation's people, set in opposition to its ruling elite, as an essentially homogeneous body whose interests were all united. The united people, and consequently the leaders to whom they delegated their authority, were seen as incapable of tyranny for, as John Adams put it, "a democratical despotism is a contradiction in terms." Sacrifice for the sake of the common good was deemed the essence of virtue; opposition to the acts of the people's representatives was fundamentally unacceptable and unprotected. These underlying principles combined to generate a severe and at times brutal response, not only to blatant opposition and loyalism, but to disaffection as well. They also lay the groundwork for making participation in the Revolution mandatory. The belief that the will of this supposedly united and homogeneous people was the only legitimate basis of government encouraged the Revolutionary leadership to do whatever was necessary to secure expressions of popular consent for their actions. It is in the dangerous years of the war, when the Revolutionaries faced their greatest insecurities, that we can see, through the eyes of dissenters and the disaffected alike, the lengths to which the Patriots would go to extract the popular support that legitimized their Revolution and the ways in which a belief in government by the will of the people could, in tragic irony, lead to terrible acts of oppression.[12]

The redcoats came to Philadelphia two years after the war broke out in New England. They stayed only nine months before retreating back to their stronghold at New York City. Yet, though it was relatively brief in comparison to the prolonged occupation of New York, the British occupation of Philadelphia spanned the turning point in the American War for Independence and in the war for the hearts and minds of many Americans. When the redcoats came to Philadelphia the Revolutionaries stood alone against the British Empire. With only a few, albeit crucial, exceptions, their armies had been consistently outmaneuvered and outfought on the battlefield. It often seemed that only the apathy, or perhaps the sympathy, of Britain's commanding general saved the Revolutionary forces from total annihilation. A new invasion was already sweeping south from Canada toward Albany, threatening to isolate New England from the rest of the nation. Boston remained a tattered shadow of its former glory as a port, New York was firmly in British hands, and now America's de facto capital and largest city, the seat of the Congress and birthplace of independence, had fallen despite a committed effort to defend it. A year later, the change was dramatic. Great Britain was now locked in a war against its most feared and hated rival, France, severely weakening its ability to project force in America. The Patriots had won an unparalleled victory at Saratoga, forcing the surrender of an entire British army, severely shaking public sentiment in Britain and bolstering the flagging spirits of Revolutionary Americans. And finally, without the Patriots firing a shot, the king's army had abandoned Philadelphia, never to return, a move which immediately and deeply disillusioned Loyalists and British officers alike.

The occupation was a remarkable occurrence, not only for *when* but for *what* it was. The term "occupation" is one we should use cautiously, particularly in light of the many and varied instances of occupation that the United States has experienced since the beginning of the twenty-first century.[13] "Occupation," in its modern sense, is military control by a foreign power without claims of sovereignty. It is, consequently, distinct from both conquest, wherein a foreign power declares itself to be sovereign over the newly controlled territory, and martial law, wherein the controlling military presence is domestic.[14] This definition can be applied fairly comfortably to the United States' recent military occupations in the Middle East but immediately presents problems when applied to the American Revolution. Identifying the British as "occupiers" subtly implies that their role in the Revolution should be viewed as that of *foreign* invaders, that Great Britain possessed no sovereign right to the territory its armies controlled, and that the presence and control of those armies could not (or should not) have brought about a change in allegiance for the "occupied" territory and populace. While this perspective would certainly have suited the ardent Revolutionaries, it would not have reflected the sentiments of the British, many Americans, or, before 1778, the other European powers.[15] Nevertheless, to the modern reader the language of occupation carries with it a sense of the many moral and practical difficulties that are unavoidable when an unfamiliar army attempts to exercise control over an ambivalent and at times hostile population. This connotation *is* appropriate to 1777; for that reason, and in the absence of a less cumbersome alternative, I use the language of occupation despite its technical demerits. We should strive to remember, however, that for many Philadelphians the British regulars in their midst were hardly more foreign than the American soldiers from New England.

A Particular Place

The Philadelphia of the 1770s would have been at once startlingly alien and curiously familiar to a resident of the modern city. Philadelphia was, by the standards of its time, no frontier village but a true metropolis of the empire; only Dublin, Edinburgh, and London were larger. A tourist out for an evening stroll could meander along broad, lamplit streets on paved sidewalks. A modern map would be remarkably useful in navigating the Revolutionary city, so long as one remained in the "historic district." Perhaps more than any other major eighteenth-century port, Philadelphia has retained its basic layout, with numbered streets running north to south crossing perpendicular streets named, often, for trees.

For example, to reach the old State House from the Drinker residence, you might head south down Front Street for half a block before cutting west through Elfreth's Alley to Second, then turning south again. At the first intersection you see Betsy Ross's house off to the right down Arch Street, but continue on south for two more blocks, past the high steeple of Christ Church, to Chestnut. Resist the urge to continue on to the City Tavern, now visible at the next intersection, and follow Chestnut west for three and a half blocks, past the entrance to Benjamin Franklin's place on your right, and you'll have arrived. These directions apply as well today as they did in 1776, and while Drinker's house and fine garden are, regrettably, no more, the other landmarks are still present.

Though the similarities are striking, the differences between the modern and Revolutionary cities are, of course, almost beyond counting. The sidewalks were paved; the streets, generally, were not. The buildings were shorter and quite different in style. The smell of mud, dung, human waste, and smoke, among other things, would have been immediately apparent and difficult to forget. And while some street directions carry over from century to century, in the Revolutionary city one could not walk in any one direction for an extended period of time without finding oneself in the country. Though among the largest cities in the empire, Philadelphia in 1770 extended only eight blocks west from the Delaware and, even generously including Northern Liberties and Southwark, ran just fourteen blocks north-to-south, from Callowhill to Christian streets. Beyond those limits the cityscape gave way to fields and farmland, small groups of trees, and the occasional country house. Logan Square, the Philadelphia Museum of Art, City Hall, Thirtieth Street Station, Rittenhouse Square, and the modern campuses of Drexel and the University of Pennsylvania all sit on land far outside the bounds of Benjamin Franklin's Philadelphia.

Perhaps an even more intriguing difference between Franklin's city and our own lies in their responses to the Revolution itself. Modern Philadelphia is striking for its celebration of the event. Tourists flock to see Independence Hall, the Liberty Bell, the National Constitution Center,

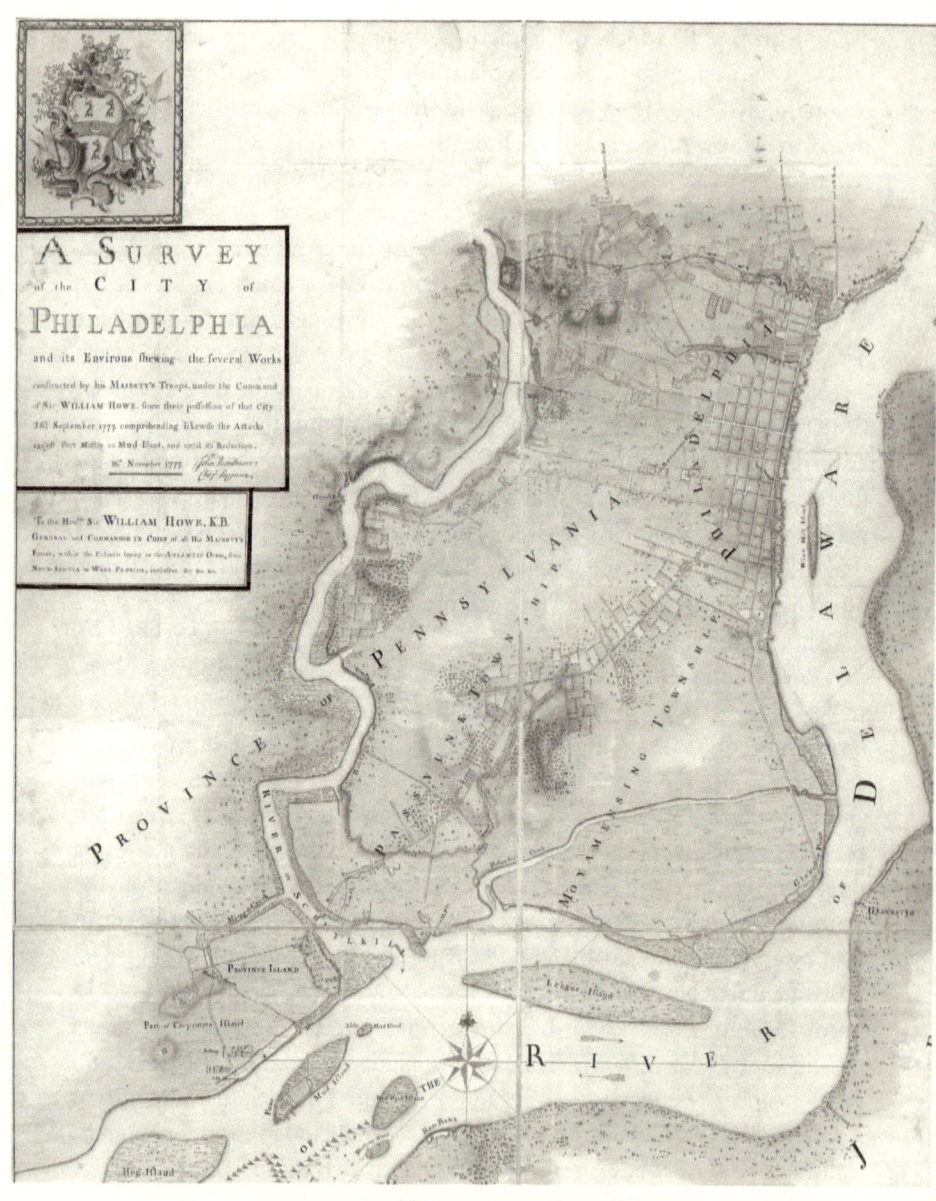

FIGURE 1. Philadelphia in 1777. Detail from Pierre Nicole and John Montrésor, *A survey of the city of Philadelphia and its environs shewing the several works constructed by His Majesty's troops, under the command of Sir William Howe, since their possession of that city 26th. September, comprehending likewise the attacks against Fort Mifflin on Mud Island, and until it's reduction, 16th November* (s.n., 1777). Library of Congress, Geography and Map Division.

Carpenter's Hall, the Betsy Ross House, the Declaration House, and the Tomb of the Unknown Revolutionary War Soldier in Washington Square. Flags at these historic sites have thirteen stars as often as fifty, and in the summer an observant bystander can generally spy several Continental soldiers telling stories about the Revolution, demonstrating pieces of historical equipment, or leading guided tours through the bustling streets of the city's historic district. Today's Philadelphia is staunchly, publicly, and economically committed to celebrating American independence.

Yet such was not the case when the nation was born. Though it housed the seat of the Congress, and thus was the de facto capital of the new nation, Pennsylvania was one of the last colonies to condone a formal separation from Great Britain, and it approached that breach with the greatest reluctance and hesitation, prompting one impatient Philadelphia Patriot to complain that "there is more opposition to independence in this Province than in all the Continent beside."[16] Though many Pennsylvanians raged against the authoritarian or tyrannical acts of the British king and Parliament and demanded that their rights as British subjects be respected, when the Revolution transitioned into an attempt to establish a new, sovereign nation in America and began to restructure existing political and economic hierarchies, it threatened to leave many residents of the Quaker colony behind.

Pennsylvania was a deeply fragmented society. A refuge for diverse settlers and long governed by relatively tolerant Quaker principles, the province sheltered men and women from a wide range of religious, ethnic, and political backgrounds.[17] The colony was simultaneously marked by radicals who fervently, and at times violently, longed for political and economic reform, and strongly influenced by pacifists, like the Drinkers, who abhorred violence and prioritized the maintenance of order and stability. Philadelphia, as America's largest city, was fertile soil for enlightenment thinking, radical political theory, and mass mobilization, yet it was also closely tied to the British networks of commerce, culture, and religion that stretched across the Atlantic. This lack of unity made the process of assembling a powerful and dominant coalition difficult for anyone who hoped to either enflame or suppress a rebellion. In Pennsylvania, America's most radical and democratic elements of Revolutionary change confronted some of the nation's staunchest forces of peace, security, and stability. The confrontation proved to be deeply revealing on both sides.

Until the summer of 1776, Pennsylvania politics were officially controlled by the General Assembly, a staunchly conservative group dominated by the counties around Philadelphia. As the colonies generally moved toward independence, the assembly resolutely ordered Pennsylvania's congressional delegation "to dissent from and utterly reject any Proposition... that may cause, or lead to, a Separation from our Mother Country."[18] When efforts to change the minds of the assemblymen failed, advocates of independence set out to change the assembly itself.

Both the city of Philadelphia and the rural counties of the backcountry had long been underrepresented in government. Believing that these were strongholds of pro-independence sentiment, the radical Committee of the City of Philadelphia demanded that they be allocated additional assembly seats. Under considerable pressure, the assembly acquiesced and created four new seats for Philadelphia and thirteen for the western counties. The May 1, 1776, election to fill these new posts offers a useful, if still imperfect, indication of the electorate's opinion on independence, for the question of changing the government's instructions to the congressional delegation was the foremost electoral issue. The city proved itself to be nearly evenly split on the question; by a small margin, the voters rejected independence and filled three of their four new seats with conservatives who supported the assembly's existing orders. Backcountry voters were somewhat more favorably disposed toward independence, but even there the returns suggest that a large percentage of the populace believed plans to sever the colonies from Great Britain were wrongheaded, or at least premature.[19] James Allen was elected almost unanimously by Northampton County, despite, as he wrote in his diary, "having openly declared my aversion to [the independents'] principles & had one or two disputes at the coffee-house with them." He assumed his seat "determined to oppose them vehemently in Assembly."[20] Northumberland County sent James Potter, Bedford County chose Thomas Smith, and York County overwhelmingly elected James Rankin; all three were moderates or conservatives and profoundly leery of American independence. To the immense frustration of the radicals, the newly enlarged assembly merely reiterated its stance against declaring independence.[21]

Unable to secure enough popular support to sway the General Assembly, those Revolutionaries who supported independence next sought to simply abolish that institution altogether and replace it with a government more amenable to their own objectives. The Patriot committees, supported by the more radical elements of the Continental Congress, declared that Pennsylvanians lacked a "government sufficient to the exigencies of their affairs" and began the process of creating a new, radically democratic, constitution founded on the premise of independence from Britain. Hoping to undercut this insurgency, and distressed by reports that George III intended to employ foreign mercenaries to fight in America, the assembly finally altered its instructions to the congressional delegation. Never positively supporting independence, the body merely withdrew its firm prohibition and freed the delegates to vote as they thought best. Even so, there was never a majority of Pennsylvania delegates in favor of separation from Britain. Only through the abstentions of John Dickinson and Robert Morris did the radical members of the delegation succeed, by a single vote, in throwing Pennsylvania's support behind independence. Such was the hesitation with which the "keystone" was finally added to the new American political edifice.[22]

The months that followed saw the steady decline and eventual collapse of the colony's old government and the deeply controversial, chaotic, and uncertain creation of a new constitution founded, its backers declared, "on the authority of the People only."[23] By November of 1776, when that new government held its first elections for the assembly, a growing number of Pennsylvanians were weary of involvement with Revolutionary politics or had become alienated and disengaged. By some estimates, of an expanded electorate of approximately fifty thousand, only two thousand appeared at the polls and a scant seven hundred voted in Philadelphia.[24] The city of Philadelphia, Philadelphia County, and Bedford County chose legislators whose avowed intent was to inhibit and replace the very Revolutionary government they were elected to participate in. Though too few to control the government, these opposition members were numerous enough to deprive it of a quorum and cripple its activities.[25] When the redcoats came, then, they came to a province and a city that was still divided, still uncertain of its destiny. They faced a new state government that had yet to fully gain control over its people, that still struggled to demonstrate its legitimacy and authority. Though few Pennsylvanians felt great affection for the British Empire, many wondered if the new state government was truly any better.

These, then, are the people, the time, and the setting for the story of the British occupation. It is, I hope, now clear that the Revolution presented here is a messy affair, without the majesty of a straightforward struggle for liberty or even the clean lines of a civil war. It is a Revolution that was not just a "glorious cause" to be won, nor an "unnatural rebellion" to be defeated, but a dangerous and costly calamity that, for so many Americans, simply had to be *endured*. In that way, it is a Revolution not so different from those of our own time: full of people simply hoping to come through the storm with their lives, their families, and their property intact. It is a Revolution drained of much of its romance, and yet still, perhaps for that reason, all the more human.

CHAPTER 1

CONSENT

> That it shall and may be lawful . . . to arrest any person or persons within this commonwealth who shall be suspected from any of his or her acts, writings, speeches, conversations, travels or other behavior, to be disaffected to the community of this or all or any of the United States of America . . . and that no judge or officer of the supreme court or any inferior court within this common wealth shall issue or allow of any writ of habeas corpus or other remedial writ to obstruct the proceedings.
> —"An Act to Empower the Supreme Executive Council,"
> September 6, 1777

Through the 1760s and early 1770s, James Allen, a young Philadelphia lawyer and member of one of Pennsylvania's most influential families, saw himself as a committed friend of American liberty. He bitterly objected to Britain's attempts to control and tax the colonies, policies with which he was intimately familiar. As a lawyer and brother to the attorney general, he repeatedly found himself asked to prosecute fellow Americans for breaking laws he, personally, detested. Though his legal talents often allowed him to secure convictions, the experiences left him "fully persuaded of the oppressive nature of those laws," and in time he began refusing to prosecute cases that seemed particularly unjust. In 1765 Allen became a leader of the Stamp Act protests in Philadelphia and was found at the head of large crowds demanding the resignation of the local stamp distributor. In the wake of Lexington and Concord, he embraced the idea of armed resistance against a king he considered "despotic" and a mother country that was "running fast to slavery." Voluntarily taking up arms in the militia, Allen described himself as part of "a great & glorious cause" which would determine not only the future of America, but of humanity itself. "If we fall," he wrote in 1775, "Liberty no longer continues an inhabitant of this Globe."[1]

Yet as time passed and the nature of the Revolution continued to evolve, Allen became increasingly uncomfortable with its goals, tactics, and leadership. He had little faith in the extralegal Revolutionary committees and deeply distrusted the crowds of middling and lower sort Philadelphians who periodically threatened or punished Loyalists and dissenters. His own legal background and elite upbringing likely exacerbated this distress, as did his growing fear that the "great & glorious cause" was being subverted by something altogether different and less noble. When radicals began to clamor for independence, Allen found himself suddenly caught between two equally distasteful alternatives. The bloodshed in New England and word that King George was sending tens of thousands of new soldiers to America only strengthened his belief that Britain was pursuing a despotic approach toward the colonies. Yet while Allen thought the king was denying key British constitutional liberties to Americans, he also suspected that the American radicals were determined to throw that cherished heritage out entirely, forcibly imposing a new order led by demagogues and rabble-rousers. To Allen's mind, a declaration of independence was not the culmination of the cause he had so proudly taken up but a total betrayal of its values and objectives, a leap from the frying pan of despotism into the fires of anarchy and mob rule. "I love the cause of liberty," he declared in 1776, "but cannot heartily join in the prosecution of measures totally foreign to the original plan of Resistance. The madness of the multitude is but one degree better than submission to the Tea-Act." Disheartened and disillusioned, he abandoned the militia and retreated to his country estate, hoping in vain to avoid participation in the conflict happening on his doorstep, and wondering what had become of his country and the glorious cause of liberty in which he had once believed.[2]

Allen was not alone in disengaging from the struggle. Though Pennsylvania's capital was the birthplace of independence and seat of the Continental Congress, the province's commitment to the Revolutionary cause was questionable at best. Pennsylvanian Revolutionaries, having deemed the established provincial assembly far too conservative for their purposes, were forced to create their own government and constitution in order to take control of the province. Yet the evidence suggests that a great many Pennsylvanians had no strong attachment to that new regime or the cause of independence it represented. The final elections of the old government show an electorate, at best, evenly split on the issue, while the paltry turnout in the first elections of the new government imply widespread disengagement from the populace. The community fissured as those who joined and persisted in the local militias looked with shock and fury on their many neighbors who either felt no need to take up arms or, like Allen, abandoned militia service when the terms of the conflict shifted. As 1776 came to a close, the new state government was still lost in chaos, its legitimacy still hotly debated, its powers neutered by internal opposition and widespread protest. Legal proceedings had ground to a halt as judges and justices of the peace refused to serve under the new constitution. The new state assembly struggled to maintain a quorum as elected representatives refused to convene for any business except reform. The old colonial government, which continued to meet through September 26, 1776, repeatedly blasted the Revolutionaries' regime as illegitimate and tyrannical.[3] When George Washington led his retreating army across the Delaware into the state that December, he wearily confided to his brother "between you and me, I think our Affairs are in a very bad way." Though he had only just escaped destruction at the hands of the redcoats, Washington's foremost concern in that moment was not the British army but the decline in popular support he had discovered among the general populace, including what he described as the "defection" of Pennsylvania.[4]

Yet if the people of Pennsylvania were not the zealous Revolutionaries Washington desperately needed, neither were they the devoted Loyalists some Patriots feared and the British hoped they would be. Those seeking tales of ardent warriors for the king will be disappointed by events in Revolutionary Pennsylvania. By many measures, there were relatively few Loyalists in the state. During and after the war, Americans who had lost property or income because of their loyalty to the king would file claims with Britain, asking to be reimbursed or at least supported by the British government. Only a fraction of Pennsylvanians made such claims, a smaller proportion than in almost any other colony. On a per capita basis, residents of neighboring New York and New Jersey were, respectively, seven and two times more likely to register as claimants. Similarly, of the inhabitants of the many major cities occupied by British forces during the war, Philadelphians were the least likely to register claims with the British government. Even those who did identify as Loyalists in Pennsylvania proved to be subdued in their support for the empire. They were unlikely to actually enlist as soldiers for the king, and many of the Loyalist leaders had been outspoken opponents of Britain's policies in the early days of the resistance. Though some benefited from the economic connections the empire fostered, they brought no great affection for the British government when they joined the redcoats. Historians have since described loyalism in Pennsylvania as "equivocal," "neutral," "subtle," and "weak"; the province was "a stronghold of moderates, pacifists, and neutralists." It was disaffection, not loyalism, which muted their support for the Revolutionary cause.[5]

Yet even if Pennsylvania's disaffection did not create new soldiers for the king, the Patriots of Pennsylvania nonetheless perceived any absence of support as a significant threat to the Revolution. Revolutionary leaders were well aware that the strength of their cause was proportional to the level of support it received from the populace. While their foe could call upon an army of thousands of trained regulars and hire thousands more from other nations, the American Patriots depended entirely on a civilian populace willing to leave their homes, families, and economic pursuits in order to enforce and maintain the new Revolutionary governments and defend independence. Anything, or anyone, that called into question the desirability or utility of such endeavors threatened to rob the movement of its most valuable resource.

Beyond the realm of manpower and materiel, popular apathy and disaffection were also seen as threatening the ideological underpinnings of the Patriots' cause. The republican ideas on which the Revolution was founded held that government existed solely to pursue the common good and was legitimized to the extent that it received the common consent of the people to do so on their behalf. The Patriots had condemned the British government's policies as illegitimate because the American colonists did not truly consent to Parliament's actions; their own governments were thus particularly vulnerable to accusations that they too were imposing acts on the people against their will. Consequently, the nascent independent regimes of America felt a desperate need for the people to positively express consent for their governments. Disaffection, a simple withholding of consent, even if not coupled with active support for the empire, seemed to present a profound threat to the legitimacy of the whole Revolutionary enterprise. At times it would seem even more threatening than outright loyalism. The rare Loyalist who lauded submission to royal authority and took up arms against his neighbors was far easier to demonize and disregard than were the peaceful inhabitants whose inaction and silence on the question of independence implicitly rejected the Patriots' assumed authority.[6] Driven by this need for visible signs of consent and convinced that disaffection represented a significant threat to the common good, as they perceived it, the Patriots pursued various means of forcibly encouraging participation in the Revolution, persecuting dissenters and eventually mandating active expressions of consent.

Consent Expressed

The Pennsylvania Revolutionaries' need for consent and intolerance of opposition is readily apparent in their efforts to limit freedom of expression in the province. Dissenting speech directly challenged the radicals' claim that their new governments represented the will of "the people" of America. Both in the State House and in the street, ardent Patriots came to believe that if the struggle for liberty was to be preserved such voices must be stopped. Through both public pressure and explicit legislation, sometimes subtly and sometimes directly, Pennsylvania's Patriots set out to either convert or silence those who opposed them.

As the primary means of mass communication and key sites of political debate, newspapers were invaluable to the Revolution; Patriots and Loyalists alike strove to control them, amplifying their own influence and giving no place to the arguments of their opponents. In 1774, moderates and conservatives in Philadelphia felt increasingly excluded from the press and struggled to have their stories told. Their difficulty in securing space in the local papers became, itself, an issue they wished to make known. John Drinker, Elizabeth Drinker's brother-in-law, composed a series of "observations" on recent happenings in America, suggesting that elements of the Revolutionary leadership were acting out of self-interest more than concern for the public and asserting that "the freedom of the press here has . . . been interrupted by the illegal menaces and arbitrary frowns of a prevailing party, to the exclusion of an honest, unprejudiced and unawed investigation."[7] As he might have expected, Drinker encountered great difficulty in finding a printer who would publish his remarks. He contrasted the printers' refusal to publish his material against their apparent willingness to reproduce the "scandalous handbills" of radical Revolutionaries, such as the self-described "Committee for Tarring and Feathering," which responded to the Tea Act of 1773 by openly threatening violence against individuals who participated in importing British tea. Such writings had been "publickly exhibited to terrify such as were disposed for the preservation of peace and good order. For such kind of publications," Drinker allowed, "there was, indeed! A freedom of the press."[8] Other writers turned to the papers of New York to carry remarks that would not be printed in Philadelphia. "Veritas" suggested in *Rivington's New-York Gazetteer* "that the presses in Philadelphia are held under an undue influence" while another writer complained that "the Printers [in Philadelphia] were so closely watched, and held in such awe, that not one of them dared to print any piece that appeared to reflect upon the conduct of those sons of violence." "And this," he added sardonically, "is LIBERTY!"[9]

The following year, three new papers opened in Philadelphia to capitalize on the frustration of those who could not make themselves heard. The new diversity was not to last, however. Before the year was out, the conservative-leaning *Pennsylvania Mercury* had been consumed in a fire. The year after, the *Pennsylvania Ledger* was shut down when an anonymous individual accused James Humphries Jr., the printer, of reprinting pro-British articles from Loyalists in New York. The accuser declared that the Pennsylvania Council of Safety would be "very justifiable in silencing a press whose weekly labors manifestly tend to dishearten our troops."[10] Humphries promptly packed up his press and fled the city. Of the three new papers, only the pro-independence *Pennsylvania Evening Post* survived without interruption, due in large part to its printer's skill at conforming himself to whichever party happened to be in power at the time.[11]

An exchange in the *Pennsylvania Gazette* offers unusually clear insight into how advocates of Revolution could, on the one hand, fiercely denounce British impositions on their liberty while, on the other, work to silence those who opposed them. In a cautiously composed letter to the printers of Philadelphia, "An Anxious By-Stander" entreated them "to reflect on the immense importance of an open, and uninfluenced Press . . . to admit a free and fair discussion of subjects, which eventually concern the happiness of millions yet unborn."[12] The author scrupulously avoided any direct accusations of partiality in the press and sheltered his words amid support for Congress and denunciations of the British. In the following issue, one "Philadelphus" responded by assuring the printer, "Your press, and I trust all others in this city, are open to every publication, wrote with decency and truth, and containing no public or private scandal." However, in Philadelphus's view, daring to "censure the proceedings of the late Congress . . . is neither just, decent or politic" and therefore such remarks could and should be suppressed. The justification laid out for this policy deserves careful consideration:

> Unanimity and mutual confidence are allowed to be the only sure basis, on which the fabric of American liberty is to be reared. . . . How can we expect resolutions and associations . . . will be observed, if those, who profess themselves friends to the American cause, studiously endeavor to divest them of all title to our respect or regard? . . . The American cause derived its principal weight and dignity from the late Congress. . . . But let it once be thought that it wants the support and confidence of the people, all its terrors vanish. . . . All authority and government is founded in opinion, more or less—theirs is peculiarly so.[13]

In short, "Philadelphus" argued that unanimity and mutual consent were absolutely necessary for American liberty; dissenting from or disrespecting the acts of the Revolutionary governments weakened that unanimity; to suggest that the Congress lacked the confidence of the people, to fail to place confidence in it yourself, was to threaten the liberty of all Americans. On this basis, then, it was in the defense of the cause of liberty that such dissent and disrespect may be and must be silenced.

This kind of suppression, driven by what John Drinker called "the illegal menaces and arbitrary frowns of a prevailing party," was eventually given the support of law. The convention ostensibly created to draft a new state constitution also took upon itself the task of limiting freedom of expression in Pennsylvania. In September of 1776, an ordinance was passed to muzzle the "evil disposed persons" who "may, by speaking or writing, endeavor to influence the minds of weak or unwary persons, and thereby impede the present virtuous opposition." The convention made it illegal for anyone to "by advisedly speaking or writing, obstruct or oppose, or endeavour so to do, the measures carrying on by the United States of America, for the defence and support of the freedom and independence of the said States." The determination of what sorts of words qualified as attempted obstruction or opposition was left, not to a jury, but to a justice of the peace, who could demand that an individual provide security, "in such sum or sums of money as the said Justice may think necessary," against their future good behavior. Should two justices declare that an individual was "too dangerous, unfriendly, or inimical to the American cause," they could have him or her thrown into jail "for such time as they shall deem proper, not exceeding the duration of the present war with Great Britain."[14] The ordinance thus granted immense power and discretion to justices of the peace, who were in the main men with little or no legal training. Furthermore, since many of the more conservative and moderate justices refused to serve under the new Revolutionary government, those who continued in office or were appointed to fill vacancies tended toward the radical end of the political spectrum. The ordinance did allow appeals to the Council of Safety, but the council itself was composed of justices of the peace, and there was no appeal beyond them. An ill-timed word of dissent could thus condemn one to indefinite imprisonment without the benefit of being heard by a jury or even of a trial.[15]

Pennsylvania's soon-to-be-dissolved colonial assembly, in its final meeting, took this as an opportunity to lecture the Revolutionaries on their own principles. The assembly reminded the convention "that no Freeman can be constitutionally restrained of his Liberty, or be sentenced to any Penalties or Punishment whatsoever, but by the Judgment of his Peers, and a Trial had by a Jury of his Country." It therefore declared that the ordinance punishing dissent was "a dangerous Attack on the Liberties of the good People of Pennsylvania, and Violation of their most sacred Rights and therefore ought not to be considered as obligatory." By this point, however, few Pennsylvanians heeded the words of the increasingly impotent assembly, least of all the radical Revolutionaries who were working to replace it.[16]

Dissenters feared persecution, not only from the Revolutionary governments, but also at the hands of pro-independence neighbors, many of whom had come to believe that the preservation of American liberty depended on unanimity of consent, that dissent was the same as opposition, and that opposition placed one beyond the protections guaranteed to "the people." In November of 1776, more than seventy Philadelphians came together at the Indian Queen Tavern to form an unauthorized and entirely extralegal courtroom for the examination and trial of any fellow citizen who they suspected of being "an Enemy to the liberties of America." Participants accused their neighbors of such high crimes as singing "God Save the King," toasting the British army, and having said that the opposition to Britain was unjustified. Members went forth to collect the accused who were then interviewed by the body as a whole. Those who failed to pacify the crowd or, like Joel Arping, were foolish enough to admit that they "would as leave take up arms on the one side as the other," were seized and confined until they could be seen by the Council of Safety.[17]

One particularly unfortunate victim of this proceeding was Joseph Stansbury. Along with several others, he had been accused of singing "God Save the King" in a tavern. However, by the time he was made to appear before the assembly at the Indian Queen, he had already stood trial before the Council of Safety, been examined, and dismissed. Stansbury explained to the crowd that he had previously been acquitted of any wrongdoing and was even able to produce a certificate to that effect, but neither it nor his continued denials of having sung the British anthem were of any avail; by the end of the night he had been lodged in New Jail. After nearly two weeks of confinement, Stansbury penned a remarkably polite letter to the Council of Safety asking to be released. The following week, still in jail, he wrote a somewhat more perturbed missive, complaining that he had been "cruelly treated in being confined to this Jail without the least shadow of Reason whatever . . . in violation and defiance of the Bill of Rights, and every authentic declaration held up to the People."[18] Three more days would pass before the council finally intervened and ordered Stansbury and four other prisoners released from the jail, but even then they were to be confined to their own homes.

These unofficial tribunals rendered their judgment on members of the lower and middling sort as well as the wealthy. One humble shoemaker was made a great deal more humble when a gathering at the Coffee House "exalted [him] as a spectacle to a great number of reputable citizens" for "vilifying the measures of Congress, the Committee, and the people of New England." Only when he "very humbly and submissively asked and entreated their pardon and forgiveness" was he released.[19] A butcher was similarly made to grovel by a militia company outside the College of Philadelphia "for speaking disrespectfully of their proceedings."[20] Arthur Thomas, a skinner, was accused secondhand of "cursing the congress" but had the good sense to run for it when a crowd appeared to bring him to justice. Unable to find Thomas himself, the mob "wreaked their vengeance on his house," destroying or confiscating his money, furniture, and other property.[21]

This hypervigilance and suspicion on the part of the more radical Revolutionaries could sometimes reach comical heights. On January 9, 1776, Christopher Marshall heard a report from a housekeeper who claimed that a servant boy had told her that he had been told by his sister, a housemaid, that one James Brattle, a servant man to James Duane, was secretly in the employ of William Tryon, British governor of New York. On the basis of this fourth-hand accusation, Marshall immediately launched an investigation. The case seemed to fall apart immediately: the housemaid denied having ever said any such thing about Brattle, Duane dismissed the claim against his servant as ridiculous, and a thorough search of Brattle's room and possessions revealed nothing suspicious. Undeterred, Marshall, now joined by two fellow investigators, tracked down the servant boy, carried him to his sister, the housemaid, and forced her to either support the accusation against Brattle or implicitly accuse her brother of lying to the Revolutionary leadership; she promptly changed her story, assured the gentlemen that her brother was an honest boy, and offered to stand by whatever he had told them. Bolstered by this "confession," Marshall and his fellows again interrogated Brattle, "but all to no purpose" and once more the little committee began a thorough search of his room and effects. At this point, likely seeing the writing on the wall, Brattle disappeared out a back door and ran away. "Thus he escaped," reflected Marshall without any apparent doubt as to Brattle's guilt.[22]

Though it merely turned James Brattle into a fugitive, the Patriots' suppression of dissent and persecution of supposed "Enemies to the liberties of America" often produced behavior the Revolutionaries desired. Much disaffection and dissent faded from view and ceased to threaten the radicals' aspirations of apparent unanimity. Following his own interrogation by the Council of Safety and having heard the fate of other disaffected citizens, James Allen wrote that he had become "afraid to converse with persons here, or write to my friends in Philadelphia; & a small matter, such as a letter intercepted or unguarded word, would plunge me into troubles." He "never knew, how painful it is to be secluded from the free conversation of one's friends" and found it "odd to reflect that I am taking as much pains to be in obscurity, as others are to blaze in the publick Eye & become of importance." Such aching silence on his part achieved the Revolutionaries' goal of isolating him and others who shared his sentiments, rendering their opinions largely irrelevant.[23]

Yet the enforcement of Revolutionary edicts was most successful when it not only silenced opposition but converted opponents into, at least nominal, allies. Such a conversion appears, in its most benign form, in the writings of the Reverend Henry Muhlenberg, who conformed himself to the will of the Revolution in obedience to the biblical admonition that every soul should "be subject to the authority that has power over him," a passage he repeated to his journal and to himself many times after the radicals came to power and he was made to pray for the United States as well as, or instead of, King George.[24] A more explicit and forceful conversion process was used on Robert Owings of Hanover, who had "taken the liberty to speak in an unbecoming manner against the measures now pursuing for the maintaining our invaluable rights and privileges." This was not a liberty the Patriots were willing to allow. Upon being tried and convicted by the York County committee, Owings experienced an immediate and profound change of heart, declaring "his entire disapprobation" of his former conduct. He then "expressed his hearty and unfeigned sorrow" by signing a confession the committee had thoughtfully prepared on his behalf, ostensibly becoming one more citizen demonstrating his consent.[25]

Even as they took action to silence speech and writing which opposed or questioned them, the Patriots of Pennsylvania also began mandating direct, verbal expressions of consent from those who had remained silent. From its inception, the new Revolutionary government created by Pennsylvania radicals was surrounded by a defensive wall of oaths. Unwilling to let self-interest or disaffection sully or confuse the supposedly unified voice of the virtuous people, the Revolutionaries first guaranteed that only those willing to vocally and publicly embrace the cause of liberty, as they saw it, would have a hand in shaping the new constitution. Once that framework was complete, new oaths were deployed in an attempt to protect it from alteration and to prevent dissent from becoming visible within the new legislature. In the end, oaths of allegiance were implemented in order to guarantee that the new government had the vocal consent of the entire community by wringing that consent out of the recalcitrant or, if they persisted in dissenting, effectively nullifying their social identities.

On June 20, 1776, the Provincial Conference, created to outline plans for a state constitutional convention, established an oath renouncing allegiance to the British monarch that was to be taken by all those who wished to vote for convention delegates.[26] The conference went on to stun all but the most avid advocates of revolution by declaring that all delegates to the upcoming convention would also have to submit to a religious test, a requirement almost unprecedented in Pennsylvania and fundamentally antithetical to the colony's long history of religious freedom. The test, which required one to profess belief in a Trinitarian God and the divine inspiration of scripture, was aimed squarely at the moderate Quaker population.[27] Christopher Marshall, a strong supporter of the radicals, was shocked at the widespread outrage that followed. The oath, he remarked, "is highly censured. . . . I strenuously supported it [and] I am blamed, and was buffeted and extremely maltreated by sundry of my friends."[28] Unsurprisingly, the delegates of the constitutional convention, as beneficiaries of these oaths, quickly incorporated them into the framework of government they created. A new religious test was to be required of all elected members of the new legislature before they were seated, and no citizen was to be allowed to vote in the general election unless they swore to uphold the new constitution.[29]

These oaths and tests were meant to both purify the political voice of the people and to silence dissenters by providing no legitimate means of expressing their disapproval. Had the last requirement been enforced, there would have been no way, without breaking one's oath, to cast a ballot for a candidate who meant to overturn and replace the radical constitution. In the event, enforcement was uneven; in a massive town meeting Philadelphians chose to ignore the oath requirements and overwhelmingly elected an entire slate of candidates who opposed the new constitution.[30] These opposition legislators and other dissenters in the government crippled the operation of the new assembly for months but ultimately failed to enact the changes their constituents had hoped for. As the radicals finally secured effective control over their government in the early summer of 1777, they implemented yet another oath requirement for the people of Pennsylvania. Past oaths and tests had been used to secure the political framework the Revolutionaries desired and then to protect it from alteration by dissenters. Now the radicals would use a new oath to demonstrate and guarantee the continued legitimacy of that government and the Revolutionary struggle for independence by forcing the entire adult male population to declare their consent for the new regime.

Facing the fact that "sundry persons have or may yet be induced to withhold their service and allegiance," the newly installed state legislature devised a new oath for the general population. Known as the Test Act, this legislation first required Pennsylvanians to "renounce and refuse all allegiance to George the Third, king of Great Britain, his heirs and successors" and to "be faithful And bear true allegiance to the Commonwealth of Pennsylvania as a free and independent State" and "not at any time, do or cause to be done any matter of thing that will be prejudicial, or injurious to the freedom and independence thereof, as declared by Congress." This was sufficient for a declaration of allegiance; the remainder of the Test entailed a pledge of service. All citizens were to swear to "discover and make known to some one justice of the peace of said State all treasons or traitorous conspiracies which I now know or hereafter shall know to be formed against this or any of the United States of America."[31] In short, all citizens would vow to be informers against their friends, families, neighbors, or strangers.[32]

Previous oaths were theoretically avoidable if one was willing to forgo the privileges of voting or holding office, but now simple disengagement and isolation would provide no protection, for the Revolutionaries needed the people to consent to their Revolution and its structures lest they be made hypocrites and tyrants according to their own republican logic. The Test was to be taken before justices of the peace who would dutifully document which individuals had and had not yet sworn allegiance. Individuals who took the oath were to receive certificates stating as much which could be used to shield them from persecution should their allegiance be challenged in the future.[33] In creating the Test Act, the assembly declared that "allegiance and protection are reciprocal, and those who will not bear the former are not nor ought to be entitled to the benefits of the latter" and so it moved to strip the protections and privileges of citizenship from those who refused to swear allegiance.[34] As the Rev. Muhlenberg observed, anyone who failed to "swear an oath of allegiance and acknowledge the new government as the lawful authority . . . within the appointed time is to forfeit all rights and privileges and protection in the *Republic*."[35] In addition to being stripped of the right to vote or hold office, those who refused the oath were forbidden from serving on juries or suing to recover debts; they could not purchase, sell, or otherwise transfer real estate; and any weapons they possessed were subject to confiscation. Prolonged refusal could result in imprisonment or forced exile. In short, the Test Act was intended to guarantee that "the people" consented to the government's rule by driving committed dissenters into a sort of political, legal, and economic nonexistence.[36]

The Test Act also became the final temptation of Henry Drinker and his fellow prisoners in the summer of 1777. Arrested and imprisoned on the basis of vague accusations of having "evidenced a disposition inimical to the cause of America" and, in unspecified ways, threatening to "subvert the good order and regulations" of the new government, they vainly waited for an opportunity to defend themselves in court. Elizabeth Drinker joined other wives and family members in visiting the prisoners as often as her son's continuing illness allowed. She recorded the rising and falling of her husband's spirits, and her own, as days passed and the prisoners wrote their petitions, undertook periods of stillness and prayer, and considered the limited choices offered by the government. In light of the radicals' earlier efforts to forcibly secure unanimous consent, these choices were unsurprising. As always, the regime's preferred outcome was to have accused dissenters publicly express their support for the Revolution and so the prisoners were first offered the opportunity to embrace the Test Act, to swear true alliance and support to the state that had illegally arrested and imprisoned them. A few accepted this offer, mouthed the prescribed oaths, and were released. Those who would not join "the people" in unified consent were to be cast out from among them. In this case, the severance was not merely social and commercial but became a physical banishment from the state.[37]

Elizabeth's diary makes no mention of her, or any of the family, asking Henry to submit to the Test in exchange for his freedom and he rejected the government's offer. On the evening of September 10, Henry made a surprise appearance at home, having been granted a temporary release for that one night: an act of mercy, perhaps, or an attempt to remind him of what he had to lose by continued dissent. After breakfast the next day the couple parted and Henry dutifully surrendered himself to the authorities and was returned to the Masonic lodge. The remainder of Elizabeth's day soon fell into chaos. About mid-morning Philadelphians became aware of a sound like thunder rolling up from the southeast, the distant echoes of artillery fire. The sounds of war could be heard, intermittently, throughout the rest of the day and rumors soon circulated of warships moving toward the city up the Delaware. As panic slowly spread, Elizabeth returned to the lodge to find Henry and prisoners gone, moved by the state, their whereabouts undisclosed. Working her way back home through the "great Confusion" that filled the streets, she waited until, shortly after dinner, Henry burst through the door to announce that he and the other prisoners were being moved out of the city immediately. Henry was rushed to the lodge where the prisoners were loaded aboard wagons. Elizabeth followed as soon as she could, but finding the area crowded with men and few other women in sight, "bid [her] dearest Husband farewell, and went in great distress." Elizabeth and her daughter sought refuge and sympathy in the Pemberton home as their husband and father was carried into exile.[38]

Consent Enacted

The American Revolutionaries' attempts to mandate consent for their movement went far beyond controlling the people's speech and the public press. Actions, as well as words, were capable of carrying political messages and one of the Revolution's great strengths was that it gave Americans varied and diverse ways to signal their unity and support for the cause. Direct statements of consent at the ballot box or in the form of oaths, pamphlets, and public declarations were, of course, always welcome. But other, more tangible, means of expressing support were also available to most Americans and, to the extent that they involved greater personal sacrifice, were often seen as more sincere than words alone. The boycott and the outright destruction of British goods triggered in response to the Stamp Act, Townshend Duties, Tea Act, and Coercive Acts, created a new political language of commerce and material goods through which colonists could express themselves. A colonial man's or woman's choice of what to buy, to wear, or to drink came to be interpreted as a political statement, as did the origin of such goods. Imported tea and linens were seen as symbolic of the British Empire and acquiescence to its policies while, in a form of conspicuous nonconsumption, wearing homespun garments and drinking beverages brewed from local herbs stood for liberty, American self-sufficiency, and independence. Participation in these movements was available to a wide range of individuals who, due to status, sex, or the social and legal mores of the time, were commonly excluded from traditionally political spheres. The average colonial man and woman might lack the education or talent to compose a political treatise on the illegitimacy of the Townshend Duties, but they could certainly express themselves by refusing to purchase any of the goods that were taxed under those acts or castigating, with varying levels of violence, those who submitted to such taxation. Participation in the boycotts became, as James Madison put it, "the method used among us to distinguish friends from foes." As time passed, that binary distinction became a fundamental, but flawed, feature of Revolutionary ideology.[39]

As with speech so too with commercial choices, the Revolutionary governments in Pennsylvania eventually came to mandate direct expressions of support for the cause and their new republican regimes. In so doing they left no space for those who would have preferred to separate themselves from the conflict or who felt no loyalty toward either side. Where early attempts at persuasion failed, the Patriots deployed other, more coercive, measures in a somewhat paradoxical attempt to forcibly extract voluntary consent from a resistant populace. Notably, because consent, or at least the appearance of consent, was seen to be essential, the economic, social, and physical pressures the Patriots applied to the disaffected were generally designed to do more than merely force compliance. Rather, they were designed to demonstrate that the Revolution was universally embraced by everyone, even the dissenters who were being persecuted by it. The penalties the Revolutionaries inflicted upon those who violated their boycotts and commercial ordinances were thus generally aimed at extracting a public confession from the accused and securing (at least the appearance of) their consent for the Patriot committees and their resolutions.

In extracting these confessions, the Patriots were often less interested in confirming a true change of heart in the accused than in sending a message to the public, and in some cases the words of the confession were penned in advance by the committee; the confessor merely had to sign and publicly read the paper he was handed. Select confessions received an even wider audience when they were published in newspapers or as pamphlets. It was crucial in these performances that the subject not only confess his guilt as a violator of congressional and committee resolutions, but also that he make it clear he accepted his condemnation as just by expressing great personal shame for his misconduct or lauding the rules he had violated as legitimate and desirable. Thus did Alexander Robertson, when apprehended for violations of the Townshend boycotts, confess "To the Publick" that "I am truly sorry for the Part I have acted; declare and promise that I will never again attempt an Act contrary to the true Interest and Resolutions of a People zealous in the Cause of *Virtue* and *Liberty*."[40] So too did Solomon Cowles and his wife come to "voluntarily, in this public manner, utterly disapprove of and condemn" their own conduct in daring to secretly sip tea as being "to the manifest injury of the public interest of British America."[41] Such statements were presented as claims that even those who violated the boycott were actually in agreement with the committees about the "true Interests and Resolutions of the People." They might, for a time, put their own greedy desires above the good of their country, but they did so with shame and full knowledge of their selfishness. The notion that there might have been honest disagreement about the legitimacy or utility of the Revolutionaries' edicts was not entertained.

Consider too the amusing and unusual experiences of Ebenezer Withington, a laborer from Dorchester, Massachusetts, who, shortly after the

Boston Tea Party, discovered an unopened chest of British tea floating in the marshes near Boston. Withington plucked the treasure from the water, had it brought home, and promptly began selling it off in direct contravention of Revolutionary edicts. To their surprise and distress, Boston Patriots learned that the tea they had risked so much to destroy was circulating in Dorchester; an investigation soon traced the illicit commodity back to Withington. Unsurprisingly, Revolutionary committees quickly had the remainder of the tea consigned to the flames and undertook efforts to track down the portions that had already been sold. More remarkable is that, having apprehended Withington, the Patriots of Dorchester declared that his conduct had "proceeded from Inadvertency" and, having published his admission of the same, released him without further inquiry.[42] This explanation, implausible though it was, served the interests of all involved: Withington escaped a harsher punishment and the Revolutionaries could maintain that his defiance was merely the result of ignorance, not true dissent.

Though Philadelphia had no "tea party" to compare with Boston's, the crisis surrounding the Tea Act nonetheless served to demonstrate the power and methods of the Patriots within that city. It also brought the family of Henry and Elizabeth Drinker into direct confrontation with those Revolutionary forces, ensuring that Henry's name would come quickly to mind when the Patriots later made lists of potential enemies to banish from the state. Drinker and his partner, Abel James, had been appointed agents of the British East India Company and charged with the sale and distribution of taxed British tea in Philadelphia. In the autumn of 1773, as the ship *Polly*, laden with company tea, slowly made its way across the Atlantic, Drinker and James faced increasing pressure from extralegal Patriot committees to reject their appointments and promise not to sell the tea when it arrived. Hoping to demonstrate that they were "persons concerned with the Reputation and Peace of the City & who have a thorough regard for the security & preservation of the Civil Rights and true Interests of the Country," the partners offered to have the tea sealed within a warehouse where it would remain safe and unsold until the crisis could be resolved or, failing that, until it could be shipped to some other imperial port.[43]

This failed to satisfy the Revolutionaries, and as pressure mounted against James and Drinker, ominous publications began to appear in the city, threatening in no uncertain terms that "TAR and FEATHERS will be his Portion, who pilots her [the *Polly*] into this Harbour." More warnings were issued toward the *Polly*'s Captain, Samuel Ayres. A self-described "Committee for Tarring and Feathering" first threatened to set fire to the *Polly*, should she come up the river, and concluded by asking Ayres what he thought of "a Halter around your Neck—ten Gallons of liquid Tar decanted on your Pate—with the Feathers of a dozen wild Geese laid over that to enliven your Appearance?" Ayres was encouraged to "fly to the Place from whence you came—fly without Hesitation—without the Formality of a Protest—and above all . . . fly without the wild Geese feathers."[44]

It is unclear whether Drinker personally faced similar threats, but he was undoubtedly aware that any continued resistance on his part would make him the target of this same committee. On December 2, James and Drinker formally declared that they would not land the tea at all or act as agents of the East India Company. The *Polly* never reached the custom house at Philadelphia. Faced with threats from Philadelphia radicals, public protests in the city, and a formal request from the Continental Congress, the *Polly* anchored off Gloucester and, shortly thereafter, set sail for England, her hold still full of tea.[45]

In the statement declining their appointment as agents of the company, James and Drinker claimed they were yielding to "the general Opinion of the People," noting that "no considerable number of the Inhabitants" had spoken out in favor of landing the tea in Philadelphia. They did not, in that publication, address the question of whether the Patriots' widely propagated threats of torture and humiliation had contributed to that silence. By publicly declaring that the Patriots' position reflected the opinion of "the People," Drinker joined the many targets of Revolutionary coercion who not only yielded before threats of violence but found themselves lauding the legitimacy and justice of those who threatened them. This is all the more ironic given that, had "the People" as a whole *truly* been united in opposing the sale and distribution of taxed tea, the Patriots need not have ever bothered turning back the *Polly* or polluting the waters of Boston. Surely a more convincing and less provocative means of demonstrating "the People's" rejection of the Tea Act would have been to simply let the tea sit, unpurchased and rotting, in the warehouses of the company's American agents. The Patriots' ferocious efforts to prevent the tea from ever being brought ashore make sense only if they believed that "the People," given the opportunity, would in fact voluntarily purchase it and so submit to the tax. The perpetrators of the Tea Party in Boston and the Committee for Tarring and Feathering in Philadelphia acted not to enforce the people's choice to reject the taxed tea but to make certain that the majority of the people never had the opportunity to make that choice one way or the other.

Naturally, such strategies proved effective only when their targets, like Drinker and James, could be made to yield under pressure and at least mouth acceptance of the Patriots' position. In the face of intransigent dissenters who could be neither "converted" nor ignored, a different response was called for. Mobs and elements of the militia might attempt to force compliance more directly, but the committees generally preferred a less violent approach that maintained the perception of a fully unified American resistance. If an individual was so lacking in virtue that he steadfastly refused to join with the community in defending its liberty, then it followed that he could not truly be part of the community at all. The Articles of Association issued by Congress in 1774 called for Americans to "break off all dealings" with "such foes to the rights of British-America."[46] Commercial and social interactions between the violators and their community were to be entirely severed; they were to be made strangers in their own lands. A committee in North Carolina memorably referred to this penalty as "civil excommunication," succinctly capturing its gravity and intent.[47] The intended message was clear: true Americans were united in their love of liberty and consented to the Revolutionary platform; those who did otherwise were thus not internal dissenters but, necessarily, outsiders and enemies. Henry Drinker's decision to abandon his connections to the East India Company during the Tea Crisis spared him this fate in 1773, though in the end it would prove to be only a temporary reprieve.

Service in the colonial militia, like participation in the boycotts and nonconsumption movements, made it possible for relatively apolitical segments of society to actively express themselves and declare their support for the Revolutionary cause. Prior to the Revolution, Pennsylvania lacked the formal, organized militia structures typical of colonies farther north. The bloodshed at Lexington and Concord triggered a hurried, though still uncertain, attempt to organize and assemble a local defense in the Quaker colony.[48] Because widespread militia service was rare in Pennsylvania before the imperial crisis, participation in the new regiments was seen as sending a clear political message. Enlistment suggested the individual thought that armed resistance by American civilians was a legitimate and proper response to British policy while continued service past 1776 marked one as supportive of American independence. Militia service was available to (and later pushed upon) a wide swath of the male population, elevating dozens of hitherto little-known men to civil office as county lieutenants and sub-lieutenants. Consequently the militia empowered many who were outside the traditional avenues of political expression to make their voices heard.[49]

Unsurprisingly, as they had in speech and commercial choice, Pennsylvania's Revolutionaries eventually mandated expressions of consent in the sphere of military service, offering the people no choice when it came to participation in the militia. The arguments used to justify many of the punishments and fines levied on those who refused to join the Revolutionary militias were strikingly similar to those which justified the enforcement of nonconsumption. When first established, militia companies were wholly voluntary organizations. However, as relations with Britain worsened and it became increasingly apparent that many eligible men had no intention of volunteering, Pennsylvania began mandating service. To that end, Pennsylvania's colonial and, later, state governments enacted a series of escalating fines against those who refused to participate, or as they were called by contemporaries, "Non-Associators."[50] These fines began in November of 1775 with the relatively mild fee of two shillings sixpence for each absence at a mandatory drill, or a potential grand total of £2 10s. 0d. for the year.[51] Four months later, the fines were raised to three shillings sixpence for each absence.[52]

This leniency came from the moderate and hesitant colonial assembly, but by September of 1776 that body was all but defunct and responsibility for enforcing militia attendance had been taken up by the radical and controversial convention established to create a new constitution for the state. That body discarded both the methods and leniency of the old assembly and declared "that every Non-Associator, between the ages of sixteen and fifty years, shall pay for and during the time of his continuing a Non-Associator, at the rate of twenty shillings for each and every month." To this explosive increase in the fine for Non-Association, the convention added "that every Non-Associator, above the age of twenty-one years, shall pay, in addition to the aforesaid fine, at the rate of four shillings in the pound on the annual value of his estate."[53] The old assembly lashed out at this ordinance, giving voice to the disaffected among their former constituency. In language that should have been familiar to all Revolutionaries, the assembly reminded the people that "it is the sacred Right of Freemen to give and grant their own Money; and that all Taxes, levied without their Consent, are arbitrary and oppressive" and that the convention, created for the sole purpose of establishing a new state constitution, had "derived no

Authority from the good People of *Pennsylvania* to levy Taxes and dispose of their Property."[54] By this time, however, the moderate assembly was too weak to stem the tide; early in 1777, the new government created by the convention more than doubled the fines for Non-Association and declared that, if necessary, the money could be recovered through the seizure and sale of Non-Associators' personal property. Willing to offer a carrot along with the stick, the Revolutionary government expanded the voting privileges of active militiamen, waiving property and naturalization requirements laid on the rest of the population.[55]

The official justification for this series of punishments was rarely that the Non-Associators were true dissenters who rejected the independent American governments or opposed armed resistance to Britain. While admitting that there were some who were "conscientiously scrupulous against bearing Arms," the early advocates of a mandatory, universal militia service held that these individuals were "but few in Comparison to those who . . . make *Conscience a Convenience.*"[56] These more numerous and self-serving Non-Associators were implicitly assumed to desire the same ends, even the same means, as the Revolutionaries: they simply wished others to do the heavy lifting while they pursued personal profit. The justifying assumption was that all Pennsylvanians, whether they had voluntarily joined the militia or not, were united in the beliefs that armed resistance was desirable and that a firm opposition to Britain would bring about an end devoutly to be wished. Because "the Cause is common," declared one revolutionary committee in its report to the assembly prior to the first imposition of fines, "and the Benefits derived from an Opposition are universal, it is not consonant to Justice or Equity that the Burdens should be partial."[57] The militiamen themselves were adamant that all Non-Associators would "reap equal advantages" and "are to be equally benefited" by the militiamen's service and, therefore, whether they wanted to or not, should equally contribute.[58]

Later in the war, the provincial convention deployed the same logic even as it discarded the leniency of the initial fines and levied crushing economic burdens on those who refused to serve. Non-Associators had selfishly "pursued their business to advantage" while more virtuous men fought what had now become a War for Independence, "which," the convention ruled, "is a common benefit."[59] By explaining their actions in terms of common cause and universal benefits, the Patriots furthered assumptions of universal consent and implicitly denied the existence of any middle group of Americans who might have shunned the militia because they doubted whether there was really anything worth fighting for or questioned whether there truly were "advantages" and "benefits" in the pursuit of war and independence.

James Allen experienced the shifting powers and purposes of the Pennsylvania militia firsthand. A willing participant in 1775, Allen's "zeal for the great cause we are engaged in" led him to don a uniform and practice maneuvers. Even then, however, he recognized that the organization was more a political than a military force. He doubted that they would be of any use in defending the city from an actual attack, complaining that the common militiamen "have no subordination" to their officers and betters. More importantly, however, he perceived that the mere act of *not* appearing for militia exercises made one a target of Revolutionary suspicions. Non-Associators were increasingly labeled selfish, if not treacherous, and their opinions on the conflict disregarded or suppressed. Even as the militia radicalized far beyond his own tastes, Allen continued to serve "hoping by this means to have some right to speak freely." His hope of restraining the movement from within proved to be in vain.[60]

Following the Declaration of Independence in 1776, Allen stopped participating in militia gatherings and exercises. From his perspective, the province he had sworn to protect no longer existed, having been usurped by a new, independent regime. He was, consequently, discharged from any obligations to it. Neither the Revolutionary leadership nor his former comrades in the militia shared this point of view. Allen woke one morning that December to find his country estate "surrounded by a Guard of Soldiers with fixed Bayonets." The commanding officer presented a warrant from the Pennsylvania Council of Safety authorizing him to arrest Allen and bring him in for questioning. The council informed Allen that he was only one of many former militiamen in his region who had recently ceased to participate. Perhaps uncomfortable with the idea that this falloff represented a widespread rejection of independence or the new Revolutionary government, the council believed that some influential demagogue was actively seducing men out of the ranks. Allen was a prime suspect. He freely confessed he was "unfriendly to the present views of Independence, which I had strenuously opposed before it was declared." However he denied any responsibility for the state of the militia, declaring that he "had not interfered in publick matters, further than in confidential conversations with my friends," and that he had no plans or desires to do so while the war continued. Upon further investigation, the council concluded that Allen, as he claimed, had largely kept to himself since July. He was made to swear "not to say or do anything injurious to the present cause" in the future and then released with a warning not to venture too far from his home in the country.[61]

This satisfied the Revolutionary leadership, at least for a time, but apparently did not guarantee Allen any protection from the militia itself. In 1777 he noticed that the local militia companies had begun targeting anyone who failed to join their ranks for plunder and persecution. Tragically, it was not Allen himself but his wife and daughter who most directly experienced the militia's fury. Traveling in the family carriage to visit a friend, the women were surprised to encounter a militia company coming down the road toward them. Their driver pulled aside to make room, but the militiamen, likely recognizing Allen's vehicle, followed him off the road. The driver was pulled down and beaten while the bulk of the company turned their wrath on the carriage. As Allen's wife and daughter screamed and begged to be let out, the militiamen smashed the carriage windows and drove their bayonets through the walls. They were attempting to turn the carriage over with the women still inside when the Continental Army's commissioner of supplies for the county, David Deshler, happened by and put a stop to the violence.[62]

The incident left Allen in a mixture of fury and despondency. With the justice system still in chaos and his own loyalty suspect, he knew there was no chance of seeing the militiamen punished for the assault. Moreover, he strongly suspected that the Revolutionary leadership was actively encouraging such depredations against those who refused to support them. "The Province of Pennsylvania," he despaired, "may be divided into 2 classes of men, viz. Those that plunder and those that are plundered. . . . To oppress one's countrymen is a love of Liberty." It would not be the Allen family's last encounter with the Pennsylvania militia.[63]

In the languages of speech, commerce, and military service the Patriots of Pennsylvania strove to make participation accessible to the general population and, when large segments of that population still refused to participate, to bring the people into the Revolutionary camp by force. Though this coercive approach to securing consent may at first seem antithetical to the Revolution's ideals of liberty and popular sovereignty, in many ways it was a direct outgrowth of the ideas and values at the heart of Revolutionary rhetoric. Because the Revolutionary governments claimed to directly represent "the People," there came to be no conceptual room for legitimate dissent, no place for what might, with some irony, be called a "loyal opposition" to the Revolution: supportive of the rights of Americans but opposed to independence.[64] Within the framework of Revolutionary republican ideology, "liberty" was a corporate term. The people as a whole were to be liberated from the oppression of the powerful; that an individual person might desire liberty from "the People" themselves was still an alien notion.[65] After all, as a South Carolinian asked rhetorically, "who could be more free than the People who representatively exercise supreme Power over themselves?"[66]

The ways in which the Revolutionary governments and committees went about punishing and incorporating those who defied or disregarded them suggests that this conception of a corporate, homogeneous "people" was not merely assumed; it was also enforced. No group threatened this conception so directly as did the disaffected. Unqualified support of royal prerogative and parliamentary taxation or service alongside British regulars against Americans easily marked one as an outsider and oppressor, distinct from and in opposition to the unified American "people." But apathy, disinterest, and hesitancy were harder to demonize and dismiss, particularly when they appeared in individuals who had been advocates of resistance in the early days of the Revolution. These internal challenges directly threatened the very heart of radical ideology by calling into question the unity of the people and the legitimacy of actions purportedly taken on their behalf. Unsurprisingly, then, a tremendous amount of energy was expended in trying to nudge, persuade, or force this uncertain and reticent multitude into the Revolutionary camp.

All these efforts to generate evidence of popular consent, either in word or deed, or to suppress dissent relied on the Revolutionaries' control of coercive force, on their ability to project violence, or, as Muhlenberg put it, on their possessing "the strongest arm and the longest sword."[67] The absence of any serious counterweight to the increasingly coercive militias and, later, the Continental Army, allowed the Patriots to carry out their agenda with limited interruption and relatively little fear of retaliation. Unlike New York and Massachusetts, Pennsylvania had no significant British military presence in the decade before independence. Its conservative leadership was strongly intermixed with pacifists and slow to embrace armed force.

Aware of their need for a monopoly on firepower, in January of 1776, the Continental Congress recommended that all the states take steps to disarm disaffected persons.[68] Four months later, the colonial assembly moved hesitantly to "recommend" that Non-Associators turn over their arms and that the electorate in the towns and boroughs choose a few men to collect them. Later that year, the radicals' new government moved swiftly to replace this polite recommendation with more effective measures. Noting that many of the Non-Associators had "either refused or neglected to deliver up their Arms," the provincial convention removed enforcement from the hands of locally elected men and turned it over to the militia battalions, who would directly benefit from collecting as many arms as possible and were unlikely to be sympathetic toward those who refused to serve alongside them.[69] Consequently, between the summer of 1776, when the radicals erected their own governing bodies and disarmed the Non-Associators, and the early autumn of 1777, when the British marched into the state, no force existed in Pennsylvania capable of opposing the militias or sheltering those who provoked the ire of the Revolutionary leadership, nor was it at all likely that such a force could be assembled from the disarmed, isolated, and cowed population of dissenters. Any examination of the region in the early years of the war or of the British occupation that followed should bear this situation in mind; it undoubtedly bore down on the minds of the disaffected people of Pennsylvania.

Given the near total lack of armed opposition, the Revolutionary committees, militias, and occasional mobs destroyed surprisingly little and killed very few as they overthrew the colonial government and worked to stamp out dissent.[70] This speaks to their difficulties in obtaining sufficient support from the populace but also to their objectives. There was certainly violence: sometimes spontaneous, often unofficial, and generally public; and the *threat* of violence was ever present for those who, in word or deed, openly rejected the legitimacy of the new regime.[71] Yet the outright destruction of dissenters was never the goal. Time after time, the violence could be suddenly stopped or the threat ended by a humble apology for one's misdeeds, an act of solidarity with fellow Patriots, or a firm declaration of support for the Revolutionary cause, even if these acts of penance were manifestly the product of extortion rather than a true change of heart. Like so much else in the Revolution, the threat of violence was deployed to obtain the consent, or at least the outward manifestation of consent, that was seen as necessary to legitimate the organized resistance to British policy and the creation of a new nation in America.

On one level, this campaign to create the appearance of common consent was successful. The threats of ostracism, fines, violence, and banishment convinced many of those who, internally, opposed or disregarded the Revolutionary movement to outwardly embrace it. They conformed their commercial transactions to the dictates of the Congress and committees; they took part in militia exercises; they refrained from publicly questioning the legitimacy of independence or the Patriot regime. Yet these same efforts also placed the Pennsylvania Revolutionaries in a perilous position as the summer of 1777 approached. Despite the outward signs of conformity which could be extracted from the people, disaffection remained widespread; many seemingly compliant Pennsylvanians supported the cause, not from a deep affection for its goals and principles, but only to avoid further persecution.[72] Consequently, the Patriots' ability to govern the state, control its flow of commerce and materials, and enlist its men in their military, depended upon the Revolutionaries retaining a monopoly on coercive force in the province. That monopoly was soon to be challenged; the British were coming.

INTERLUDE

THE BROTHERS ALLEN

James Allen's three brothers came to New York in December of 1776, nine months before the British captured Philadelphia. They came to save themselves and, they hoped, to secure the salvation of their home in Philadelphia. New York was, at that time, firmly under the control of the British army, having been captured the previous summer in a campaign that went disastrously for the nascent United States and very nearly saw the total destruction of General George Washington's entire army. The Allens hoped the king's army would offer them protection from the new Revolutionary government of Pennsylvania, a regime which was already applying considerable pressure to dissenters. Moreover, having come to believe that only the might of the British military could end the "tyranny" of the Revolutionaries, they soon undertook the awkward task of lobbying for the invasion of their own homes.[1]

Thus by the end of 1776, the three brothers were unquestionably Loyalists, fully committed to British victory in America and dependent upon the king's forces for protection. Yet their politics were more complex than that simple label suggests and the journey that ultimately led them to British-occupied New York was far from straightforward; only a year before they had all been outspoken advocates of American liberty and committed opponents of British oppression. Their father, Chief Justice William Allen, was the colony's most prominent opponent of royal government and had, in both Pennsylvania and England, publicly opposed Parliament's right to tax Americans.[2] John, the eldest son, served on Philadelphia's Committee of Inspection and Observation, helping to regulate and enforce the commercial boycott of British goods. He was later a delegate to the Provincial Convention of New Jersey. Andrew Allen was the attorney general of

Pennsylvania and, before 1776, engaged in resisting British encroachments on almost every level. In 1774, as tensions mounted between civilians and the British army in Boston, Andrew joined the First Troop of Philadelphia City Cavalry, a voluntary unit created to protect American liberties from imperial overreach. In 1775 he became a member of the local Committee of Safety and then a delegate to the Continental Congress itself. William Allen Jr., the youngest Allen brother, had risked his life for the American cause, serving as a lieutenant colonel in the Continental Army during its ill-fated invasion of Canada in 1775.

Yet even those who risked their blood and treasure denouncing British policy as tyrannical and engaging in battle with the king's forces might balk at declaring independence. Knowing, as we do now, the ultimate outcome of events in the 1770s, we tend to think that such individuals would go *only so far* down the road of resistance, that independence represented the limit of their commitment. Yet for the Allens, among others, independence was not a step *too far* but a step *off the path* of legitimate resistance altogether, a wrong turn which took the country in a new and disastrous direction. They were committed to securing the liberties of the British constitution for subjects in America; severing America from Britain entirely struck them as a sinister and foolhardy corruption of that great cause. And so, as the Declaration became inevitable, John left the Convention of New Jersey, Andrew ceased to attend the Continental Congress, and William, returning from Canada, resigned his commission. They left the Revolution and retreated to their various homes in the countryside of New Jersey or Pennsylvania. But their rejection of independence was remembered, sometimes bitterly, by those who came to lead the new American governments. Driven by a legitimate fear for their safety and a growing, sometimes elitist, disgust for the new Revolutionary regimes, they made their way to New York. They turned for refuge to the empire they had once denounced as oppressive and pleaded with it for liberty.

It was fortunate timing for such a request. As 1776 came to a close, the commander in chief of the British army in America, General Sir William Howe, was pondering where the empire should strike next. Numerous potential targets presented themselves, and each had its own advocates. There was considerable pressure on Howe to return part of his army to New England, and particularly to wreak royal vengeance on Boston and erase the shame of his retreat from that city the previous March. A new British army was being assembled in Canada, led by the flamboyant general

John "Gentleman Johnny" Burgoyne, who planned to march his troops south into New York. If Howe's main army moved north and west, it might meet Burgoyne at Albany, thus drawing a red British line across the state and cutting off New England from the rest of the colonies. Alternatively, Howe could, as the Allens hoped, go south and strike directly at the de facto American capital in Philadelphia. By capturing or destroying the available watercraft along the Delaware, Washington had thus far prevented the British from crossing into Pennsylvania, but there would be little he could do if Howe chose to launch a naval invasion and bring his army up the river from the south. Given that the general's own brother, Admiral Lord Richard Howe, commanded the Royal Navy in America, there would be no great barrier to planning a coordinated attack.

Even before the Allens and other Pennsylvania refugees arrived to plead their case, Howe felt inclined to make Philadelphia his primary objective for 1777. News coming down from the north combined with Howe's own experience in Boston to convince him that the militia companies of New England were too numerous and too determined to risk returning the seat of war to that region.[3] In Pennsylvania, however, he believed "the prospect was very different. The increase of force which that country could afford Washington was small in comparison." Though the region was well populated and, indeed, home to America's largest city, Howe strongly suspected that the Pennsylvanians would be slow to oppose him. With sufficient reinforcements he believed he might take the main army to Pennsylvania while simultaneously sending a small force to meet Burgoyne's invasion at Albany, should that be required. Regardless, any move he made against Philadelphia would be certain to assist the Canadian invasion by forcing the Continentals to divide their strength.[4] More importantly, Howe had come to believe that the destruction of the Continental Army was "the surest road to peace" and that the only objective Washington might risk his entire army to defend was Philadelphia.[5]

Though he made his initial decision before they arrived, the Allen brothers sought diligently to bolster Howe's confidence in his planned invasion of Pennsylvania. Within a few weeks of reaching New York, the Allens became friends with Ambrose Serle, a British military secretary in his mid-thirties who was sympathetic toward American Loyalists and, more importantly, had immediate access to the Howe brothers. They were also reacquainted with Joseph Galloway, a fellow Loyalist refugee from Pennsylvania and former delegate to the Continental Congress. Together, the Allens and

Galloway launched an unremitting campaign to convince the British leadership that Pennsylvania was a stronghold of British Loyalists, oppressed by a Patriotic minority, who needed only arms, ammunition, and the support of the British army in order to rise up and reclaim the colony for the king. By the end of March, Serle had met with either the Allens or Galloway at least thirty-four times, and almost invariably the conversation had turned to Pennsylvania and how Britain might secure the support of more Americans for their cause. The Allens assured Serle "that the Force of the opposition was breaking" in Pennsylvania and "that the Congress was much declined in the Opinions of the People at large, that it had been openly opposed in the three lower Counties upon Delaware." William Allen was "positive that three forths of the People are against Independency." Most importantly, they declared "that there is no Doubt of their [Pennsylvanians'] making a formal Renunciation [of Independence] when the Army shall advance to support them." Galloway echoed these claims and more, describing elaborate plans for the creation of vast Loyalist regiments and the seizure of Congress.[6] Serle passed their remarks on to Lord Howe and within a month arranged for the refugees to meet with the admiral and general directly.

It's unclear how much influence the Pennsylvanians had on Howe's plans and outlook, though later events demonstrate that the general did form a potent, if short-lived, alliance with Galloway. Whether due to his conversations with the refugees or other factors, as 1777 began, Howe's commitment to capturing Philadelphia grew into what some would later call an "obsession."[7] Like many Britons, the general had long believed that the rebellion in America was the work of a small faction who were forcibly imposing their will on the loyal majority. Given the opportunity, he trusted that those loyal subjects would rise up in support of the empire. Consequently, while he remained dedicated to the destruction of Washington's army, he took great care not to alienate the many British sympathizers he believed existed in America. While others called for harsh retribution against the rebellious colonies, Howe preferred a softer approach.[8] He came not to conquer America, but to liberate it from a band of tyrannical demagogues. In describing Pennsylvania as an essentially loyal but oppressed province, Galloway and the Allens flattered and reaffirmed Howe's preconceived understanding of what the Revolution was and how it could be defeated. Howe was assured that the Loyalists of Philadelphia would vindicate his conciliatory approach and give him the manpower he needed to finally cut out this cancerous rebellion once and for all.[9]

While the Allens' effect on Howe remains uncertain, their influence over Ambrose Serle does not. According to his journal, the British secretary first met the Pennsylvanians' claims with dismissive cynicism, writing in December that Loyalist Americans like William Allen "all prate & profess much." Yet as the months passed, Serle lost his cynicism and began to embrace their vision of a powerful Loyalist uprising. He grew particularly attached to Andrew Allen and Galloway, and often found himself an active participant in their plots of raising American regiments and capturing the Revolutionary leadership.[10]

In July a massive British invasion force set out from New York for Philadelphia. Crammed tightly aboard naval transports, the army was carried out into the Atlantic, south along the coasts of New Jersey, Delaware, and Maryland, and ultimately into the northern reaches of the Chesapeake. From there the soldiers would travel by foot and come at Philadelphia from the west while the warships of the Royal Navy pushed their way up the Delaware River to assault the city from the south. Relying on the reports of Loyalist refugees and spies, the British knew of the widespread apathy and antipathy toward the Revolutionary cause in Pennsylvania. They believed that support for American independence was tepid, that the new state government was weak, and that the Patriots were increasingly turning to coercive force in order to maintain their control over their people. In all this, the British were correct.

Yet, based on this accurate information, the Howes and even Loyalist Pennsylvanians like Galloway and the Allens made a series of disastrously poor assumptions. They assumed that, if support for American independence was weak, support for the British Empire must be strong; that if the Revolutionary administration was unstable, a royal government, once reestablished, would be secure; and that if few Pennsylvanians would freely commit themselves to the rebel cause, many must be ready to voluntarily serve the king. In short, they assumed that if Pennsylvania held few Revolutionaries, it must hold many Loyalists. They were wrong.

CHAPTER 2

INVASION

> It being a melancholy truth, that too many of our People are so disaffected already that nothing but the neighbourhood of the Army keeps them subject to Government.
>
> —Pennsylvania Council and Assembly, 1777

Ambrose Serle, secretary to Admiral Lord Richard Howe of the Royal Navy, stood on the deck of HMS *Fanny* and watched as a British invasion force of more than ten thousand men disembarked along the shores of the Elk River in northern Maryland. It was the morning of August 25, 1777, more than four weeks since Serle, joined by Andrew Allen and Joseph Galloway, had set sail with the fleet from occupied New York, and the air was suffocatingly hot and heavy. Serle may well have feared the heat of summer in the Chesapeake more than rebel bullets, and he prayed along the way that God would protect the army "from the Fatality of the worst Climate in America at this worst Season of the Year to experience it."[1]

The long journey from New York, spent mostly in the sweltering darkness below decks, had killed a number of the army's horses and left the men themselves irritable and impatient for action. Finding the area around their landing site largely abandoned, they vented their frustration on the property of the absent inhabitants, breaking into homes and stealing anything that caught their eye. General Howe, who viewed the army as a force for reconciliation rather than mere destruction, immediately issued orders against plundering. Though he was only a secretary to the admiral, and so not in the line of command, Serle's fine clothes and general demeanor often led the rank and file to assume he was some sort of naval officer, and they were quick to fall in line when he found them engaged in illicit activities. Having no actual authority to do otherwise, Serle "graciously" allowed would-be plunderers to return to duty; those apprehended by actual officers were not so lucky.[2] When a band of marauding soldiers had the misfortune of being caught by the British commander in chief himself, Howe had one executed and the others whipped nearly to death before sparing them to serve as a living warning to their fellows.[3] Despite this and other harsh punishments by the officers, the British army remained an unruly and destructive force in Maryland.

Though distracted by the heat of summer and general destruction wrought by the soldiery, Serle considered Maryland one of the most beautiful parts of America he had seen thus far. He spent the journey on deck observing the fair countryside, the fine houses, and the breathtaking sight of more than a hundred Royal Navy ships, white sails against green hills and blue sky, serenely navigating a bend of the river. Yet for all his watching, both on ship and ashore, he saw very few of the free inhabitants. The fields and houses were mostly empty, the river largely untraveled except for the fleet. A few white faces peered down at the passing ships before vanishing over the hills or into the woods, but most of those who remained to be seen were black slaves. A handful of these came out to the fleet at various times, willing to share information with the British and doubtless curious about the appearance and intentions of the army. The sight of slave huts along the shore disturbed Serle's usually placid demeanor. His journal bitterly assaulted the colonists for treating their slaves "as a better kind of Cattle, being bought or sold, according to Fancy or Interest. . . . Such is the Practice or Sentiment of Americans," he spat, "while they are bawling about the Rights of *human Nature*."[4]

Serle was pleased that he saw no indication of fervent militiamen, like those of New England, turning out to defend their homes and protect independence, yet neither did he see any hint of a Loyalist uprising, eager to restore the region to the crown. There was, instead, only the quiet emptiness of abandoned farms and homesteads, signs of a fearful people who cared less about empire or independence than they did about being left in peace. When the war came to their doorstep, they made certain they were not at home.

Serle's was only one of many voices commenting on the pervasive disaffection of the region in the summer and early autumn of 1777. General George Washington described the people as being "in a kind of Lethargy" while Brigadier General Anthony Wayne of Pennsylvania complained of "the Supineness of some and Disaffection of Others."⁵ Yet perhaps more telling than these direct assertions of widespread apathy is the mirrored disappointment expressed by advocates from both sides of the conflict, who complained that the region had turned against them. Even as the American commander in chief complained "that this State acts most infamously, the People of it I mean as we derive little or no assistance from them," his opposite number in the British army, Howe, was grumbling about "the prevailing disposition of the inhabitants who, I am sorry to observe, seem to be, excepting a few individuals, strongly in enmity against us."⁶ While Joseph Jones of York criticized the people of Pennsylvania because they "make little or no exertions in [their] own defence, but on the contrary afford every succor and support to the Enemy,"⁷ and John Adams condemned Philadelphia as "that mass of cowardice and Toryism,"⁸ British lieutenant general James Grant wrote home that "we find [the province of Pennsylvania] if possible more inimical than any we have yet been in."⁹ We can begin to resolve these apparent contradictions by noting that the "infamous" and "inimical" behavior the civilians engaged in rarely took the form of direct opposition to either side: local resistance to Howe's landing at Head of Elk was negligible, and no armed Loyalist bands emerged to harass Washington's flank as he rushed to halt the British invasion. Each side hoped, even expected, to find active support among the peoples of the mid-Atlantic. When, instead, they found a wearied people, largely unwilling to risk their blood and treasure for either the king or the Patriots' conception of liberty, both the British and the Revolutionaries tended to interpret this disengagement as betrayal and hostility; it was not antagonism but disaffection that both sides perceived as "enmity against us."

The problem was worse for the Pennsylvania Patriots, for they had spent the preceding years turning consumer choices and militia service into badges of patriotism and signs of consent for the Revolutionary government. It was precisely along these lines that the first signs of popular disaffection appeared in the weeks after the British landing.

Aggressively Assembling a Defense

Early in the summer, with General Howe's intentions still uncertain, Pennsylvania began to gather its militia strength. Turnout was somewhat lethargic, to say the least. Tasked with rallying the troops in York County, Richard

McAllister complained that the militiamen there "will not meet together to Do any thing."[10] They would not gather to elect officers or collect arms and ammunition; officers appointed by the government were reluctant to assume the authority given them. When pressed harder, the people responded by throwing rocks through windows and making threats. "I shall Exert Every Power in me to Git them out," wrote McAllister to the president of the executive council, "but am shure of failing with at least the half or more."[11]

Similar hesitancy plagued the city of Philadelphia where, in keeping with McAllister's predictions for York County, only about half of those called up agreed to serve. Pennsylvania militiamen were called by "classes," roughly even groups of men spread across the state. The greater the need for troops, the more classes called upon. Slightly over 40 percent of the first three classes of men who were summoned into service in July and August turned out, while another 10 to 20 percent hired substitutes to serve in their stead.[12] While this was not the level of mobilization the Patriots might have hoped for, confidence remained high among the Revolution's more ardent supporters. Early in August, Pennsylvania militiaman Josiah Parker assured a friend in Virginia that "Should an attempt be made on Philadelphia by Howe, which yet seems believed, we with the Militia are sufficient to repel him."[13] Parker's faith in his fellow militiamen would soon be severely tested.

By mid-August Howe's target was no longer in question; the British invasion fleet was seen moving up the Elk River in Maryland and no one doubted that the campaign for the rebel capital would soon begin. On August 22, three days before the British began to disembark, Congress called upon the states of Maryland, Pennsylvania, Delaware, and Virginia to place their militias, or substantial portions of them, under Washington's command to aid in the defense of Philadelphia. Pennsylvania was expected to maintain a force of at least 4,000, a number that seems modest when one considers the approximately 40,000 men formally enrolled in the militia. Yet this number proved to be wholly beyond the state's capabilities.[14] A report on September 6 found fewer than 3,000 serving from the state, of whom only 2,043 were fit for duty. On the same day, Congress recommended that Pennsylvania increase its militia commitments, calling out 5,000 from Philadelphia and the surrounding counties alone. Though John Hancock assured General Washington that he had "no Doubt of their Compliance" in meeting this new quota, the Pennsylvania militia not only failed to rise to this higher standard but soon made itself even more scarce than before.[15]

Howe's landing in Maryland and subsequent march toward Philadelphia drastically altered the calculus of loyalty and commitment among Pennsylvania's militiamen. It was now plain that military service would soon place them under the fire of British and Hessian regulars. Yet perhaps more importantly, the invasion of Pennsylvania called into question the Revolutionaries' ability to enforce the militia laws they had created. The Patriots' monopoly on coercive force was severely strained and in some areas entirely broken; the very survival of the Revolutionary government in the state was now in doubt.

This crisis was immediately visible in the militia. Though Philadelphia had managed to send approximately half of the militia classes called up before the British landing, a mere 15 percent answered from the first class summoned in September. Shocked by this paltry turnout, the Revolutionaries immediately called out the next class, but again only 15 percent appeared, prompting still another call for the next class, yet here, too, fewer than 20 percent responded. Service slumped to the lowest rate of the war; the city's militia was actively evaporating.[16] Out in York County, Richard McAllister also registered the sudden change in disposition among the people. He no longer complained about their refusal "to meet together to Do any thing," for now more than two hundred of them had gathered "to bind themselves to each other that they wd not muster nor go in the Militia any way, nor suffer their effects to be sold to pay any fines, and to stand by [each] other at the Risque of their lives, to kill every man who wd Distress them." Far from concerned about broken windows, McAllister now worried that these supposed militiamen meant to "either kill me or beet me so that I should not truble them any more."[17] Few of the disaffected men of York County or those like them intended to declare for the British monarch or offer the British the services they denied to the Revolutionaries; as McAllister recognized, they simply wished that no one would "truble them any more." They were quick to realize that, with a British army on Philadelphia's doorstep, the radicals were no longer in a position to harass nonparticipants, impose fines, or punish dissent.

As the supply of fresh men for the militia withered, the incidence of desertion among those already in service exploded; one in four of the Philadelphia militiamen who turned out deserted, primarily from the later classes who faced longer service in a contested theater. Most of them likely returned to their homes in the city, submitting peaceably to the British occupation.[18]

The collapse of the Pennsylvania militia shocked some and infuriated others. "It is true this State wants punishment & suffering if ever one did," roared Elias Boudinot, an American commissary general, "We have mustered from the whole State, by exerting every Nerve about 4000 Men, who as soon as a Gun was fired within ¼ of a Mile of them would throw down their arms & run away worse than a Company of Jersey Women."[19] Doubtless his irritation would have been all the greater had someone told him that only about two thousand were left in service when he penned these words.[20] Adjutant General Timothy Pickering was equally furious, declaring to his brother that "No militia can be more contemptible than those of Pennsylvania and Delaware." Yet behind his fury lay genuine surprise and bewilderment. "How astonishing is it," he exclaimed, "that not a man is roused to action when the enemy is in the heart of the country, and within twelve miles of their grand capital, of so much importance to them and the Continent! How amazing, that Howe should march from the head of Elk to the Schuylkill, a space of sixty miles, without opposition from the people of the country."[21]

Pickering, a native of Massachusetts, was quick to remind one and all that "Such events would not have happened in New England!"[22] The unfavorable comparison was soon driven home by events near Saratoga. Even as Howe's forces marched smoothly past abandoned farmhouses and militia turnouts plummeted in Pennsylvania, British general John Burgoyne's army to the north was being smothered beneath the seemingly endless streams of men rushing to turn back his invasion of New York. Continental general Horatio Gates's victories at Freeman's Farm and Bemis Heights were due in no small part to the outpouring of militia support he received from New York and New England.[23] News of such triumphs would later inspire Pennsylvania's Revolutionary leadership to hope that a similar show of force might yet wrest the capital back from British control, but even they were forced to concede that, had Pennsylvanians risen with the zeal of the New Englanders, Howe would never have reached Philadelphia in the first place.[24]

As turnouts continued to slide, Washington too expressed surprise and distress at his precarious manpower. In letters to Thomas Wharton, president of Pennsylvania's Supreme Executive Council, he made his expectations clear: "When the Capital of your State is in the Enemies hands, and when they can only be dislodged from thence, by a powerful reinforcement of Militia ... at least one half of the Men capable of bearing arms should be called into the Field." As an absolute minimum, Washington demanded that Pennsylvania at least assemble the four thousand men ordered by Congress. He considered it "a matter of astonishment ... that Pennsylvania, the most opulent and populous of all the States, has but Twelve hundred Militia in the Field, at a time, when the Enemy are endeavouring to make themselves compleatly [sic] masters of, and to fix their winter Quarters in her Capital."[25] In time, Washington's "astonishment" would fade; by the end of 1777 he would come to long for even twelve hundred Pennsylvania militia but would not have them.[26]

Even as the erosion of the Pennsylvania militia severely limited Washington's ability to impede the progress of the British army, a different sign of widespread disaffection was empowering his enemy. Howe's decision to land at Head of Elk and march overland to Philadelphia was a perilous one, for it left his men isolated from their supply lines and the support of the Royal Navy. The British commander and his generals looked to the people and farms they passed to provide, voluntarily or otherwise, sustenance for the army until the men reconnected with the fleet on the Delaware. "Provisions we could not carry," recalled General James Grant, "Proceed we must & of course trust to the country for subsistence." He had not "the smallest apprehension" of this trust being disappointed so long as the army was able to keep moving, and his faith was rewarded.[27]

The majority of the people near Howe's landing site neither resisted nor assisted the invaders but rather, after briefly gawking at the unprecedented sight of hundreds of warships and transports filling the river, vanished into the interior.[28] As the army traveled north toward Philadelphia, however, more and more civilians remained in their homes to see it pass and, in some cases, strike a deal.[29] Not all of the inhabitants supplied these provisions voluntarily, but some did, particularly when they learned that the British would pay good prices in hard currency. The army absorbed a tremendous number of livestock as it moved along, gathering some from abandoned pastures in Maryland and purchasing more from entrepreneurial herders in Chester County.[30] The long passage from New York had taken a terrible toll on the mounts of the British cavalry, leading to such a premium on horses that even some Patriot dragoons were persuaded to sell their animals to the redcoats.[31]

The British fleet conducted its own commercial exchanges with civilians, both along the shores of the Chesapeake and on the Delaware. Captain

Friedrich von Muenchhausen, General Howe's aide-de-camp, recorded the arrival of small groups of Marylanders, including some African Americans, rowing out to supply the fleet with produce as it approached the landing site; trade between the Royal Navy and the peoples of Chester, Wilmington, and New Castle later became a painfully recurrent theme in Washington's correspondence.[32]

With material goods came an even more precious resource: information. Aside from a handful of local Loyalists traveling with the army, the British had little knowledge of the terrain they were traversing, a dangerous predicament in the face of an enemy who had, on more than one occasion, demonstrated the ability to use geography to its advantage. Howe desperately needed more information about the lay of the land and the location of his foe. Time and again, the British commander received this precious data from the civilians who traded with the army. Much of this information gathering was incidental; men and women answered questions about the area when asked and repeated what they had heard about the movement of American troops. One did not have to have great affection for the empire to describe a landmark or pass on a rumor when interrogated by a patrol of armed men.[33] Few served as actual spies or intentionally sought out information on the American army, though some committed Loyalists did volunteer or hire themselves out as guides.[34] Like the material goods they received, the British put this information to good use, turning superior knowledge into victory in the battles of Brandywine and Paoli.[35]

However, neither the absence of a strong militia, nor the supply of provisions, nor the slow trickle of information was enough to truly convince the British that they had entered a friendly or supportive region. Empty houses and agreeable, talkative traders provided a better reception than the redcoats might have received from the militias of New England, but such passive affability was still a far cry from the kind of enthusiastic and committed support much of the British leadership had hoped to find here. Even General Howe, who eventually came to see the area as favorably disposed toward the British cause, admitted that he first encountered nothing more than "an equivocal neutrality."[36] Several officers expressed their disappointment with the level of intelligence they were able to extract from the populace, primarily because so many civilians had left the area; this was not the sort of behavior one hoped for from a truly loyal population.[37] Grant, in particular, was frustrated by the short supply of civilian guides to help him navigate the fields and woods and later grew furious when no civilians came forward to warn him of a surprise attack by the Continentals.[38]

Yet in another telling contradiction, even as Grant grumbled and Howe complained that information remained "extremely difficult to procure," Washington wrote to Hancock that he was maneuvering amid a people "from which I could not derive the least intelligence being to a man disaffected."[39] Though both generals made the best use they could of civilian intelligence networks, neither felt he was operating in friendly territory and each was painfully aware of how blind the people's reticence made their armies. The mirrored complaints and accusations point us once more toward a people who sought, above all else, to limit their involvement in the war that had suddenly burst into their homes and lives.

This caution and hesitancy was problematic for both sides of the imperial dispute. The British and their allies needed a steady stream of material supplies and expected to raise a sizable force of provincials to police and safeguard the regions pacified by the main army.[40] The American situation was more dire still, for they hoped to win a Revolutionary war and establish a republic. The former objective required the people's active labor; the latter depended on their willing and expressed consent. Popular disengagement was not merely inconvenient, it was dangerous.

Over the preceding years of resistance and revolution, the Patriots of Pennsylvania had developed a variety of ways to quiet popular dissent and encourage widespread involvement with, or at least nominal acceptance of, the Revolutionary cause. Yet behind all these techniques for uniting people under the banner of revolution there had always been the coercive power of the crowds, radical committees, and state militias. The appearance of the British army on Pennsylvania's doorstep severely undercut the effectiveness of these means of control and made it possible for many disaffected Pennsylvanians to express their dissatisfaction with or disinterest in the Revolutionary cause. The redcoats cowed Revolutionary mobs, chased away the committees, and seemingly deflated the militia by their mere presence. The Patriot leadership, desperate to reassert and demonstrate their control of the divided and disaffected state, soon turned to the only source of militant power that might successfully stand up to the British: Washington's army.

The Continental Army was the most powerful coercive force the Patriots had at their disposal and the Revolutionary leadership intended to make the most of it in Pennsylvania. Even as the unprecedented sight of the

British invasion fleet dropped jaws and widened eyes along the Chesapeake, Washington made plans for an impressive show of his own in the capital. Already marching south to meet Howe's invasion force, the Continental Army was diverted directly through the streets of Philadelphia, an inescapable demonstration of the new nation's martial power. Washington sent four divisions of Continentals through the city. Cavalry, with the commander in chief himself at their head, led the way, followed by interspersed waves of infantry and artillery, all arranged to appear as clean, professional, and intimidating as possible. The men on foot proceeded in a single column, twelve ranks deep, marching in quick step to the rhythm of drum and fife. They entered the city from the north along Front Street, following the river south as far as Chestnut, a course that led them all directly past the front of Elizabeth Drinker's home. Turning right at Chestnut, the procession marched west past the State House, not coming to a halt until it was approximately a mile outside the city. The specified route along Front and Chestnut took the army through the commercial and social heart of Philadelphia, passing the homes of the elite and many of the more prosperous businesses. Of necessity it followed the wider and more traveled streets, avoiding the stalls along Market Street, which would have split the infantry columns and posed challenges for the artillery. Though the men marched quickly and made no stops they took more than two hours to pass by, giving onlookers plenty of time to observe and reflect upon the martial power of the new nation.[41]

This demonstration served multiple purposes. For worried and fearful Patriots, the sight of the army supplied a much-needed boost of morale, an opportunity to rediscover their enthusiasm for the cause. For the commander in chief, it was a chance to quiet criticism of his troops and their general, to show the world that he commanded more than just a disorderly rabble. For the men of the army, it was a way of instilling martial pride in themselves and their fellows. And for the state and Continental authorities, it provided a means of assuring the people that their leaders would protect them and defend their newfound independence.[42] Yet more than this, the march through Philadelphia was intended to warn all those who looked to the pending British invasion for a chance to rise up and reassert royal authority, or even simply for relief from Revolutionary domination, that the Patriot leadership was still very much in control of the province and still capable of dealing with disaffection and dissent. This was, above all else, a show of force.

That the disaffected ranked highly among Washington's intended audience is readily apparent. In his letter to John Hancock explaining his decision to send the army through Philadelphia, the general did not reference the impact on troop morale, patriotic pride, or his own reputation but immediately declared he had chosen this course "that it may have some influence on the minds of the disaffected there and those who are Dupes to their artifices & opinions."[43] Alexander Graydon, a former Continental captain, watched the troops pass from the Coffee-House at the corner of Front and Market, recording that "the General [Washington] thought it best to show both Whigs and Tories the real strength he possessed." Yet some onlookers did not fit comfortably into either of those groups. As the soldiers swept past, Graydon spotted "a very anxious spectator" watching from an upstairs window. This was Benjamin Chew, former chief justice under the empire and future justice of Pennsylvania's High Court of Error and Appeals, one of the many inhabitants Graydon thought "perhaps, equally disclaimed the epithet of Whig or of Tory."[44] If Chew's "anxious" appearance as he surveyed the Patriot army was any indication, the march was having its desired effect even on the uncertain and uncommitted. In these final days before the British challenged the Revolutionaries' monopoly on force, there was no better image to leave in the minds of the disaffected and potentially disloyal than of a powerful army, capable and willing to enforce, as well as defend, the new American order.

Washington did what he could to enhance the martial aspect of his soldiers and the apparent strength of his army. He "earnestly enjoined" his officers "to make all their men who are able to bear arms (except the necessary guards) march in the ranks." The distance between the ranks of soldiers was "to be exactly observed in passing thro' the City, and great attention given by the officers to see that the men carry their arms well, and are made to appear as decent as circumstances will admit." Thirty-nine lashes awaited any soldier who, for any reason, broke ranks while passing through the city. Camp kettles were to be left with the baggage, which would take a different route in order to remain out of sight, and green sprigs were added to the men's hats to signify vitality. Finally, Washington firmly mandated that "not a woman belonging to the army is to be seen with the troops on their march thro' the city."[45] Like all eighteenth-century armies, Washington's force included numerous female camp followers who provided a variety of necessary services to the soldiery. Though the army could not have functioned without them, the contemporary ideal of a pristine, masculine fighting force made them an embarrassment to the military leadership. Consequently, Washington tried to separate them from the troops at public events, in this case sending them on a longer march around the outskirts of Philadelphia while the majority of soldiers paraded through the streets.[46]

Results were mixed. Rhode Island congressman Henry Marchant thought the troops passed "with a lively smart Step," while an ever-worried John Adams wrote to his wife that "they dont step exactly in Time. They dont hold up their Heads, quite erect, nor turn out their Toes, so exactly as they ought. They dont all of them cock their Hats—and such as do, dont all wear them the same Way."[47] The less discriminating Graydon surmised that the army, "though indifferently dressed, held well burnished arms, and carried them like soldiers." Most importantly, they looked "as if they might have faced an equal number with a reasonable prospect of success."[48]

Less satisfactory, at least to Graydon, was the civilian response. He trusted that the display would be effective in securing a healthy respect for the army's power, if only due to "the propensity of persons unaccustomed to the sight of large bodies of men, to augment them." However, turning his gaze to the watching crowds, he found that the popular display of enthusiasm for the cause "was very disproportioned to the zeal for liberty, which had been manifested the year before."[49] It was that very absence of zeal, as much as anything, that made such shows of force so very important for the cause.

Graydon's belief that the Continentals were prepared to meet "an equal number with a reasonable prospect of success" was soon put to the test. Having paraded through Philadelphia, the American army marched south and west to meet the British force that was sweeping up from Maryland. Washington chose to make his stand just north of Wilmington, Delaware, on Pennsylvania's threshold. Marking Brandywine Creek as a line he would not let Howe cross, he ordered his men to assume a strong defensive position on the north bank. There, on September 11, as Henry Drinker and his fellow prisoners were being led out of Philadelphia and into exile, the two armies collided in one of the longest and bloodiest battles of the Revolutionary War.

Few Pennsylvanians experienced the Battle of Brandywine Creek, in all its danger, excitement, glory, and horror, as closely as Joseph Townsend, then a twenty-one-year-old Quaker living in Chester County. The young Quaker's journal captured the uncertain and divided sentiments that swirled around the British army's arrival. "Some," he wrote, "were of the opinion that a general devastation would be the consequence. Others concluded that the country was now conquered, and peace and tranquility would be restored." Some countenances "wear a serious aspect, and . . . appeared gloomy, others somewhat brightened up from the pleasing prospect before them."[50] Townsend himself was unsure how to feel; his own internal conflict had little to do with politics, however, but rather pitted his pacifist sentiments and obligations to his family against his eagerness to see soldiers on the march and witness the excitement of battle.

That latter would win out. On September 11, the young Quaker and his brother, "possessed of curiosity and fond of new things," rode out along the banks of Brandywine Creek, searching for the redcoats.[51] He found them, and the army of King George III presented a spectacle that stirred all the suppressed martial passions that had lured the brothers away from home. "Our eyes were caught on a sudden by the appearance of the army coming out of the woods into the fields," Townsend remembered, "In a few minutes the fields were literally covered over with them, and they were hastening towards us. Their arms and bayonets being raised, shone as bright as silver."[52] Townsend and his brother encountered the British flanking parties and were allowed to pass through in order "to see the army." They were soon surrounded by marching redcoated columns, troops of horsemen, and rumbling baggage wagons, and were accosted by British officers eager for information on the countryside and the location of Washington's Continentals. The journey home again brought even more excitement, for Townsend was still among the British lines when they crashed into elements of Washington's right flank near Osborn Hill. Musket fire erupted from the trees ahead and a Hessian officer took the opportunity to draft the gawking civilians into a work detail, commanding them to remove fences that blocked the army's advance. Townsend was in such a state of shock that he immediately began following orders and had taken down the first two rails of the fence before he "was forcibly struck with the impropriety of being active in assisting to take the lives of my fellow being" and quietly snuck away from the battle.[53]

The days of the invasion took a grim turn for Townsend and his neighbors. Samuel Kern, a fellow Quaker who had also gone to see the army, was shot through the thigh by a Continental scouting party on his way home, possibly by mistake, though Townsend recalled that Kern was enthusiastically describing the Americans' defeat just before the soldiers opened fire.

He fretted through that night about what might happen to him if word got out that he and his brother had mingled with the British soldiers before the battle. For their part, the British and Hessians did little to endear themselves to Townsend's neighborhood, confiscating goods, livestock, and lumber. The dead from Brandywine were buried in shallow graves, and a series of torrential rains soon exposed the bodies, presenting Townsend and others with the unenviable task of reinterring the decaying corpses. Experience of the invasion left the young man and his acquaintances much where it had found them: conflicted, uncertain, afraid, with no great enthusiasm for either the British or the Revolutionaries.[54]

The British were victorious that day at Brandywine Creek. While one arm of the army held Washington's attention to the south, a separate force crossed the creek at a northern ford of which the American general, blighted by poor intelligence, was unaware. These were the soldiers Townsend and his brother stumbled upon and followed. Caught off guard by the sudden appearance of redcoats on their right flank, the Continentals' defensive position collapsed. Sensing their moment, the southern branch of the British army surged across the creek as well. In the confusion, some of Washington's soldiers simply dropped their arms and fled. Others, maintaining their discipline, managed a more orderly fighting retreat, surrendering the ground but at least saving the army from total destruction. In the weeks that followed, Howe pressed on for Philadelphia.

Howe Takes the Capital

The redcoats would not reach the capital until September 26, but chaos came to the city well in advance of the British vanguard. Though still preoccupied with her husband's recent banishment and her youngest son's illness, Elizabeth Drinker could not help but marvel at the frenzy of activity and emotion that swirled around her. A scattering of Continental soldiers who had fled the fighting at Brandywine and run all the way to Philadelphia brought exaggerated accounts of the army being broken and routed. Thousands of inhabitants packed up and attempted to leave the city before the British arrived. Their plans were hampered by the simultaneous efforts of some industrious Patriots who, eager to make life hard for the British, removed the bridge across the Schuylkill River, cut the ropes on the ferries, and began confiscating horses. Though she rarely left her son's bedside,

Drinker heard the seemingly constant rumble of carriages sweeping past her house on Front Street, carrying fearful families and individuals north into the countryside. As order broke down, theft became more common. Drinker's cellar was burglarized and she heard reports of other Quakers who had been similarly targeted.[55]

The chaos peaked on September 19. In the early hours of the morning a letter from Alexander Hamilton, then Washington's aide-de-camp, arrived informing Congress that the British army was advancing toward the Schuylkill River. Hamilton's report, combined with sightings of British scouting parties reconnoitering the Swede's Ford, led many Philadelphians to believe that Howe's army had already crossed the river and was mere hours from marching into the city. By two o'clock that morning panic had taken hold. Men ran from door to door, waking the inhabitants and encouraging those who feared persecution at the hands of the British to take flight. The ensuing mass exodus, led in part by members of Congress and the Pennsylvania government, created chaos in the streets as civilians, militiamen, and politicians scrambled past one another in a headlong rush away from the redcoats. With Howe's army approaching from the south and west, the evacuees flowed to the north leading more than a few of them past James Allen's home in Northampton. He recognized a number of congressmen and military figures and later proclaimed the road in front of his house "the most travelled in America."[56] From her home on Second Street Sarah Logan Fisher observed "wagons rattling, horses galloping, women running, children crying, delegates flying, & altogether the greatest consternation, fright & terror that can be imagined." Elizabeth Drinker's servants elected not to wake her when the evacuation began, doubtless knowing that she had no intention of leaving the city and, after many days of tending to little Henry and enduring her husband's absence, desperately needed her sleep. She arose in the morning to witness the last of the frenzied departures and soon learned about the misunderstanding that had given rise to the panic in the first place. Nearly a week would pass before the British vanguard actually reached Philadelphia. Later in the day, as the truth spread, a handful of congressmen and other inhabitants sheepishly returned to the city.[57]

In the wake of this excitement there was finally a period of calm. Walking about the following day, Drinker found the streets oddly quiet. Many of the shops and businesses were shuttered; the docks along the river were almost all vacant. Continental soldiers drifted from house to house, making a final confiscation of horses, blankets, metal, and other goods that might be of use to the army. The remaining congressmen gathered their papers in anticipation of reconvening elsewhere. In the confusion of the final days, Congress's official journals were somewhat haphazardly left in the hands of John Roberts, a disaffected Quaker of ambivalent loyalties. Roberts, despite his distaste for Congress, had the journals carried to his home in Lower Merion for safekeeping.[58] The following days were filled with a brooding uncertainty as the British moved ever closer and inhabitants who had taken flight on the nineteenth returned to arrange for a somewhat more orderly departure. When it became clear that Howe was, in reality, on the verge of taking the city, reports spread that some especially radical Patriots intended to set fire to Philadelphia before the British could capture it. Fears of Revolutionary arsonists were not new; James Allen caught word of similar plots to burn the city back in July when Howe's fleet first left New York, but with the imminent arrival of the redcoats, they surfaced again. Such rumors were soon silenced, however, and the streets were emptied by a long, heavy downpour of rain. Yet while the skies grew steadily darker on the eve of the occupation, Elizabeth Drinker's day brightened as little Henry's illness finally began to fade. For the first time in more than a month, she was able to dress her eight-year-old son and help him walk unsteadily across the room. The next morning, while Washington's forces sat impotently out of position to the north, Lieutenant General Charles, Second Earl Cornwallis led the first ranks of the British army through the streets of Philadelphia. The occupation had begun.[59]

Philadelphia greeted the British army with a fractured ambivalence not unlike that which it presented to Washington's Continentals when they passed through on their way to Brandywine. Before even reaching the city, Howe's forces encountered what Drinker referred to as "a great number of the lower sort of the People": the poor and laboring classes, who likely recognized that their survival and prosperity would depend on the military authorities in power.[60] In some pockets, the city wore a somber face. Reflecting back some years later, J. P. Norris recalled that "a number of our citizens appeared sad and serious" and flatly stated that "there was no huzzaing."[61] An unnamed "lady" told contemporary historian John Fanning Watson that "it was a solemn and impressive day—but I saw no exultation in the enemy, nor indeed in those who were reckoned favourable to their success."[62] Elsewhere, however, the military bands' choruses of "God Save the King" were all but drowned out by "the loudest acclamations of joy" from the inhabitants.[63] Lieutenant Colonel Francis Downman, with the

Royal Artillery, noted that "the roads and streets were crowded with people who huzzaed and seemed overjoyed to see us."[64] Captain John Montrésor, a British engineer, appreciated "the acclamation of some thousands of the inhabitants," though he noted that they were "mostly women and children," another group whose immediate fate would rest with the army's forbearance.[65] As Captain John Peebles, commander of the Forty-Second Royal Highland regiment's grenadier company, walked along "streets crowded with Inhabitants who seem to rejoice on the occasion," he could not help but reflect on the fact that, "by all accounts many of them were publickly on the other side before our arrival."[66] Elizabeth Drinker too had noticed that many of the "warm people," as she described the seemingly zealous Patriots, "continue here that I should not have expected."[67]

Some among the cheering crowds were doubtless committed Loyalists, who exuberantly gave voice to their feelings of triumph and relief. Yet taken together, the contemporary accounts suggest a population that was more hesitant and compliant than truly enthusiastic or hostile. Those who most needed the army's friendship turned out to express their friendship in return. Recent history had taught many residents that a brief but vocal expression of consent for whoever presently held power could spare one from a host of troubles; making an appearance was a small price to pay if it bought protection from charges of treason. Whether they were celebrating the arrival of a Washington or a Cornwallis was, to some extent, beside the point. The reigning emotion may have simply been one of "great confusion," a description Nathanael Greene applied to the entire colony of Pennsylvania in the summer of the invasion and which Drinker invoked five times in the month of September alone.[68] In less than a year's time, Philadelphia had gone from the capital of a proprietary colony, to the seat of a Revolutionary commonwealth, to the headquarters of the British army in America. It can hardly be surprising that more than a few residents were learning to bend with the shifting winds of power, or that they had begun to develop strategies for surviving, and perhaps even prospering, in the midst of the storm.

The Revolutionary forces outside Philadelphia were similarly forced to adapt their strategies in the face of chaos and misfortune. The fall of the capital was only the last in a series of blows to American morale in the preceding weeks. Howe had defeated Washington at Brandywine and then gone on to surprise and smash General Anthony Wayne's Continental division at the Battle of Paoli, tellingly remembered by some as the "Paoli

Massacre." Torrential rains soaked Washington's ammunition, forcing him to abandon plans for another major engagement in the wake of Brandywine. After the armies managed to dry out, Howe deftly outmaneuvered the Continentals yet again and crossed the Schuylkill unopposed and secured unimpeded access to Philadelphia. Despite the best efforts of the American army, the British had kept coming.[69]

Worse still, the British continued to receive supplies from disaffected and Loyalist Americans. Trade between civilians and the British army, both during the campaign and later in occupied Philadelphia, was immensely distressing to the leadership of the Revolution. Hancock referred to it as a practice "extremely dangerous to the Cause of America" and wrote forcefully of "The absolute Necessity of cutting off all Supplies and Intelligence from the Enemy . . . and thereby preventing any Intercourse between them and the disaffected in the State of Pennsylvania."[70] Yet it was easier said than done. Before the invasion, the Revolutionaries had looked to local Patriot committees, backed by the coercive power of the militias, to see to it that Americans acquired, used, and exchanged material goods in politically responsible ways. Now these means of enforcement, which had never been totally effective, were severely crippled; Revolutionary committees could not operate in the presence of the British army and even outside the lines their authority was powerfully undermined by the unanticipated collapse of the militia. State and local authority was in disarray, yet it was clear that the Patriots could not rely on the good will and patriotism of the people to keep them from supplying the redcoats with goods and information. Only the Continental Army had any chance of guaranteeing that the people of Pennsylvania would continue to voice their support for the Revolution in the ever-important language of commerce. As the Philadelphia campaign wore on and the capital fell to the British, Congress leaned ever more heavily on the coercive powers of the military, waiving personal and property rights and granting Washington more authority over the populace than Americans would ever have tolerated under the king.

Shortly after the defeat at Brandywine, Congress grudgingly admitted that "the city of Philadelphia notwithstanding the brave exertions of the American army, may possibly, by the fortune of war, be, for a time, possessed by the enemy's army."[71] As such it was "absolutely essential to the liberties of the United States" that any and all goods needed by the army or potentially useful to the British be secured. Further recognizing that certain "enemies to the liberties of America" might elect not to sell their goods to the army at a reasonable price and might even supply them to the enemy, Congress authorized the commander in chief "to take, wherever he may be, all such provisions and other articles as may be necessary for the comfortable subsistence of the army under his command, paying or giving certificates for the same" and "to remove and secure, for the benefit of the owners, all goods and effects which may be serviceable to the enemy."[72] Given that the British were often willing to pay for goods at a higher price and in a more valuable currency than the Americans, it's questionable how many of the owners looked upon this policy of confiscation as beneficial. Here again we see signs of the Revolutionary perspective in which independence was assumed to be of universal benefit to a unified "people," outside of which existed only "enemies to the liberties of America," whose property deserved no protection.

On October 8, with Philadelphia fallen and all hopes of quickly reclaiming it gone, Congress, now taking refuge in York, went further still and formally declared martial law. In so doing, the legislature granted the army powers not only over goods and effects but over the people themselves. "The process of the municipal law," Congress declared, "is too feeble and dilatory to bring to a condign and exemplary punishment persons guilty of such traitorous practices" as communicating supplies or intelligence to the British. The process of inflicting "exemplary punishment" on treasonous civilians would now fall to the military. Any inhabitant who served the British as a guide, provided them with any information, "or in any manner furnish them with supplies of provisions, money, cloathing, arms, forage, fuel, or any kind of stores [will] be considered and treated as an enemy and traitor to these United States." Washington was empowered to arrest any person within thirty miles of the British army, to try them by court-martial, and upon conviction of any of the above mentioned offenses, to sentence them "to suffer death or such other punishment as to [the courts-martial] shall seem meet."[73] In short, the military itself was now free to arrest, try, and execute civilian citizens without recourse to civilian justices or juries. Washington immediately requested duplicates of the resolutions in order to make them "known among the inhabitants, who are in this Neighbourhood, and who have been guilty of such practices"; Hancock ordered a thousand copies for distribution.[74]

Yet even Washington's new authority over the civilian population paled beside the powers the Pennsylvania government bestowed upon itself in response to the crisis. Here again, the presence of the British army led a panicked Revolutionary leadership to surrender the rights of the people into the hands of a few key individuals. In the opinion of the Pennsylvania Assembly, which was just completing its first term under the new constitution, the capture of Philadelphia had resulted in a time "of such danger and confusion [that] the ordinary powers of government cannot be regularly administered." Furthermore, there would soon be a break in legislative governance between the final recess of the sitting assembly and the election of its replacement. In this interval, they feared, "evil-minded persons may be encouraged, by open or secret practices, to assist the common enemy." To prevent these evils, the legislature resolved, "for a limited time, to vest fit persons with summary and adequate powers, to punish offenders, and restrain abuses."[75] Thus was born the 1777 Council of Safety, a body composed of the Supreme Executive Council and twelve individuals specifically named by the assembly.

On paper, at least, the powers of the Council of Safety were truly breathtaking and made a mockery of the much lauded Declaration of Rights included in the 1776 state constitution. In the enabling legislation, the assembly granted the council

> full power to promote and provide for the preservation of the commonwealth, by such regulations and ordinances as to them shall seem necessary, and to proceed against, seize, detain, imprison, punish, either capitally or otherwise, as the case may require, in a summary mode, either by themselves, or others, by them to be appointed for that purpose; all persons who shall disobey, or transgress the same, or the laws of this state heretofore made, for the purpose of restraining or punishing traitors, or others, who from their general conduct or conversation may be deemed inimical to the common cause of liberty, and the United States of North America.[76]

In other words, not only was the council empowered to pass its own regulations against supposed traitors and then summarily execute those who violated them, it was also free to summarily punish anyone who, regardless of their actions, in general conversation seemed inimical to the cause. Furthermore, the council was authorized "to take and seize, where it may be needful, provisions and other necessaries, for the army or the inhabitants" and "in general regulate the prices of such articles as they may think necessary, and compel a sale thereof where the same shall be wanted." Council members were also vested with the power "to call to their aid all officers and other persons, civil and military," to assist them in executing their decisions.[77] The people's supposed constitutional rights to "public trial, by an impartial jury of the country," to "hold themselves . . . and possessions free from search and seizure" except by warrant, and "to freedom of speech" were all disregarded.[78] "Oppressions multiply," wrote James Allen from his house in the country, "it seems determined to make this country intolerable to all who are not actively its friends. The most discreet, passive, & respectable characters are dragged forth." Over the last year he had often wished to see his brothers return from New York, but he now envied their being "happily out of the way" and did what he could to remain out of the way himself.[79]

More so than perhaps at any other moment in the history of the Revolution, the door was opened for an official and authorized "reign of terror" against those who would not support the cause. That very few Loyalists and dissenters were in fact executed speaks to both the weakness of the state government and its hesitancy to fully deploy the coercive powers at its disposal.[80] Despite their claims to represent a unified "people," the Patriots lacked the committed manpower to carry out a true purge of the opposition. The populace was never neatly divided into friends and foes. Many Americans remained uncertain of their neighbors' actual allegiance. Many remained uncertain of their own. In early December, as the shock of the invasion passed and the two armies prepared to settle into winter quarters, the Council of Safety was abolished by the Supreme Executive Council.[81]

The Continental Army's position as the coercive force behind Pennsylvania's Revolutionary government was just beginning, however. Its vital role in this respect became apparent as Washington began considering where and how to deploy his troops for the duration of the winter. In a council of general officers on November 30, the commander in chief put the question before his fellows and requested their advice.[82] It appears that three primary alternatives were under consideration: the army could retire to the interior of the state, assuming a position between Lancaster and Reading, relatively far from the occupied capital; the army could take up a post at and around Wilmington, close to Howe's lines; or the Continentals could not go into winter quarters at all, but instead pursue a winter campaign against the British and possibly dislodge them from Philadelphia. The response he received to these alternatives, not only from the generals but from the civilian governments as well, is telling.[83]

After sorting through many pages of correspondence, Washington concluded that "the general sentiment" of his commanding officers was that the army should fall back toward the Pennsylvania interior where it might best recover from its losses and prepare for the next year's campaign.[84] The advocates of this position were strongly of the opinion that caring for the army itself must be the highest priority, outweighing any concerns about the political vulnerability of the local Revolutionary regime. Brigadier General Johann de Kalb explained that "Rest, recruiting & Cloathing" the army were of the highest necessity and that "more tranquility & safety could be expected between Lancaster and Reading."[85] Major General Henry Knox concurred that "the ease and safety of the troops" were "the greater objects and all inferior ones should give place to them."[86] The young Marquis de Lafayette advocated placing winter quarters deep in the backcountry; "there" he argued "we schall be quiete."[87] These generals and their like-minded counterparts recognized that this course of action would leave the region around occupied Philadelphia open to the British. Nonetheless, they believed that the fate of the Revolution hinged first and foremost on the survival of the Continental Army, and that army required time to rest and recover. The worst-case scenario would be one in which the British were able to force the army into a winter campaign that would further sap its already depleted strength. The Patriots of Pennsylvania would have to look out for themselves over the winter. Knox optimistically suggested that "the militia of the state . . . will cover the Country" around the British lines. Notably, these advocates were almost entirely men from outside Pennsylvania and had little understanding of the fragility of the Revolution in the state.

Alongside this "general sentiment," Washington also heard "powerful advocates" for placing the army at Wilmington, or some other nearby location, where it could far more effectively cover the surrounding region and maintain Revolutionary authority.[88] This was the position advocated by the majority of the Pennsylvanians. Their justifications for this choice reveal that they were not only motivated by a desire to protect as much of their home state as possible but also by the dire political consequences of withdrawing the last vestige of Revolutionary force from the region. "The Disaffection of the Country, Distress of the Whigs, recruiting & refreshing the British Army—a general Despondency & above all, a Depreciation of the Currency stare me in the Face as a Consequence of Retirement to distant Quarters,"[89] warned Joseph Reed, who clearly had little faith that his fellow

Pennsylvanians would maintain the Revolutionary struggle in the absence of the army. Should Washington fall back toward Reading, he predicted that the population around Philadelphia would "seek Protection, take the Oaths, & throw themselves under the Enemy's Government. A Circle of 30 Miles at least including Jersey will be under the Command of the Enemy."[90] James Irvine also worried that "to leave so large a proportion of the most valuable part of the state uncovered . . . may have a very unhappy effect upon the minds of the inhabitants."[91] He predicted that the result would be a further reduction in the number of Pennsylvanians willing to fight for the Revolution, not only with regard to the militia but in the Continental line as well. John Cadwalader's analysis sought to take into consideration the youth of the new nation; "the situation of the american states is very different from that of a nation whose independence is acknowledged and established," he explained. "It requires great management to keep up the spirits of the well-affected & to subdue those who have taken a part against us." Like Reed he predicted that if the Continentals withdrew "the inhabitants, within this great Circle . . . must swear allegiance to the King, & deliver up their arms."[92] Doing Irvine one better, Cadwalader not only predicted a future reduction in manpower, but warned Washington that, if he failed to adequately cover the region, "those men who are to compose a very considerable part of your army the next Campaign will be engaged against you."[93]

The state and Continental legislatures, both of which had long been residing in Philadelphia, were staunchly on the side of the Pennsylvania officers and adamant about keeping a Revolutionary military force in the region. Congress dispatched Robert Morris, Elbridge Gerry, and Joseph Jones to meet with Washington and impress upon him the desirability of "carrying on a winter's campaign with vigour and success."[94] This pitted the politicians directly against the majority of Washington's generals, who believed that such a campaign would spell disaster for the army, whatever its benefits to the Revolutionary spirit in the Delaware Valley. Having interviewed a number of officers and observed a near confrontation between the two armies at Whitemarsh in early December, Congress eventually conceded that a winter assault on Philadelphia was impractical, but remained committed to covering the area around the city.[95]

The Pennsylvania state government, which arguably knew its people even better than Congress did, was driven to panic when it received erroneous information that Washington had chosen to pull the army out of the region for the duration of the winter. In a "Remonstrance of Council and Assembly to Congress," the legislators openly confessed the "melancholy truth, that too many of our People are so disaffected already that nothing but the neighbourhood of the Army keeps them subject to Government." Take away that final foundation of coercive force and the authority of the regime would collapse. Furthermore, echoing Cadwalader's dire predictions, the assembly and council warned that, without the army to keep them in check, "the Torys & Disaffected will gain Strength, & in many places perhaps declare openly for the Enemy."[96] In short, deprived of an army or at least an active militia to enforce it, the Revolution in Southeast Pennsylvania would be over.

Though initially inclined to adopt the "general sentiment" of his officers and fall farther back into the country, Washington eventually concluded that, without the assistance of the army, the Revolutionary regimes in the area would indeed collapse. Unwilling to let that happen, he sought to place the army where it might still exert some influence on the minds of the inhabitants.[97] The bulk of the army would assume a position west of the Schuylkill in and around Valley Forge to cover the country there and block Howe's access to the Pennsylvania interior; a detachment of Continentals would be sent across the Delaware to aid New Jersey in maintaining order and fending off British foraging parties; the area north of Philadelphia between the Schuylkill and Delaware rivers would be entrusted to the collective strength of the Pennsylvania militia, aided by a troop of Continental cavalry. The army would thus be kept partially in camp and partially in the field, poised to cover the civilian population but spared the rigors of a full offensive campaign and aided in their task by the state militia. It was not a decision without risk, for it placed winter quarters, such as they were, within the reach of a British offensive and, for good or ill, bound the army tightly to the unstable and conflicted government of Pennsylvania.[98] The months that followed proved how dangerous such a predicament could be, both for the army and for the divided and weary people who lived around it.

Settling the army at Valley Forge so it could keep the disaffected "subject to Government" was only one in a series of steps taken to counteract the troubling lack of Revolutionary enthusiasm in the region around Philadelphia during the invasion. Among the earlier steps were some of the most extreme measures taken by the Patriots in the course of the war, measures which, in different circumstances, might have opened the door for the sort of tyrannical purges and mass executions carried out by later revolutions.

The severity of these measures stemmed in part from the very real material and symbolic problems Howe's invasion posed for the Revolutionary regime in Pennsylvania, problems which would have existed even if the population had been fervently loyal to the Patriot cause. The political capital and agricultural breadbasket of the united colonies was under assault by the largest military force the region, and most of those living in it, had ever seen. The British commander in chief had consistently demonstrated his ability to outgeneral Washington and he continued to do so during the push toward Philadelphia. The Continental Army had failed to save the city and then failed in an attempt to retake it; the Continental Congress had taken flight; local government was in disarray. Franklin may have quipped that "Philadelphia has taken Howe" for the benefit of his French audience, but others like Nathanael Greene privately admitted that the loss was "a distressing circumstance notwithstanding we affect to despite it."[99] Far too much blood and treasure was lost in the Philadelphia campaign for us to casually accept the Patriots' public claims that the outcome was of no great importance to them.

Yet more threatening still were the *internal* crises of loyalty and consent triggered, or at least made evident, by the British invasion and occupation. Over the preceding decade the Revolutionaries had worked tirelessly to unite the American people in opposition to Britain and, more recently, in support of independence. As proof of that unity, which they saw as necessary to legitimate their actions, they pointed not only to explicit declarations of support but to the ways in which the people chose to spend their time and money. Surely service in the local militias signified consent to the Revolution; surely the rejection of British imports and acceptance of homemade alternatives were signs of support for an independent America. Yet if these practices were the markers of true republican citizens, willingly sacrificing their own interests for the greater good of a new nation, what did it mean when the people abandoned them the moment they were free to do so without punishment?

The collapse of the militia and the exchange of goods and information between the British military and Pennsylvania's civilians would have been intensely problematic under any circumstances, but it was especially dire in light of the ideological significance the Patriots had come to place on such activities. Service and material sacrifice were the "foundation of trust" among the Patriots, and in the summer and fall of the British invasion, deep cracks appeared in that foundation, endangering the entire Revolutionary edifice built upon it.[100] The Revolution's leaders could neither admit nor allow that instability. Consequently, they turned in desperation to the Continental Army, granting Washington authority they would never have acknowledged in the king or Parliament, in the hopes that he might somehow restore the image of a unified, consenting "people" that had been shattered by the arrival of the British army. Simultaneously, the state government entirely discarded any pretense of tolerance or freedom of expression in a desperate attempt to enforce its authority on an obstinate people.

The invasion of Pennsylvania, then, revealed with striking clarity that the young American governments in the region as yet relied, to a great extent, on coercive force, not merely to defend themselves from external dangers but also to achieve and maintain the expressions of popular consent that ultimately legitimated them. The arrival of a military counterweight to their own forces and the precipitous collapse of their primary internal enforcers thus called into question their very survival and understandably provoked a panicked reaction. In many ways, it was the Patriots' very aspirations to government by consent of the governed that led them, in a moment of crisis, to embrace such desperate measures in the quest to secure that consent.

INTERLUDE

THE ROAD TO VIRGINIA

As General Sir William Howe led his British army north from Head of Elk toward Philadelphia, Patriot forces in Pennsylvania herded some twenty civilian prisoners, Henry Drinker and his fellow Quakers among them, on a parallel journey, first west, but ultimately south to exile in Virginia. On September 11, not long after the competing armies came to battle along Brandywine Creek, a smaller, more intimate conflict erupted around Philadelphia's Masonic lodge where the prisoners were being held until their removal. The task of escorting Drinker and his fellows into exile fell to a troop of the city's light horse cavalry led by Samuel Caldwell and Alexander Nesbit. Arriving at the lodge, they found it surrounded by a sizable crowd which was outspokenly sympathetic to the prisoners' plight. Perhaps bolstered by this show of support and as yet denied any sort of trial, Drinker and those with him refused to submit themselves to the soldiers' authority, demanding to see written orders for their removal and denouncing the whole process as a violation of both civil law and natural rights. Unmoved by these objections, the troopers pressed their way through the crowd and began forcibly carrying the prisoners to the wagons meant to take them into exile. The situation soon became dangerously tense. One soldier bitterly hurled expletives at Thomas Wharton as he forced him out of the lodge but was soon confronted by a civilian bystander who threateningly described, in graphic and decidedly un-Quakerly terms, what he and crowd would do to the troopers if they attempted to abuse the prisoners. Rather than test the limits of the Friends' peace testimony, the soldiers finished their task in a more orderly manner.[1]

The wagons did not get underway until late in the afternoon of the eleventh and so the prisoners' first stop was Palmer's Tavern, not far outside

FIGURE 2. Silhouette of Henry Drinker. From Amelia Mott Gummere, *The Quaker: A Study in Costume* (Philadelphia: Ferris & Leach, 1901).

the city. Drinker was lodged in a nearby home where he claimed to have a "comfortable Nights Sleep in this Hospitable House." Writing to his wife, Elizabeth, early the following morning, he was surprised to find that he maintained "a serene tranquil state of Mind," an achievement which gave him "a degree of pleasing admiration." Appealing to Divine sovereignty for comfort, he urged Elizabeth "to be resigned & given up, to best direction . . . it will comfort my Heart to hear thou hast attain'd to this state." He could only hope his own tranquility would be of some comfort to her in return.[2]

Howe's invasion made the process of banishing the prisoners infinitely more difficult. The most straightforward route to their final destination in Winchester, Virginia, would take them straight into the arms of the British army. Washington's failure to stop the redcoats at Brandywine put an end to any hopes of proceeding directly southwest. A quickly devised alternative took them on a longer, winding course off to the northwest as far as Reading with the hopes of turning south again once they were well clear of the British. Furthermore, with Philadelphia now under imminent threat, committing an entire troop of the city's own cavalry to escorting a bunch of pacifists from the state no longer seemed like an acceptable allocation of resources. Caldwell and Nesbit were instructed to find some other authority to take charge of the prisoners and return to the city as soon as possible.[3]

The immediacy of the war posed other problems as well. With the Continental Army requisitioning nearly all the wagons and horses it could find for military use, the prisoners' escorts had failed to secure enough transportation for their baggage. His third day on the road, Drinker reported that several of the prisoners were still dressed in the same clothes they had worn departing Philadelphia. "With much difficulty" he and his fellows persuaded Samuel Caldwell to linger at Pottsgrove in the hope that their clothing and effects might catch up with them; Caldwell grudgingly agreed to halt the procession for a single day. "An unfeeling & inflexible Man is this Caldwell," Henry wrote to Elizabeth, revealing small cracks in his tranquil serenity.[4]

The delay in Pottsgrove proved to be a pivotal moment for Drinker and his fellows, though they would not know its full import until nearly a year later. As the party lingered, two very different men, each sympathetic to the injustice of the prisoners' plight, were pursuing two very different means of delivering them. Unbeknownst to Drinker, John Roberts, the Quaker from Lower Merion who would later act to protect Congress's official journal from the redcoats, had quietly rushed south to meet the British army near Brandywine. There he sought out Joseph Galloway, an old acquaintance, and proposed that the British launch a rescue mission to liberate the exiled Quakers before they could be carried too far into the Pennsylvania backcountry. Galloway immediately approved of the scheme and carried it to Howe, but the cautious British commander demurred. Disregarding his pacifist principles, Roberts then offered to assemble and lead the expedition himself if Howe would only lend him the necessary horses. Again, the general refused, and Roberts despondently rushed back toward Philadelphia, thankful that at least his futile expedition had not been noticed by the Revolutionary authorities.[5] Meanwhile, a different sort of deliverance was being attempted through Pennsylvania's legal system. In fulfillment of the prisoners' long-standing hopes, a writ of habeas corpus arrived from Thomas McKean, the state's new chief justice. Caldwell and Nesbit were ordered to bring the prisoners before the court where the state would have to either formally charge them with a crime or else release them. Whatever rise this gave to Drinker's hopes was short-lived, however, and McKean's judicial rescue was no more effective than Roberts's military solution. At nine the next morning, in blatant defiance of the court, the party of prisoners and escorts set out again for Reading, the next stop on their long road to Virginia. It marked the beginning of a long and challenging day.[6]

The people of Pottsgrove, most notably the Potts family itself, had been sympathetic and supportive toward the exiles; the inhabitants of Reading were less so. Easily accessible by road but still relatively far into the country, Reading had become an ideal location for housing British, Hessian, and Loyalist prisoners. Both the Continental Congress and the Pennsylvania government used it for this purpose, despite the loud and continuous objections of the local citizens who complained that their town lacked resources to support so many new people, to say nothing of the dangers inherent in living among so many enemy soldiers. Upon learning that Philadelphia was sending them even more prisoners, the outraged people of Reading poured out in protest. Lining the roads, they threw insults and more than a few stones at the exiles as they passed by. The prisoners were all hurriedly crowded into a single tavern which was then surrounded by armed guards, less to keep the exiles in than to keep the increasingly agitated mob out. The guards offered little protection, however, for the first pair of sympathetic friends who foolishly tried to press through the crowd and visit the exiles; they were swiftly turned back by a volley of stones and fists. The only visitor to reach the prisoners that day was Samuel Morris, who volunteered to provide their food at his own expense, a necessity Caldwell and Nesbit had apparently overlooked.[7]

Drinker's days in Reading were difficult ones. Though the mob that surrounded their tavern on the first day eventually dispersed, the prisoners were forced to remain inside for their entire time there, presumably for their own protection. They eventually learned that the depth of the town's animosity was due, in part, to Caldwell having sent letters in advance of their arrival in which he accused the exiles of plotting a violent escape assisted by armed Loyalists. It's unclear whether Caldwell had sincere fears of such a rescue attempt or whether he simply wished to stir up trouble and make the prisoners less sympathetic in the eyes of local civilians. Regardless, he and Nesbit soon surrendered control of their charges to the Reading militia and set off for Philadelphia.[8]

Other tribulations followed. Local authorities wanted the prisoners removed from Reading as quickly as possible, but the transportation crisis made this impractical. The baggage wagons which had followed them up from Pottsgrove, and which had been so difficult to secure in the first place, were requisitioned by the military almost as soon as they arrived at Reading. New ones would have to be procured. The state had not given any thought to how the exiles were to be supplied or fed along the road; sympathetic friends provided for them while they were confined to the tavern, but other provisions would have to be found for the journey to Virginia. Word arrived that Chief Justice McKean, who apparently was not amused by Caldwell's and Nesbit's decision to ignore his earlier writs, had now ordered the prisoners to be released. Yet not only did the local authorities ignore this order too, but the state government responded by retroactively granting itself the power to arrest and punish any inhabitants it thought suspicious and explicitly declaring itself immune from all judicial interference in such matters. Moreover, Nathanial Walker, a young man who had volunteered to deliver McKean's orders respecting the prisoners, was forcibly detained as he tried to leave Reading and ordered to swear an oath of loyalty to the Pennsylvania government in keeping with the Test Act. When he refused to commit himself to a regime which had just, before his very eyes, so blatantly disregarded the rights and liberties enshrined in its own constitution, he was summarily arrested and thrown into prison.[9]

Through it all, Henry Drinker remained "easy & placid" in his mind, or so he claimed in his letters to Elizabeth. His greatest anxiety, he wrote, was "a fear & care that I might be enabled so to pass [through] the tryals which may be permitted to come upon me . . . that my conscience may not accuse me at a future day of baulking my Testimony or flinching in the Day of Battle." He asks for prayers, not that he would be released, but that he would "be preserved & favour'd in stability & uprightousness of conduct." Conditions were less than ideal for writing, with three prisoners all huddled around a single tea table where they could lay their paper, constantly being jostled as their fellows or guards pressed past them. Nonetheless, on at least four occasions during the company's five days in Reading, Drinker found the opportunity and space to write letters home. Uncertain of when they would depart or if there would be any opportunity of contacting their families again once they'd left Pennsylvania, the exiles used their time to give final instructions to loved ones.[10]

Henry addressed each of his children individually and personally. His overriding message was one of restraint and self-control in the face of frustration or persecution, and it is not hard to imagine that he worried about their ability to hold their tongues in the aftermath of his banishment. "Watch over your Tempers and passions," he warned, "never returning any thing harsh or unkind to any thing which you might think offensive or wrong." Painfully aware of how dangerous an ill-timed criticism of the Revolutionary regime might be, he urged his oldest daughters to "watch over thy words and actions every hour of the day" and avoid unnecessary communication with those outside the family. His ten-year-old son he simply commanded not to leave the house at all except for religious services. To his baby girl Mary, then not more than three, he sent "a kiss and much Love with a charge to be a good Girl—and to think & talk of Daddy sometimes."[11]

Drinker's letter to his namesake, "little Henry," was the first he wrote and was sent earlier than the others. Elizabeth recorded that "our little sick Son received a letter from his dear Father . . . he has ordred it to be put in his Pocket-Book Wile he larns to read writeing." Perhaps because it was stored separately in little Henry's "Pocket-Book," this letter was not preserved with the others and so it cannot be known what Drinker wrote to his youngest son, who at that time remained bedridden with a seemingly interminable disease, except that Elizabeth considered it "well worth the store he [little Henry] sits by it."[12]

To Elizabeth herself, Henry wrote a mixture of devout reassurance and warning. He assured her that "for wise and good purpose are tribulations & afflictions permitted" and that "all things shall work together for good to them who love & fear the Lord." Yet he also cautioned her, clearly if indirectly, that she herself remained in danger of sharing a fate similar to his own. He warned against anyone writing to him about "the state of Public Affairs," as even "a plain relation of Facts as they occur . . . might by the ingenious Men of the present day, be represented as Inimical." Twice he declared that any "Man or <u>Woman</u>" was liable to face banishment for failing to support the Patriot cause in their communication, pointedly underlining "<u>Woman</u>" each time. Having seen the legislation through which the Revolutionary government had retroactively justified his arrest, Drinker knew that it took the unusual step of inclusively referring to potential suspects as either male or female, rather than relying on the male generic. He did not want Elizabeth laboring under the impression that her sex would spare her if she ran afoul of the powers that had sent him into exile. Instead of political affairs he wished for information only on the wellbeing of his family and friends. He wanted to hear nothing about "the State of Fleets & Armies," as "these are subjects which leave melancholy Sensations on the Humane & feeling Mind."[13]

On the twenty-first the exiles, now passed off to the keeping of Daniel Levan, sheriff of Berks County, finally departed Reading. They would spend almost every day of the next week on the road. First from Reading to Lebanon. Then on to Hummel, where several of them were allowed the enjoyable distraction of visiting a network of limestone caves along Swartara

Creek. From Hummel to the home of John Harris along the Susquehanna River. The Harris family had long operated a ferry and their sizable mansion offered spacious, if not necessarily clean, accommodations. The site would, in time, become Harrisburg, Pennsylvania's modern capital. Having crossed the Susquehanna and now well clear of the British invasion force, the prisoners were finally turned south toward the state border. The following days took them through Carlisle, Shippensburg, and Chambersburg, out of Pennsylvania, briefly through Maryland, and at last across the Potomac at Watkins Ferry and into Virginia. The journey brought several small comforts in the form of supportive individuals along the road. It also brought challenges. The mundane hardships of difficult roads and poor accommodations mingled with darker moments wherein the exiles encountered open hostility and more threats of violence. As had been the case at Reading, unsupported accusations and insinuations had been circulated ahead of them in order to preempt local sympathies. Late on September 29, eighteen days after leaving Philadelphia, Henry Drinker arrived at Winchester, his home and prison for the foreseeable future.[14]

CHAPTER 3

SIEGE

> The friends of the revolution excuse this tyranny by saying
> that liberty for all must be forced on a few by despotism.
> —Captain Johann Ewald, March 21, 1778

On the evening of October 3, 1777, Captain Johann Ewald walked through the growing darkness around the village of Germantown, some five miles north of occupied Philadelphia. Ewald was a *jäger* officer of the Hessian Leib Infantry Regiment serving with General Sir William Howe's British forces in America. It had been more than a week since the American capital had fallen, and while a significant British force was camped in and around the city, the bulk of Howe's army had been placed near Germantown, a position better suited for guarding against attack by Washington's army, which still lurked somewhere out in the darkness. Ewald had only one eye, his left having been lost in a duel some seven years earlier and replaced with an occasionally uncomfortable glass prosthesis, but he used it, along with his fellow light infantrymen, to maintain a constant lookout for any sign that the Continentals were planning an assault to retake Philadelphia. Thus far, they had seen and heard nothing of consequence. That was about to change.[1]

Ewald walked with William Smith, provost of the College of Philadelphia, Anglican clergyman, and an American of complicated loyalties. Long an advocate of expanded liberties for Americans, Smith had spoken against British oppressions for more than a decade and served on the Philadelphia Committee of Correspondence early in the Revolution. Yet he abhorred the chaos and violence that came with the war and mostly refrained from active involvement in the struggle. Though his heart lay with the Patriots' cause, his decision to remain at Philadelphia even when it fell into British hands, his association with the Anglican Church, and past disagreements with Patriot luminaries like Benjamin Franklin marked him as a Loyalist in the eyes of many Revolutionaries. When the College of Philadelphia was superseded by the University of Pennsylvania in 1779, the government pointedly rejected Smith as either a trustee or the head of that new institution. He later moved to Maryland and founded a new college which he named in honor of George Washington.[2]

Though Smith often resided in Philadelphia itself, he also owned an estate in the country situated quite close to Ewald's post. The Hessians had a reputation for pillage and plunder, but Ewald and his *jägers* had treated Smith's property and family with the utmost respect and, moreover, had offered him protection from both the more dastardly elements of the British military and Continental forces who might have requisitioned Smith's belongings for their own army. Though their acquaintance was new and their backgrounds wildly different, it seems that Ewald, the *jäger* warrior, and Smith, the college provost, had quickly developed a respect for each other and even a friendship. It was that personal relationship, running counter to Smith's own political loyalties, which took him to Germantown that evening and led him to seek out the Hessian captain.

Smith led Ewald on a leisurely walk about the British encampment, talking idly of small matters until, at length, they came to a place out of the sight and hearing of any other soul. At that point Smith's manner transformed and he turned toward Ewald with sudden seriousness. "My friend," he began, "I confess to you that I am a friend of the States and no friend of the English government, but you have rendered me a friendly turn. You have shown me that humanity which each soldier should not lose sight of. You have protected my property. I will show you that I am grateful. You stand in a corps which is hourly threatened by the danger of the First attack when the enemy approaches. Friend, God bless your person! The success of your arms I cannot wish.—Friend! General Washington has marched up to [Norristown] today!—Adieu! Adieu!" Without another word, Smith turned and fled the British camp, returning as quickly as he could to Philadelphia, leaving Ewald stunned and alone. From Norristown the Continental Army could reach the British camp within a matter of hours. Having somehow eluded all the patrols and scouts meant to find him, Washington was poised for a potentially devastating surprise attack. How Smith learned of the Continentals' movements, Ewald did not know and he likely did not care; whatever its origins, the provost's warning might yet save the army if steps were taken quickly and defenses made ready.[3]

Yet, somehow, nothing was done. Whether due to miscommunication, bureaucratic delay, or simply because more powerful officers doubted Smith's reliability, Ewald's warning went unheeded and never even reached the upper ranks of the army. And so as evening turned to night the bulk of the British army slumbered, unaware of its danger, while Johann Ewald and his men prepared for war and stared anxiously out into the night.[4]

Early the next morning the inhabitants of occupied Philadelphia awoke to a sound like "the crackling of thorns under a pot, and incessant peals of thunder": the rolling echoes of musket and cannon fire which swept down from the village of Germantown to the north.[5] Having failed to defend the city, Washington now strove to retake the American capital, launching a four-pronged surprise attack on the main body of the British army. James Allen considered it "the most general & important battle ever seen in America." The Battle of Germantown marked the Continentals' only attempt to reclaim Philadelphia by force. Numerous factors contributed to their defeat, and several might be seen as harbingers of greater troubles to come.[6]

Washington's plans for the battle were complex, relying on the coordinated movement of four separate columns of men, determined action by the militia, cooperation from the weather, and the complicity of local civilians, at least to the extent of not alerting the British in advance. None of these factors proved to be fully reliable. Inexperience, ignorance of the local terrain, and the challenges of communicating effectively across large distances in the midst of battle all conspired to turn what was supposed to be a simultaneous assault from multiple angles into a staggered series of attacks directed mostly against the British center. A thick fog covered the region and, as one participant reported, "made such a midnight darkness that a great part of the time there was no discovering friend from foe."[7] The militia, which made up the flanking prongs to the left and right, failed to contribute anything significant to the engagement; the militiamen from Pennsylvania provided little more than a distraction for some Hessians on the British left, while those from Maryland and New Jersey never succeeded in reaching the enemy at all. Finally, as Ewald's encounter with Smith demonstrates, the local civilians, even those inclined to support the American cause, were not entirely to be trusted. Loyalties were complicated and secrets hard to keep.[8]

The attempt on Germantown cost Washington approximately a thousand men, and though the soldiers initially remained in good spirits despite the defeat, the loss signaled that the only hope of removing the British from Philadelphia before the next campaign season would be by starving them out. In pursuing that goal, the Continentals faced perils not unlike those which had thwarted their plans at Germantown. Dangerous weather, unhelpful civilians, an unreliable militia, and the constant challenge of "discovering friend from foe" in the midst of civil war continued to threaten the American cause even as the focus of the Philadelphia campaign steadily shifted away from reclaiming territory and toward the acquisition of basic supplies. The danger of crippling shortages and potential starvation first haunted the British in Philadelphia, as Continental forces worked to isolate the city from waterborne supplies and local produce. Yet the same specter soon appeared at Valley Forge, as logistical disorganization and the behavior of the surrounding populace drove the Patriot military toward a material crisis. Increasingly, through their commercial choices and pursuit of personal interests, Pennsylvania's disaffected civilians threatened to accomplish what British guns and bayonets could not: the destruction of the Continental Army. Consequently, outside the British lines, the focus of the Americans' coercive power increasingly shifted from the British forces of occupation to the local civilian population. The result was a bitter and destructive spiral of disaffection and brutality that appeared, in the early spring of 1778, to presage the collapse of the Revolution in Pennsylvania.

Isolating the Occupied City

During the first months of the occupation, it still seemed possible that, in capturing Philadelphia, Howe had inadvertently led his army into an elaborately set trap meant to destroy it.[9] "I almost wish he [Howe] had Philadelphia," wrote an optimistic John Adams shortly after the British landed at Head of Elk, "for then he could not get away. I really think it would be the best Policy to retreat before him, and let him into this Snare, where his Army must be ruined."[10] The New Englander's willingness to sacrifice Pennsylvania's capital as a poisoned pill was not widely embraced by his fellow Patriots, but when the city nonetheless fell into British hands, more than a few onlookers either hoped or feared that it would prove to be the redcoats' undoing. George Walton, Congressional delegate from the state of Georgia, wrote triumphantly to Benjamin Franklin in France of "General Howe being shut up in Philadelphia, scarce of provisions, and surrounded by conquering troops." Writing from Savannah in late December, he confidently, if erroneously, assured Franklin that "the fate of Howe is surely determined by this time; when I came away the prevailing opinion was, that his safety depended upon his flight."[11] Even Washington expressed hope "that the acquisition of Philadelphia may, instead of being his [Howe's] good fortune, prove his ruin."[12] Among the British themselves, Lieutenant General James Grant found that a majority of his fellow soldiers believed that the city would have to be abandoned. "Quitting Philadelphia after We had once taken possession of it," he worried, would render "all the advantages which had been obtained during the campaign of no effect . . . [and] must have ruined the cause of Great Britain—What to think of it at present I know not."[13] If the Continentals could send the main British army slinking back to New York, or better yet force it to surrender for want of provisions, then the end of the war might well be in sight and America's already declared independence all but achieved.

Such a quick victory was not to be, but the Revolutionaries took three crucial steps which, combined, very nearly put it within their grasp. The first was to strip Philadelphia of anything that might be of use to their enemy. Arms and ammunition, horses, carts, and all river-going vessels, bells, presses and other potential sources of metal including some lead pipes from people's homes, and most importantly, provisions and stores were confiscated and carried away. In their turbulent wake the Revolutionaries left only "what was immediately wanted for the present Use of the Inhabitants," what the ingenuity or influence of individual families allowed them to retain, and a simmering resentment in the hearts of those who stayed behind.[14] Not only did the British find nothing in Philadelphia to use for their own needs, they also, almost immediately, faced a subsistence crisis among the civilian population.

Having left Howe little in Philadelphia, the Patriots then sought to deny him his own provisions by cutting him off from naval support along the Delaware. In one of the war's most valiant defenses, Continental soldiers in Forts Mifflin and Mercer kept the river closed to British shipping, defying the overwhelming combined firepower of Britain's army and navy for more than a month. So long as he was cut off from his waterborne supplies, Howe could not seriously contemplate a further offensive into the Pennsylvania interior, and as the weeks passed and repeated assaults failed to dislodge the American defenders, soldiers on both sides began to question his army's ability to survive the approaching winter.[15] Though eventually battered into retreat, the forts' defenders effectively guaranteed that the British would only gain a foothold in Pennsylvania in 1777.

Prevented, at least temporarily, from accessing their shipborne provisions, the redcoats turned to the countryside to provide the supplies they desperately needed, both for themselves and the more than twenty thousand civilians who were now under their care.[16] Here again the Revolutionaries moved to cut the occupied city off from material relief. On October 8, Congress had declared Philadelphia and the surrounding counties to be under martial law; granted Washington complete freedom to unilaterally arrest, try by court-martial, and even execute civilians who traded with the occupation forces; and further urged him, as well as all officials and "good people of these states, to be vigilant in apprehending, securing and bringing to condign punishment all such offenders."[17] Two weeks later, the Pennsylvania Council of Safety stepped forward to declare that anyone carrying provisions to Philadelphia was, on that basis, "contributing as far as in them lies, to increase the distresses of their injured country" and had "wickedly joined themselves to our unnatural enemies." Further, since "it is highly unjust, and repugnant to the practice of all nations, to protect and preserve the property of their avowed enemies," commissioners were appointed to seize the property of all such traitors, keeping 5 percent of all seized goods for themselves. The exchange of goods between the countryside and the city, a commerce that had been ongoing for generations and represented the foundation of economic life in this corner of the province, was now tantamount to treason.[18]

In order to enforce these edicts, Washington deployed the men at his disposal in a broad arc around the city, centered on Valley Forge and stretching from Wilmington in the southwest to Trenton in the east. Specific regions of responsibility were fluid during the campaign, but once the army moved into winter quarters the lands west of the Schuylkill River were to be guarded directly by the Continental Army, primarily in the form of patrols regularly launched from Valley Forge. The region north of Philadelphia, between the Schuylkill and the Delaware, was given over to the Pennsylvania militia, anchored by detachments of Continental cavalry along the Schuylkill and at Trenton.[19] Across the Delaware, the New Jersey militia was charged with overseeing the countryside along the river and as far inland as the British could reach, an overwhelming responsibility for so small a force.[20]

Throughout October and November, the Continentals' stranglehold on occupied Philadelphia held fast, slowly choking the life out of the forces within. "Washington keeps the army so tightly bottled up by his parties," complained Ewald, "that the market people must sneak through at the risk of their lives."[21] It was a risk few of them were as yet willing to take. Various writers within the city echoed Elizabeth Drinker's distress in finding that "the people round the Country dose not come near us with any thing."[22] With the British military intently focused on securing control of the Delaware River, the Continental Army was largely free to impose its will on the countryside. Even in late November, British secretary Ambrose Serle noted that there was only a "very small Extent of Country at this time under our Command."[23] Beyond that small patch of land, the Revolutionaries proved to be remarkably successful in identifying and shoring up any weaknesses that appeared in the embargo they were imposing on Philadelphia.[24] Observing the effectiveness of the Continental cordon from the outside, Allen recorded that "Genl Howe's situation in Philadelphia becomes much strait'ned, provisions & other necessaries very dear"; he suspected that the British were doomed unless the Royal Navy could overcome the Patriot fortresses guarding the Delaware River. Also watching the occupation from the outside, but knowing that his daughter was contained within, the Reverend Henry Muhlenberg fretted "that the American army had occupied the passages to Philadelphia so that no food could enter the city, whether by land or by sea. Poor Philadelphia! So thine inhabitants are to be frozen and starved!"[25] He went on to compose a prayer for the Lord's mercy. The need for such mercy was soon felt by the city's elite as well as its poor, for even the wealthy could not purchase what wasn't there to be sold. "Money will not procure the necessaries of life," wrote Sarah Logan Fisher from Philadelphia, "for as the English have neither the command of the river nor the country, provisions cannot be brought in."[26]

Only stealth and the cover of night allowed a meager, but crucial, trickle of supplies to reach the city. So long as Fort Mifflin was defended, few navy transports dared approach the wharves, and so military provisions were unloaded down the river and conveyed by wagon over miles of difficult and exposed terrain or laboriously guided up narrow channels in small boats before finally reaching British lines and bellies.[27] Well-connected civilians, like Fisher, learned where small packages of butter and eggs could secretly be obtained from a handful of individuals willing to risk arrest, or worse, in order to exchange their goods for hard money, but quantities were severely limited and the price was terribly steep.[28] Such smuggling was all the more important for the populace because the few supplies the British were able to secure were generally retained for the use of the army.[29] Even the managers of the Bettering House, one of the few institutions of poor relief still operating in Philadelphia during the occupation, were told that the military had nothing to spare for them or the people under their care.[30]

Change was coming, however, beginning with a long-awaited British victory on the Delaware. Though it cost him hundreds of men, two warships, untold quantities of munitions, and, most importantly, nearly the entirety of the remaining campaign season, Howe finally succeeded in driving the Americans from Fort Mifflin on November 15. Six days later, Fort Mercer was also in British hands.[31] The Royal Navy moved swiftly to rid the river of its final impediments and to deliver long-awaited provisions to the docks of the occupied city. Yet while access to the sea might offer the army a lifeline, being forced to rely entirely on imported provisions while ostensibly in the process of "liberating" one of America's premier agricultural regions would be embarrassing, expensive, and politically disastrous. Depending on if and when the Delaware froze, the Royal Navy might manage to fulfill the army's material needs for the winter, but there were more than military mouths to feed in the occupied city. Even as ships advanced up the now undefended Delaware, Captain John André worried that "we have reason to fear grave scarcity of provisions in Philadelphia this winter unless by driving off Mr. Washington the country people can be emboldened to bring in their product."[32] The survival of the army would matter little if the thousands of civilians under British protection were driven out by starvation and forced to sell their allegiance for food and fuel. If the British cause, as well as the British army, was to endure the winter in Philadelphia, the flow of goods from the countryside to the city had to be reestablished.

Fortunately for the British, as early as December of 1777, significant cracks were appearing in Washington's embargo of the city; provisions and supplies were beginning to seep in from the countryside and, despite the looming threat of Revolutionary retribution, commerce between Philadelphia and the surrounding region was being restored. Though seemingly insignificant at first, this initial trickle was the harbinger of a turning tide that, in the months to come, would threaten the Continental Army with the same deprivation it had hoped to impose upon the British. For Philadelphia's civilian population, scarcity and brutally high prices were matters of constant concern, but in the waning weeks of the year, worries over the local farmers' inability or unwillingness to reach the city and remarks about the effectiveness of Washington's patrols faded away and were increasingly replaced by reports of individuals successfully crossing the lines to bring much-needed, if painfully expensive, food to those under occupation. While Sarah Logan Fisher had previously waited at the river by night in hopes of obtaining a pound of butter and declared that "provisions cannot be brought in," she was now able to obtain large quantities of butter and honey from one source and pork, beef, and a goose from another. "If we can but be favored to get flour," she mused, "bread & honey will be an excellent substitute for many other things that we have been used to."[33] It's unclear whether or not Fisher found flour for sale in December, but Elizabeth Drinker did.[34] On December 18 she wrote to reassure her exiled husband that "food and raiment are much more plenty, than some time past."[35] Sixteen-year-old Robert Morton noted that, while provisions were still scarce, he daily learned of people crossing the lines in order to pursue them. Even Robert Proud, a typically pessimistic Philadelphian merchant and Quaker, wrote to his brother that the threat of starvation "appears now in a likely way to be removed," not only by the arrival of the British fleet but "by Reason of some Part at least, of the Country being in a much fairer Way to be speedily opened than heretofore."[36]

This opening of the country seems to have begun in the region immediately north of the city and between the Delaware and Schuylkill rivers. By mid-December, Hessian major Carl Leopold Baurmeister was able to report that "The highways from Philadelphia to Germantown and Frankford, and the road to Trenton by the way of Jenkintown, are open to anyone" and that people, food, and intelligence flowed continually over them. The flow would increase as time passed such that a month later he found "nothing remarkable" in the news that men and women came from "the most distant parts of Pennsylvania to sell food for hard money." His fellow Hessian, Ewald, reported that "an abundance of provisions has been brought in by the country people" and, as a result, "the city came to life; trade and commerce began to flourish again."[37]

These same currents were also apparent to observers outside the British lines. As the new year approached, Washington increasingly found himself confronted with reports of civilians successfully reaching Philadelphia with food and other supplies. Again, the most significant breaches appeared to the north of the city in the direction of Bucks County. By mid-December,

Major John Clarke, Washington's spy-master in the region, had issued repeated warnings from Newtown that the embargo was on the verge of collapse. On the nineteenth he wrote the commander in chief to "again tell your Excellency that the country people carry in provisions constantly."[38] In Whitemarsh, Major John Jameson estimated that "not less than two hundred [inhabitants] a day" left the city with empty sacks and returned loaded down with meal and flour while those in the countryside made the reverse trip in order to buy salt.[39] During the first week of January, Christopher Marshall, having evacuated Philadelphia before the occupation began, recorded that there was "a great concourse of market folks from Bucks County, who attend the markets constantly; that this day week [sic] fifty or sixty men went inside of their [British] works at Kensington, and after some time returned back."[40] Less than a week later, Brigadier General James Potter confirmed that "there is a smart trade carried on between the country and the city" and that wagons loaded with flour and other provisions were safely reaching British lines.[41]

Relative to the needs of city, the quantities carried by each individual were small, but as the number of inhabitants doing business with the city grew, their combined impact became increasingly significant. In late January, Colonel Walter Stewart wrote Washington from Smithfield, not far from British lines, and tried to impress upon him the extent of the problem: "I can assure your Excellency not less flour than is sufficient to maintain eight or ten thousand men goes daily to Philadelphia, carried in by single persons, wagons, horses &c. The quantities of other provisions are great. . . . Were these articles taken in for the use of the poor inhabitants I should think nothing of it, but from all I can learn, tis a traffick, and make no doubt that the British Army receive the greatest Benefits of any persons therefrom."[42] Washington expressed surprise and alarm over the quantities involved and requested that Stewart do what he could to discover how so much material was able to get past the militia and Continental cavalry that ostensibly patrolled the roads north of the occupied city.[43]

Across the river in New Jersey the situation was, if anything, even worse. Having taken forts Mifflin and Mercer, the British now had full control of the Delaware up to and along Philadelphia itself. Supported by the Royal Navy, Howe could easily deploy forage parties to the opposite bank to collect supplies and trade with Loyalist or disaffected civilians. Having tasted British specie and largely unhindered by the meager forces of the state militia, those same civilians felt a powerful pull toward the open markets of

Philadelphia. "The Coast is Very Extensive," complained Colonel Joseph Ellis, who found himself in command of the New Jersey militia in January, "and I fear it will not be in our power to Guard every part effectually. Considerable Quantities of Provision are carried to Philada which it is Not in our power totally to prevent." The militia had managed to arrest numerous civilians for carrying goods toward the city, but for every would-be trader they pursued, many others slipped past them. "The Coast is so Extensive," Ellis repeated, "that many Escape." In fairness to Ellis, "extensive" hardly began to describe the country he was expected to oversee. The swath of New Jersey which lay exposed to British foraging and vulnerable to the allures of Philadelphia's markets represented approximately the same amount of territory as was then being covered by the combined forces of the Pennsylvania militia and the Continental Army, yet Ellis's small force of militia was largely alone in guarding it.[44]

The ineffectiveness of the militia in both New Jersey and Pennsylvania was due, in no small part, to the remarkably poor turnout it experienced throughout the occupation. The decline in militia service which began with the British landing over the summer continued throughout the fall campaign and worsened as the winter turned into early spring. The collapse was so severe that, at several points in early 1778, the Pennsylvania militia, which the state's Revolutionaries had worked so hard to create and forcibly maintain, was practically nonexistent.

In mid-October, Washington estimated that Pennsylvania had about twelve hundred militia in the field. At that time, he had been "astonished" and penned a scathing letter to the state government decrying so paltry a turnout in the face of invasion and occupation.[45] By late December, however, Washington had become more familiar with the disaffected condition of the region. Where before he had demanded at least four thousand Pennsylvania militiamen, the number called for by the Continental Congress, he now came to an agreement with the state's military and political leadership for a mere one thousand men for the winter, provided that they were "regularly reliev'd." Washington tactfully said that he accepted the smaller number in order to spare the state "expense & inconvenience," but by that point he was likely also aware that obtaining a larger force was wholly unrealistic.[46]

By the winter's end, even the agreement to supply one thousand militia would reveal itself to have been hopelessly optimistic, a revelation that disappointed no one more than twenty-two-year-old Brigadier General John

Lacey Jr. From the moment he took command of Pennsylvania's militia in the first weeks of 1778 through the end of the British occupation, Lacey was crippled by a lack of manpower. In an effort to assemble the one thousand men it had promised Washington, the state government called up seven classes of militia in early January and ordered them to join Lacey in policing the region between the Schuylkill and Delaware Rivers. Additionally, to provide a more mobile force for patrolling the roads, Philadelphia and Bucks Counties were ordered to contribute twenty light horse apiece.[47] Thomas Wharton Jr., president of Pennsylvania's Supreme Executive Council, estimated that this would put at least fifteen hundred troops at Lacey's disposal.[48] Yet by the end of the month, none of these new recruits had materialized. Lacey was left with four hundred and fifty men spread across four different posts, and nearly all of these were due to return to their homes in early February. On the fifteenth of that month, Lacey reported to Washington that his "force is at last reduced to almost a cipher. Only sixty remain fit for duty in camp." Of the fifteen hundred militiamen called for by the state government, he had as yet been joined by no more than seven individuals. Of the forty cavalrymen supposedly sent from Bucks and Philadelphia Counties, he could report the arrival of only two.[49]

Unable to maintain a guard on all the roads leading into Philadelphia, Lacey's men fell back to a single post and even then struggled to keep scouts and pickets deployed for self-defense. Aware that even a small British detachment might surprise and destroy their meager force, the militia moved their headquarters to a tavern some seventeen miles from Philadelphia, a distance which, one officer concluded, "puts it out of his power the doing of any thing of Consequence."[50] Washington, and even Lacey himself, expressed agreement with this assessment.[51]

The region north of Philadelphia was thus almost entirely bereft of Revolutionary authority and, as a result, the people there were free to trade with the occupied city without fear of retribution. Major Francis Murray of the Thirteenth Pennsylvania Regiment, who was visiting his family in Newtown, was surprised to find that his neighbors had fully reestablished commercial relations with Philadelphia, trading just as they had before the occupation commenced. He blamed this on "there being no guards on the Road between here and the City," though it also reflected the people's general stance toward the Revolution.[52] This same absence of Revolutionary forces, combined with the constant flow of goods and information between Newtown and Philadelphia, helps to explain why, less than a week after penning these words, Murray was captured and made prisoner by a detachment of provincial cavalry sent from the city.[53]

This near-total collapse of the Pennsylvania militia can be traced to a continuation, or even acceleration, of forces first seen during the early weeks of the invasion. The continued presence of a strong British force in and around the city, along with the increasingly apparent weakness of the Revolutionary government, led to what Major General Armstrong called a "very infamous falling off of the Militia which may with great justice be called desertion."[54] This, in combination with the scheduled departure of men who had completed their term of service, steadily sapped away Lacey's strength, while an ever-increasing hesitancy and at times total refusal of new classes of militia to turn out prevented his numbers from being restored.

Throughout the winter and early spring, Pennsylvania's inability to convince its militia to march became ever more apparent. From within Philadelphia, Baurmeister noticed the disappearance of enemy posts and estimated that "less than a third of the new militia" had actually taken the field.[55] The much oppressed Colonel Richard McAllister, whose York County militia were supposed to provide two of the seven classes ordered to support Lacey in January, reported that "the Militia of this County seems determined not to march" and, further, that "it is allmost Impossible" to find anyone, including the local law enforcement officers, who would assist him in collecting fines from those who refused to serve.[56] Some escaped service or punishment by seeking shelter within Philadelphia. Somewhat ironically, among the few people Lacey's crippled force was able to apprehend on their way to the occupied city in mid-February were three "young fellows" who "were flying to escape their fines in the militia."[57] By late February the state's failure to field an effective militia had become so well established that Anthony Wayne, seeking to castigate the people of New Jersey for their refusal to turn out, could think of no better insult than to claim that they were "(if possible) more toriesetically inclined than those in the State of Pennsylvania."[58]

Eventually Washington himself took steps to address the pitiful state of Lacey's militia forces east of the Schuylkill. Dividing the responsibility for isolating Philadelphia between the Continental and state troops had been intended to free Washington from the hassle of micromanaging the entire region and, perhaps more importantly, to let the state have some visible role in its own defense. Yet the division increasingly proved to be untenable as Lacey's force withered away to almost nothing. Though he remained steadfast in his demand that the militia, not the army, control the region north of Philadelphia, Washington eventually found himself in the awkward position of chastising Pennsylvania's political leadership on behalf of its own militia officers. After Lacey's repeated pleas to the Supreme Executive Council for more men went unanswered, the commander in chief stepped in. In a letter to council president Thomas Wharton Jr., Washington painstakingly reviewed his past agreements with the state and reminded Pennsylvania's leadership that they had pledged a force of at least one thousand men which "should be regularly kept up." He then explained that, despite these promises, the militia had "by some means or other dwindled away to nothing."[59] A chagrined Wharton wrote back with a litany of explanations and excuses, but assured the commander in chief that well over a thousand men would soon arrive to strengthen Lacey's force.[60] Though Lacey never came close to commanding a thousand militiamen, following Washington's intervention his command did return from the brink of extinction and in March his numbers crept above six hundred, allowing him to redeploy closer to the occupied city and participate in the increasingly ruthless effort to isolate Philadelphia.[61]

Washington's success in revitalizing the Pennsylvania militia proved to be short-lived, however. Lacey's numbers peaked in early March as the surge of militia, such as it was, originally called for in early January finally arrived. From that point forward he experienced a steady decline due to defection, desertion, casualties, and the state's inability to replace the lost. By early April, he was reduced to half his peak strength; by the end of that month, the Pennsylvania militia had once again "dwindled away to nothing." As of the twenty-seventh, Lacey reported a mere fifty-seven men fit for duty; the five classes called up the previous month had never materialized. Just as he had in February, Lacey abandoned the roads to the British and collected his meager force together at a single post.[62]

As this second collapse was in progress, Congress obliviously passed a new resolve giving Washington the authority to command even more militia forces. Despite the fact that Pennsylvania was then struggling to maintain a force of three hundred militiamen in the field, on April 4 Congress empowered the commander in chief to call up a force of five thousand from Pennsylvania, Maryland, and New Jersey.[63] This suggests an alarming disconnect between Congress's perception of recent events and the actual situation in the field. In a carefully composed response, Washington politely thanked Congress for his expanded powers before letting some of his frustration slip out by suggesting that assembling so many militiamen might be impractical, "to evince which, I need only recur to the experience of last Campaign on similar occasions—and to remind you, that it was not possible to obtain 1000 Men, nor sometimes even one hundred from this state, although the former number was required, and promised, for the purpose of covering, during the winter, the Country between Schuylkill & Delaware."[64] Though Washington had learned better than to expect five thousand militiamen, he did use the congressional resolve to try one last time to get the one thousand men Pennsylvania had promised him. Presenting his new authority to the state's Supreme Executive Council, he demanded that a "Body of one thousand to be sent into the field as expeditiously and for as long a time as possible." Wharton admitted that in the past the militia "have not turned out to my wishes" and somewhat ambiguously promised to give "such orders as I hope will answer your Excellencies expectations," though almost in the same breath he began suggesting excuses for why they might not turn out this time either.[65]

Across the river in New Jersey, Colonel Joseph Ellis, Lacey's counterpart in that state, was undergoing a similar trial. Shortly after taking command, Ellis wrote Washington to confess that "the Militia dont turn out so well as I could wish" and that, while he was never certain exactly how many of his men remained in the field, the number "Seldom or Never exceeds 500." His situation would not improve. While on a foraging mission in New Jersey, Brigadier General Anthony Wayne wrote bitterly to Washington about "the Supine[ne]ss and Disaffection of every part of this State" and declared "I don't expect a Single man of the Militia to turn out more than those already under Col. Ellis." He could not have been far from right; the state's militia numbers had already slipped below three hundred. Yet where Washington pressured Pennsylvania into pushing more men into service, at least temporarily, the same cannot be said of New Jersey. On the contrary, Washington tended to increase rather than relieve Ellis's burden, ordering his militia to assist in constructing batteries along the Delaware and to guard the Continental artillery placed there.[66]

The weakness of the New Jersey militia and their vulnerability to British forces in Philadelphia created a vicious cycle for Ellis's command. As the number of active militiamen decreased, service with them became increasingly dangerous, and so fewer and fewer men were willing to answer the call and take up arms. In March Ellis wrote to the state governor with a woeful tale. He had repeatedly tried to summon militia from Burlington, yet "not a single man of them appears, nor do I hear there is any motion of the kind among them." One of his battalions amounted to fewer than twenty men and another had essentially defected, taking their own officers prisoner. By the twenty-third Ellis admitted that "we have little to expect from the Militia," estimating that he had about fifty men who would still follow his orders. As to the prospect of more men joining him, he concluded that upon seeing how hopelessly outnumbered his force would be in the event of the British incursion, "each one naturally consults his own Safety by not being found in Arms."[67]

In Pennsylvania, at least, the question of whether the militia would ever be able to cover the country north of Philadelphia received a decisive answer from the British in early May. For the past months, Lacey's men had continuously pestered, threatened, and otherwise alienated much of the local civilian population. Those same civilians, often engaged in trade with Philadelphia, were well positioned to inform the British of the militia's strength and location. It was a perilous situation for so small a force to be in and on May 1 Lacey's good fortune, such as it was, ran out. Having received word from the inhabitants that the militia was camped near Crooked Billet, the British chose to finally rid themselves of that particular irritant. In the early morning a column of British light infantry and dragoons, not incidentally aided by locally raised provincial troops, surprised and demolished Lacey's camp. The militia suffered heavy casualties and reports soon circulated of atrocities committed against the dead and dying.[68]

The raid on Crooked Billet all but eliminated the Pennsylvania militia as an effective force for the remainder of the season and forced Washington to finally abandon goals he had been doggedly pursuing throughout the winter and spring. No longer seeing the point in repeatedly demanding the thousand men he had been promised but never given, he now requested that the state do its best to scrape together a mere four hundred. Those troops would be aided by, and implicitly subject to, a force of Continentals; on May 7 the task of covering the region between the Schuylkill and Delaware was handed over to Brigadier General William Maxwell of the Continental Army. Washington's attempt to leave the state in direct control of at least some portion of the embargo was given up.[69]

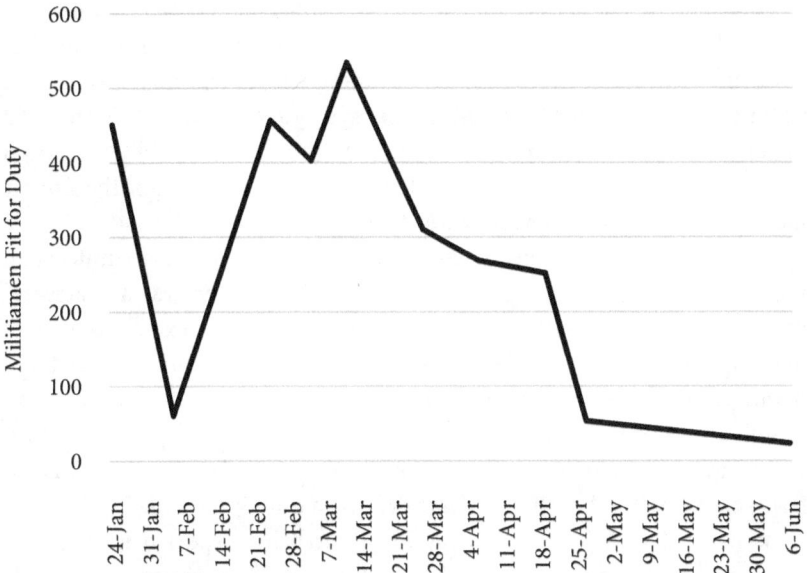

FIGURE 3. Pennsylvania militia under Brigadier General John Lacey Jr., 1778. These figures reflect Lacey's own reporting of his numbers, combining those fit for duty at camp and on command. Note the temporary recovery following Washington's intervention on February 12 and the militia's failure to recover following the British attack at Crooked Billet on May 1. See Hazard, *Register of Pennsylvania*, 3:305, 307–308, 342, 357; *Pennsylvania Archives*, 1st ser., 6:297; "To Thomas Wharton Jr.," February 12, 1778, *PGW*, 13:519.

The Embargo Collapses

Absent a powerful coercive force to restrain and control their behavior, the people were free to follow their own interests and inclinations. Enthusiastic Loyalists and Revolutionaries sought to advance their respective causes, but the disaffected looked instead to their own profits and security. Increasingly, this led them to look toward Philadelphia. Though the Revolutionary governments were sometimes quick to condemn civilians who traded with the British or the Philadelphia markets as traitors and enemies, the military officers who dealt with and tried to stop such individuals rarely attributed their actions to political motivations or allegiance. Far more often they concluded that the root causes of this illicit traffic were economic.[70] As General Howe's aide succinctly put it, the farmers of Pennsylvania "take all sorts of food to the market for the sake of profit." Ewald believed that the people "braved all dangers" to trade with the city, not out of loyalty, but "to collect our guineas."[71] After investigating why it was that "even those who pretend to be our best friends, hide their Stocks from us," Continental major general Stirling wrote to Washington that he had finally settled on "what I really belive [sic] to be the true Cause of it, vizt from the Enemy they are sure to get hard Money for it."[72]

The movement of produce from countryside to city was a familiar and reliable part of life in the Delaware Valley. Philadelphia was a "gateway" city, a grand entrepôt that absorbed and exported the excess harvest of the Pennsylvania countryside, transforming it into precious imported and manufactured goods which were dispersed back into the country. Like the mouth of a great commercial river, Philadelphia was the point to which overrunning streams of flour and produce, springing from a thousand farms and pooling briefly at inland depots, naturally flowed. By the early 1770s more than half of the wheat and flour being exported from North America departed from Philadelphia's wharves.[73] The reemergence of trade with Philadelphia in early 1778 was not indicative of any particular affection for the forces occupying that city, but rather speaks to the popular indifference of the people who, when not restrained from doing so, promptly took up their traditional pursuits with little concern over who controlled the port.

Struck by Pennsylvanians' hesitancy to serve with the redcoats but their willingness to trade with them, one Hessian officer in Philadelphia concluded that "if any people worships money, it is the Americans, for everyone is in business."[74] The Americans might have disagreed with this assessment, but some of those from other regions developed their own harsh critiques of the people living near Philadelphia. New Englander Israel Angell recorded a humorous story told around the camp at Valley Forge which, he claimed, showed "in what manner Some people live in this part of the Country." The tale told of Pennsylvania farmers who raised turkeys and sold them to the army, but when asked how to dress the birds for roasting replied that they did not know, for they had never eaten turkey themselves but always sold every last one for cash.[75] It may have been that the people of the Delaware Valley were unusually avaricious, but a more likely explanation for this impression is that the disaffected people of the region put personal profit over patriotism, not from an overabundant love of the former but from a relative deficit of the latter.[76]

Poor economic policy and incompetence only aggravated the situation for the Patriots, alienating many inhabitants who did initially choose to trade with the Continentals and guaranteeing that some would, thereafter, take their goods to the British instead. Even as the British put increasingly scarce gold and silver within reach of the civilian populace, the paper Continental currency, already on the decline, tumbled to unprecedented lows, driven down by repeated, unfunded emissions and a waning confidence in the Revolutionary government. From an exchange rate of three-to-one against silver in the summer of 1777, it slipped to four-to-one by the end of the year and dropped to five-to-one in April of 1778. Simultaneously, even accounting for inflation, the prices of many basic necessities were on the rise as the presence of two armies increased demand and the general disruption and dislocation of war limited supply, making people especially loath to accept money that was daily losing its value.[77]

The immediate impact of this imbalance was readily apparent to contemporaries. Joseph Reed spent the early months of 1778 bemoaning "the baneful disease" of depreciation and warning that it threatened "to produce fruit more pernicious than that of ancient Eden." He noted that the worst depreciation was to be found in the region immediately around Philadelphia, where the money was of so little value that even people he considered "good Whigs" hid their stores of provisions from Continental commissaries in order to avoid having to accept it.[78] About the same time, Christopher Marshall was recording in his diary that his neighbors' agreeable manners and "sweet countenances" changed remarkably as soon as he asked about purchasing forage or foodstuffs "to be paid for in Congress money." "Then," he found, "their serene countenances are all overcast, a lowering cloud spreads all over their horizon; they have nothing to say, nay scarcely to bid you farewell."[79] Though the de facto rate of exchange between Continental paper and hard money rose continually throughout the occupation, Congress persisted in valuing their currency at the rate it had held over the summer of 1777. Maximum prices were fixed on a variety of goods that were needed by the army and Continental commissaries were ordered to enforce them. The politics of the Revolution, rather than the needs of the market, became the decisive factor in determining what goods were worth. As one quartermaster callously quipped, "if the farmers does not like the prices allowed them for this produce let them choose men of more learning and understanding the next election."[80] Once the embargo on Philadelphia began to fail, those who were close enough to the British lines had another option: to smuggle their goods to the occupied city.

In addition to further incentivizing trade with occupied Philadelphia, Revolutionary price controls created problems for Continental officers trying to purchase goods in Pennsylvania. Washington's Commissary of Prisoners, Elias Boudinot, was charged with purchasing flour for Patriots held as prisoners by the British but discovered that Pennsylvania's fixed price of £2 5s. per cwt. was so far below the going rate of £6 that no one would sell to him. He was eventually forced to look for flour in New Jersey, where he could offer more for it, though even there he faced the challenge of finding wagons and drivers willing to work for what he was able to pay. Congress relieved him of this challenge by empowering him to forcibly press wagons into Continental service whether the owners liked his prices or not.[81]

To make matters worse, even those who were willing to accept (or at least found themselves unable to refuse) the Revolutionaries' fixed prices did not always receive what little they were promised. Both armies foraged heavily throughout the region, giving the former owners of what they confiscated certificates to be exchanged for payment at their respective headquarters. As the Continentals learned, bad faith on the part of army commissaries could have a profound effect on the sentiments of certificate-holders and drive them to the enemy. Writing from Radnor, Major General Stirling warned Washington that, while the British were paying debts in hard currency, "when our Certificates are produced to the Commissary of purchase & forage Master Genl at Camp, they are treated with the Utmost Contempt. the people are told to Call again & again 'till tired of making further application & in despair of payment they go home with a determination [sic] to Sell to the Enemy rather than to us."[82] From the other side of the Schuylkill, Major Jameson also complained that the commissaries were not paying for receipts his officers were handing out in exchange for provisions, while Colonel Stewart blasted the commissaries as "in General Stupid good for Nothing fellows" and blamed them for the continued flow of goods into Philadelphia.[83]

This system of payment often served British interests by giving a number of farmers, who might have initially been alienated by the foraging parties, an incentive to enter Philadelphia and be paid for what they had already lost. Having once made the trip past the lines and returned home with hard currency in their pockets, they may well have been more inclined to make the trip again later, this time bringing more goods with them.[84] Foraging parties, either British or American, may have further prompted the collapse of the Continentals' containment efforts by encouraging farmers to risk rushing their produce to Philadelphia in the hope that the British would pay more for property sold voluntarily than either side would offer for goods taken by force.[85]

One peculiar challenge Washington faced in his attempts to isolate the city lay in the Revolutionaries' inability to recognize women as a threat. Despite the fact that nonconsumption and the movement toward homespun gave new political weight to the actions of colonial women, many of the Revolution's men still struggled to recognize female choices and actions as important enough to be potentially dangerous to their cause. A male who brought provisions to the British-held city was "considered and treated as an enemy and traitor to these United States," fit to be arrested, courtmartialed, and potentially executed, but a female caught in the same role was apt to simply be labeled "a poor woman" and sent off with most of her goods intact and possibly with money in her pocket.[86] This blindness toward the significance of their actions allowed women to more freely defy the edicts and military forces of the Revolution by slipping past sentries and through the lines, possibly becoming, at times, the primary conveyors of provisions and intelligence between the countryside and British-held Philadelphia.[87]

Throughout the early months of 1778, Washington was repeatedly informed by officers in the field that "the intercourse [between the country and the city] is chiefly carried on by women."[88] Henry Muhlenberg's journal records a steady stream of women, alone or in small groups, passing his home in Trappe on their way to or from Philadelphia, often carrying correspondence or packages of provisions. Much of Christopher Marshall's information about conditions in the occupied city came to him through women who ventured out for food and other goods.[89] James Allen also relied on women for news from the city and concluded in December that "Women are suffered to come out of Philada without enquiry."[90] The American commander in chief responded in early February by identifying "women in particular" as responsible for the "pernicious consequences" that had resulted from people freely passing Continental lines. Such consequences ostensibly included not only the conveyance of goods and information but also the loss of manpower, as the women were supposedly sent to "intice the soldiers to desert." Washington ordered his men to immediately stop giving passes to women headed into the city and to apprehend those who attempted to come near the Continental camps.[91]

One officer theorized that women and children were specifically chosen to drive carriages full of provisions into the city because "they think indulgence will be allowed on account of sex and age."[92] In a great many instances it seems that they were right. Major General John Armstrong, of the Pennsylvania militia, found that his patrols tended to arrest and detain the men they intercepted carrying goods into the city, but women caught in the same predicament "were dismissed by the parties who intercepted them." Colonel Israel Angell not only released a woman caught carrying a load of meal and flour, along with multiple turkeys and other fowl, but "lett her have the greatest part of her truck, and paid her for the remainder."[93] Certain that the commerce between the city and countryside was undermining the Revolution, Joseph Reed desired that a proclamation be issued to the inhabitants that "under some severe Penalty they should not go into the City on any Pretence whatever without Leave" and that such Leave "be granted to no Men on any Pretext" unless directly in the service of the cause. However, when it came to women seeking passes and crossing the lines, Reed's language softened considerably and he weakly suggested that the officers involved "must act according to their Discretion."[94] Such "discretion" at times took a darker turn. One young woman apprehended on her way into Philadelphia was told by her militiaman captor that, "if she would permit him to use certain freedoms with her (which her modesty and virtue would not admit of) he would let her pass to the enemy with the provisions." In this particular instance, the militiaman may have been surprised to discover that his captive was one of Clarke's spies and that word of his conduct moved rather swiftly up the chain of command to Washington himself.[95] We cannot know how many similar, unrecorded propositions were made to women who lacked such official connections.

In at least a few instances the Revolutionary soldiers not only neglected to apprehend or stop women carrying on commerce with the occupied city but actively assisted them in their work. In December Major Baurmeister was amused to discover that, upon encountering them along the road, "the rebel light dragoons frequently carry the women's packages [of foodstuffs bound for Philadelphia] on their horses as far as their vedettes." It seems that, in addition to bearing such burdens, the dragoons also grew to be rather chatty with their female companions, for Baurmeister noted that it was "from these [women] we receive most of the news about the rebels."[96] Such practices persisted well into the new year. In late January, Colonel Walter Stewart wrote Washington to complain that the militia were "too well acquainted with the girls and people from the Town" and were "Seizing flour &ca from one person, and delivering it their favorites."[97]

Patriots who *did* recognize women's ability to invisibly slip past male sentries put that knowledge to use in order to gain intelligence about the British army and to obtain supplies that were difficult to get from the countryside. On one particularly memorable occasion, a pair of women pretended to be pregnant in order to smuggle a quantity of salt and leather past the British pickets.[98] One unusually bold and inventive American cavalry officer hoped to take advantage of the soldiery's tendency to overlook women by disguising himself in a dress when he went to meet an informant from the city near British lines.[99]

The Continental Crackdown

The army's inability to isolate and starve Philadelphia was deeply distressing to the Revolutionary leadership, both civil and military, as was the population's obstinate commitment to trading with the city in spite of all orders to the contrary. The flow of goods toward British lines not only sustained the occupying forces and contributed to the crippling shortages experienced at Valley Forge, but also undermined claims that the people of Pennsylvania were responsible and consenting citizens of the new Republic. As the occupation continued, the state and Continental authorities' attempts to end trade with the city and secure provisions for the Revolutionary military became increasingly desperate and brutal.

As early as mid-December, when the first signs began to appear that the embargo was failing, the Continental Congress wrote to Washington, urging him to take more drastic steps. Reminding the commander in chief that they had authorized him to confiscate "all goods and effects which may be serviceable to the enemy" and to arrest, try, and even execute those carrying supplies past British lines, they now pushed him to exercise this authority more aggressively. Tactfully attributing "his forbearance in exercising the powers vested in him by Congress . . . to a delicacy in exerting military authority on the citizens of these states," they explained that this was "a delicacy, which though highly laudable in general, may, on critical exigencies, prove destructive to the army and prejudicial to the general liberties of America." Henceforth, he was encouraged to strip the country around Philadelphia of anything that might be of use to the British, to take "from all persons without distinction," and to leave behind only what was "necessary for the maintenance of their families." What he lacked the manpower or equipment to confiscate, he was to simply destroy. Furthermore, Congress suggested that he order the people of the country to assist him in confiscating their produce by promptly threshing all their grain so it could be more easily collected by the quartermasters and commissaries.[100] Since the British had not been driven from the state during the fall campaign, Congress also voted to extend the period of martial law through April 10 of the following year. About the same time, Brigadier General James Mitchell Varnum wrote Washington with similar sentiments, arguing that, although "it will make your Excellency unhappy," the time for maintaining "virtuous Principles," with regard to securing provisions was past.[101] For the foreseeable future, at least, it seemed that "the general liberties of America" were to depend upon the unflinching and indiscriminate exercise of military power over the people and their possessions.

Initially Continental forces were often uncertain of how to handle civilians intercepted on their way to the city. Some of those captured had their goods confiscated, others were simply turned around and sent home, while still others were arrested and brought before courts-martial.[102] When Matthias Tyson, of Bucks County, was apprehended carrying eggs and butter into Philadelphia, the militia confiscated his goods, tied him to a tree, and spent a jolly afternoon bombarding him with his own merchandise. They then dismissed him, bruised and sticky perhaps, but otherwise unhurt.[103]

By mid-January, Washington began pursuing a more organized response by taking up the recommendations of Congress and putting aside his "delicacy" regarding the army's treatment of civilians. In response to one expression of uncertainty about what means were open to the military, he wrote that in order to prevent "a Continuation of Intercourse between the City & Country" the troops were "hereby instructed to take the most immediate & Coercive Measures . . . I must repeat my desire that you will adopt the most rigorous Means (if nothing less will do) to put a Stop to this practice."[104] The parenthetical qualifier expressed a lingering hesitation which would not last.

Before the month had ended, Washington began to accept that, given the limited manpower available, stopping the flow of supplies headed to Philadelphia was a goal that "perhaps with the utmost vigilance cannot be totally effected."[105] If it was not possible to apprehend all, or even most, of those who violated the embargo, then the punishment inflicted on those who were caught had to be particularly severe. Washington became increasingly convinced that this was the best, and perhaps the only, way to discourage commerce with the city and in letter after letter he began calling for "proper objects to make examples of" in order "that the rest may be sensible of a like Fate should they persist." A "proper object" would be a man, caught in the act, against whom witnesses could be found. In such a case, and given a guilty verdict from the court-martial, the condemned was not to face mere confinement or confiscation but, according to Washington's orders to General Lacey, execution.[106]

In the event, neither Washington nor Lacey officially executed many, if any, civilians solely for trading with Philadelphia. At first Washington may have hoped that the threat alone would be sufficient, and on more than one occasion he went out of his way to make certain that the military's authority to execute civilians was made public.[107] Achieving a guilty verdict at all was often challenging; the constant arrival and departure of new militiamen and the widespread refusal of the civilians to testify against each other made it all but impossible to bring witness testimony before the court.[108] The most common sentence for those found guilty was a number of lashes, ranging somewhat haphazardly from twenty-five to two hundred and fifty, the number apparently more dependent on who sat on the court than on the severity of the offense. In addition to corporal punishment, the courts-martial imprisoned some civilian offenders and sentenced others to forced labor or to service in the Continental Army. Terms of confinement and labor were generally limited to however long the British remained in Pennsylvania.[109]

Though he continued to call for "proper objects to make examples of" throughout the winter and spring, by the end of February, Washington was willing to admit that the current regimen of punishments was ineffective. "I don't well know what to do with the great numbers of people taken going into Philad[elphi]a," he wrote to Lacey in early March, "I have punished several very severely, fined others heavily and some are sentenced to be imprisoned during the War," and still the trade with the city continued and even expanded.[110] Facing renewed pressure from Congress to stop shipments of flour from reaching Philadelphia and aware that he lacked the manpower to place guards on all the roads, Washington took another step away from the "delicacy" that had previously restrained his actions and ordered that all the mills within easy reach of Philadelphia be disabled or destroyed. This measure may well have made it more difficult for the British to obtain flour from the countryside, but it also presented dire challenges to the civilian population that had long relied on those same mills. When word of the destruction reached Philadelphia, one perplexed redcoat noted that the loss of the mills "does not hurt us very much because we are always sure of provisions from England, while they ruin their own country by such acts."[111] The indiscriminate nature of the destruction and the collateral damage associated with it distressed some of Washington's own officers. The commander in chief made it clear that his orders must be kept secret, not only from the British but also from Revolutionaries whose friends or families relied on the mills. Only the officers directly involved in the plan were to be made aware of it, and they "should be such who have no connections in the part of the Country where the Mills are."[112] Even Major Jameson, who sympathized with Washington on the need for desperate measures to stop the trade with Philadelphia, expressed qualms about disabling the mills of those who had already pledged not to do business with anyone from the occupied city. Nonetheless, he dutifully agreed to carry out the orders he was given.[113] New and more desperate strategies followed.

In order to induce the men "to be more active and zealous in the execution of their duty," Washington granted them the right to keep for themselves whatever they confiscated from civilians trading with Philadelphia. The Revolutionary soldiery now had a personal financial stake in apprehending as many traders as possible. This new incentive was first granted to the militia east of the Schuylkill, but by mid-March it had been extended to the rest of the army as well. Washington was painfully aware that this policy opened the door for rampant abuse, and with every mention of it worried that it would be "made a pretext for plundering the innocent inhabitants." To check this tendency, he ordered that a commissioned officer always be present during confiscations, but given the desperate shortage of manpower, especially in the militia, such a requirement was not always feasible.[114] As Washington had feared, this step only further alienated the civilian population, who accused the military, and particularly the militia, of indiscriminate plundering. General Armstrong decried the confiscation policy as "a step undoubtedly wrong in every point of view," but others, like Joseph Reed, argued that while there were many instances of abuse, they were only a "partial evil" in comparison to the "Extensive Mischief" of the illicit trade they were intended to stop.[115]

Continental soldiers and militiamen also took upon themselves the task of carrying out harsher punishments while patrolling the roads. Circumventing the challenge of winning a court-marital conviction, officers increasingly rendered their own verdicts in the field and issued sentences for lashes and, occasionally, death.[116] Rumors that Revolutionary forces were summarily shooting civilians caught carrying goods to Philadelphia began early in the occupation, but it wasn't until the desperate months of February and March of 1778 that such practices were given official approval.[117] A severely vexed Washington wrote to General Lacey that "the communication between the City and country, in spite of every thing hitherto done still continuing, and threatening the most pernicious consequences," the militia patrols were henceforth empowered to determine for themselves whether or not those they intercepted with provisions intended to trade with the occupied city. If so, and the patrols deemed it necessary, they were now authorized "to fire upon those gangs of mercenary wretches who make a practice of resorting [to] the city, with marketing."[118] At the time this order was given, Lacey's numbers were so reduced that they could do little more than huddle around their distant headquarters and await reinforcements, but when the militia ranks briefly swelled to several hundred the following month, the young general quickly acted on his new authority. In orders to his scouting parties, Lacey vividly described the message he wanted his men to send to the local populace: "If your parties should meet with any people going to market, or any persons whatever going to the city, and they endeavor to make their escape, you will order your men to fire upon the villains. You will leave such on the roads, their bodies and their marketing lying together. This I wish you to execute on the first offenders you meet; that they may be a warning to others."[119] Fortunately for those carrying goods to Philadelphia, popular disaffection and a widespread refusal to turn out for militia service prevented Lacey from ever commanding a sizable force. The scarcity and fragility of Revolutionary sentiment in the region around Philadelphia may have made such brutal strategies all the more necessary, at least from the Patriots' perspective, but it also made them almost impossible to carry out with any consistency or regularity. Nonetheless, it is worth recognizing that, though generally limited to words rather than deeds, both Washington's persistent desire to "make an example" out of a handful of individuals and Lacey's willingness to leave bodies piled in the road as a "warning," speak to a continuing evolution in the nature and methods of the Revolution. In the face of an enemy they could not beat militarily nor compete with economically and in the midst of a population that was largely indifferent to their cause, the Revolutionary army, like many militant forces before and after, found itself increasingly drawn to terrorism as a means of controlling the countryside and the people who lived there.

An increasing acceptance of extreme and violent action marked the Continentals' attempts to procure supplies for their own use, as well as their efforts to keep them from the British. In late January Washington considered competing with the economic lure of Philadelphia's markets by creating a market of his own near Valley Forge. He called for his officers and "the most intelligent Country-men" to create a plan for the operation of said market and the establishment of its prices. On January 30, Washington issued a proclamation outlining the prices and announcing that the market would begin operation the second Monday in February. The language he chose for this advertisement is telling, reflecting both the connection he saw between allegiance and commerce and his awareness that the army had hitherto done much to alienate the local population.[120]

Life between the lines had given these people a number of legitimate concerns when it came to trading with the military and Washington sought to address these head on by assuring the prospective marketers that they would be protected "from any kind of abuse or violence that may be offered to their persons or effects," that "their carriages and cattle shall not be impressed or otherwise detained," and that they would actually be paid for the articles provided to the army. Aware that, for some, the soldiers from New England were only a shade less foreign than those from Britain, he promised that the clerk of the market, who was in charge of protecting the people who traded there, would be a Pennsylvanian. Finally, Washington expressed his hope that "all persons well affected to their country" would take this as an opportunity to "manifest their zeal" for the cause.[121] Here again was the belief that commercial choices represented political affections.

Problems began almost at once. The day before the market opened, no clerk had been appointed to look after the marketers' rights; the officer in charge of the local piquet guard received last-minute orders to enforce the regulations. Washington worried that few people would come.[122] Greater challenges to the army's détente with the local farmers loomed just ahead. The opening of the Continental market came just as several factors, including poor management, bad weather, local disaffection, and insufficient transportation conspired to plunge the Continental Army into one of the worst logistical crises it would ever experience. Washington wrote that what had once been "occasional deficiencies in the Article of provisions . . . seem now on the point of resolving themselves into this fatal crisis—total want and a dissolution of the Army."[123] The situation no longer allowed for the development of amiable relations with the local populace based on voluntary and mutually beneficial commerce at the new marketplace. The times had become exceedingly desperate and the Revolutionaries' response would be no less so.

Less than a week after the Continentals' market opened for the first time, Washington drafted orders for Nathanael Greene to carry out a massive and unprecedentedly merciless foraging expedition. Washington wanted the area between the Schuylkill and Brandywine rivers, stretching as far as twenty miles inland from the Delaware, entirely stripped of livestock and provisions. No distinction was to be made between friends and enemies of the cause. For the first time, Washington took no steps to guarantee that friendly residents would be left with at least some basic provisions to subsist on.[124] What Greene could not safely carry off he was to destroy. Those who lost goods to the army because of this expedition were to be given special certificates which could one day be used to apply for payment, but the specifics of when that day would be, where the certificates could be turned in, and to whom, were still yet to be determined as Greene and his men began their mission. Given the Continental Army's poor reputation for honoring its debts in the region, these mysterious pieces of paper were likely of little solace to those who watched as the last of their horses, cattle, sheep, and provender were taken from them.[125]

Over the course of the following weeks, Greene's expedition drained the countryside of what little supplies and good will remained. The Continental officers themselves struggled with the severity of the duty set before them. "The inhabitants cry out and beset me from all quarters," Greene wrote to Washington, "but like Pharoh I harden my heart . . . I [am] determin[ed] to forage the Country very bare. Nothing shall be left unattempted."[126] Though he took all that he found, Greene found that there was little left to take from these people who had for some months been trapped between the lines of two hungry armies. "The face of the Country is strongly marked with poverty and distress," he reported, and "has been so gleaned that there is but little left in it."[127] As word of the foraging expedition and its methods spread, the people's pleading gave way to desperation and subterfuge. Those who could rushed to get their goods to market in Philadelphia before all was lost to the Continentals. Others carted their provisions and drove their livestock and wagons off into the wilderness to conceal them. Greene followed, sending his men "to search all the Woods and swamps after them."[128] Farmers who tried to hide their property from the Continentals were to be arrested, while those caught trying to make it to British lines were severely whipped. Aware that dire circumstances at Valley Forge required that Greene maintain his "hardened heart" and committed to the hope that brutally punishing a few might yet terrorize the many into obedience, Washington did what he could to steel Greene's resolve along the way, urging him to "make severe examples" of anyone who tried to reach the occupied city and assuring him that "our present wants will justify any measures you can take." Greene assured his commander that "examples shall not be wanting to facilitate the business I [am] out upon."[129]

While Greene made his grand forage in Pennsylvania, Washington sent Wayne to carry out a similar program in New Jersey. There the story was much the same: residents hid what they could from the Continentals and the army punished them for it harshly. Wayne took what he could and burned much of the rest; his men plunged into the swamps after hidden livestock and set fire to hundreds of tons of forage as they swept along the banks of the river. Like Greene, Wayne grew troubled by the severity of his task, and though assured of "the *policy necessity* and *Justice* of the Measure," by mid-March he began interpreting his orders more flexibly. "Anxious to save as much from the Fire as possible," he began allowing civilians to keep some of their forage provided they carried it farther back into the state where, he hoped, the British would be unable to find it.[130]

Unfortunately for the Revolutionaries, the forage mission in New Jersey backfired dramatically when Howe, sensing that Wayne's detachment was vulnerable and cut off from the main army at Valley Forge, launched an assault across the river to surround and destroy it. Wayne's force escaped the British and fled back to Pennsylvania, but the damage was done. Having crossed into New Jersey for battle, the British detachment remained to forage and to systematically disassemble what remained of the state militia. "I doubt not," Wayne informed Washington, "that they [the British] are now Employed in Collecting the Cattle &ca which the Inhabitants in that Quarter took great pains to hide from us—finding means at the same to give the Enemy exact Intelligence of our Numbers and Rout." Washington sent more troops to counteract the British presence, but the region soon descended into a vicious civil war as Revolutionaries and Loyalists rose up to wreak retribution on their enemies when friendly troops came near only, in their turn, to suffer the vengeance of their former victims as soon as the tides of power shifted. By April Washington concluded that, as much as the Revolutionaries of New Jersey might clamor for him to send more Continental troops to their state, "considered in the true light" such deployments "rather do more harm than good" since they inevitably provoked an overwhelming response from the British in Philadelphia.[131]

In the end the provision crisis proved to be fatal, not to the army itself, but to the army's ability to actively project the Revolutionaries' vision of a cleanly divided society, friends and foes, a unified "People" against a treasonous minority. Over the long months of the occupation more and more local inhabitants forsook Revolutionary rhetoric and made their own private, economic peace with the occupied city. The percentage of inhabitants who fit the model of the virtuous, committed Patriot, who legitimated the Revolution and deserved its protections and privileges, diminished until, in the dark days of Greene's grand foraging expedition, the Continental soldiers went forth treating everyone they encountered with the cold brutality once reserved only for alleged enemies to the cause.

Nonetheless, the Continental crackdown on trade with Philadelphia and the new foraging policies implemented in February met with some initial success. As the Revolutionaries began to embrace more rigorous and coercive means of stopping farmers on their way to the occupied city, the effects were felt by the British and their allies. Ewald noted that Washington had begun "to make the highways around Philadelphia so unsafe with parties from his fortified camp at Valley Forge that the country people no longer dared to bring provisions to market." This brought an end to the period of "sweet tranquility" he had been enjoying throughout the first weeks of the year.[132] Again, in February, when Lacey's militia received authority to open fire on civilians along the road, Ewald noticed that trade with the city dipped noticeably. He concluded that the execution of farmers bringing food to the city, several of whom were reportedly "bound to the tails of horses and lost their lives in this sad way," terrified the people into submission.[133]

Such episodes of success were not to last, however. Whenever the Revolutionaries' crackdown on trade began to place too much pressure on Philadelphia, the British and their allies responded in force to protect their access to local provisions. British and provincial patrols took to the roads, providing armed escorts for farmers en route to the city. At times the country people themselves took up arms to protect their wagons from Continental and militia soldiers who might try to take their produce, or possibly their lives, for trading with Philadelphia. In March, when the Patriots' campaign against the populace was at its most terrifying, Howe's aide-de-camp recorded that every day saw the deployment of "small and sometimes strong commands against the enemy parties in support of the peasants who bring in food." Eliza Farmar's small family depended upon "poor folks who got thro the lines and got flower [sic] at the Mills . . . tho they frequently had it taken from them by the Americans." However, as she also recalled, "when the spring came on we were a little better off for the Ridgment [sic] of Queens Rangers were Posted on the River side opposite our house."[134] The proximity of the Rangers not only eased the pressure on those attempting to carry flour toward the city but also protected the Farmars from being plundered or threatened by the Patriot militias. Greene found that the mounted provincial units, like the Queen's Rangers, who were more familiar with the countryside and the people in it than were their British counterparts, were particularly effective in this regard.[135] Due in part to such patrols, the Continental crackdown was never able to recreate the provisions crisis that had threatened the British hold on Philadelphia at the end of 1777 and the continuation of trade between the city and the countryside remained a constant source of irritation and concern. Prices remained high in the city and the civilians occasionally complained of shortages in one sort of good or another, but the tone of desperation never returned and the British army in particular was able to enjoy a season of relative plenty and relaxation. Not only did the British response thwart Washington's efforts to isolate Philadelphia, it also allowed the redcoats to take on a protective role, casting themselves as the defenders of the commercial interests and liberty of the local populace against the dictates and requisitions of the Revolutionary regime.[136]

As the trade continued despite all the vigilance and violence the Revolutionaries could muster, despair set in. By April Lacey and Washington had each come to suspect that trying to control the farmers' trade through coercion was a doomed effort; short of physically restraining the entire population, there was little to be done.[137] Congress's decision to allow the resolution declaring martial law to expire on April 10 suggests a similar degree of discouragement from that quarter.[138] In desperation, some Revolutionary officers drew up a bold but impractical plan for forcibly evacuating all inhabitants who lived within fifteen miles of the occupied city. Civilians who learned of the scheme decried it, not only as materially impossible but cruel.[139] Before the outcry could spread, Washington explicitly swatted the idea down; sympathizing with the planners' motivations, he nonetheless explained that "the horror of depopulating a whole district, however little consideration the majority of the parties concerned may deserve from us, would forbid the measure."[140]

Though it never succeeded in isolating Philadelphia from the surrounding countryside, much less in forcing the British to choose between starvation and retreat, the Continental crackdown in 1778 did have a profound, if unintended, effect on the local populace. The confiscations, destruction, arrests, imprisonment, whippings, and executions carried out by the Continental Army and the Pennsylvania militia began to slowly but steadily alienate more and more civilians in the Delaware Valley. Though perhaps no more firmly attached to Great Britain than they had been previously, the disaffected grew increasingly wary of and hostile toward the Revolutionaries who strove to control them. More alarming still, previously committed Revolutionaries began to abandon the cause, unable to reconcile their prior devotion with the coercive acts carried out by their fellow Patriots and the commercial benefits of reengaging with the British-Atlantic trade via the occupied city.

Observers on both sides took note of these shifting political affections, though few Patriots captured the effect so clearly as did Joseph Reed. "The intercourse between the Country & the Town has produced all the consequences foreseen by many in the beginning of the Winter," he fretted. Yet it was not the supply of provisions to the enemy that so concerned him; indeed, he counted such material losses as "the least pernicious" of those the cause was suffering. It was not simply the War for Independence but the Revolution itself, John Adams's Revolution of hearts and minds, that Reed saw collapsing in the face of a persistent British presence and the people's ability to take advantage of it. He despaired that "the Minds of the Inhabitants are seduced, their Principles tainted & opposition enfeebled—a familiarity with the Enemy lessens their abhorrence of them & their Measures. Even good Whigs," he worried, "begin to think Peace at some Expense desirable."[141] While Reed blamed the ongoing trade with the city, others recognized dangerous consequences arising from the actions of the Revolutionaries themselves. In the eyes of J. B. Smith, it was "the conduct of the different departments" and "the impositions & irregularities of some of the agents" that were responsible for the people's declining confidence in the Revolution and its leaders. Yet it was more than "irregularities" that drove the people away. He suggested to Reed that "if it were possible to avoid seizures & except in particular cases acts of force, many disaffected persons, more of the indetermined [sic], & all real Whigs would be with us." Yet whether they held that trade itself or the Revolutionaries' harsh and ineffective attempts to stop it were responsible, both agreed that "by the present system of conduct, we suffer a fearful increase of disaffection."[142]

The British also registered the change. Even Major General James Grant, who had at first decried Pennsylvania as "more inimical than any [province] we have yet been in," came to believe that, had the war gone as well elsewhere in America, events surrounding the occupation of Philadelphia "must have put an end to the Contest, for tho' factious leaders may be unwilling to part with the power they have got into their hands, individuals are tired of the business, & tho' they have no attachment to Great Britain they would be glad to rescind Independency if they knew what terms they are to expect. They see their interests but dare not declare their opinions."[143] The British commander in-chief also took note of the changing sentiments and, like Grant, came to believe that by the spring of 1778, whatever Revolutionary fires had once burned in the Delaware Valley were now all but extinguished. Yet as Howe informed Parliament, "this favorable disposition . . . did not appear immediately. An equivocal neutrality was all I at first experienced." As time passed he watched as the flow of provisions and information to the city not only strengthened his position but also steadily undermined his opponents. "The difficulties of the Congress in raising supplies and in recruiting Mr. Washington's army," he wrote, "then indeed became real, and had the appearance of being insurmountable." All this he "could not but attribute . . . to the possession of Philadelphia."[144]

This shift in political affections came as the result of a self-reinforcing cycle of disaffection which was initially triggered by two crucial imbalances between the Revolutionaries and the British. The first and primary imbalance was economic: British wealth and access to hard currency allowed them to offer prices the Patriots could not afford to match. Combined with this was a second, ideological imbalance: the Revolutionaries, much more than the British, relied on expressions of popular consent and popular participation to legitimate their rule. They had, consequently, placed tremendous and at times coercive pressure on the population in an effort to elicit demonstrations of consent. The result was a sizable population that, even absent any particular affection for British rule, had developed a distaste for Revolutionary edicts and which mimicked patriotic behavior, not from a strongly felt commitment to the cause, but in order to avoid persecution. Taken together, these imbalances meant that, when the British army successfully established a foothold in Pennsylvania and crippled the Revolutionaries' ability to exercise control over a large region, a multitude of previously acquiescent colonists were primed to forsake their prior compliance with the patriotic program, abandoning Revolutionary activities and rhetoric and embracing a remunerative but, in the eyes of some, disloyal trade with the occupied city. This alarmed and surprised the patriotic regime and triggered a series of increasingly brutal punishments and confiscations, meant to preserve both the material survival and the legitimacy of the Revolution. These crackdowns, in turn, only further alienated the political affections of the people and provided them with greater incentives to get their produce to the Philadelphia markets as quickly and surreptitiously as possible.[145]

Meanwhile, because local farmers were voluntarily bringing their goods to the occupied city, the British were allowed to reduce the extent and frequency of their own foraging expeditions. This not only let them limit the number of negative interactions between their own soldiers and the civilian populace but increasingly encouraged the people to view the British patrols as their defenders, shielding them and their goods from Continental foraging parties.[146] Terrified by Greene's desperate foraging efforts in February and Lacey's lethal "examples" in March, civilians outside the city began crying out to the redcoats for help as soon as Revolutionary forces drew near their homes. Lacey complained that, as his patrols approached the towns and farmsteads near Philadelphia, the inhabitants took to their horses and "repair directly to the city with the intelligence that the rebels are in the neighborhood."[147] By the end of March he despaired that "but few real friends to America [are] left within ten miles of Philadelphia."[148] Reed's wife, Esther de Berdt Reed, feared for her husband's safety whenever he remained at home for more than a day. "There are so many Disaffected to the cause of their Country," she explained to a friend, "that they lay in wait for those who are active in it."[149] From within the city, Joseph Galloway, who had long since believed Pennsylvania was eager to embrace a renewed allegiance to the crown, interpreted the people's behavior as a vindication, declaring that "there is no Place in America where the Persons attached to Government are so numerous, where there are so many good Intelligencers, guides and faithful refugees."[150]

In his enthusiasm and desperate desire to keep the British in Philadelphia, Galloway no doubt exaggerated. The most explicit and direct evidences of a people being "attached to government," declarations of loyalty and service in that government's defense, never emerged in great numbers from the people in or around the occupied city. Throughout the entire course of the occupation, a mere two thousand of the city's civilian inhabitants stepped forward to take the oath of allegiance to the king. They were joined by an approximately equal number of Continental and militia deserters who took the oath in order to escape punishment.[151] Galloway had hoped that the Loyalists of Pennsylvania would be so numerous and committed that, once the threat of the Continental Army was countered, they would rise up, overwhelm their Revolutionary neighbors, and restore the province to the empire on their own. Even Howe had hoped to raise a force of at least five thousand provincials while the army was at Philadelphia.[152] Like their Revolutionary counterparts, who also looked to the people of Pennsylvania to voluntarily and enthusiastically offer up their devotion and service, they were met with disappointment. Yet while it did not raise the grand army of provincial soldiers that some British leaders desired, the growing popular disaffection toward the Revolution did much to empower the British army at the expense of the Continentals. It was sufficient to sustain the British occupation of the American capital through the winter of 1777/78, to rob Washington of a considerable part of his military strength, and to constantly challenge the Patriots' depiction of the war as a defensive struggle for liberty.

By the spring of 1778, as trade with the occupied city flourished, the state militia ceased to function, and the people suffered under a brutal series of Revolutionary policies, the conflict looked less and less like a simple defensive struggle which pitted the inhabitants against would-be conquerors from Britain. Rather, despite Washington's attempts to keep the Continental Army from wholly dominating Pennsylvania's defense, it became increasingly apparent that not one but two militant forces, one only slightly less foreign than the other, were struggling to conquer the region around Philadelphia and to secure its resources and people for their respective nations. Each could claim allies among the local populace; neither could achieve explicit, broad-based support without resorting to coercion. As the year advanced and a new campaign season approached, the economic and ideological vulnerabilities of the Revolutionaries, which were especially crippling in the midst of a disaffected population, steadily pushed the material support and the political affections of the region into British hands. It remained to be seen whether the British would let such an advantage slip through their fingers.

INTERLUDE

CROSSING THE LINES

James Allen called it "Trout Hall." Located well outside the immediate environs of Philadelphia in what is now Allentown, Allen's country home was a two-story stone structure built with such care that it still stands today, the town's only remaining house from before the Revolution. In 1777 it became Allen's refuge, a place to try to wait out the storm of war when the British occupied, and the Continentals lay siege to, the capital. He hoped those stone walls would isolate him from the conflict, but he was soon disappointed.[1]

From Trout Hall Allen observed and shared in the wartime sufferings of his fellow disaffected civilians and recorded the increasing brutality, callousness, and desperation that marked the Continentals' efforts to secure supplies for themselves and deny them to the British. "The prevailing idea now," he wrote, "is that no man has any property in what the publick has use for." Allen and his neighbors watched the army carry off their blankets, shoes, stockings, wagons, and livestock, often without any compensation. When an army hospital was established nearby, Allen offered to supply it with timber from his property at a reduced priced, hoping that such an arrangement would prevent the Revolutionaries from simply taking the wood without paying anything. However, his efforts seem to have done little more than alert the army that he had a supply of good trees at hand. The hospital ignored his offer of sale but soldiers soon arrived to cut the timber and, while they were there, also made off with his fences and a stockpile of bricks.[2]

Allen had particular trouble from the local militiamen, who seem to have still resented his departure from their ranks the year before, and he generally found that the militia officers were neither inclined nor able to restrain the rank and file from plunder and destruction. His tribulations were shared by various other Non-Associators, particularly those who lacked Allen's wealth and so faced not only direct persecution but also economic ruin in the face of mounting fines for refusing to serve. The lack of restraint on the part of the militiamen, combined with the near total collapse of the justice system which followed the new constitution and the British invasion, soon gave those who were friendly toward the Revolution a chance to settle grudges against those who were not. "It is a fine time to gratify low private revenge," Allen remarked in October, "few opportunities are lost." Those who ran afoul of the militia or its favorites risked suddenly finding themselves the targets of an unrelenting campaign of plunder for which there was no recourse. Allen's neighbor, who raised poultry, came to Trout Hall one day desperately trying to sell off his whole supply of turkeys, having discovered that an old adversary whom he had sued some three years earlier had convinced the militia to single him out for confiscation. Allen bought the fowl but doubted that he would be allowed to keep them long. Life for the disaffected was lived, as Allen wrote, "in perpetual fear of being robbed, plundered & insulted."[3]

Allen's refusal to submit to the Test Act, his confinement, and the general turmoil of the justice system prevented him from practicing law, and thus his income relied almost entirely on what he received from his various tenants in and around Philadelphia. Unsurprisingly, the occupation and siege entirely cut him off from monies within the city, which accounted for the majority of his holdings. Meanwhile, the rapid depreciation of Continental paper money quickly eroded the payments he did manage to collect from those in the countryside. Though rents were originally established in terms of specie, many of Allen's tenants now began paying him in Continental dollars instead. Consequently, as inflation continued to decrease the value of the paper money, Allen's income dropped to as little as a sixth of what it would have otherwise been. Worse still, tenants who had become indebted to Allen took advantage of this opportunity to settle accounts for a fraction of the cost. Though he considered himself "as much robbed of 5/6ths, of my property, as if it was taken out of my Drawer," Allen studiously avoided complaining about his predicament outside the walls of his house. He had no legal recourse and, more importantly, he had learned that refusing to accept Continental currency or demanding a higher exchange rate tended to provoke the wrath of the Revolutionary authorities.[4]

Yet, for all his troubles, at least Allen was not lonely. In addition to the immediate Allen family, Trout Hall soon became the home of James Hamilton, Allen's uncle, former deputy governor of Pennsylvania, and a dear friend. Like Allen, Hamilton's loyalties were considered suspect by the Continental Congress and, though they had no specific charges to bring against him, the Revolutionaries ordered him confined to the house and its immediate surroundings. Once the military hospital was set up nearby, Allen regularly played host to Dr. William Shippen, the director general of hospitals for the Continental Army, and his associate Dr. Thomas Bond. Though diverse in their opinions on American independence, the group succeeded in jovially passing the evenings together and, Allen thought, "we make out a good Society, & we endeavour to banish Politics."[5]

Their good society was interrupted in December, though for familial reasons rather than political ones. Allen's wife, Elizabeth, had been in the latter stages of pregnancy throughout the preceding months of the occupation. In late December, as the birth drew near, complications convinced the family that she should seek the assistance of medical professionals in Philadelphia. Allen wrote to General Washington, whom he had met on multiple occasions before, requesting permission for his wife to cross the Continental lines and enter the besieged city. He initially viewed the petition as a mere formality, knowing full well that dozens of people, particularly women, regularly crossed the lines without permission and often with more sinister motives. Allen was, consequently, shocked when his request was denied; the Continental Army would allow help for Mrs. Allen to leave the city and join her at Trout Hall, but it refused the family permission to enter Philadelphia. In response, Allen set off for Valley Forge to take up the matter with the commander in chief in person. There he met and dined with Washington, whom Allen found to be "very civil" if somewhat surprised to see him. He returned home with the general's promise that his family would be allowed passage to Philadelphia. Washington was adamant, however, that any of them who crossed into the city would not be permitted to leave it again while the occupation continued.[6]

This proposal perfectly suited Mrs. Allen, who had long wished to join her family within the city, but it was a disappointment to her husband. Though he dearly missed the company of his brothers who had joined the British, Allen's desire to remain uninvolved in the war prevented him from going to them. Relocating to the British-occupied city might easily be interpreted by the Patriots as a declaration of allegiance to the king and would, simultaneously, leave all his properties outside the British lines vulnerable to plunder or confiscation. He had previously thought that, should Mrs. Allen end up returning to Philadelphia, he would prefer to leave the British Empire altogether and travel to Europe for the duration of the war, but his experience of the American siege thus far convinced him that it would be best if he remained to watch over his estate.[7]

Consequently, on January 7, Allen escorted his wife and children from Trout Hall as far as the British lines outside Philadelphia where they bid each other farewell for the present. To Allen's immense joy, as his wife was taken into Philadelphia, all three of his brothers came out. John, Andrew, and William met James, and the brothers Allen spent the remainder of the day sharing dinner and conversation in the ribbon of space between the siege and the occupation. Having been separated from his brothers for more than a year, Allen described his joy at the reunion as "inexpressible" and later reflected that "never did I pass a happier day." Throughout their time together Allen was accompanied by an officer from the Revolutionary cavalry who had been "so polite as to meet us on our way down & escort us near the City." Whether such politeness was primarily intended to protect Allen or to see that he followed Washington's orders is unclear.[8]

Allen parted with his brothers that evening, they returning to the city and he setting off on the journey back to Trout Hall. Allen's conversation with his brothers provoked an inner reevaluation of his choice to remain in the countryside. Though still disinclined to become involved in the imperial dispute or throw his support behind the British, Allen was particularly drawn toward his brothers' descriptions of the "ease & security, & freedom of speech" available in the occupied city. It was, admittedly, an "ease & security" only available to those, like the Allens, who could afford it. Yet the inflation of the Continental dollar and the mounting fines for remaining a Non-Associator made life in the country increasingly expensive. Moreover, after months of constantly worrying that some ill-timed expression of dissent might make him the target of further Revolutionary persecution, Allen was sorely tempted by the notion of living under a regime which would, unless provoked, largely ignore him and his politics. Nonetheless, after some anguish, he again chose to remain at Trout Hall to watch over his property and household. He comforted himself with the thought that, even if in principle the laws of the Revolutionary regime threatened to make it impossible for the disaffected to live in the province, in practice the Patriots still lacked the unity and power to fully enforce their edicts, a situation unlikely to change so long as the redcoats remained in control of the capital.⁹

Yet all Allen's reasoning was shaken and his life unalterably changed on the fifth of February when word came to him that his oldest brother, John, was dead. In mid-January John Allen had become suddenly and severely ill, slipping quickly into a persistent state of delirium and unconsciousness which lasted more than two weeks before he finally passed. The loss hit Allen hard; he became acutely aware of the distance which separated him, not only from his remaining and grieving brothers, but also from his wife and his children. In the light of John's death, Allen's concerns for his property and houseguests in the countryside seemed suddenly shallow; he felt "compelled" to be with his family, regardless of the dangers to his estate or the political implications of such a move, and was willing to accept Washington's offer of a one-way pass through the Continental lines. On February 13 he packed his baggage and said farewell to the stone walls of Trout Hall. He would never see them again. Later that year, having learned of his decision to enter occupied Philadelphia and disregarding the permission he had sought and received from Washington, Pennsylvania's Supreme Executive Council formally accused James Allen of high treason against his home and country.¹⁰

CHAPTER 4

OCCUPATION

> My principal object . . . was, to afford protection to the inhabitants, that they might experience the difference between his majesty's mild government, and that to which they were subject from the rebel leaders.
> —General Sir William Howe, 1779

Through the first months of the British occupation, Elizabeth Drinker steadfastly defended her home from incursions by the British army. With the exception of one soldier who, under orders, requisitioned a single blanket for use by the army and "with seeming good Nature begged I would excuse his borrowing it," the Drinker house remained inviolable even as the homes of many neighbors became the quarters of British officers and were marred by plunder or fire. The family's respite came to a sudden end, however, on November 25 when Drinker's own home suddenly became the site of an armed invasion.[1]

Toward nine that evening Drinker's sister, Mary Sandwith, who also lived in the house, discovered a British soldier inside the walled backyard, apparently flirting with the family's female servant, Ann Kelly. Sandwith demanded to know who the man was and, receiving only a slurred "What's that to you?" in reply, quickly retreated back into the house, bringing Kelly with her. The soldier followed, entering at the kitchen where he encountered Drinker. Though the family succeeded in getting him to acknowledge that this was not the house where he was barracked, Drinker complained that "we could not get him out." In the next room was Chalkley James, the twenty-four-year-old son of Henry Drinker's business partner, who was

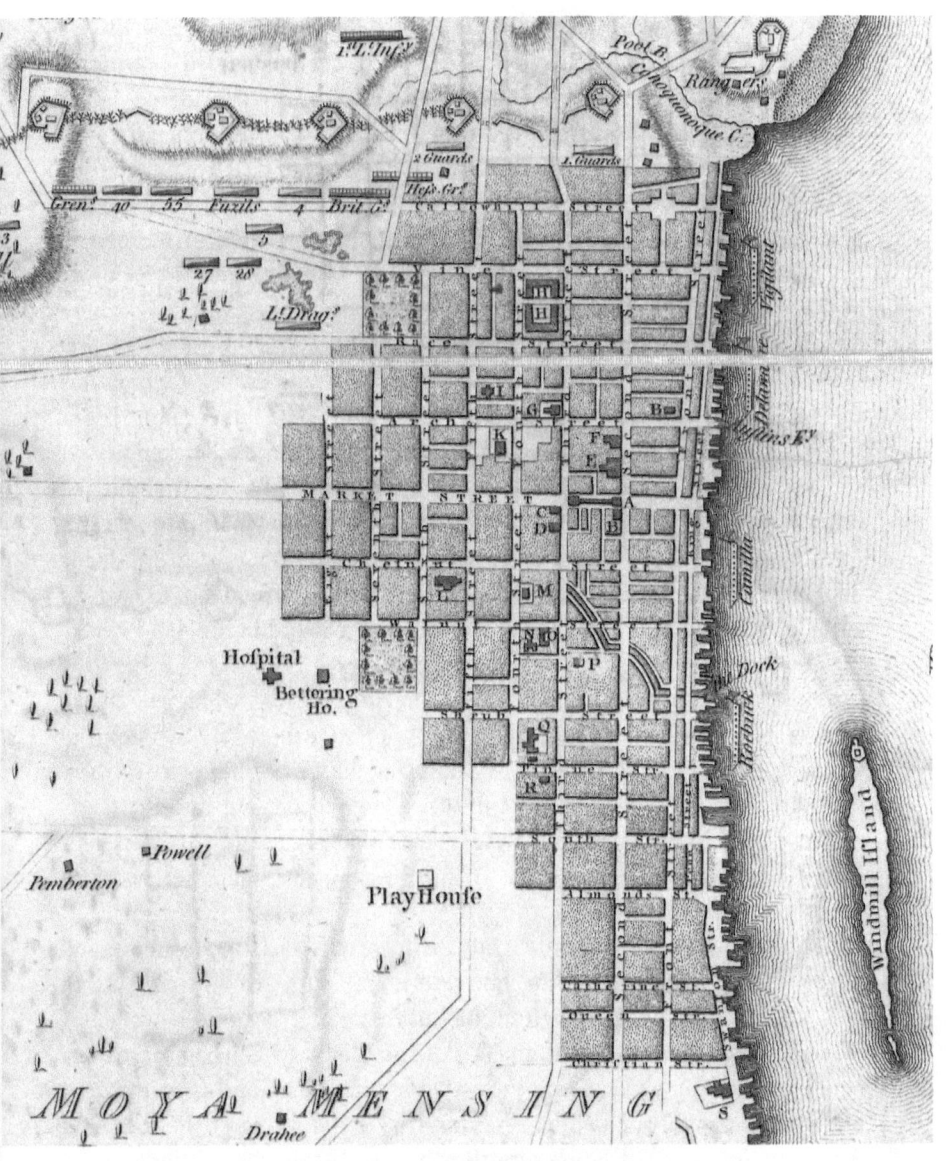

FIGURE 4. Philadelphia under British occupation. Detail from William Faden, *A plan of the city and environs of Philadelphia: with the works and encampments of His Majesty's forces under the command of Lieutenant General Sir William Howe, K. B.* (London: s.n, 1779). Library of Congress, Geography and Map Division, 74692213.

visiting for the evening and now moved to the kitchen to see what was going on. Upon being challenged by James, the soldier issued a string of curses and drew his sword. Acting with what Drinker considered "great resolution," James promptly ripped the sword away and restrained the redcoat while Sandwith locked the weapon in a drawer and Drinker sent for reinforcements. Still held by James, the soldier alternated between contrition and threats, at one moment praising the good nature of the people around him and, at the next, declaring that he intended to murder James in the street. At length the redcoat was escorted out the front door where he was released and had his sword returned to him. Yet, instead of leaving, the man remained on the doorstep, hurling curses and eventually burst his way back into the house. Acting quickly, Drinker locked James in one room so he could not get out to confront the soldier again and then locked herself and the rest of the family in the parlor. The soldier blundered about the otherwise empty house, occasionally banging on the parlor door and "desireing we would let him in to drink a Glass of Wine with us." "Our poor dear Children," Drinker recorded, "was never so frightend, to have an enrag'd, drunken Man, as I believe he was, with a Sword in his Hand swareing about the House."[2]

Finally help came in the form of Joshua Howell and Abel James, Chalkley's father. The men convinced the soldier to depart, at least for the moment. Drinker would meet him again. For reasons of her own, the servant girl, Ann, left the house and followed the redcoat out into the darkness. Drinker locked and bolted every door that night and Chalkley slept over. Nonetheless, badly shaken, Drinker remained awake and watchful into the early hours of the morning.[3]

The following week Drinker sat down to write a letter to her exiled husband. She wrote of sending him additional shirts, of visiting friends, and of their youngest daughter having a cold. About the events of November 25 she told him only this: "Ann Kelly, who I have not been able to keep from ye Gate and Front-Door since ye troops came in, went off last week with one of them—I don't in the least regret the loss." Of the home invasion, of James wrestling a sword from the soldier's hands in the kitchen, of cowering in the parlor with their children, she said nothing.[4] Nor did she tell him of stray cannonballs smashing into houses during the fight for control of the Delaware River, of the thunder that rolled down from the Battle of Germantown, of the many times the army asked to use their home to house officers or as a place to put some of the wounded, or of the British-made infernos which consumed so many houses north of the city.⁵

Henry Drinker made his own assumptions about the state of things in the city, but could not truly know what life was like for his family there. Though he asked for no news about "the State of Fleets and Armies," he was desperately curious about the material well-being and safety of his wife and children. Did they have sufficient food and fuel? How were they obtaining it? Was the house still safe? Perhaps most importantly, in Drinker's eyes, were the children being kept away from the corrupting influence of the British soldiery? Similar questions, though on a larger scale, plagued the minds of the Revolution's political and military leadership. What were the material conditions of the British army and the civilian population in occupied Philadelphia? How much damage had been done to the city? And, crucially, what influence was the presence of the king's army, and the absence of the Revolution's own enforcers, having on the loyalties and political affections of the people? Though the armies fell back to winter quarters, the war for hearts and minds raged on.⁶

Events transpiring outside the British lines gave the Revolutionaries legitimate cause for concern. The state militia had evaporated, the provisions trade favored the British army over the Continentals, and the Revolutionaries were being pushed toward increasingly desperate, brutal, and terrifying measures in order to control the populace. British commander in chief Sir William Howe firmly believed that, if given a safe opportunity to do so, the American colonists would shake off the new Revolutionary governments and accept a peaceful return to the empire. The fragility of the Continental siege around Philadelphia seemed to suggest that Howe's beliefs would be vindicated. As the new year unfolded, Joseph Reed wailed that "the Minds of the Inhabitants are seduced, their Principles tainted & opposition enfeebled . . . even good Whigs begin to think Peace at some Expense desirable."⁷ His concerns reflected the realities he bore witness to, but his perception of events in the region was incomplete and his perspective skewed.

Reed posited that the people's "familiarity with the Enemy lessens their abhorrence of them & their Measures." This formulation may have been true for those outside the British lines, whose "familiarity" with the British, aside from the occasional instance of foraging and plunder, was primarily economic and light-handed. The British were a desperately needed source of specie at a time when paper currency was undergoing dizzying inflation.

Able to reach but unable to secure areas beyond the immediate boundaries of Philadelphia, the British shattered Revolutionary control of such communities but could not enforce their own edicts or demands on the inhabitants. The people's "familiarity" with the occupiers was thus distant and highly selective.

The remaining inhabitants of Philadelphia, Elizabeth Drinker among them, were the ones most familiar with the British army and all the benefits and terrors that came with it. They met the invading army with weighty expectations for what the occupation would mean for themselves, the war, and the future of America. The army brought its own expectations of how American civilians would (or should) behave and the ways in which they would contribute to an eventual imperial victory. As Drinker and her family learned on the night of November 25, familiarity did not always lead to affection. Even as events in the surrounding countryside told a story of alienation from the Revolutionary cause and acceptance of the British, the army and inhabitants of occupied Philadelphia lived out a very different tale of destruction, disaffection, and profound disappointment.

Great Expectations

For their part, the inhabitants' expectations of the British were diverse and often uncertain. The most ardent Patriots, congressmen, and others who, regardless of their politics and involvement in the Revolution, feared living under the British military fled the city well in advance of the redcoats. Left behind were the Loyalists, many of the disaffected, women, children, the poor, and others, some of them Patriots, who could not (or simply *would* not) abandon their homes and businesses. In all perhaps a third of the city, nearly ten thousand souls, departed. Many would return in the months that followed when it became clear that the occupation would be neither as brief nor as bloody as the Patriots had predicted.[8]

Even those who voluntarily chose to remain in the city met the army with some fear and uncertainty. The Hessians, in particular, put some of the residents "in great fear." One young observer later recalled how the drums which accompanied the Hessian grenadiers seemed to sound a steady beat of "—plunder—plunder—plunder—," a rhythm he found "dreadful beyond expression."[9] Sixteen-year-old Robert Morton, whose sympathies lay decidedly with the king, nonetheless fretted about the practical implications of military occupation and "the dreadful consequences of an army however friendly."[10]

Yet alongside such fears there was also considerable hope, particularly among those inclined through politics, religion, or Patriot oppression to look upon the British as liberators more than occupiers. Despite his fears of the occupation, Morton recalled that Lieutenant General Charles Second Earl Cornwallis arrived, "to the great relief of the inhabitants who have too long suffered the yoke of arbitrary Power; and who testified their approbation of the arrival of the troops by the loudest acclamations of joy . . . we had some conversation with the officers, who appeared well disposed towards the peaceable inhabitants, but most bitter against, and determined to pursue to the last extremity the army of the U. S."[11] Morton looked to the redcoats for relief from the tyranny he felt the Patriots had been imposing upon the people. Such sentiment was more than mere partisan hyperbole. In the months and years that preceded the occupation, the Revolutionary governments had taken steps to control private purchases and consumption, demanded near-universal military service in the militias, outlawed opposition speech, mandated oaths of allegiance to their newly formed states, imposed martial law, and threatened those who opposed, or even simply tried to ignore, them with ostracism, imprisonment, exile, and death. Morton's own stepfather, James Pemberton, had been among the nineteen men the Revolutionary government had arrested, denied habeas corpus, and condemned, without trial, to banishment from the state. Elizabeth Drinker, though she lacked Morton's explicitly Loyalist sympathies, also found some comfort in the arrival of the British vanguard, supposing that the orderly and peaceful nature of the soldiers' entry would be of great satisfaction "to our dear Absent Friends, could they but be inform'd of it." Her husband's business partner, Abel James, soon brought his family into the city, "thinking it more safe to be here" than among the Revolutionary forces that dominated his previous residence in Frankford.[12] Quaker merchant Robert Proud wrote to his brothers that he had lived "almost as a Prisoner now for several years," "scarcely ever departing above two Miles from my Place of Abode" for fear of drawing the attention of the Patriot regime. He had looked on in horror at the arrest and banishment of Pemberton, Drinker, and their fellow exiles and believed that only "the Arrival of the Royal Army prevented further Proceedings of this kind."[13] Having faced the "arbitrary Power" of the Patriots, the remaining inhabitants of Philadelphia now dearly hoped that the British would be different.

Several early signs were promising. Morton was comforted by conversations with the British officers. The grenadiers exchanged greetings with the onlooking civilians, calling out "'How do you do, young one—how are you, my boy'—in a brotherly tone" to one young man and shaking his hand, as he later recalled, "not with an exulting shake of conquerors, as I thought, but with a sympathizing one for the vanquished."[14] In some quarters cheering crowds lined the streets as the army marched past, while in others "Everything appeared still & quiet." Yet whether jubilant or somber, the city suffered little violence as it was first taken by the British and, though several fences quickly fell victim to the army's need for fuel, there were no reports of plundering. These first peaceable days led Sarah Logan Fisher to call for "great humility & deep gratitude."[15]

Initially the British placed a far lighter burden of loyalty on the populace than did the Revolutionaries, who had so determinedly imposed oaths and mandatory militia service. No sooner had Howe landed at Head of Elk than he issued a proclamation to "assure the peaceable inhabitants of the province of Pennsylvania" that he was "desirous of protecting the innocent" and was committed to "the preservation of regularity and good discipline." He extended his protection, not only to Loyalists and neutrals, but also to Revolutionaries who served "in subordinate stations," asking only that they peacefully return to their houses. Even those actively bearing arms against the empire were offered "a free and general pardon." Continental and militia units were encouraged to surrender themselves to the nearest British detachments, but the only essential requirement Howe placed on his enemies was that they stop fighting and go home.[16] Howe renewed the proclamation shortly after taking possession of Philadelphia, having already instructed the inhabitants of the city, through merchant Thomas Willing, that they had only "to remain quietly and peaceably in their own dwellings and they should not be molested in their persons or property."[17] To many Pennsylvanians who were weary of the Patriots' constant demands for consent and seeming eagerness to declare fellow colonists "enemies to the liberties of America," such an offer must have sounded refreshingly easy and open.

In the days immediately following Lord Cornwallis's entry into the city, a new sense of order and stability prevailed, at least for those not affiliated with the Revolutionaries. Drinker described the early days as being ones of "great quiate," Jacob Mordecai recalled that "Great order was preserved in the city, the inhabitants were not interrupted, the officers were polite & the soldiers civil," and Proud went so far as to proclaim that the city had "not had so much good order and Tranquility these several years, as we have had since the British Forces came hither."[18] Much of this early tranquility came through the efforts of Joseph Galloway who, having been an invaluable resource for the British on their march to Philadelphia, now undertook the task of calming and organizing the remaining inhabitants of his home city, smoothing out their interactions with the occupying force. He promptly implemented a loyal town watch, took steps to thwart any attempts at arson the Patriots might have considered, disarmed citizens suspected of supporting independence, and began creating a network of spies who could obtain information on the Continental Army and the situation outside British lines. Though only an unofficial liaison for the army initially, his role was formalized in early December when Howe appointed him superintendent general, adding regulatory authority over the city's commerce to the list of powers Galloway had already assumed as the de facto chief of the civilian inhabitants.[19]

With the bulk of the army stationed in and around Germantown and nearly six hundred empty homes in the city, abandoned by those who had fled to the countryside, the British could initially afford to accommodate the preferences of various inhabitants when it came to quartering their officers. Deborah Norris wrote that her mother's house had been selected as the residence of Lord Cornwallis, but when Mrs. Norris found herself entirely overwhelmed by the general's guards, baggage, servants, and aides, Cornwallis "behaved with great politeness to her, said he should be sorry to give trouble, and would have other quarters looked out for him." He and his men were gone by the end of the day. Elizabeth Drinker also managed to repeatedly turn away officers looking for a place to stay and was given hope that those women who were living without their husbands present, of whom there were many in the early days of the occupation, would be spared the trial of military boarders.[20]

Morton also rejoiced in the arrival of the British because their coming "put a period to the existence of Continental money in this city." For more than two years Congress had been promoting this new currency in order to fund the war effort. Those with political or religious objections to the Revolution were hesitant to take up such bills, but so were those who foresaw the inflationary effects of a newly established government attempting to finance a war via printing press. By the summer of 1777 the bills issued by Congress had already lost at least half their value, beginning the steady decline that would eventually see them fade to utter worthlessness in 1781.[21] Nonetheless, the Revolutionary government interpreted any reluctance to accept the currency as an open assault on itself, the Revolution, and the people of America. As early as January 1776, Congress resolved that anyone "so lost to all virtue and regard for his country, as to 'refuse to receive said bills in payment,' or obstruct or discourage the currency or circulation thereof . . . shall be deemed, published, and treated as an enemy of his country and precluded from all trade or intercourse with the inhabitants of these colonies."[22] The threat was not idle. Before the month was out the Philadelphia committee of inspection and observation pounced on John Drinker and Thomas and Samuel Fisher for refusing to accept Continental bills. Dismissing the accuseds' defense that they did not support the war and, therefore, should not have to accept the money that funded it, the committee decried the trio as working "to subvert the most essential rights and liberties of their fellow citizens" and daring "to expose their lives and properties to unavoidable ruin."[23] The political sins of the Drinker and Fisher families were not soon forgotten by the radicals. The following year, as the currency began to falter, Congress moved again to reinforce it, this time focusing on those "enemies of American liberty" who, aware of its declining worth, accepted the Continental currency only at a discount. No longer content to merely ostracize and boycott offenders, Congress now demanded that they "forfeit the value of the money so exchanged, or house, land, or commodity so sold or offered to sale."[24] If the currency could not stand on its own or rest on the patriotism of the people, it would be upheld by force. The coming of the redcoats eliminated such threats and ended the circulation of Congress's money in the city.

Across the ideological spectrum from the Continental bills, and complicating the currency issue in Pennsylvania, was what remained of the paper money issued, under royal sanction, by the colonial government before the outbreak of war. Striving to uphold the value of its own issue, the Revolutionary government had worked to suppress the colonial bills and, by the end of 1777, was moving to make them "utterly irredeemable" by law.[25] Rejected by more ardent Patriots, these bills had accumulated in the possession of the Loyalists and disaffected, who held them in "full confidence, that the money which had received a royal sanction would be restored to its proper value" upon a British victory in the war.[26] The sight of redcoats marching through Philadelphia led many to expect that such a restoration would happen immediately and that the old "legal paper money," as they called it, would soon "be of equal value with gold and silver."[27]

In the opening weeks of the occupation, it seemed these high expectations would be met. Howe approved the circulation of the old currency. Some British commissaries and officers accepted it, both for their own use and for paying the soldiery.[28] A listing of the currency's value relative to various coinages was published in the newspapers only days after Cornwallis's troops arrived. By the end of October, the money was, at least for the moment, declared to be "generally current."[29] Even in Chester County, outside the British lines, groups began banding together to reject the Continental money and return to the older colonial currency.[30] With the support of the army it seemed as though it would be only a matter of time before the "legal paper money" was once again the common currency of the land, a vindication for all those who had hoped for, or simply expected, an eventual reconciliation with Great Britain.

Though he generally had no cache of colonial currency nor any exceptional loyalty to Great Britain, few people looked to the British occupation with greater hope than did Mike High. High arrived in Philadelphia alongside the British in 1777. Though he came in the company of the redcoats, and would not have come without them, he was not himself part of the army. Chance, security, and profit all conspired to bring men and women across the British lines, but for High, a black slave, the presence of the army in Philadelphia meant something far grander; it meant liberty. In passing from the Patriot-controlled fields of Maryland to the British-occupied city, Mike High passed from slavery to freedom.

Six feet tall, muscular, and fit, High was a quick, strong fieldworker and known for his remarkable speed. His former master, John Bolton, claimed High could "run almost as fast as a horse," a useful trait for one who wants to escape enslavement. Yet even the fastest fugitive must have somewhere to go, some safe haven that will not return him to bondage. Bolton, a merchant, "son of liberty," and committed Revolutionary, lived in Chestertown, Maryland, where he owned multiple slaves and substantial property, including a sizable plantation northwest of the city where High probably spent most of his days. The plantation put High no more than a few miles from the shores of the Chesapeake. When the Royal Navy swept up toward its landing at Head of Elk in the late summer of 1777, High recognized his chance. As most Maryland whites fled away from the sight of the British ships, seeking shelter in their homes and cities, High took advantage of the suddenly empty roads to run, "almost as fast as a horse," toward the redcoats and freedom, plowing through the flowing waters, and finally clambering aboard a British warship. He may well have been one of the black fugitives from Maryland whom Ambrose Serle encountered in September.[31]

No group saw the British army as a force of liberation quite so clearly and literally as did the men and women of color held as slaves by the Revolutionaries. Even before the war slaves in America began to suspect that, should violence break out between their masters and the empire, British forces would offer freedom to bondsmen who revolted.[32] When Lord Dunmore, the besieged royal governor of Virginia, declared free all slaves and servants held by rebels and willing to bear arms on his behalf, he only reinforced the expectation that the British were a force of liberators.[33] Shortly thereafter, the *Pennsylvania Evening Post* reported that, in the streets of Philadelphia, "a gentlewoman . . . was insulted by a Negro" who, upon being reprimanded, warned the white onlookers that a "black regiment" of formerly enslaved men, now free, would soon come and put an end to his subjugation.[34]

Henry Muhlenberg's journal neatly captured the high expectations of Americans in bondage, recording a conversation he overheard between two slaves owned by Patriots fleeing Philadelphia in the days before the British captured the city. The slaves, he reported, "secretly wished that the British army might win, for then all Negro slaves will gain their freedom." Muhlenberg suspected that "this sentiment is almost universal among the Negroes in America."[35] The months that followed lent credence to this suspicion as enslaved men and women from around the region, like Mike High, sought sanctuary and freedom with the British army in or en route to occupied Philadelphia.[36]

The occupation offered an especially promising opportunity for enslaved women. Female slaves were more likely to have developed the sort of domestic skills, such as sewing or cooking, that retained their value in the crowded city. For those living in the midst of thousands of bored soldiers for months on end, prostitution also offered a potential means of survival, if all else failed. Though men made up the majority of fugitive slaves throughout the eighteenth century, the ratio of women to men rose sharply during the Revolution. As a result of the British occupations of New York City and Philadelphia, more enslaved women fled from their masters in New York and New Jersey during the years of the war than in all previous years combined.[37]

Thus, in the opening days and weeks of the occupation, Philadelphians of many stripes looked upon the British with a mixture of fear, hope, and confusion. Ardent Patriots fled or fretted in the face of the redcoats, but Loyalists, the disaffected, and others who were more open to a positive interpretation of events developed, or brought with them, a set of key expectations about the intentions of the occupying forces. They looked to the British to reestablish peace and order, to relieve those who had suffered at the hands of the Revolutionaries, to restore economic stability and reward those who held colonial currency, and to grant freedom to those held in chains by the so-called "sons of liberty." Though at first it seemed that many of these expectations would be fulfilled, the people of the occupied city soon entered a long season of surprise and disappointment.

Disappointments

Howe's initial proclamation upon landing at Head of Elk, repeated immediately after the army took Philadelphia, represented an open offer of security and protection for the inhabitants and a free pardon for all rebels, even those actively in arms. As the population began to respond to his offer, however, Howe altered this policy. Having observed the flow of people back toward their homes and the first trickle of defectors from the Continental lines, the British commander now deemed it "both reasonable and necessary that all such persons, as a proof of the sincerity of their intentions to return to their due allegiance . . . should take the oath of allegiance to his majesty." Those who refused to do so would forfeit the promised security and protection of the army, no longer be covered by Howe's general pardon, and "be considered as persons out of his majesty's peace, and treated accordingly."[38] Hemmed in on one side by Pennsylvania's Test Act and on the other by Howe's oath of allegiance, it now seemed that those who hoped to avoid participating in the conflict would be left with no place to hide. Whatever course they took, an army stood ready to strip them of their rights and declare them enemies and traitors; silence on the question, rather than sparing them, threatened to raise the ire of both combatants.

In practice, the redcoats paid little attention to who had and had not taken the oath, only pressing it upon select individuals and defectors. Over the course of the occupation, only about two thousand civilians swore allegiance to the king, suggesting that even committed Loyalists preferred to avoid an act that would so obviously mark them as targets for Revolutionary retribution. The overwhelming majority of civilians who did take the oath did so in October, when those previously affiliated with the Revolution faced the greatest threat of arrest and before events made it so abundantly clear that swearing allegiance to the king did little to stay the hands of the king's men when it came to plunder.[39]

Acts of plunder and destruction had marked the campaign almost from the moment the British stepped ashore in Maryland. Howe's belief in the peaceable and loyal nature of most Delaware Valley inhabitants and his fears of alienating them encouraged him to crack down harshly on soldiers who stole or damaged private property. Yet despite the general's explicit and threatening orders to the contrary, the troops under his command immediately descended upon the largely vacant homes and farmsteads around their landing site and began pillaging.[40] Before the day was out, the army had executed at least one of its own for plundering and whipped several others.[41] Such punishments failed to reform the soldiery. William Rawle later recalled Howe's march toward Philadelphia as "the path of one of those tornados which, between the tropics, traverse the country in dreadful fury, and leave a mournful picture of devastation and destruction."[42] If, as observers like Drinker and Fisher reported, the arrival of the British in Philadelphia was free of plundering and theft, it represented an exceptional and carefully constructed performance. Cornwallis led only a select group of soldiers through the streets; Howe kept the bulk of his forces at Germantown and forbade any "Woman or follower of the Army" from attempting to reach the city.[43]

Germantown immediately suffered at the hands of British forces and Philadelphia's peaceful respite soon came to an end.[44] The grim tale of stolen property, produce, and livestock, of fear and destruction, echoes not only through civilian letters and journals but also in the multitude of orders and proclamations the British leadership issued in its attempt to keep the soldiery in check. On November 7, Howe issued a proclamation admitting that numerous inhabitants in and around Philadelphia had complained of being "injured in their property by disorderly persons" and promising to inflict "the most exemplary punishment" on those engaged in plundering.[45] The same proclamation was reprinted five times in the following months and joined by others focused on protecting the people's farmland, produce, and livestock.[46] In March a separate edict broadly forbade taking "the property of any of his majesty's well affected subjects without their consent," a rule many might have thought would have gone without saying.[47] Fences, being readily available sources of firewood, were particularly enticing targets and were repeatedly singled out, both in Howe's orders forbidding theft and in civilian accounts of plundered property.[48] The ineffectiveness of such proclamations was apparent in the general orders of December 18: "Notwithstanding the repeated orders that have been given against plundering and depredation, the Commander-in-Chief continues to receive daily complaints from the inhabitants on that head; he is very much mortified at being again under the necessity of calling upon the commanding officers of corps for their exertion to suppress such shameful and unsoldierlike behavior."[49] Patrols were ordered to keep an eye out for "straggling soldiers or disorderly persons," but given the crowded nature of the city, maintaining strict discipline was all but impossible. Philadelphia became home to as many as fifty thousand souls during the occupation. Remaining and returning inhabitants, refugees from the countryside, and merchants from abroad brought the civilian population back to its preinvasion levels of approximately thirty thousand. Late in the occupation, these men and women shared the city with more than fifteen thousand British soldiers, sailors, and camp followers.[50]

Most of the more ardent Patriots having fled and not returned, the victims of theft and looting within the city were primarily Loyalist and disaffected. Yet many found it particularly disturbing that even on the outskirts and at Germantown, where the allegiances of the inhabitants were more mixed, British plundering appeared to be at best indiscriminate and at times to fall hardest on those who had supported the imperial cause. Fisher complained that the army "was plundering & ruining many people" regardless of their affiliations; Drinker noted that "a number of friends of government about the country have lately been plundered and ill used by the British troops"; and Morton recorded that the British had "abused many old, inoffensive men."[51] Even Revolutionary observers noticed the redcoats' casual disregard for expressed loyalties. Solomon Bush, a Patriot and militiaman wounded at Brandywine, was recovering at his home near Germantown when a detachment of British soldiers passed by. Bush wrote to a friend that the redcoats "treated our family with the utmost respect: they did not take the least trifle from us." However, he observed, "our neighbors, the poor Tories lost every thing."[52] One of Robert Morris's correspondents wrote him from north of Philadelphia to report that the British were freely destroying the property of pacifist Quakers alongside that of outspoken Revolutionaries. He snidely, but accurately, added that "this is a kind of proceeding that was not expected from friend Howe."[53]

The darkest moments came in late November and early December. On the morning of November 22, the chimney of the Reverend Henry Muhlenberg's house in Trappe caught fire, prompting a frantic scramble of activity to put it out before the roof ignited. Though the chimney was extinguished without incident, later that same day Muhlenberg's attention was once again captured by the flickering lights of an unexpected conflagration. Staring perplexedly toward the east, he and his companions "saw high flames in the direction of Philadelphia" and pondered what ill fate had befallen the people there. Other eyes were also drawn toward the lights as across the occupied city the inhabitants turned their attention toward the smoke and flames that had suddenly erupted in Germantown. Deborah Logan's family gathered on the roof of her mother's house in Chestnut Street to watch in horror as British soldiers set homes and outhouses ablaze. They counted seventeen fires that day, doing their best to determine which buildings were being consumed, and experienced an especially painful shock when they saw the flames take Fairhill, a country seat built by Logan's own grandfather.[54]

The soldiers attempted to justify the destruction by claiming that the houses provided shelter to Revolutionary marksmen who harassed their picket lines, but such excuses were met with little sympathy from the people. Many were shocked to discover that no distinction had been made between the homes of Loyalists and Patriots. More astonishing still, at least to Robert Morton, was "their burning the furniture in some of those houses that belonged to friends of government, when it was in their power to burn them at their leisure." Logan mourned the loss of not only the house and furniture but also the substantial library that had been at Fairhill; the army had given the family no opportunity to remove it.[55] When Muhlenberg finally learned the cause of the flames, he castigated Britain as an abusive parent: "O Mother, Mother! How wretchedly dost thou deal with thy children!"[56]

Two weeks later the city's attention was once again drawn to the ominous sight of burning houses. Frustrated British and Hessian soldiers, drearily returning from yet another tiring and anticlimactic attempt to achieve a decisive engagement with Washington's Continentals, vented their aggression on the civilian structures they passed. The villages of Cresheim and Beggarstown, northwest of the city, suffered repeated burnings as each wave of passing soldiers selected their own set of houses to ignite. High winds whipped at the flames, pushing them from house to house and generating a firestorm that nearly prevented the British rear guard from making it through the town. Hessian captain Johann Ewald was horrified by the spectacle and grimly recorded "the cries of human voices of the young and old, who had seen their belongings consumed by the flames."[57] Once again, as Fisher observed, "those who had always been steady friends to government fared no better than the rest." Once again, the residents were given no time to collect their belongings or save their treasures from the inferno. And once again, no convincing justification was offered for the destruction. Indeed, it seemed to Morton "as if the sole purpose of the expedition was to destroy and to spread desolation and ruin."[58] Many began to wonder just where the destruction would end.

The sudden and indiscriminate nature of these burnings prompted fears that the army might, with little notice, put whole swaths of territory to the torch. Drinker heard rumors that the British planned to create a no-man's-land around the city by burning every house within four miles of the lines. One Germantown resident was so convinced that the entire village would be destroyed that he spent two days carting his most valuable possessions away for safekeeping.[59] The British officers did little to put such fears to rest. Captain John André actively believed that the army needed to engage in harsher measures, both to match the coercive steps taken by the Revolutionaries and as a way of forcing the rebellion, and perhaps all of America, to its knees. "Have we not fire as well as the sword," he asked suggestively, "a horrid means yet untried!"[60] Major Nesbit Balfour, one of Howe's aides, freely suggested in front of civilians that all of Germantown and everything for twelve miles around it might be destroyed in retaliation for Washington's surprise attack there. Ironically, he asserted that the widespread destruction of homes and livelihoods would be justified because the people had failed to assist the British army in its mission "to preserve the liberties and properties of the peaceable inhabitants."[61]

In the early days of the occupation, many Philadelphians had worried that the Revolutionaries would burn the city to the ground rather than see it occupied by the redcoats. They readily recalled the suspicious fires which had been set in New York City just as it was seized by the British.[62] In late September men had patrolled the streets into the wee hours of the morning, keeping a lookout for potential Patriot arsonists.[63] As the year waned, however, those same anxious souls began to worry that the British, not the

Patriots, might burn down the entire region even as they held possession of it.

Such acts of plunder and destruction severely undercut British attempts to win the hearts and minds of Pennsylvanians and deeply disappointed those who had hoped the occupation would bring greater peace and security to the area. The more sensitive officers recognized the damage being done to their cause, though they struggled to remedy it. "We have been going too far and have done infinitely more to maintain the rebellion than to smother it," wrote Hessian major Carl Leopold Baurmeister. "These excesses, though we gain but little by them, may have very serious consequences."[64] Writing to James Pemberton, who had been exiled to Virginia by the Revolutionary government, Philadelphian Thomas Parke listed off a series of outrages committed by British and Hessian troops. Having considered moral objections to their behavior, he pragmatically added that "it is certainly bad Policy & must be detrimental to their Cause."[65]

Wherever the army set foot it seemed to spread destruction and alienation. Observing the effect of British foraging expeditions from outside the lines, Jedidiah Huntington observed that "[Howe] makes Whigs wherever he marches."[66] Yet if the mere passage of the army left a trail of disaffection, its extended presence did even more to sour whatever Loyalist sympathies its hosts had once possessed and to dissuade the disaffected from embracing the British cause. Not only were those within the occupied city witness to repeated instances of bad behavior by the British military, they also became intimate enough with the army to recognize the arbitrary nature of the destruction. Morton's joy at seeing the Revolutionary regime removed from power had initially given him a limited tolerance for some degree of unofficial confiscation by the British soldiery, but this steadily evaporated as he came to understand that the army often had no real need for the goods it plundered and was quite capable of compensating victims but regularly refused to do so. He predicted that, "had the necessities of the army justified the measures, and they had paid a sufficient price for what they had taken, then they would have had the good wishes of the people, and perhaps all the assistance they could afford." Instead, however, British confiscations appeared to serve no purpose except "to dispose the inhabitants to rebellion by despoiling their property."[67]

Inhabitants in the city were also exposed to the futile and seemingly endless series of orders and proclamations which forbade plundering and threatened to punish those who engaged in it. In composing these edicts,

Howe sometimes demonstrated a surprising insensitivity toward the public. The oft-reprinted proclamation of November 7, which began by acknowledging the "complaints from the inhabitants," immediately moved on to blame those same inhabitants by declaring that the theft and destruction of civilian property was "encouraged by citizens purchasing from the soldiers" and that anyone who purchased stolen merchandise would be subject to the same "exemplary punishment" as the plunderers. Whatever limited reassurance these edicts may have initially brought, their ineffectiveness eventually became a source of even greater frustration and fostered a sense of betrayal among the inhabitants. Civilians who recorded incidents of destruction often referred to these pledges of protection and how they were being violated. Even John Adams noted that the victims of British destruction had been made even more "angry and disappointed because they were promised the Security of their Property."[68] For his part, Robert Morton grew increasingly incensed over the army's routine failure to keep its word. His descriptions of British wrongdoing were soon peppered with sarcastic references to "the gracious proclamation of his Excellency" and "the General's candor and generosity."[69]

Galloway, positioned as the aggrieved public's foremost ambassador to the military, did his best to limit the depredations of the army but chafed at his limited powers in this regard. Though given great latitude in dictating the lives of Philadelphia's civilians, Britain's refusal to reestablish civilian government meant that the superintendent general had little authority over the actions of the military, and Galloway grew increasingly frustrated with Howe's failure to keep his soldiers in check. The establishment and maintenance of a civil police force became Galloway's foremost means of limiting the army's opportunities to abuse the city's inhabitants. Though it did little to prevent plundering or punish destructive acts by the soldiery, Galloway's administration was at least able to shield civilians from the full rigor of military law.[70]

The extensive burning of Germantown forced even staunch Loyalists like Morton to reevaluate their earlier comparisons between imperial and Revolutionary forces. Though he had derided the Patriots as "a liscentious mob," a "deluded multitude," and a "lawless power," Morton now confessed that this was "an instance that Gen'l Washington's Army cannot be accused of. There is not one instance to be produced where they have wantonly destroyed and burned their friends' property."[71] The Revolutionaries were quick to conflate neutrality or disaffection with enmity and could be ruthlessly intolerant toward such perceived enemies, but their violence was not so indiscriminate, nor so seemingly pointless, as that carried out by the redcoats. Where the Patriots harassed the population with incessant demands for consent and allegiance, the British seemed to be wholly indifferent to the loyalties of the people. When the occupation first began, Morton had rejoiced that, at last, the inhabitants would be able to escape "the yoke of arbitrary power." As the year came to a close however, it seemed that many had only escaped the frying pan to find themselves, quite literally, in the fire.[72]

In addition to acts of plunder and outright destruction, crimes of other sorts continually plagued the city.[73] Accusations of burglary, rape, and assault, sometimes carried out by soldiers, sometimes by civilians, run throughout the period. Theft, in particular, was rampant and the newspapers almost always contained new descriptions of stolen items. Drinker worried that "these are sad times for thieving and plundering, tis hardly safe to leave the door open a minute."[74] Courts-martial assembled regularly to try and punish offenders, both military and civilian. Only when Galloway's Magistrates of Police were able to claim jurisdiction were civilians spared trial by the army.[75] Yet the army's attempts to restrain and punish criminals occasionally succeeded only in further alienating the victimized populace.

Sentences meted out by the courts-martial were generally brutal and public. Penalties for plundering or theft ranged from five hundred lashes to death by hanging. Desertion was most often punished with one thousand lashes. Striking an officer was a capital offense. Civilians were executed and whipped alongside military offenders, but were also subject to special punishments including impressment and various public shaming rituals.[76] Wagoners Robert Brown and John Dillion were convicted of raping two servant girls. Each was sentenced to suffer one thousand lashes, be drummed through town to the "rogue's march" with a noose around their necks, and then be expelled from the city. Sixteen-year-old Mary Fygis was convicted of perjury against a British captain. The court deemed itself merciful in banishing her from Philadelphia and threatening her with time in the pillory and prison should she attempt to return home. James Duncan, master of the private ship *Rose*, was one of several men accused of trying to poach British seamen from the HMS *Zebra* for his own crew. Duncan confessed and was merely charged a fine of twenty pounds per sailor he had approached. His boatswain, Thomas Buck, refused to confess and, in a reversal of the criminal scheme, was compelled to take up service in the Royal Navy.[77]

The army took few, if any, steps to shield the city's inhabitants from the more gruesome aspects of military justice. A "public place of execution" was established in the courtyard behind the State House, in the very center of the city, but floggings and hangings could be witnessed in various places.[78] Returning home from surveying the destruction British soldiers had wreaked on Israel Pemberton's estate, Robert Morton's company passed the grisly sight of a corpse hanging from the gallows. Morton had no knowledge of what the man's offense had been.[79] Corporal William McSkimming, of the Fifteenth Foot, was convicted of assaulting a commissioned officer and hanged behind the State House on the morning of November 1. His body was labeled "Condemned for Mutiny" and left to sway in the breeze until sunset.[80]

The level of brutality deeply disturbed some inhabitants. The Quakers, in particular, were distressed by the violence, even when they themselves had been the victims of the condemned criminals' actions. Morton's family estate outside the city was robbed and damaged by a group from the British Sixteenth Light Dragoons who were, shortly thereafter, identified and caught. After learning that the men were to be "severely punished," Morton approached their commanding officer, Colonel William Harcourt, to plead for mercy on their behalf. Harcourt had no interest in discussing the matter with Morton beyond making certain that he would testify against the men at the trial. Morton's mother, Phebe Pemberton, also attempted to secure a more lenient punishment for the soldiers that had robbed her. The officer responded to her with more gentility but no less resolve, assuring her "that he could not admit her application as the orders of the General must be obeyed, and that the soldiers were not suffered to commit such depredations upon the King's subjects with impunity." Morton's diary entry for the day bitingly follows this pronouncement with a reminder that not only had the family's house been ransacked but British troops had also lately made off with a large quantity of their hay without leaving any money or receipt. Mary Pemberton also petitioned General Howe to mitigate the death sentence issued against the soldier who had broken into her house.[81] Young Rebecca Franks interceded to spare the life of Corporal John Fisher, of the Twenty-Eighth Foot, who was sentenced to hang for the rape of nine-year-old Maria Nicholls. It's unclear whether Franks's pleas for mercy influenced Howe's decision, but Fisher was granted a pardon "in consideration of his

Youth, and the very good Character given of him by the Field Officer of his Regiment."[82]

British courts-martial records also shine a spotlight on troops engaging in various lesser crimes which likely offended the sensibilities of their civilian hosts. Violent altercations between soldiers were common, as were attempts to desert and seek a new life in the Pennsylvania countryside, a crime the courts punished quite severely. A standard defense against charges of desertion was that the accused had simply been deliriously intoxicated. Their having crossed the lines without a pass or plotted to desert with others was attributed to the wayward wanderings and senseless babblings of a drunk. This line of defense sometimes failed and sometimes succeeded, but its ubiquity and the fact that the court often made unsolicited inquiries as to the sobriety of the accused indicates the severity of drunkenness as a problem for the army within the lines.

The court-martial of Lieutenant Nathanial Fitzpatrick of the Queen's Rangers highlights another common vice of idle soldiers confined to the city. Fitzpatrick was officially charged with "behaving in a scandalous infamous manner such as is unbecoming the character of an officer and a gentleman," meaning, in this case, that he had been instrumental in the spread of venereal disease to his fellow soldiers. The lieutenant, who was the first in his unit to acquire the disease, was accused of having slept with and thus knowingly infected one Mary Duche, a woman known to live with and "belong to" Captain Murray, also of the Queen's Rangers. Murray was himself infected shortly thereafter. Testimony during the trial revealed that Duche slept with a great many of the Queen's Rangers throughout the occupation. Fitzpatrick avoided a formal conviction but was ordered to publicly apologize to his fellow officers. For her part, Duche received nothing from Fitzpatrick, aside from the disease, and it seems that the court chose to view her as a dangerous seductress rather than a victim.[83]

The city's inhabitants were increasingly confronted with such distasteful scenes following the army's transfer from Germantown toward Philadelphia itself in mid-October.[84] Over the following weeks, as the campaign season came to a close and the weather grew steadily colder, more and more men sought semipermanent quarters in the increasingly crowded city. Many Philadelphians, particularly women who had been led to believe they could maintain the privacy of their homes, soon found themselves forced to accept military boarders. Elizabeth Drinker's steadfast efforts kept her home free of British guests throughout the autumn and early winter, even as the steady influx of soldiers gradually filled the homes of her friends and neighbors. Yet as the year waned she confessed, "I fear we shall have our Family disagreeably encumbered." Her fears were soon realized.[85]

On December 18 Drinker was once again asked to accept a British officer into her home, this time by one Major J. C. Crammond. As before, she demurred and hoped to be left in peace, but Crammond returned to repeat the question on the nineteenth and again on the twentieth. Though his persistence was irritating, Drinker had to admit that he was remarkably polite compared to many of the officers who had taken up residence with her neighbors. She found herself talking at length with him about the poor behavior of his comrades in arms, even relating to him the details of that terrifying night when the drunken officer had stalked through her house with a sword, events she was still keeping from her absent husband. To his credit, the major made no attempt to justify or excuse the actions of his fellows, but on the contrary worried that worse might come as the city became ever more crowded. Arguing that the family's best protection from poorly behaved soldiers would be to house a well-behaved officer, Crammond offered himself as an ideal candidate for the Drinker home. Having payed careful attention to her complaints and fears, he systematically listed his qualifications: he was quiet, solitary, and sober; rarely had guests; and kept early hours. As a reference, he offered Joseph Galloway, a close acquaintance of the family. Drinker again said no, but promised to consider his offer.[86]

A week passed before Crammond called again, during which time Drinker desperately sought advice and looked for any means of keeping her home clear of soldiers. She could find no way out. Prior assurances proved to be false, pressure was mounting, and it seemed that soon she would have to accept a military guest whether she wanted to or not. Already a number of officers, particularly those who came from elite British families, were expressing bitterness at having to sleep in taverns or aboard ships because the colonists they were ostensibly fighting to "liberate" wouldn't offer them a place in their homes. On the twenty-ninth the major returned to hear Drinker's answer. "Cramond here this morning," she recorded, "we have at last agreed on his coming to take up his abode with us." Two days later she wrote to her husband, "our Family is somewhat increas'd; I made many efforts to be excused, but am led to believe tis best to make a virtue of necessity. I have reason to think that I am quite as well of[f] as any of my neighbours, and find the matter much easyer than I expected." To herself she wrote "I hope it will be no great inconvenience, tho' I have many fears." For the first time in months, there was a man living in Drinker's home, though not the one she wanted.[87]

Time would prove Drinker fortunate in her choice of guests. Crammond was not the ideal boarder he had claimed to be, but aside from a tendency for keeping company late into the evening, he was generally sober and well-behaved. Over the following months he and Elizabeth Drinker would form a remarkably positive bond, given the circumstances of their acquaintance. Others were not so lucky. Deborah Norris's mother had managed to persuade Cornwallis to leave her property back in September, but he was soon replaced by two artillery officers she could not so easily dissuade. Shortly thereafter two additional gentlemen from Lord Admiral Howe's staff arrived to fill her home's remaining space.[88] Many officers damaged or destroyed their hosts' property and confronted homeowners with threats, insults, and other sorts of "very rude and impudent" behavior. Drinker's friend, Mary Eddy, was forbidden from using her own front door and forced to come and go through a back alley in order to avoid the rooms her resident officer had claimed as his own. She was further scandalized when her guest invited his mistress to move in with him.[89] The soldiers' tendency to simply take over whatever space seemed most desirable to them prompted a reprimand from Howe in mid-December. Even then, however, he demanded only that the officers seek the permission of their military superiors, not of the inhabitants, before they occupied a dwelling, office, or outbuilding.[90]

In the first days of the occupation, when only Cornwallis's chosen troops were present in the city streets, observers like Drinker and Proud had praised the "great quiate" and "good order and Tranquility" that accompanied the British army. It is hard to imagine that such sentiments long endured as the rest of the army and its legion of followers descended upon the Quaker city that winter.[91]

The changing seasons and the arrival of new faces not only cost inhabitants control over their homes but also threatened the value of their money. Hopes that the army would oversee a reestablishment of the old Pennsylvania currency were soon dashed. Though October had witnessed the disappearance of Continental bills and the promising rise of the older colonial currency, November brought change. The Patriots' early success in cutting the British off from the countryside and in maintaining the river forts led to inflated prices regardless of the currency offered, but concern over the army's ability to hold the city seems to have led also to a wavering of the "legal paper money's" value relative to specie.[92] Several prominent civilians had anticipated this eventuality and already taken steps to prevent it. As early as October 3, only a week after the British first arrived in the city, activists were traveling throughout Philadelphia requesting that prominent citizens sign a pledge to "engage to each other and to the public, that we will not ask or receive, in our dealings, for any commodity whatever, a greater sum in the said legal paper money than in gold or silver."[93] Within a month more than six hundred of the most prominent civilians remaining in the city had signed. Joseph Galloway's name was the first one added to the list. When the value of the currency first began to tremble in early November, its supporters, in a move which echoed the earlier tactics of the Revolutionaries, had the names of all subscribers published in the newspapers, a reminder to the public and to the subscribers themselves of their commitment.[94] Bolstered by such efforts, the old bills continued to circulate for a time, but greater challenges were soon to come.

On November 15, after withstanding weeks of bombardment from the British army and Royal Navy, the Revolutionaries finally evacuated Fort Mifflin and Fort Mercer on the Delaware River. With the river finally clear of American defenses, the navy advanced to the docks of Philadelphia itself, bringing long-awaited and desperately needed supplies to impatient British commissaries. In its wake came a separate flotilla of merchant vessels from New York and Britain, eager to do business with the occupying forces and to reconnect Pennsylvania's capital to the Atlantic trade network and to the empire of goods the Revolutionaries had dared to reject. With no investment in the colonial money and unbound by any pledge to uphold its value, these "merchant-strangers," as Joseph Stansbury called them, paid little heed to the local community's posted rates of exchange.[95] Hesitant to risk their profits on a currency which was valued in only one city and which, should the British withdraw, might soon become entirely irredeemable, they rejected paper money altogether and set their sights squarely on the hard currency and bills of exchange held by Philadelphia's elites and, more importantly, by the British army. Though their economic reasoning was sound, the foreign merchants' choices spelled disaster for the civilians' efforts to reestablish the "legal paper money," restore their fortunes, and secure a common medium of exchange in the occupied city.

The civilian leaders responded with a furious and desperate campaign to uphold the old currency's value and to isolate the "merchant-strangers" who threatened it. Desperate to win the support of the army, they not only presented their case in terms of public utility and economic justice but also of allegiance. Just as the Continental Congress had conflated rejection of their new money with treason, so now the elite Loyalists of occupied Philadelphia struggled to transform the old colonial bills into symbols of loyalty toward Great Britain and the old colonial government. A public letter published in late November explained that the people had "continually negotiated off their continental money for legal paper, at a considerable loss" because "in their hearts they adhered to the old constitution." Moreover, they argued, the money itself, combined with Congress's attempts to eliminate it, turned the people who held it into "friends of government" by necessarily tying their fortunes to a British victory.[96]

The same authors were also quick to execrate the newly arrived merchants as well as local traders who had begun refusing or discounting the old currency in the face of foreign competition. Such men, they cried, were "characters of so selfish and cruel a temper, that they would starve the widow and orphan, and sacrifice a whole country to rise upon their ruin." Knowing that Congress desired the extinction of the "legal paper money," these misers nonetheless took steps which advanced that goal and so put themselves in the service of the Revolutionaries. Worse still, if the old paper ceased to be of any value, all commerce in the city would have to be done in specie, which would inevitably leak out to the countryside and into the hands of the rebels, leading to consequences "which every Frenchman, who imports arms and ammunition for the use of the congress, can readily explain." Selfish and treacherous, they were also defeatists. Loyalist writers interpreted the merchants' concern that the colonial money might turn out to be irredeemable as "declaring to all the world that they are doubtful of the success of the English arms, and that with an army and a fleet around them they will not risque a farthing of their property upon the issue." "Does it not speak the language of distrust and despair?" asked one anonymous author, "Does it not disgrace the men under whose very banners they import their goods?"[97]

On the other hand, argued the same advocates, "if paper should be restored to its old credit . . . in defiance of all penal laws of either assembly or congress it would be received by the farmer in preference to continental dollars," accelerating the inflation of the Revolution's currency and driving the empire's enemies toward bankruptcy. A symbol and creator of loyalty, a much-needed medium of exchange, and now a weapon to be wielded

 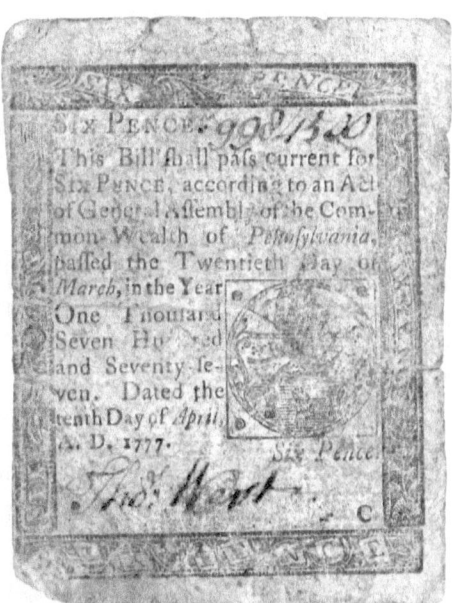

FIGURE 5. Counterfeit six pence note of Pennsylvania currency. Original at the William L. Clements Library, University of Michigan. In an effort to undermine the Revolutionary governments, British forces in the occupied cities printed and distributed counterfeit Continental and state currency. See Jackson, *With the British Army in Philadelphia*, 287.

against the Congress and the Revolution, the currency of colonial Pennsylvania became all these things in the words of those who were desperately trying to defend it. For these reasons they were "determined to support its credit, at every hazard." [98] Yet in so doing they necessarily embraced the perspective of their Revolutionary opponents: that money and loyalty were inextricably linked, that the rejection of a bill and treachery against the nation were, in the final analysis, two sides of the same coin.

In this arena as well, then, the neutral ground was quickly vanishing beneath the feet of anyone who hoped to avoid taking sides in the imperial conflict. Already hemmed in by demands for oaths of allegiance from both the Revolutionaries and the British, Philadelphians now found all their mediums of exchange likewise tainted with loyal or treasonous import. By embracing the rhetoric of their Revolutionary opponents, the advocates of the colonial paper suggested that all those who retained the old currency had already implicitly chosen the British side in the war. In so doing they also implied that the British had a duty to support them and their newly symbolic wealth. The fate of the "legal paper money," and the loyalty it symbolized, would ultimately rest on the decisions of the British army.

Yet while the coercive powers of the Revolutionary governments were frequently deployed to support the Continental currency, British support of the colonial money remained halfhearted at best. Howe never rescinded his permission for the provincial bills to circulate within the city, but neither did he make any move to support them. Pulled on the one side by local civilians who wanted to see the currency reestablished and on the other by the "merchant-strangers" who wanted the freedom to reject it, the British commander eventually sided with the latter. Though not averse to issuing economic proclamations in general, Howe chose not to make the provincial currency legal tender in the city. Shortly after the opening of the river, it seems, the officers of the army and navy, now supplied by the fleet and able to avail themselves of the newly arrived merchants, also stopped accepting the provincial currency, to the great disappointment of the local populace.

Some, such as Joseph Stansbury, cautiously suggested that Howe's decision was shaped by his personal financial involvement with certain merchants, though the charge remains unproven.[99] However, other, more pragmatic factors also argued against establishing the "legal paper money." The local inhabitants had warned that, if the paper currency was not supported, gold and silver would inevitably leak out into the countryside and into the hands of the Revolutionaries. Yet as the British officers were well aware, it was primarily the availability of specie that convinced the largely disaffected population dwelling outside the British lines to bring their produce to Philadelphia and to withhold it from the Continental Army.[100] The advocates of the provincial currency had also argued that support for their cause was linked to one's confidence in the army's ability to hold Philadelphia and expand its lines deeper into Pennsylvania. This connection may well have worked against them with regard to the British commander in chief. As the campaign to establish the provincial currency reached its peak near the end of 1777, Howe himself seems to have lost confidence in his ability to break out of his lines around the occupied city. On October 22 he had, in fact, written to Lord Germain requesting permission to resign his command.[101] Confirmation of Burgoyne's defeat in New York only further convinced Howe that the army was incapable of simultaneously pressing farther into America and maintaining its current possessions. This belief was finally cemented when Howe attempted one last time to provoke Washington into a general engagement near Whitemarsh in early December, an attempt which resulted in little more than an awkward and ultimately pointless series of maneuvers followed by a disheartening march back to the city. Greater conquests in Pennsylvania would require the abandonment of New York or Rhode Island, actions which Howe believed "would operate on the minds of the people strongly against his majesty's interests."[102] Given his doubts about the future, simple prudence dictated against forcing the merchants to accept provincial currency or encouraging his own officers to receive it.

Bereft of official support and faced with intransigent merchants from abroad, the value of the provincial currency crashed to near zero by the end of the year. From the first days of December, Washington's spies within the occupied city were able to report that "Money is very ill to be got. Numbers of people in town will take no paper money of any currency," and that there continued to be "great confusion and dissentions among the citizens."[103] Morton's diary entries for the month chart the steady collapse of the "legal paper money," a decline he blamed on "a deficiency of public virtue." By the eighth the boycott and subscription efforts were failing and there was "No prospect of the paper money being established." Four days later it had become "Hard to pass the paper money" at all and provisions were scarce. On the fourteenth Morton reported "Paper money entirely dropt, and not passable."[104] Other residents and observers presented similar chronicles of woe throughout December.[105]

The collapse of the local currency, the plundering and destruction carried out by British soldiers, the dogged persistence of the Revolutionaries defending Fort Mifflin, and Washington's limited success in isolating the city all combined to make the closing months of 1777 truly desperate for the civilians who remained in the occupied city. By November, even resolute Revolutionary Christopher Marshall sympathetically recorded that "the poor inhabitants of Philadelphia are in a dreadful situation for the want of provisions and firewood."[106] From within the city, Muhlenberg's daughter, Margaretta Kunze, informed her father that her family was "now living on potatoes and bread" and praised God that, unlike others, she still had those. "It is a good thing, in these times," she added, "not to have a large family."[107] In a letter to his brother, dour Quaker Robert Proud neatly summed up the fate of his fellow inhabitants in two words: "Beggary and Ruin."[108]

Faced with such dire prospects, the people turned to the army for assistance, assuming that his majesty's forces would provide for his American subjects living under military occupation.[109] The officers of the army, however, thought otherwise. Lieutenant Loftus Cliffe acknowledged that thousands of civilians were in need of provisions, but held that relief for them would have to somehow come from the countryside, past the Continental patrols, for "our shipping are only to supply *us*."[110] As supplies of food and fuel dwindled, the army steadfastly asserted that its own needs must be met first; the people under its protection would, with few exceptions, simply have to make do on their own.[111]

Before and after the war, colonial Philadelphia was home to an unusually large number of organizations designed to combat the effects of poverty. In addition to the Alms House and publicly funded outrelief systems, the city boasted any number of private societies focused on relieving particular subsets of the poor, such as widows, prisoners, sailors, and immigrants. With few exceptions, these private relief organizations ceased to function during the occupation. Their disappearance placed a terrible burden on the already strained sources of poor relief that remained, making assistance that much harder to get.[112] Consequently, no inhabitants were in more desperate need of military assistance than those residing in the city's Alms House, and yet none were more cruelly rebuffed when they reached out to the British for aid.

The Alms House continued to operate throughout the occupation, but was struggling to keep up with rising poverty even before the British took over the city. The war had entirely disrupted attempts to raise money to support the poor; only a single tax had been levied for that purpose in the two years preceding the occupation, and that had been only partially collected. The Overseers of the Poor ceased to operate while the British controlled the city, leaving the managers of the Alms House without an organized way of collecting additional funds. In December of 1776, the Continental army had taken over the east wing of the house to serve as a military hospital, forcing the managers to relocate all their charges to the west wing, which was known as the House of Employment. The east wing continued to house sick and wounded soldiers during the British army's stay in Philadelphia.[113]

Conditions in the Alms House grew increasingly desperate as winter approached. In late November the managers sent a petition to General Howe explaining that in spite of their "utmost exertions in borrowing and begging money" they had "not more provisions than will sustain them [the poor in the house] three days." The treasurer, who carried this petition to the general, was at first informed that Howe was too busy to attend to him. He returned the next day, and the next after that, only to be similarly rebuffed each time. Finally, after four days of waiting, the treasurer was given an audience with the general. Howe expressed concern for the city's poor, but quickly passed the man off to the commissary, where he was informed that the British army had nothing to spare for the residents of the Alms House. Worse still, the treasurer's repeated requests seem to have drawn the army's attention to the Alms House as a potential resource for the troops. Two nights later the British barracks master approached two of the house managers and informed them that he would be commandeering the entirety of the Alms House the following day. All the managers met together early the next morning to oppose such a move, but despite their objections, the poor were hurriedly relocated to the Free Mason's Lodge, the Friends' Meeting House, and Carpenter's Hall.[114]

On December 17 the managers assembled to reevaluate their situation. By this time, they had long since exhausted their supplies of meat and bread for the poor; desperate action was called for. Citing "the peculiar Hardships to which the Poor are likely to be reduced to if they continue in this City," the managers agreed to "discharge a number of them who are most likely to be able to provide for themselves." Approximately forty men and women, about a third of the poor on public relief, were discharged and presumably encouraged to look for work or assistance outside Philadelphia. Winter in Pennsylvania was a bad time to be seeking employment; with the ground and river frozen there was little demand for agricultural labor or dockworkers, and the cold weather could be lethal for those without shelter. Nonetheless, in the winter of the occupation, the managers of the Alms House apparently felt that the city's impoverished would be better off searching for subsistence on their own than they would be if they remained on public relief in the city.[115] These refugees were merely one of many groups who made an exodus from the city. Beginning in November, observers in and around Philadelphia reported the flight of many other poor people who, while they had not previously been so destitute as to end up in the Alms House, now found themselves desperate for food and warmth and without hope in Philadelphia.[116]

For its part, the army was largely protected from the "beggary and ruin" taking place around it. The paper currency's collapse, which so devastated many of the city's inhabitants, worked to the advantage of the British soldiers, who found that their access to hard currency and bills of exchange was more valuable than ever. Though forced to live off preserved rations until the river fortifications were taken, the army never suffered the level of distress felt by the civilians.[117] Once the Delaware and countryside were opened as sources of supply, many British officers found themselves living quite well. The demand for provisions created by the army allowed sellers to maintain their high prices and continue to demand specie for payment. As a result, inhabitants found themselves continually unable to take full advantage of the goods and produce that began to fill up the market stalls in the spring of 1778. Even as Robert Proud worried that "most of the Capital I have is in that [colonial] Currency; so that I, as well as many others, am in a very great straight, for present spending Capital," the better-off members of the occupying forces cheerily commented on the wide array of fresh meats and vegetables now available to them and how far their shillings would stretch in the market.[118]

Having recorded the shortages experienced by their civilian hosts, Hessian captain Johann Ewald added that "one must not conclude that the army suffered want because of the dear prices of provisions." On the contrary, he boasted, "never in this world was an army as well paid as this one during the civil war in America. One could call them rich." Though he would not have called himself "rich," Lieutenant Loftus Cliffe "established a sober, comfortable mess" with his fellows, including a steady supply of port. "I want nothing to make me completely contented," he declared in late January, "but the title of Captain and a more frequent correspondence from my friends at home." Considering the situation of his men generally, Lieutenant General James Grant wrote home that "we have been well and plentifully supplied," despite the sometimes high prices, and that "every body is in good humor & the men in great health, equal to any thing which should be expected from their numbers." Grant's only concern was for his junior officers who, unoccupied by military distractions, threatened to bankrupt themselves through extravagant drinking, entertaining, and gambling.[119]

The dichotomy between the experience of the British and their hosts was not lost upon the Americans in and around the city. The wintertime refugees from Philadelphia who passed by Christopher Marshall reported that "Howe lives there in great plenty." From the reports that reached him, Washington concluded that the "British Army is well supplied with almost every Article." Robert Proud's account of the economic hardships suffered by civilians was accompanied by the bitter observation that "the Royal Army appear to be in want of nothing."[120]

Conditions within the city would improve substantially for civilians as 1778 wore on, the Continental embargo collapsed, and ships brought supplies up the Delaware. Help for the poor would eventually come from Joseph Galloway, who oversaw the raising of private, civilian funds to benefit them in the opening months of 1778. Beginning in February of that year, money started to trickle into the Alms House coffers. Several of the managers had personally gone into debt trying to keep the paupers they had not discharged from starving. They had been able to secure supplies of beef and flour only by promising payment in increasingly costly gold or silver. The funds raised by Galloway helped pay off these debts in April.[121]

Yet by that time the inhabitants' distress and the British Army's response to it, or lack thereof, had already soured the affections of many Philadelphians. Not only had the army left the civilians to fend for themselves, forcing the most vulnerable to seek sustenance in the cold Pennsylvania countryside while the officers lived comfortable and even extravagant lives, but these weeks of deepest desperation coincided with the most horrifying and pointless acts of destruction carried out by the king's men.

Runaway slaves who fled to occupied Philadelphia also encountered sights which challenged their more optimistic expectations about the British army. Many were no doubt encouraged by the bands of blacks serving with the army, such as the Black Pioneers, a black fatigue unit established by British general Sir Henry Clinton, dressed in new, British-issued clothing and paid approximately the equivalent of what their white comrades received.[122] Even if such units were more likely to be armed with shovels than with muskets, they still sufficed to strike terror into the heart of white colonials like Muhlenberg, who expressed fears that such units were "fitted for and inclined toward barbarities, are lacking in human feeling, and are familiar with every corner of the country." Fleeing slaves would also have found some comfort in encountering other runaways, all seeking the same freedom and security, all with similar tales of escape from servitude. Yet those who, like the fugitives Muhlenberg overheard, believed a British victory would mean that "all Negro slaves will gain their freedom" must have been sorely disappointed with their early experiences in Philadelphia.[123]

Though British policies toward runaway slaves changed over the course of the war, at least one truth remained relatively constant: those owned by masters not in opposition to the king were excluded from any offers of liberty.[124] While the slaves of Loyalists, neutrals, and the disaffected would continue to run away throughout the occupation, the British gave them no protection from recapture. Runaway ads for slaves appeared in Philadelphia newspapers at a rate of approximately 1.6 per month, excluding repetitions, while the British controlled the city, down from an average of 2.4 per month from the beginning of 1776 to the beginning of the occupation. The decline may reflect the number of slaves removed from the city by fleeing Patriot owners; the civilian population of Philadelphia had declined by roughly 30 percent by the time General Howe took his census of the occupied city. None of the ads published in the city during the occupation mention the possibility that the runaways might be found with the army, suggesting that the slaves of Loyalists knew better than to seek safety there.[125] Some may have fled to the countryside, hoping that their masters' reach would be limited outside the besieged city. Others found work on warships and merchant vessels filling the Delaware. Still others, like Samuel Hudson's slave Tony, chose to remain within the lines, hoping that the crowd of unfamiliar faces would help them disappear. Tony was eventually captured and returned to servitude; he would try to escape again, but not until after the British army left the city.[126]

The thoughts and emotions of those still enslaved because of their masters' loyalty must have been deeply conflicted at the sight of runaways flocking to the city. Well-dressed house servants saw their liberty denied them while rough field hands and country-bred slaves celebrated newfound freedom. What must the runaways have thought upon seeing that the British had no intention of extending such freedom to their friends and neighbors held by Loyalists in the city? This becomes terribly significant when one remembers that, since few slave owners in Philadelphia owned more than one or two slaves, slave families were generally spread out among multiple owners. A husband belonging to a Patriot who had fled the city might run back to Philadelphia and find that his wife and children were still the slaves of a Loyalist master.[127]

This strange confluence of newfound freedom and continued servitude was underscored by the continuation of slave sales in the city. The average number of slaves advertised for sale in the local papers each month actually increased slightly during the period of the occupation. Slaves primarily brought up to labor in the fields were of little use to Loyalist masters trapped inside Philadelphia. Some were retrained to learn new skills, such as driving coaches or waiting tables, others were simply added to the many being sold "for want of employ." Philadelphian Andrew Duche advertised the sale of his female slave in the *Pennsylvania Evening Post*. Though he assured prospective buyers that she was familiar with "both town and country work," Duche's advertisement admitted that the slave "has chiefly been used in the country, and for which she would be of most service."[128] Other slaves were sold because their owners were leaving the city altogether and liquidating their assets. Thus in March of 1778, "a stout negro man" was offered for sale because his owner was "going to England, [and] has no farther occasion for him." Duche made no mention of why he was selling his slave, but the fact that his ad appeared in the final weeks before the British withdrawal and that he was also selling a house and lot implies that he intended to leave the city.[129]

Perhaps the most distressing sight for runaway slaves expecting to find an army of liberation was that of British officers buying and selling Africans alongside their Loyalist allies. In December of 1777, Hessian officer Carl Leopold Baurmeister wrote to inform Baron von Jungkenn, a compatriot in Germany, that he would be sending him a special souvenir from America: "a negro boy about thirteen years old," tutored in "the German language and also in the Christian religion." The evacuation of the city made shipping the slave problematic, but Baurmeister wrote to von Jungkenn again in the final days of the occupation to assure him that "if we return to New York there will still be an opportunity to send him."[130]

Though welcoming enough to runaways who would deplete the labor supply of their enemy, the British had no compunction about actively pursuing their own slaves when they tried to escape from bondage. When George fled from Captain Smyth of the Queen's Rangers, his owner immediately placed an advertisement in the *Pennsylvania Ledger* offering a reward for his capture. The surgeon of the Sixteenth Regiment of Light Dragoons also offered a reward for the return of his runaway slave, William, and a valuable case of lancets that William had carried off.[131]

Those runaways who did find refuge with the British in Philadelphia soon began the search for a secure place in the occupied city and a chance to earn a living. With outrage over Lord Dunmore's proclamation and the fear of black units still echoing across the colonies, some slaves no doubt ran to Philadelphia looking for a chance to join the army and fight alongside the soldiers of Britain. Yet in Philadelphia they found an army not at all eager to increase the number of black men in its service. The Black

Pioneers raised by Clinton expanded its ranks only slightly during the occupation, and a separate, smaller unit with the same name disbanded while in the city. Seven months before the army took Philadelphia, Howe had ordered that "all Negroes, Mollatoes [sic], and other Improper Persons who have been admitted into these [provincial] Corps be Immediately discharged" and instructed the inspector general of provincial forces to prevent the recruitment of such individuals in the future. Howe's motivation in issuing such decrees lay in his desire to see the provincial regiments "put on the most respectable Footing." It was his intention that such units "be composed [only] of His Majesty's Loyal American Subjects," and thus slaves and their ilk must be expelled. Independently formed Loyalist regiments were not under as severe restrictions in recruiting blacks, but neither were they so well paid or supplied. They too came to fear that the inclusion of blacks resulted in a loss of respect from the British regulars and began to expel former slaves from their ranks.[132] Rather than carrying the fight to their former masters, the black men who remained in British service spent the occupation attending to tasks white soldiers found distasteful. In March the Black Pioneers were assigned the duty of "removing all Newsiances [sic] being thrown into the Streets."[133]

Employment outside the army could also be elusive. The constant arrival of runaways and refugees from the Pennsylvania countryside, all looking for work, and the economic disruptions caused by the occupation severely depressed the market for hired labor, particularly once the British completed their line of fortifications. The number of employers actively seeking servants and willing to accept free blacks plummeted during the occupation.[134]

Howe's reference to former slaves as "Improper Persons," who damaged the propriety of the provincial corps and were not among "His Majesty's Loyal American Subjects," was symptomatic of a widespread disrespect, or even disdain, many officers felt toward the escaped slaves in their midst. The Hessians, in particular, often looked upon the runaways with a sense of wry amusement. Baurmeister and his fellows found their slave boy so intriguing that they were sending him home to Germany. As the army continued to strip the surrounding countryside of provisions, Private Johann Döhla chuckled at the sight of blacks driving the commissary wagons "with a solemn expression while under the left arm they carried one or two young pigs."[135] When the British prepared a massive and elaborate fete to celebrate the Howe brothers upon their departure from America, black participants were made to don "Oriental dresses, with silver collars and bracelets," and ordered to bow humbly before and serve the white ladies and officers in attendance. The former slaves had a place in even the most romantic of British imaginings, but only as the submissive and decorated servants of the elite.[136]

Such mockery could easily give way to disdain and antipathy, especially when the army felt stressed. Later in the war, Ewald would describe the runaways that sought shelter with the British in Virginia as an "Arabian or Tarter horde," and compare them to "a swarm of locusts." As more and more former slaves flooded into occupied New York, a general there began ordering his subordinates to keep out the women and children, for fear that they would become "a burden to the town." Not all British officers shared these views, but those who did doubtless left an impression on the former slaves who waited at their tables, tended their horses, and cleaned the streets under their command.[137]

What Mike High made of the British occupation is impossible to say. He left no record of his thoughts or experiences. His abilities as a fieldworker would have been of limited use within the confines of the city, but he also knew his way around an axe and had practiced at least some carpentry while owned by Bolton, skills which might have given him at least temporary employment. Whatever he thought of the occupation, he remained in the city as long as the British were there. When the redcoats marched out the following summer, High also departed. Yet though he had come to the city in the company of the redcoats, and was doubtless grateful for the freedom their war made available to him, his time in Philadelphia did not convince him to journey with them any farther. While the British army marched north toward still-occupied New York, High traveled east, across the Delaware, to find work in the fields of New Jersey, pursuing the opportunities, liberties, and risks that existed outside the British lines.[138]

Indulgence and Disaffection

The hardships and disappointments that accompanied the occupation were not felt equally by all Philadelphians. Select Loyalists benefited greatly from the presence of the army. Men like Joseph Galloway were elevated to positions of immense power and prestige, and all Loyalists were now protected from the rage and retribution of their Revolutionary enemies.[139] Even disaffected residents and refugees, such as James Allen, appreciated not having to constantly be on their guard lest a poorly timed criticism of the Revolutionary regime or a lack of patriotic enthusiasm endanger their liberty or property. Though he had confessed to being equally disgusted by Britain's "despotic" policies and the Patriots' Revolutionary "madness," within the occupied city Allen nonetheless found "an ease, security & freedom of speech" that he had sorely missed living outside the lines.[140]

At least a few canny and politically flexible businessmen found ways to profit in spite (or even because) of the disruption and dislocation of the city. Benjamin Towne's *Pennsylvania Evening Post* was the only English-language newspaper to continue Philadelphia operations before, during, and after the occupation. The arrival of the British army had scattered the Patriot printers and the withdrawal of that same army banished the Loyalist presses that had sprung up under its wings; only the *Evening Post* endured, its printer deftly pirouetting to politically align himself with whatever power ruled the city. Consequently, the pages of the *Post* received not only a steady stream of official declarations from various branches of the military administration, but also a flood of commercial advertisements as change and dislocation roiled the marketplace. Newly arrived merchants from New York, Britain, and other imperial ports struggled to make their presence known; many resident traders relocated to newly abandoned shops in better parts of the city and needed to announce both their continued residence and their change of address; businessmen of all stripes clamored to inform the residents, refugees, soldiers, and sailors of their wares and prices. Out of the chaos came a host of other advertisements as both residents and newcomers lost, found, and sought-after goods, people, and employment. All these voices sought the volume and reach that only print could provide. The result was a "heyday of commercial newspaper advertising" and a surge of prosperity for men like Benjamin Towne.[141]

For wealthier Philadelphians, the British possession brought a different kind of opportunity: not for material gain or power but for the sort of lavish, luxurious lifestyle that the British Empire made possible and that the Revolution denounced and threatened to destroy. Alongside advertisements for fine consumables from Europe and the West Indies, sellers offered "HATS, CAPS, CLOAKS, BONNETS, &c. in the newest fashion," silver and ebony place settings, china dishes, shoes and buckles.[142] Young Rebecca Franks wrote excitedly of new hair styles with a "great quantity of different coloured feathers on the head at a time besides a thousand other things. The Hair dress'd very high," while a less approving Elizabeth Drinker recorded encountering "the highest and most ridiculous headdress that I have yet seen."[143] As the army lingered idly in the spring of 1778, the officers set about creating the many engagements of high society found in the metropolis: balls, concerts, gambling, races, and theatrical performances.[144] "The military have lived a very gay life the whole winter, & many very expensive entertainments given," James Allen recorded from within the city. He also noted that he had personally attended most of these entertainments since his crossing the lines.[145]

Such entertainments were all the more significant because of the status of the men and women who attended. Philadelphia's elite did not merely attend concerts, balls, and plays; they did so alongside peers of the realm, mingling and sharing concerns with men of far higher social positions than were customarily at their disposal. In letters to his wife, Sir Henry Strachey, Admiral Lord Richard Howe's secretary, reflected on the "great pride" Philadelphians took in playing host to the military elite, observing particularly that when serving high ranking officers tea in china cups with silver spoons the mistress of a Philadelphian house "thinks herself a very eminent personage."[146] Nowhere was this more apparent than at the oft remembered and much reviled eruption of opulence that was the Meschianza. Here the elite young women of Philadelphia, dressed and regarded as princesses from foreign lands, watched as the elite officers of Britain's army, literally dressed as knights in shining armor, fought on their behalf, proclaiming their "wit, beauty & accomplishments." There followed a lavish banquet and ball. In all, recalled British commissary Charles Stedman, "This entertainment not only far exceeded any thing that had ever been seen in America, but rivaled the magnificent exhibitions of that vain-glorious monarch and conqueror, Louis XIV of France."[147] The Meschianza was a once in a lifetime opportunity for a colonist in Philadelphia to fully embrace, and be embraced by, the power, grandeur, and wealth of the world's preeminent empire.

Yet such opportunities for power, wealth, and luxury proved to be more the exception than the rule within occupied Philadelphia. Though the presence of the British army made loyalism safe within the lines, the actions of that army guaranteed that few would commit themselves to the Loyalist cause. Though some Philadelphian businessmen and outside merchants found profit amid the chaos, their stories of success are overwhelmed by the many complaints of poverty, shortages, and stagnation experienced by their fellow inhabitants and witnessed by outside observers. Though the restoration of British trade brought fashion and opulence to the elite, the ostentatious displays and extravagant performances may have alienated as many as they charmed in the Quaker city and certainly excluded the majority. Drinker decried the "Scenes of Folly and Vanity" that surrounded the Meschianza, and Stedman recalled that it "did not escape the severest satire, both in private conversation and in printed papers."[148]

For most inhabitants, the occupying army brought neither the security, nor the stability, nor the prosperity, nor the liberty they had expected or dared to hope for. Allen was quick to recognize that his own well-being was exceptional, remarking that "this City swarms with refugees, & living is very expensive." Though quick to condemn the "misery" and "cruelty" of life under the Revolutionary regime outside the British lines, he was not slow to acknowledge the troubled lives of the people around him, declaring that "within the lines, little regard is paid to the discontents of the people, & no satisfaction for the injury of their property. It is impossible to exist another winter, as rents are ill paid, every thing dear & no means of acquiring anything by business."[149] Howe's stated goal in controlling American territory was "to afford protection to the inhabitants, that they might experience the difference between his majesty's mild government, and that to which they were subject from the rebel leaders."[150] Yet the distinction was not one that always worked in his majesty's favor, and it seems strange that Howe thought military occupation would be interpreted as "mild government." As Colonel James Murray dryly remarked in early 1778, "it has not been generally observed that any quarter was endeared to an army by six months' possession."[151]

In place of a Revolutionary regime which seemed at times obsessed with expressions of consent and declarations of support, the city was now ruled by an occupying force that, at least in practice, often seemed not to care where the allegiances of the people lay and did little to relieve those who suffered beneath the chaos and destitution wrought by the war. All too often the "friend of government" fared no better than the rebel at the hands of the British plunderer or arsonist. Promises of protection failed, crime and brutality were rampant, civilian poverty was laid bare alongside military opulence, and the reality of British liberty often fell short of expectations for those who needed it most of all.

Furthermore, as the occupation continued, the disaffected found themselves with less and less space for neutrality and disengagement. Both sides now demanded oaths of allegiance; all paper currency was tainted by political affiliation and obligation; and liberty and security were promised only to those who aligned themselves with one side against the other. Though from a distance the British army appeared to offer hope and shelter to the Revolution's disaffected, those who lived in the midst of it soon learned otherwise. The coming of the British army to Philadelphia brought despair for its enemies, profound disappointment for those who might have become its friends, and, for all peoples, the destruction which inevitably surrounded the seat of war.

The British too found a mixture of promise and disappointment in Philadelphia. Howe's prediction that the Pennsylvania militia would do little to augment Washington's forces was borne out, as were reports about divisions among the people and opposition to the Revolutionary governments. Such opposition, however, was not the product of latent Loyalist sympathies but of a widespread ambivalence toward the Revolution and a distaste for the policies and persons that governed it. The British general grew concerned even as the army disembarked amid the abandoned farms at Head of Elk. Pleased though he was to find no opposition, he had been led to believe that the people would rally to his standard. Undeterred, Howe's Loyalist guides continued to assure him that he would find the populace "more and more loyal, as [he] advanced towards the Capital of Pennsylvania." "This information," Howe later reflected, "proved equally false."[152]

Attempts to transform the disaffected population into loyal soldiers faltered badly. In October Howe ordered enough clothing for some five thousand provincials so that he could equip "the new levies expected to be raised in this and the neighboring provinces." Yet despite repeated calls for recruits, offers of land bounties, and "the most indefatigable exertions, during eight months," by the time of Howe's departure for Britain the army had failed to raise even one thousand men from Pennsylvania. The redcoats even struggled to secure volunteers for noncombat service, such as the construction of fortifications around the city.[153] This was a frustration Washington and Howe shared: each experienced shock, anger, and finally discouragement in the face of a people who expressed little enthusiasm for either side in the imperial dispute and were obstinately determined to avoid involvement in the war.

A British victory in the 1778 campaign would have to come at the hands of the redcoats themselves, without assistance from the thousands of provincial soldiers Howe had expected to secure. Given the rising antipathy toward the Continentals in the countryside and the relative health of the British army, such a victory still seemed possible as late as April. Instead, however, 1778 would deal a crushing defeat to the British in the war for the hearts and minds of Americans, undo all the gains of the previous campaign, and convince more than a few participants and observers that the struggle for American independence had, effectively, been won.

INTERLUDE

ELIZABETH DRINKER GOES TO WASHINGTON

"Our new guest behaves unexceptionally," Elizabeth Drinker declared on January 1, 1778, "and much like a Gentleman." She was writing to her exiled husband in Virginia and, perhaps unsurprisingly, hoping to put the best possible face on an inherently awkward situation. Major Crammond of the British army had moved into the Drinker home two days previously and brought his own personal army of attendants with him. The officer kept three horses, three cows, two sheep, and numerous birds, all of whom now took up space in the Drinkers' yard and stable. Three servants, two white and one black, attended to the major's personal needs while three or four Hessian soldiers served him as messengers and orderlies. Thankfully, only the major himself slept in the house, though he nonetheless had appropriated both the front parlors, an upstairs room, and the stable for his exclusive use; the kitchen and yard became shared spaces. Though such actions might well have been "unexceptional" for the British officer class, they left Drinker and her children in a house which suddenly seemed much smaller and constantly abuzz with movement, activity, and people. In Drinker's words, "we have enough of such company."[1]

More company was soon to come. Crammond had sold himself to Drinker as an ideal houseguest, or at least as good a boarder as might be hoped for in the midst of a military occupation. Having carefully listened to Drinker's fears, he had cannily presented himself as their opposite. Where she had experienced the terror of a drunken soldier staggering about her home in the wee hours and worried over the corrupting influences of the army on her children, he had promised that he was reliably sober and quiet, kept early hours, and would only rarely play host to other officers. This rosy self-portrait turned out to be only partially true to life. The major

Figure 6. Silhouette of Elizabeth Drinker. From Amelia Mott Gummere, *The Quaker: A Study in Costume* (Philadelphia: Ferris & Leach, 1901).

did reliably maintain his sobriety and civility; in a city plagued by intoxicated soldiers and outbursts of violence, Crammond never gave Drinker cause to complain of his drinking or fear that he might harm her family. He also seems to have maintained a strict discipline among the men who served him, confining them to the kitchen when they were in the house and doing what he could to limit their interaction with the family; if they participated in the more riotous activities of the occupation, they did so on their own time and in other parts of the city.[2]

Yet, as decorous and composed as he might have been, Major Crammond was not, in fact, averse to late hours or inviting over company. Within the first week of his lodging there Crammond was hosting dinners for as many as a dozen fellow officers at the Drinkers' home. Though relatively restrained, these gatherings regularly stretched into the early hours of the following morning. Drinker, either because she feared the worst or simply because the noise of their party kept her from sleeping, made a habit of staying up to chronicle these events, repeatedly recording in her diary how long the major's gatherings lasted. At first she viewed this turn of events as a minor irritant, writing gratefully that "the late hours he [Crammond] keeps is the greatest inconvenience we have as yet suffered by having him in the house." The problem seemed especially trivial in comparison to the horror stories she heard from neighbors whose military boarders were prone to either personal violence or the destruction of their property. Yet as the weeks wore on she grew increasingly impatient with the major's nighttime activities. "I shall soon be tired of such doings" she announced in January and late one night in mid-February Drinker finally declared "I am all out of patience with our Major." It's unclear precisely what transpired between them the following day. One might not expect a Quaker woman, living without her husband in the midst of an armed occupation, to take to task a British military officer residing in her very home, but something of that nature seems to have happened. "I gave him some hints," Drinker wrote, "and he has behaved better since." Thereafter Crammond's gatherings were quieter, less common, and invariably concluded before midnight.[3]

Such confrontations aside, Crammond and the Drinker family slowly but steadily developed a rapport as the weeks of the occupation rolled past. Two weeks after moving into the house, the major joined the family for coffee for the first time. Thereafter a week rarely passed without Drinker recording that Crammond had joined them for coffee or tea. In March he began taking dinner with the family, and this too soon became a regular occurrence. What Drinker's sister or the children thought of Crammond is unknown, but early on she noted that "most of our acquaintance seems much taken with our Major." Drinker's own assessments, at least those she was willing to record, were that Crammond was "of a good c[h]aracter" and that "he behaves like a Gentleman and a man of sence [sic]."[4] Whatever she thought of the major, Drinker was not afraid to use his residence in her home to advantage when the opportunity presented itself. By chance in January she spotted, through her doorway, the soldier who had invaded her home that terrifying night the previous November and then run off with the family servant girl. Stopping the man in the street, Drinker berated the redcoat as having "no sense of religion or virtue," and proceeded to lecture him on the subject of duty and "what you soldiers call honor." The flabbergasted soldier could scarcely get a word in as Drinker proceeded to demand he pay her for the servant that had run off with him and then pointedly reminded him that she and her friends were now closely acquainted with the various British officers who lodged in their homes. She left him with an ultimatum: he could either send her the money or have a detailed account of his behavior that night reported to his superiors. "Well, well, well," was the best the beleaguered soldier could manage as he hesitantly continued his way down the street.[5]

While Drinker managed to eventually reconcile herself to the presence of a British major in her home, and even discovered some advantage in having him there, her absent husband found it much more difficult to take the situation in stride. The discovery that a strange man, and a soldier at that, was living in the same home as his wife and children severely tested Henry Drinker's religious tranquility. His situation was made inestimably worse by the fact that answers to his questions about the arrangement and his family's safety only reached him, when they reached him at all, after days or weeks of delay and multiple levels of censorship. "Who is it that could urge to be received into my House, after a proper representation of the situation the Master was in?" he demanded. Questions tumbled out into multiple letters back to Elizabeth. "How many have intruded themselves into the Habitation of a Banished Man?" "What part of the House do they occupy?" "Do they demand Food, Firing etc. as well as House-Room?" With questions came warnings and admonitions. "I hope the strictest care is exercised by the Mother & Aunt of my Children," he fretted, "keep them both young & the older, altogether from the Comp[any] & conversation of such Strangers." Letters from Elizabeth, when they finally reached him, gave Henry some peace of mind, as did reassuring reports of Crammond's conduct and character from other correspondents in the city. Still, knowledge of the major's residence made his imprisonment in Virginia that much harder to bear, and Henry continued to warn his wife that "the Children cannot be kept too distant, nor too much care & circumspection pursued by & with them."[6]

Henry's concern for his family might have been all the greater if he had known what his wife was planning that spring. The winter of 1778 had been a season of reflection and transformation for Elizabeth Drinker. In December she had been plagued with anxieties and guilt about Henry's predicament. "Here am I alone, full of thoughts, which I know not how to communicate," she wrote, "when I think of setting here inactive, while my dear Husband remains a prisoner, I cannot easily reconcile it." Yet her drive to act was negated by a deep and sometimes self-deprecating feeling of powerlessness, causing her to cry out "what can such a poor weak creature as myself do?"[7] Yet surviving the worst of the winter and invasion of her home seems to have given Drinker a greater sense of her own abilities and the new year brought an opportunity to test her resolve. In February Drinker learned that her acquaintance, Susanna Jones, was making plans for a journey to Valley Forge where she could petition General Washington on behalf of her son, Owen, who was among those exiled to Virginia along with Drinker's husband. "She would like me to go with her," Drinker recorded, but as of yet she felt unready for such a step. Still, she wrote, "my heart is full of some such thing, but I don't see the way clear yet." In the weeks that followed the idea circulated among the wives and mothers of the exiles and remained in Drinker's thoughts. She talked over the possibilities with her friend, Mary Pemberton, whose father was among the exiles, and gradually her notion of what was possible began to shift. "Perhaps," she wrote, "it might be in my power to do something for my dear Husband." In March Jones again suggested that Drinker accompany her on a journey to petition for the exiles' freedom, this time proposing they go before the Congress; again, Drinker demurred. The events of the next two and a half weeks would finally change her mind.[8]

Drinker was sitting with Mary Pemberton when word arrived from their mutual friend, Rachel Hunt, that Thomas Gilpin was dead. Gilpin was the first of the exiles to die in Virginia, and though rumors of his passing had arrived in Philadelphia earlier, the confirmation was still a shock. The same letter mentioned that John Hunt, Rachel's husband, was also ill. So was Henry Drinker. Shortly thereafter, the female relatives of the exiles met together and signed an address to Congress asking for the return of their sons, fathers, and husbands. The group then chose four women to physically carry it out of the occupied city and across the lines: Susanna Jones, Phebe Pemberton, Mary Pleasants, and Elizabeth Drinker. "I wish I felt better both in Body and mind for such an undertaking," Drinker confided to her diary that night. Two days later Drinker went to visit Rachel Hunt and found her "writing to her Husband." Though the latest news Drinker had heard suggested John Hunt's condition was deteriorating, it seemed that his wife "had flattered herself from some of the letters that he was getting better." As Drinker stepped out of the house and back into the street she was met with ill tidings: "John Hunt was no more . . . the Account of his death was just come to Town." Leaving Rachel to write letters which could never be delivered, Drinker took the news to Mary Pemberton and Joyce Benezet. They agreed that Rachel was not ready to accept the loss of her husband; Pemberton volunteered to send her a recent letter describing Hunt's failing health. "She thought it would prepare her," Drinker recalled, "after which Joyce and Mary went to break the sorrowful news to her." That day Drinker shrugged off the last of her reluctance about the journey out of the city. "I concluded in mind," she wrote, "that to the care of kind providence, and my dear Sister I must leave my dear little ones." She would go with her fellows, outside the lines and into the war. She would travel, first to the headquarters of the army besieging her city, and then on to meet the Revolutionary government that had arrested and banished her Henry without hearing or trial. And she would bring her husband home.[9]

The women left Philadelphia on April 5, making it some ten miles beyond the city by the end of the day. Drinker spent that first night in the country home of John Roberts, who, though she likely did not know it at the time, had tried to convince the British to rescue her husband as he was being carried into exile seven months previously. There she was "kindly entertain'd by the Woman of House and her Daughters," Roberts himself having fled to Philadelphia to avoid arrest, or worse, by the Revolutionaries.[10] Within a week, Elizabeth Drinker found herself at Valley Forge, sitting beside Martha Washington, who she considered "a sociable pretty kind of Woman," waiting for an audience with the commander in chief of the Continental Army. Their interview with Washington was amiable but brief. As a Continental officer, Washington felt he could do little for them beyond offering the women safe passage on to Lancaster, where the Revolutionary government then sat. This he did, along with inviting their company to join him for a supper where Drinker found herself dining alongside Nathanael Greene, Charles Lee, and a dozen or so other noteworthy officers of the army. Drinker and her party left for Lancaster the next morning. Had their visit to Valley Forge been only slightly delayed it might have gone rather differently. Even as Drinker waited upon, petitioned, and dined with Washington, Pennsylvania's Supreme Executive Council was composing a message to the general informing him that Congress had chosen to order the exiles brought back from Virginia. In fact, Pennsylvania's government, facing immense and growing condemnation for having arrested and banished nearly two dozen innocent men without trial, had requested that Congress return the prisoners on March 7, weeks before Drinker resolved to undertake her venture beyond the lines. However, the wheels of power turned slowly; Henry Drinker would not learn that he was to be released until April 8; the news would catch up to his wife, still walking the rough roads to Lancaster, the following day.[11]

Knowing that their primary wish had been granted before they could even ask it, the women spent the next two weeks waiting at Lancaster, doing what they could to smooth out the details of the exiles' return and release. On April 24 the first of the prisoners, James Pemberton and Samuel Pleasants, arrived. They assured Drinker that Henry was well but traveling more slowly than some of the others; he would be along the following day. "I can recollect nothing of the occurances of this Morning," Drinker wrote on the twenty-fifth, "about one o'clock my Henry arrived."[12]

The next several days were spent obtaining a formal release from Supreme Executive Council and securing safe passage across Continental lines for their return home. Washington, whose sympathies had been won over during the women's brief meeting with him earlier that month, freely granted them passes to enter the occupied city. The council, eager to put the entire matter behind it with as little fuss as possible, promptly ordered the prisoners and their families to be transported toward Philadelphia as far as Pottsgrove and then officially discharged. Though Henry Drinker and James Pemberton succeeded in meeting with the council's president, Thomas Wharton Jr., the council as a whole refused to grant the exiles an audience. They released the prisoners without explanation, trial, pardon, or apology. And, notably, without reimbursement for the considerable expense they had endured in being forced to pay for their own lodgings and food in Virginia and along the road.[13]

On April 30, Henry and Elizabeth returned, together, to their home in Philadelphia and to the well wishes of more friends and neighbors than Elizabeth could count. She found their children and sister all safe and well, "for which favour and Blessing," she wrote, "and the restoration of my dear Husband, may I ever be thankful." What Henry Drinker and Major Crammond made of each other upon first meeting is unknown, though little more than a week passed between Drinker's return and Crammond once more being welcomed to join the family for tea. On May 14 Elizabeth pointedly recorded that Crammond "came into our Parlor, and had some talk with my Henry" through the evening. She provides no further details of what the American Quaker and the British army officer discussed, but by the end of the month Crammond was again to be found sharing dinner with the Drinkers. Whatever their relationship, it would be brief. The British army's invasion a year before had triggered Drinker's hasty banishment from the state; now the return of the exiles, it seemed, was a harbinger of the army's departure.[14]

CHAPTER 5

EVACUATION

> I now look upon the Contest as at an End. No man can be expected to declare for us, when he cannot be assured of a Fortnight's Protection. Every man, on the contrary, whatever might have been his primary Inclinations, will find it his Interest to oppose & drive us out of the County. ... Nothing remains for him but to attempt Reconciliation with (what I may *now* venture to call) *the United States of America.*
> —British Secretary Ambrose Serle, May 22, 1778

On March 6, 1778, the residents of occupied Philadelphia opened their newspapers and were shocked to discover that Benjamin Franklin, the great American inventor and printer who had made the city his adopted home, was dead. According to a "very respectable authority" he had been dead for several months, having passed on November 12 at his country house just outside Paris. Franklin had been in France to negotiate an alliance between that nation and the nascent United States. "It was supposed," reported the *Evening Post*, "the late ill success of the Americans had hastened his end."[1] Accounts of Franklin's death were, of course, greatly exaggerated; the American luminary would live another dozen years before finally dying at home in Philadelphia. Far from being despondent over America's ill success, in March of 1778 Franklin was likely exuberant over the recent formation of an alliance between the United States and France, a diplomatic development as yet unknown in Philadelphia.

Further accounts from Europe soon informed Philadelphians that Franklin still lived. Yet the news of his untimely demise was only one example of the many false assurances inhabitants of the city received from British and Loyalist sources during the occupation. Each falsehood, when inevitably unmasked as a deception or mistake, served to erode the people's confidence in the British as worthy of trust, undermining the army's halfhearted efforts to win the hearts and minds of Americans for the king. No turn of events did as much damage to that campaign as the discovery that, contrary to prior assurances, Britain intended to evacuate Philadelphia in the summer of 1778, a move which caught numerous military and civilian leaders in the city off guard and left those aligned with the empire shocked, dismayed, and often embittered. Though many of the inhabitants had been severely disappointed by the army's failure to bring security, liberty, and prosperity back to the city during the occupation, they generally perceived the British ministry's decision to abandon Philadelphia as a particularly insidious act of betrayal. It demonstrated, to both American civilians and more than a few British officers, that the empire would not only fail to protect its allies and subjects, even when in a strong position to do so, but also that it lacked the resolve necessary to win the war. For the military, this revelation was simply depressing; for many of the disaffected, it proved decisive. The departure of the British army eliminated the economic incentives of defying Patriot edicts on commercial transactions and allowed the Revolutionaries to once again secure a monopoly on coercive force in the region. Meanwhile, the seeming inevitability of American independence convinced many that the prudent and self-interested course was, both immediately and henceforth, to quietly acquiesce to the authority of the United States.

The British inclination to deny or marginalize setbacks is understandable in light of the events which transpired outside the lines of Philadelphia. Though Howe's army securely held the city throughout the occupation, the larger British war effort suffered several disasters in 1777 and early 1778. These outside events proved to be more effective in driving the British from the American capital than all of Washington's muskets and artillery. In New York, Revolutionary forces under the command of Major General Horatio Gates soundly defeated the army of British Lieutenant General John Burgoyne near Saratoga, forcing it to surrender en masse in early October. Responding to this unprecedented reversal, in February, French and American negotiators on the other side of the Atlantic negotiated a long-awaited alliance, ensuring that the War for American Independence would soon become a global conflict that would compel Britain to divert resources to the defense of its many far-flung imperial holdings. Prioritizing the protection of wealthy island colonies in the Caribbean over the maintenance of military outposts in the rebellious colonies, the British government began pulling thousands of soldiers off the mainland for use in the West Indies. To facilitate this redeployment, the British army was ordered to abandon Philadelphia, surrendering the region and the fate of those who continued to live there to the Revolutionaries.

These setbacks, in and of themselves, would have severely undermined British efforts to win the hearts and minds of disaffected Americans. Yet the damage to that cause was made inestimably worse by the army's hesitation, and sometimes outright refusal, to acknowledge that these reversals had, in fact, taken place. Pro-British propaganda in Philadelphia routinely and unambiguously dismissed accounts of Revolutionary triumphs as untrustworthy and regularly assured the populace that the empire was moving steadily from one victory to another. Only the most incontrovertible evidence forced them to publicly acknowledge the rebellion's accomplishments in diplomacy or on the battlefield. When official news of the army's evacuation came late in the spring of 1778, it followed on the heels of countless deceptive and mistaken reports the inhabitants had received about the likelihood of British military success. These deceptions not only encouraged the people to perceive the British as untrustworthy, but also prepared them to see the withdrawal, not as an isolated setback, but as part of a larger and ongoing pattern of defeat.

Though Burgoyne was, in fact, beaten in battle on September 19 and October 7, the inhabitants of Philadelphia received regular assurances throughout October that he was moving triumphantly toward Albany. On October 11, the *Pennsylvania Evening Post*, which had been publishing Howe's official proclamations, reported that Burgoyne's troops had "totally routed the rebel army at Stillwater, under the command of generals Gates and Arnold, having killed near eight hundred on the field and taken a prodigious number of prisoners." On the twenty-first, four days after Burgoyne surrendered, the editor of the *Post* claimed to have met with eyewitnesses from New York who had seen him sweep the Patriot army out of Stillwater, south of Saratoga, and that he was preparing to march on Albany. On the thirtieth, the newspaper effectively announced that Albany had fallen into British hands.

Civilians struggled to weigh such assurances against contrary rumors spread by Patriot sources. On October 3, a bewildered Elizabeth Drinker chronicled, "Tis reported to day that Gattes has beat Burgoine, also that Burgoine has beat Gattes; which is the truth we know not, perhaps nither." The same day, Robert Morton received a report that the northern army had been defeated, read a letter declaring that it had been victorious, heard a visitor from New York claim that it was nowhere to be found, and learned that a hospital was being set up in Albany to tend its wounded. On these grounds he concluded, "We may infer that there has been an engagement, but which party is successful is dubious." Later reports increasingly led him to believe that Burgoyne had triumphed and that Albany would soon be taken.[2] By mid-October, Sarah Logan Fisher recorded that the British general had defeated Gates and "was on full march for Albany, where he expected to be in 24 hours." Even outside the lines, the steadfast assurances of British victory could sway expectations. James Allen, at that point still residing at Trout Hall in Northampton, confessed that "Our accounts from the Northward are confused," but claimed that "as far as we can collect, Genl Burgoyne has had an advantage over Genl Gates & will probably be soon at Albany."[3]

For their part, the British officers were generally quick to dismiss any suggestion that events to the north might have gone against the crown's interests. When confronted with the initial rumor that Burgoyne's army had surrendered, Howe, who believed the Revolutionaries' "accounts of successes are in general much exaggerated," flatly declared his opinion, "that it is totally false."[4] Lieutenant General James Grant, though admitting in late October that "we have no certain Intelligence from the Northern Army," nonetheless regarded the notion of Burgoyne surrendering as "impossible."[5] When Lord Howe's secretary, Ambrose Serle, first heard that Burgoyne was a prisoner he merely laughed at the rebel's desperation, writing that "their Leaders often make Triumphs of imaginary Victories, to keep up the Spirits of the deluded People."[6] Captain Friedrich von Muenchhausen, General Howe's aide-de-camp, waved away claims of Burgoyne's defeat, but hoped that Washington and his men would be gullible enough to believe them.[7]

After so many expressions of confidence and surety, the news of events around Saratoga was devastating when it definitively arrived near the end of October. Serle thought it "the most fatal Blow we have yet felt" while Sir Henry Strachey, secretary to the Howes' peace commission, was at a loss for words when it came to detailing what he could only call "the Catastrophe of Burgoyne."[8] In the immediate aftermath of the news, some slipped into abject despair, asking whether there was any point in continuing the war at all.[9] Muenchhausen actually hoped that the ministry would take this opportunity to abandon the struggle, as he now believed that the war could not be won without an additional twenty thousand reinforcements, which he doubted Britain could afford.[10]

Even for less fatalistic observers, word of Burgoyne's surrender settled like a weight on their shoulders. Lieutenant General James Grant, who had looked forward to seeing Congress brought to terms in the spring, now could "not see the least probability of accommodation and I think it is impossible for any man on this side of the Atlantic to form an opinion about the fate of America." Strachey had believed that the near simultaneous captures of Albany and Philadelphia would have brought the war to an end immediately. Instead, he wearily informed his wife, "we must have at least another campaign. . . . You have only Burgoyne to blame for not seeing me this Winter." Unwilling to even name the misfortune, Lieutenant Loftus Cliffe wrote, "I confess *that* unlucky affair has deranged our Plan of Operations" and he worried about the troubles it would bring in the spring.[11] On November 8, well after the last doubters had accepted the sad truth, the *Pennsylvania Evening Post*, which had so firmly and repeatedly assured the public of Burgoyne's successes, finally published, without comment, the terms of his surrender.[12]

Discovering the truth of Burgoyne's fate might have made the people and presses of Philadelphia more skeptical of positive reports and more willing to consider accounts of disaster. Yet it seems, in many instances, such was not the case. The occupied city was exposed to numerous examples of British overconfidence, but no message relating to the Revolution was delivered more regularly, confidently, and deliberately than that France would by no means enter the war against Great Britain. From October 1777 through April 1778, the *Post* alone ran at least sixteen issues including descriptions of declining Franco-American relations and outright assurances that no agreement had been or would be made between the American Revolutionaries and the French. Beginning in January, the printer set out to dispel the "most improbable and indeed evident untruths" then circulating about an impending French alliance. Having accused the Revolutionaries of propagating a "delusive tale" and fabricating evidence, he promised his readers that his analysis was "not relying upon vague reports—but upon facts founded on authentic letters and affidavits, to be seen by any candid enquirer." There followed excerpts of letters and sworn statements from British gentlemen who had been to France to the effect that they were certain France did not intend to intervene in the rebellion.[13] As late as April 15, the *Post* continued to explicitly assure its readers that reports of pending French intervention were "intirely [sic] groundless."

A repeated theme in these many assurances was the supposedly unhappy fate of Philadelphia's most famous adopted son: Benjamin Franklin. News of his death was merely part of a long series of Franklin-related misinformation reported in Philadelphia. In October readers learned that Franklin had been "so little satisfied with his entertainment at the French court, that he is said to be on the actual point of embarking for America." In November it was reported that Franklin's ship had been seized by French authorities. December brought word that Franklin was leaving France for Prussia, fearing that the French intended to arrest him and turn him over to London. With April came word that Franklin was desperately trying to negotiate a peace treaty with the British ambassador in Paris, and that since "France has given the strongest assurances of her pacifick disposition to the court of Britain . . . the agents of congress, Franklin and Dean, are totally neglected by all in France."[14]

As a result of such erroneous reports, more than a few inhabitants of occupied Philadelphia, both soldiers and civilians, remained ignorant of the looming conflict until finally, on May 8, HMS *Porcupine* arrived on the Delaware bringing confirmation that the French had indeed entered into an alliance with the Americans and that war with France was all but inevitable.[15] It was a heavy blow. Allen looked upon this turn of events as an "embarrassment" for Great Britain. Muenchhausen observed that desertions from the Continental camps dried up. Meanwhile, outside the lines, observers saw a sudden and substantial shift in the economic imbalance that had so greatly favored the British over the Continentals as consumers of local provisions. Farmers, who had previously braved arrests and beatings in order to avoid having to accept Continental dollars for their produce, became "as eager for continental Money now as they were a few weeks ago for gold" and began "to sell off cheaply the stores they have been withholding." France's supposedly imminent involvement in the war, combined with Howe's failure to launch a new campaign and expand British control of the state, prompted disaffected Pennsylvanians to once again reevaluate which political and commercial choices offered the most peaceful and profitable future for themselves and their families. As they had the previous autumn, when the arrival of the British army had so fundamentally changed the balance of power in the region, they once again adapted their speech and practices to reflect the new military reality. As one rather dubious American officer recalled, "The Tories all turned Whigs."[16]

Orders to abandon the city arrived in Philadelphia on May 8, but were initially kept secret from civilians and all but the highest echelons of the army. Like the surrender at Saratoga and the treaty negotiations in Paris, the ministry's plan to evacuate fell upon most of the inhabitants with very little warning and many were slow to accept it. The relative strength of Britain's position in the state, the ongoing work of fortifying the city, the arrival of the Carlisle peace commissioners, and a general disbelief that the empire would so blithely surrender the capital and its people all combined to persuade soldiers and civilians alike that such an event would not truly take place. Consequently, the authentic news, when it finally came, was all the harder to bear.

Even after most of the soldiers and civilians in the city learned of the American alliance with France, they still expected the British army to hold the capital and, in all likelihood, launch a new Pennsylvania offensive in 1778.[17] "It is expected the campaign will soon open," wrote James Allen in mid-May, despite the fact that "the face of politics is much alter'd" by the coming war with France. Allen had only passed the British lines in February in order to bury his deceased brother, John, and tend to his wife in the city. He had received a pass from Continental authorities allowing him to enter the city, but had been refused permission to return again to his country estate. Unable to resume his self-imposed, apolitical isolation, he found himself hoping that the redcoats would soon launch themselves toward Valley Forge, if only to make the city less crowded and decrease the demand for goods in the marketplace.[18] Loyalist chieftain Joseph Galloway had long "deplored the Languor of [British] Proceedings" and become increasingly impatient for renewed military action. He remained confident that a firm British attack would dislodge Washington's weakened forces and break the rebellion.[19]

Outside the lines, Continental major general Nathanael Greene's experience of the occupation winter had led him to conclude that Britain's "only hope" of victory in America lay in "possessing themselves of our Capital Cities." The countryside's growing antipathy toward the Revolutionaries had made Greene acutely aware of how profoundly the mere presence of the British military shaped political affections in the region. As spring arrived, he wrote to Washington that by holding Philadelphia the British "had made a deep impression upon the minds of many well affected Inhabitants who reason from the past to the future and conclude that we must be finally conquered." He emphatically declared that the Continentals "must dispossess them [the British] of some of the places they now hold" in order to "confirm the weak and wavering among ourselves, stagger the confidence of the Inhabitants now in the power of the Enemy and incline them to favour our designs."[20] Greene found the idea that Britain would *voluntarily* surrender the region, forsake the inhabitants there, and give back all that had been gained the previous autumn almost inconceivable. More than a few British officers agreed with him.[21]

Muenchhausen was flabbergasted by word of the impending withdrawal in late May. "It is maintained that our army will leave Philadelphia. Nobody knows why," he wrote, "for, counting heads, our army is twice as strong as the one of the rebels, and, with respect to courage, a hundred times as strong." The Hessian captain hypothesized that, perhaps, it was all part of some elaborate deception meant to secure a surprise attack on Valley Forge, though he worried that the British were not clever enough to have come up with such a scheme.[22] Muenchhausen's incredulity was understandable. Though he exaggerated the redcoats' numerical superiority, the balance of military power in the region still strongly favored Great Britain. In early May, Washington estimated that his army in and around Valley Forge amounted to some 11,800 rank and file infantrymen, though to reach that number he included "such of the sick present and on command, as might be called into action on any emergency." Another 1,400 were stationed in the region, though this count also interpreted "fit for duty" in the broadest possible sense. British returns from the same month show some 14,500 effective infantry at Philadelphia. Mere numbers aside, the British force was, in general, both better trained and better equipped than the Continental Army and possessed more than a thousand armed provincials who, if not nearly so numerous as Howe had wished, would have greatly improved his knowledge of the local roads and terrain. Moreover, while the Continentals had suffered a grueling winter of disease and discomfort at Valley Forge, the British, having enjoyed an almost luxurious spring in Philadelphia, were in astonishingly good health and spirits. In late April a proud Major Carl Leopold Baurmeister found it "difficult to conceive of an army in such excellent condition and such order as the army in the city." Other officers bestowed similar superlatives on the status of the army.[23] Well-fed and in good order, the soldiers in Philadelphia were almost desperate to carry the war farther into Pennsylvania. Captain Johann Ewald and his fellow jägers waited anxiously for the campaign to begin, at one point sending an emissary to Howe to make certain that they had not been forgotten. Major John Graves Simcoe of the Queen's Rangers busied himself gathering intelligence on the terrain around Valley Forge, marking off the likely placement of Continental batteries and the most promising approaches for the attack he felt certain would soon come.[24]

Much of the uncertainty surrounding the occupation was intentionally created and maintained by the British commander in chief himself. Beginning in late April, local residents observed the British embarking on immense new projects to strengthen their lines around Philadelphia. Hundreds of men labored to construct new redoubts, walls, and even a moat of sorts north of the city. Regular detachments were launched to survey and secure the region around Philadelphia and Howe himself made an appearance inspecting the works. These efforts continued, largely unabated, through May and into June even as the army quietly prepared to withdraw.[25] Such projects were intended to sow uncertainty in the minds of Continental generals and protect the army from being attacked as it marched away. However, they proved equally, if not more effective in confusing the local civilians who were anxiously fretting over the future of their city, their property, and their lives.

Within the city the people were, according to Drinker, "at a loss . . . what to think of the present appearance of things amongst us." The officer lodging in her home, Major Crammond, could do little to lessen her confusion, for he too seemed perplexed by the simultaneous preparations for battle and retreat.[26] As rumors of the impending withdrawal circulated through the city, Ambrose Serle reported that "notwithstanding appearances, some of the most sensible [inhabitants] cannot credit it. Their fortifying the principal Redoubt, Bomb Proof, is certainly very remarkable." The ongoing fortifications and strong objections of the Loyalists gave him "a Gleam of Hope that this terrible measure may be averted."[27] As late as June 11, less than a week before the final withdrawal, Baurmeister was still uncertain, noting in letters home that "in spite of the apparent preparations to evacuate Philadelphia, three hundred men are working in the lines every day. Our wood and hay magazines and our cultivated gardens and fenced-in meadows are being carefully guarded and kept up." He felt certain that the army intended to march, but could not tell whether it meant to retreat through New Jersey or assault Valley Forge.[28]

The coming of a new peace commission on June 6 only further confused the situation. Though British orders to evacuate the city were explicit and, ultimately, unaffected by their arrival, the appearance of the commissioners on the Delaware did force the army to alter its timetable. Faced with the necessity of defending the city a few weeks longer than he had planned, the British commander wearily ordered munitions and provisions returned to the city magazines; ships that had previously been loaded and made ready now found their departure suddenly postponed indefinitely.[29] The shift was immediately felt by the inhabitants and the Loyalists desperately hoped it signaled a fundamental change in British plans. "An evident Delay is made in the Embarkation," wrote Serle while he himself was still ignorant as to its import. "People hope for some good Reason: One supposes, from a Wish for further news from England; Another, for a sudden Expedition ag[ain]st the Rebels." The revelation that a new commission had arrived raised expectations even higher. "Spirits of the Town seem revived upon the Occasion. People conceiving a Hope, that they shall not now be abandoned."[30] Misinformation and confusion seemed to surround the peace delegation. They brought news that war had not yet been declared between Britain and France, but this was quickly misinterpreted as a sign that the two nations were amicably reconciled, reviving false impressions that had plagued the city for months. Due to a tragic oversight, the commissioners had not been told the city would be evacuated and so came fully expecting that Philadelphia would remain in British hands for the foreseeable future.[31] Bewildered civilians mistook their ignorance for evidence that the ministry had changed its mind. James Allen heard that the commissioners "came critically to prevent the evacuation of this City.... War with France is not declared, nor like to take place, troops are coming over here & if Congress will not treat, as there is reason to expect, this will be an active campaign."[32] Drinker too came to understand that "there is no likelihood of war with France . . . nor does it look so likely that the British Troops will so soon leave us." "The face of things seems again changed," she declared. Outside the lines, even Joseph Reed half credited such rumors about the commissioners and came to suspect that the British might not be departing as soon as his compatriots expected. "In short," he wrote on June 9, "Appearances are now as much for their Stay as they were against it last Week."[33]

Departure

Time eventually revealed to even the most hopeful observers that the expanding fortifications were a sham, that the commission's arrival would only delay, not prevent, the British evacuation, and that even the delay would be a brief one. As the army's firm intention to abandon the region and its people was steadily driven home to the inhabitants, men and women responded to the news and made preparations for the future in accordance with their various political affections, or lack thereof. The more committed Loyalists split their time between railing against the military's betrayal of their trust and packing their possessions for transport to Britain, New York, or some other imperial outpost where they would be safe from persecution, if not from poverty. Those who lacked such strong affection for Britain, who felt they had relatively little to fear from Patriot retribution, or who simply felt greater attachment to their home than to their former empire, braced themselves for the Revolutionaries' return to power.

For many of the civilians who had most closely aligned themselves with the British cause or simply come to trust in the continued presence of the king's army, the withdrawal was seen as nothing less than a betrayal, the cruel and unnecessary sacrifice of his majesty's loyal subjects to their enemies. They showed little reserve in communicating these sentiments to the departing officers. "They told us to our faces," remembered Ewald, "that the army had come only to make them miserable, They had previously concealed their true opinions from their enemies, but now their convictions had been betrayed by their association with us. Their entire reward that they now had from accepting English protection consisted in that they were unfortunate and the English lucky."[34] The men who had taken up arms to fight alongside the British were no more charitable. "They grumble and swear that the army will leave Philadelphia and would rather let them be hanged by the Congress than serve England. God alone knows what will happen to them."[35]

The Loyalist leadership, which had the most to lose if Philadelphia were abandoned, soon returned to the very same arguments that had persuaded Howe to invade Pennsylvania the previous summer. Up to the final day of the occupation Galloway continued to insist that the inhabitants of the state were "anxiously desirous of being restored to their former obedience, are ready to co-operate with the king's troops to effect that desirable purpose." He ardently urged the army to assault Washington at Valley Forge, claiming to have a list of "above three hundred gentlemen of weight & influence" who were willing to raise provincial troops and secure the province should the Continental Army be driven away.[36] Serle recorded that Andrew Allen remained unshaken in his conviction that "five Sixths of the Province were against the Rebels, our Army had only to drive off Washington & put arms into the Hands of the well-affected, and the Chain of Rebellion would be broken." The unshakable, or perhaps simply desperate, confidence such men placed in the allegiance of their fellow Pennsylvanians succeeded in once again convincing a few British officers that the region was, despite appearances, on the verge of taking up arms for the king.[37] It was not, however, enough to shift British policy or regain the support of a jaded General Howe, who departed the continent with deep resentment over the failure of Pennsylvania's many supposed Loyalists to rally to his standard in 1777.

The sad predicament of Philadelphia's Loyalists, and Britain's role in creating their plight, was not lost upon the other inhabitants of the city. James Allen observed that Howe had already "offended all the friends of Government by his neglect of them & suffering their property to be destroyed" and that now "by the late design of evacuating Philada . . . every man obnoxious to the American rulers, was offered up a Victim to their resentment."[38] Allen did not view himself as a Loyalist and so did not, as yet, expect to be personally targeted, but he felt great sympathy for those who did. British officers also found themselves sympathizing with the men and women they would soon abandon. "Now a Rope was (as it were) about their necks," wrote Serle. "The Information chilled me with Horror, and with some Indignation when I reflected upon the miserable Circumstances of the Rebels, &c." Ewald confessed that "the heart of every honest man bled on hearing these people complain, who had an absolute right to do so."[39] Howe's replacement as commander in chief in America, General Sir Henry Clinton, soon found himself confronted by desperate and at times heart-wrenching letters from inhabitants like Peter Miller, a former justice of the peace and notary public and father to ten children sheltering in the city. The economic woes of the past months and the collapse of the old colonial currency had all but bankrupted the Millers. In May the Revolutionaries had charged Miller with treason and he was terrified that the withdrawal of the army would result, not only in the loss of his family's remaining property, but also of his freedom and perhaps his life. He pleaded with Clinton for "relief, protection or assistance." Preferring the surrender of his holdings to the rebels over facing them in court, Miller made plans to follow the army to New York.[40]

The Millers were not alone in fleeing with the army. No clear account exists of precisely which, or how many, Philadelphians departed the city alongside the British forces, but contemporary estimates suggest that their numbers were considerable. Ewald heard that some fifteen hundred families were departing "and turning their backs on their property"; peace commissioner William Eden claimed as many as five thousand Loyalists went aboard the transports. Other estimates put the number closer to three thousand individuals.[41] It is uncertain how many of these were native Philadelphians, as opposed to the thousands of outside refugees and merchants who had come to the city during the occupation. The people's rush to preserve their lives and their property led to no small amount of noise and chaos. Shortly before the withdrawal, Baurmeister wrote that "Philadelphia at present greatly resembles a fair during the last week of business." Wagons piled high with personal effects clogged the streets on their way to the ships.[42]

Elizabeth Drinker's own home was soon full of commotion as Major Crammond prepared to depart with his army. Most of his extensive collection of baggage, animals, and other possessions had to be taken to the docks and loaded aboard ship; friends and colleagues visited the Drinker house to wish the major farewell. Crammond joined the Drinker family for his last supper in Philadelphia on June 8 and retired to bed early. Elizabeth Drinker remained awake as the night gave way to the early morning. Crammond was called from his bed and left to join his company shortly after one in the morning. Drinker and her sister were awake to say goodbye; they found him "very dull at taking leave." The two women remained at the door, watching until Crammond's unit marched past on its way out of the city. "J. C. bid us adieu as they went by," Drinker remembered, "and we saw no more of them." She wrote to him a few days later, sending the letter along with one of the last waves of troops to leave the city; it would not be their last correspondence.[43]

By dawn on June 18, 1778, the British occupation of Philadelphia was over. After having held the city for nearly nine months, the army had quietly withdrawn its men from the American capital. Only a handful of unfortunate officers remained, rising groggily that morning to discover that they had "inquired too late about the last orders" and lingered too long "in the houses of their tender acquaintances." They awkwardly crept across the waking city, attempting to dodge the Revolutionary forces that had arrived, almost literally, on the heels of the departing British column. As an unsympathetic Hessian officer recalled, these late risers "played Bopeep" with the Continental light horse through the streets of Philadelphia; not all of them escaped.[44]

Though thousands of civilians joined the redcoats in evacuating the city, thousands of other Philadelphia Loyalists and neutrals chose not to seek shelter with the British army in New York. Many stayed behind to protect their property from being confiscated by the Patriots, including Joseph Galloway's wife, Grace Galloway, who remained even as her husband fled. Those who privileged their homes, their businesses, and their families' security over political allegiances remained, preferring Philadelphia, even in independence, to any other home the empire might offer. The previous nine months, and particularly the evacuation itself, called into question Britain's ability and inclination to care for its American subjects. Consequently, even some who were known to have openly aligned themselves with the empire decided it was better to risk the wrath of the Patriots than to put themselves in a position of dependence on British mercies; only a minority of those proclaimed as traitors by Congress chose to depart, the rest preferred to take their chances with the Revolutionaries.[45]

A similar split emerged among the black inhabitants of the city. At least seventy-five free civilian blacks, including twenty-seven women, left Philadelphia with the British army and traveled to New York. The Black Pioneers continued to operate with the redcoats in New York and elsewhere. The British promise of freedom was a powerful lure; the risk of reenslavement by the Americans, a dreadful threat. Those who had found remunerative work serving the needs of the empire's officers had strong economic incentives to follow their employers, and the slaves held by British officers and fleeing Loyalists often had no alternative to departing.[46]

Yet others, including runaway slaves, reflected upon their situations and experiences and chose to take different paths. Mike High parted ways with the army to fend for himself as a hired laborer in New Jersey. Peg and James, once owned by Persifor Frazer and David Crane, respectively, both chose to remain in Philadelphia after the army left, hoping to disappear into the crowds and confusion that filled the streets when the Patriots returned.[47] For many runaway slaves, their first months of freedom had fallen short of their expectations. The liberty they had been given was precarious, granted only because it suited British interests and denied to the slaves of Loyalists. Those who had been unable to secure employment or support in the lean winter months would have learned that freedom from slavery did not mean freedom from suffering. Having had the opportunity to examine the attitudes of their liberators, they may have seen little reason to believe that things would be any better in New York than they had been in Philadelphia. The evacuation itself was perhaps the clearest sign that the liberty and security offered by the British was an uncertain foundation upon which to build their hopes and aspirations.

Though not threatened with enslavement, the Quaker population that remained in Philadelphia wrestled with its own peculiar concerns on the eve of the evacuation. Having already been targeted for daring to express "a disposition inimical to the cause of America," many Friends experienced "endless worries . . . expecting an unbearable fate" when the Revolutionaries retook the city.[48] Lutheran reverend Henry Muhlenberg, who had little sympathy for the religious groups that had long dominated the politics of pre-Revolutionary Pennsylvania, noted that such "so-called *Tories*" were "again in a predicament," having come to expect that the British would "protect these sects in their former liberties and accumulated possessions," protections the returning Revolutionary leadership had no intention of offering to the dissenters and the disaffected.[49] When she first learned of the coming evacuation, Sarah Logan Fisher lamented that "we may expect some great suffering when the Americans again get possession." The coming of the peace commission briefly and vainly raised her hopes, but these were soon dashed and she returned to her reflections on how "the apprehensions of again coming under the arbitrary power of the Congress are very dreadful." Elizabeth Drinker, who had less invested in the British presence, also noted that many of her fellows were "in much affliction" and that she herself felt "very forlorn" as the occupation neared its end.[50]

Consequences

As the Loyalists despaired and the civilians in general prepared themselves for the return of Revolutionary control, British and Hessian officers took the opportunity to reassess the state of the war and Revolution in light of the past year's reversals. For many, the evacuation was a culminating event. More than simply the latest in a series of setbacks, it was interpreted as a final straw, a signal that the British cause in America was not simply suffering but that it had, for all practical purposes, been lost.

"I now look upon the Contest as at an End," wrote Serle when rumors of the evacuation were finally confirmed. In the evacuation, and the betrayal it symbolized, Serle and others among the army bid farewell to any hope of a Loyalist uprising and, with it, any hope of British conquest in the North. "No man can be expected to declare for us, when he cannot be assured of a Fortnight's Protection," Serle explained, "Every man, on the contrary, whatever might have been his primary Inclinations, will find it his Interest to oppose & drive us out of the County." Serle's journal entry for the day included a telling shift in terminology, referring to his Revolutionary opponents not as "the rebels" or "the rebellious colonies" but, for the first time, as "(what I may *now* venture to call) *the United States of America*."[51]

Serle's fatalistic outlook was not unique. On the eve of the withdrawal, a despondent Captain Nesbit Balfour attempted to convey the army's sad state in a letter to a fellow officer already departed for England. "I am sure you will pity us here, insulted & ridiculed by the Americans, disgusted & unhappy amongst ourselves. . . . Tomorrow we leave town & bid adieu to America as masters." Like Serle, Balfour recognized that the abandonment of so many Loyalists and potential Loyalists shattered any hope Britain had of winning the hearts and minds of the American people, and in that loss of political affection, more than in the loss of a strategic post, he saw the loss of America. "Since you left us," he continued, "no American has been fool enough to delay one moment of submitting to the States . . . there can be no doubt their government will be first immediately much firmer than ever ours was."[52] General Sir William Erskine declared that "this Abandonment of the Town, so void of all Honor, Spirit & Policy, made him miserable in himself & ashamed of the name of Briton." He and a group of fellow officers, including Major General Charles Grey, spent a mournful evening in early June sharing their "strong Resentment of the Disgrace, wch was arising to their Country & to the British Arms."[53] The weight of the evacuation followed the army as it retreated across New Jersey. "I am most heartily tired of this cursed business," wrote a weary and depressed James Grant from his new quarters in New York, "and gave up the Game the moment we were ordered to leave Philadelphia." He believed the British capture of the American capital had been the most effective blow Britain had struck in the war. Its abandonment finally led him to conclude that the effort to conquer the colonies "is now over, and the sooner the army is withdrawn the better."[54]

Clinton expressed similar emotions as his army prepared for departure in late May and early June, confessing that he would "have wished to avoid the arduous task of attempting to retrieve a Game so unfortunately circumstanced." Though he had initially held out some hope for achieving renown as the foremost general in America, Britain's decision to abandon Philadelphia convinced him that his command was "very unenviable indeed . . . full of difficulty, and perhaps danger, without the least prospect of reputation to alleviate the weight."[55] The arrival of the peace commissioners in June only deepened Clinton's depression, prompting him to complain that "it is surely my fate to be thrown into the most extraordinary situations, such is the case at present . . . my fate is hard; forced to an apparent retreat with such an Army is mortifying." He scoffed at the notion that Britain could simultaneously surrender the American capital and expect the Revolutionaries to give up their cause. "What?" He asked rhetorically, "Is it expected that America in her present situation will agree to terms when the Army is avowedly retiring?" He soon found himself envying the departing Howes and wishing he too could abandon the war and return home.[56]

For their part, the members of the new peace commission, William Eden, George Johnstone, and the fifth Earl of Carlisle, were surprised to learn the city to which they had been sent was on the verge of being abandoned. The discovery was a source of both anger and embarrassment. Eden penned a furious letter to Lord Germain, the British secretary of state for America, accusing the ministry of entirely failing to support the commission and describing the "mortifying" spectacle of the army evacuating Philadelphia. "I have only to struggle as well as I can thro' the embarrassment in which I never deserved to be involved." He added that he would "take care not to incur or deserve any personal disgraces," but strongly implied that the surrender of Philadelphia was a national disgrace that he and all Britons would have to endure.[57] Johnstone, who took up the task of communicating with Congress, soon found that the Revolutionary leadership would not even consider his proposals and that the congressmen thought him "irrational" for imagining that they would be willing to consider Britain's terms when it appeared so weak militarily.[58] The commissioners were not immune to the effects of the army's plummeting morale. "Things go ill, and will not go better," wrote Carlisle several days after reaching Philadelphia. "We have done our duty, so we ought not to be involved with those who have *lost* this country."[59]

It would take several years before the British government finally agreed that the country had truly been lost. The year 1779 would witness a new British assault on the American South, driven in part by the same belief in a latent, widespread loyalism that had persuaded Howe to take Philadelphia in 1777. That effort too would eventually founder on misconceptions about American loyalties, priorities, and commitments, though there the story would be horribly complicated by the ever present influence of racial slavery, guerrilla warfare, and active military intervention by France. Never again would Britain seriously attempt to reconquer an American state north of Virginia. The British military would continue to occupy Newport through most of 1779 and would remain in New York City until the war came to an official conclusion in 1783, but these posts soon became defensive citadels, isolated islands of the empire, rather than footholds that set the stage for offensive operations.

The evacuation was also a pivotal moment for Pennsylvania's disaffected, transforming their world as drastically as had the British invasion nine months before. The occupation had taught the inhabitants in and around Philadelphia three important lessons. First, that despite the optimistic claims of the local Loyalists, the return of British authority did not restore the relative peace, prosperity, and stability that had existed before the rise of Revolutionary violence. Though the proximity of the redcoats offered some protection from the demands of the new Patriot regimes, the brutality, criminality, unpredictability, and indifference of the occupying army meant that its presence was, at best, a mixed blessing for all but the most elite Loyalists. In matters of currency, liberty, and security, among others, the high expectations of civilians crashed headlong into the reality of life under occupation. For many, there now seemed less to be gained from a British victory than they had once thought.

Second, it was now clear that much could be lost by openly supporting Great Britain. The seemingly resolute presence of the British army had encouraged a number of citizens, who had previously avoided committing themselves to either side in the war or even acted as Patriots, to align themselves with the redcoats. Some did so through active service, others by taking oaths, and still others by simply expressing sentiments they would never have dared to utter while the Revolutionaries controlled the city. The protective shield of passive compliance they had once sheltered beneath, an aura that had been extraordinarily hard to maintain in the face of the Revolutionaries' constant quest for explicit acts of support, was gone forever.

Hundreds were, or soon would be, accused of high treason against the state and threatened with death. Such men and women did not bear this betrayal quietly, and all those in and around the city were regularly reminded of Britain's unreliability and treachery over the occupation's final weeks.

Finally, the army's inability or unwillingness to hold the American capital, or even to stand and fight for it, convinced many who might have previously doubted the Revolutionaries' chances of success that American independence was a fait accompli. Like the British officers trudging their way across New Jersey, Pennsylvanians now struggled to see how Britain could ever possibly regain sovereignty over a region it had so brazenly abandoned and which had now maintained its own independent government for two years. The independent state government that had fled Philadelphia the previous year had only just succeeded in truly grasping the reins of power; the corpse of the previous body politic had still been warm, its denunciations of the insurgent regime as illegitimate and tyrannical still ringing in the people's ears. The Patriots returned in 1778 to fill a power vacuum, were now the only established government left in the state, and were supported by the only remaining military force. All who hoped for law, order, and security in Pennsylvania had no choice but to look to them.

Thus, in one sense, the plight of Pennsylvania's dissenters and the disaffected was once again as it had been before the British army had arrived in 1777, yet on a deeper level, the context of their decisions had been radically and permanently altered. As had been the case before the invasion, nominal support for and consent to the Revolutionary cause became the most reliable course for inhabitants who wished to live their lives in peace. Now, however, those who had once held back, fearing that commitments to the Patriot cause would bring about ruin should Britain win the war and restore the province to the empire, were free of such fears. The Revolutionaries returned to a city stripped of both its most outspoken Loyalists and of its incentives to embrace the Loyalist cause. On the issue of independence, at least, the war for hearts and minds in Pennsylvania soon became a mopping up operation. "The arduous contest for American Independence is near at an End," declared one of Reed's correspondents, "& that Brilliant Revolution is accomplished."[60]

The crowds that gathered around Valley Forge in May and June to swear allegiance to the Patriot regime spoke to how greatly the Revolution, and the people's perception of it, had changed over the preceding year. Many who had previously refused to do so now found themselves willing to accept the radical assembly's offer of protection in exchange for loyalty. They came, as Reed put it, "to sue for Grace"; they returned home as consenting citizens of the new republic.[61] Allen took the oath to the state while in Philadelphia, though his unhappy references to the "mob-government of Pennsylvania & the united states" reveal continued unhappiness with the new regime to which he had pledged his loyalty. Benjamin Towne, printer of the *Pennsylvania Evening Post*, once again experienced a political transformation and, after a brief hiatus, reemerged as a printer of pro-Revolutionary sentiments and congressional declarations. Towne's own suit for grace before the Revolutionary leadership went unrecorded, but Patriot John Witherspoon satirically composed "the humble confession, declaration, recantation, and apology of Benjamin Towne" for the public's enjoyment.[62] John Penn, last proprietary governor of the colony, also pledged his loyalty to the state at this time, if only in a largely futile attempt to preserve his property. He too acknowledged that the Revolutionary government, not Great Britain, would henceforth control the destiny of Pennsylvania's lands.[63]

As a testament to how severely Loyalist faith in Britain had been shaken and how drastically the politics had shifted, even Galloway, the most prominent Loyalist leader in the occupied city and hitherto a tireless proponent of the belief that the hearts and minds of Pennsylvania could yet be brought over to Britain's side, considered approaching Washington in the hope that he too might find amnesty and acceptance in the American republic. Shockingly, he was even encouraged toward this path by the departing Howe brothers, who were themselves deeply disheartened. Clinton, who quickly recognized that Galloway's making peace with the rebels would set a bad precedent and might trigger a mass defection of his entire provincial corps, forbade the inspector general from seeking terms with the Continentals. Nonetheless, according to Serle, word that the occupied city's leaders were close to giving up the struggle "was soon circulated about the Town, & filled all our Friends with melancholy on the Apprehension of being speedily deserted."[64] Some who heard the story came to believe the Howes' advice to Galloway was intended, not for him specifically, but for the inhabitants generally, prompting even more disaffected and Loyalist men to declare their loyalty to the United States.[65] Though he personally refrained from treating with Washington, Galloway warned the British that others "who by their attachments to the crown have rendered themselves liable to the cruel resentment of the rebels" might feel they had no alternative. The withdrawal would "deprive them of all confidence in the British Protection, and alienate their minds from the British Government, and from necessity unite them to the rebel states."[66] The severity of the situation was not lost upon those, like Serle, who recognized "that in future these People who wd. have fought for us and covered the Province are now at best neutrals, & can yield us no assistance in future, if we shd. want them."[67]

Galloway's and Serle's warnings were soon borne out during the army's long march across New Jersey to its stronghold in New York. Regions which had been, at best, disaffected toward the Revolution now turned decidedly against the British, refusing to sell their remaining provisions, assisting deserters, and passing intelligence on to the Revolutionaries. The New Jersey militia, which had been so anemic while the occupation persisted, turned out in force to harass the retreating redcoats and take part in the Battle of Monmouth. Even as the British army swept through their towns and farms, few Americans now believed their interests would long be served by aligning themselves, even tangentially, with the king's men.[68] In evacuating Philadelphia, the army not only relinquished the region to the Continentals, it also effectively surrendered the loyalties of the people who lived there and did irreparable damage to Britain's chances of ever regaining it or them.

INTERLUDE

CHANGE AND CONTINUITY

The Whitall family lived south of Philadelphia, just across the Delaware River, near Woodbury, New Jersey. The house built by James and Ann Whitall in 1748 still stands today as part of Red Bank Battlefield Park. From its windows the family could have watched the British fleet come up the river in 1777 to secure the American capital and then sail back down again when the redcoats abandoned the city in 1778. Through the intervening months the Whitalls experienced, to some degree, nearly all the trials which war and occupation brought to the region. Quakers and farmers, the family was by and large disaffected, doing what they could to avoid engagement with the politics and violence of the imperial contest, and like many of the disaffected they discovered that there was no escape, no peaceable neutrality to be found in the midst of Revolution.[1] They endured as best they could and maintained throughout a perspective which we would do well to consider. They remind us that the great events which often dominate our traditional stories of the American Revolution may not have garnered much notice from many of the Americans who lived alongside them, that some contemporaries perceived the great men whose deeds have long pressed our narrative of independence forward as neither heroes nor villains, but as distant strangers whose pursuits were not terribly relevant to everyday life. We often recount the Revolution as a moment of all-consuming transformation and change. The diary of Job Whitall, James and Ann's second son, reminds us of how even the most dramatic upheavals can be swallowed up by the steady continuity of daily life.

Job maintained his diary from at least 1775 to 1779. With few exceptions, he added to it every day, preserving the sights, news, and events he thought worth recording. It is the account of an eighteenth-century farmer and his family, driven forward by domestic concerns and flavored with the obligations of a New Jersey Quaker. But these were fraught years for the region and, in bits and snatches, the events of the war intruded into the steady pattern of Job's life. "The People Began to muster this Day," he wrote in February 1776. In May he "heard a cannonading with the rowgallies & a mannawar or two which lasted three hours or better. . . . The people a geting In arms as fast as ye can." Then, nine months later, "This Day, ye People began to Press Peoples horses & take them away to Ride."[2]

As the war came it sent ripples through the otherwise placid predictability of Job's diary. Beginning in 1776 he mentions the loss of property to the Patriots as they imposed fines and military taxes. "I, not finding fredom to pay," he wrote, "they took what they pleased," and two chairs and a pair of irons were carried out the door. Other losses would follow, along with threats of personal violence. At first Job was disinclined to take the latter seriously, waving away promises to deploy militant force against him and his family as empty words meant "to sceer us, I suppose." Yet soon enough frightful events transpired around him. Job's cousin was briefly jailed by the local Patriot committee; his servant was accosted along the road and forbidden from leaving his property; a neighbor was thrown into prison for refusing to swear allegiance to the new regime. Then, in August 1777, as the British army moved up the Chesapeake to launch its invasion, Job himself was offered the alternative of voluntarily being interrogated by the committee at once or being arrested later. He chose the former and faced a long walk to the local tavern in the company of a militia captain. Yet the committee, perhaps surprised by his choice to come at once, was unavailable and the captain, after some discussion, chose not to hold him.[3]

Like the residents of Philadelphia, the Whitalls felt uncertainty when faced with the region's many new forms of currency, pondering their values and political significance. Trading with the markets of Philadelphia in 1776, Job received his first Continental dollar bills, though he seems to have been unsure what to do with them. For the next two years he used Continental money sparingly and was careful to precisely record who he paid it to and from whom he received it. He occasionally made a list of the specific bills he gave or was given in payment and tried to carefully calculate the exchange rates in pounds, shillings, and pence.[4]

On April 16, 1777, Job walked to his parents' farm to fish and found several hundred American soldiers there systematically felling trees and piling up great mounds of earth. Despite the strenuous objections of James and Ann Whitall, the Patriots erected Fort Mercer on land which had once been the Whitall family orchard. The pacifist Quakers looked on bitterly as this symbol of war was constructed on their land, but the full weight of their loss would come later, when the Whitalls' peaceful fields were transformed into a raging and bloody battlefield.[5]

Job Whitall was not, could not have been, blind to the Revolution and war which surrounded him, and he dutifully recorded the parts of it which crashed inescapably into his life. Yet through it all his descriptions of the politics and the violence, all the loss and change brought by Revolution, are swallowed up by the steady, monotonous rhythms of his farm, his faith, and his domestic life. Weeks passed without so much as a word of the conflict seeping into his writing. Job's diary takes no notice at all of the Declaration of Independence or the changes to New Jersey's government; does not acknowledge when Philadelphia was taken by the British or when the redcoats withdrew from the city; he records no political debates or discussions; he makes no attempt to track the passage or objectives of the armies. Rather, he makes a point of carefully memorializing the common events of his daily life: what he planted and when, where he or his family visited on a given day, the progress of sickness and recovery, happenings at the Quaker school over which he sometimes had oversight, visitors from outside the area who came to Quaker meetings, his obligations and decisions regarding relief for the poor, and commercial exchanges he engaged in. When the new governments detained or harassed his own small circle, when soldiers appeared on his own property, when the war intruded, unavoidably, into his ordinary life, he made a note of it, but taken as a whole *The Diary of Job Whitall* suggests a man with almost no interest in the course of the struggle.

On October 22, 1777, the war intruded, unavoidably, into his life. The British, having then secured Philadelphia and repelled Washington's counterstroke at Germantown, moved to open the Delaware River to their shipping. This necessitated the capture or destruction of the Continental garrison at Fort Mercer which sat on Whitall family land. Howe sent a powerful force under Hessian colonel Carl von Donop to take the fort, but though the Hessians greatly outnumbered the American defenders, they were forced back after a brutal and exceedingly bloody assault, leaving the surrounding fields littered with the dead and dying.[6]

Job Whitall's record of the battle which took place on his parents' property, like most of his diary entries during the war, disregards the larger military and political import of the event and focuses closely on the specific and personal concerns of his family. He recalls working on fences with his father when "our women blode ye horn . . . ye reason was because ye English troops was close by." The rest of Job's morning and early afternoon were spent securing his and his parents' property, driving away livestock so they would not be caught in the middle of the ensuing battle. As the Hessians prepared for their assault, Job went back to evacuate his family but found that his parents refused to leave the house, trusting to God for protection and, perhaps, hoping that their continued presence would discourage the soldiers from plundering their home. Job accepted his parents' decision and left them to their fate.[7]

The walls of Fort Mercer and the carnage which ensued around them were readily visible from the upstairs bedrooms of the Whitall house where, according to family tradition, Ann Whitall sat at her spinning wheel while the battle raged just outside. As Donop's Hessians charged the walls and the Royal Navy unleashed fire and fury from the river, a stray cannonball smashed through the gable just above her, ricocheted about the attic, and then gently rolled down the stairs to stop near her feet. With considerable calm, given the circumstances, Ann carefully gathered her materials, picked up the spinning wheel, stepped past the cannonball, walked down to the basement, and resumed her work there for the remainder of the battle.[8]

Job returned to his parents' home the following morning to find the house full of blood and broken men, American and Hessian alike. Ann Whitall moved among them, doing all she could to heal the wounded and comfort the dying without regard to their loyalties or origins. One of her patients was, in all probability, Colonel Donop, who received a mortal wound during the battle and was briefly treated at the Whitall house before being moved elsewhere. Though history would fondly remember her ministries that day, the victorious Continentals offered little reward. The military claimed the entire house for its own use, forcing Ann and her husband to gather what belongings they could and move to her brother's home for the foreseeable future. Six months would pass before they could return.[9]

Job's diary, focused wholly on preserving his family and their property, offers no account of the battle. He makes no mention of who was victorious aside from noting that it was the Americans, not the British, who took control of his parents' house in the aftermath. The same disregard is apparent in his entries throughout the occupation. Indeed, an uninformed reader of his diary would have no idea that the city had fallen at all, though hints exist for those who know to look for them: nearly a year passes without Job recounting a visit to Philadelphia; there are no more accounts of fines or imprisonment for Non-Association or the failure to swear allegiance to the state; beginning in November the soldiers who occasionally appear in his entries are British, not American. Though, in truth, Job often failed to specify the affiliation of the armed men who periodically made off with his belongings. As Washington attempted to isolate the occupied city and the British grasped for provisions, the Whitalls' goods and livestock where regularly confiscated. By the end of 1777, Job and his family had lost at least five horses, as many pigs, an unspecified number of cattle, and nearly four dozen sheep to foraging parties from one army or the other. On November 21 alone he recorded that "while ye army were a passing by, they came in & took our bread, pyes, milk, chees, meet, dishes, cups, spoons & then took shirts, sheets, Blankets, coverleds, stockings, Breeches, a lite Broadax & drove our catle out of ye Brickshed & they all came Back but one big, brown ox that we workt. While here, they Broke open two doors & ransack ye hous all over but ye seller."[10]

What is perhaps most striking about Job's account of such losses, aside from the sheer number of goods taken, is how little the identity of the foragers mattered to him or influenced their behavior. At least as often as not Job referred to the men who confiscated his property only as "soldiers," a label he applied to redcoats, Continentals, and militiamen alike. He expressed no greater sense of shock or betrayal when plundered by the Americans than by the British, and neither side seemed to see him as an ally worthy of protection.

The British retreat from Philadelphia left no more of a mark in Job's dairy than did their occupation of the city nine months earlier. Visits to the city reappear without explanation for their long absence.[11] His use of Continental money becomes steadily less awkward and self-conscious. Though Job offers no remarks on the progress of the British army across New Jersey toward New York, the chaos of the period is conveyed in one of the last, and certainly one of the strangest, entries which concern plundering soldiers. About midnight on June 22, some half dozen men armed with guns and swords broke into the Whitall house. Upon being confronted, they declared that they were from the Royal Navy. Apparently recognizing that this did not induce the Whitalls to offer them support, they changed stories and claimed to be Continentals, sent to seize Job and take him for trial in Philadelphia. Operating under this assumed authority, they allegedly began a search for incriminating papers and correspondence, pulling open cabinets and rifling through drawers. The Whitalls were quick to notice that the men seemed disinterested in seizing documents but rather "took near all ye cash they come across & a good deel of wearing apperal." Having looted what they could easily carry, the self-described Continental investigators departed, seemingly having forgotten that they were supposed to arrest Job and return with him. Having been repeatedly plundered by both the British and Americans over the preceding year, in the confusion of the occupation's final month Job suffered one last loss to a group of men who claimed to be the agents of both sides but were, in fact, from neither.[12]

The Whitall family was hit hard by the yellow fever epidemics which struck the Delaware Valley in the 1790s; the disease carried off both Job and his mother, among others. Americans looking back on the family have struggled to describe their relation to the Revolution. Contemporary Continentals labeled them as "Tories" and mild opponents, citing the family's objections to the construction of Fort Mercer on their property and James Whitall's long-standing bitterness over the government's refusal to compensate him for the estimated £5,760 lost as a result. A century later his wife, Ann Whitall, would be transformed into "the heroine of Redbank" for the brief care she offered to the wounded after the failed Hessian attack on the fort. In 1905 the Daughters of the American Revolution opened an Ann Whitall chapter in Woodbury, New Jersey. Applicants traced their lineage back to this "Patriot nurse" and hailed her for having "assisted in establishing American Independence."[13]

CHAPTER 6

AFTERMATH

> Johnny Drinker was taken up today by a Mob (part of the Militia) as he came out of meeting.... Many of the Light-Horse came up and a Battle ensued, when 2 or 3 lost their lives and many were wounded—they rescu'd the Prisoners ... it seems the intent was or is to take up a number of the Inhabitants who they call disaffected and send them off to some other part; perhaps New York.
> —Elizabeth Drinker, October 4, 1779

"Sir, I congratulate you on the present happy aspect of our affairs in general," wrote Timothy Matlack in July of 1778, "as well as the particular wished for event of our repossessing of the city of Philadelphia." For the previous nine months, the de facto capital of the nascent United States had been occupied by the British army. Matlack, as a secretary to Pennsylvania's executive council and one of the state's more powerful figures, was immensely relieved to see the city back in Revolutionary hands, as was his correspondent, Pennsylvania's attorney general, Jonathan D. Sergeant. Matlack wrote to hasten Sergeant's return to the capital and inform him of the city's submission to the Revolutionary program. "Its inhabitants in general," he boasts, "Whig & Tory throughout, appear to be fully reconciled to independency, and acknowledge their detestation of the conduct of their formerly reputed best friends the British troops."[1] It seemed to Matlack that, while the clash of arms may continue elsewhere, the great war for the hearts and minds of Philadelphia's people had been won; they had "reconciled" themselves to an independent America. It remained to be seen, however, if the independent United States could reconcile itself to them.

Almost from its inception, the Revolutionary movement expressed a steadily growing intolerance of neutrality, apathy, and ambivalence; a bitterness and suspicion toward the disengaged, disinterested, and disaffected. Such antipathy surged and broke into open violence when the British army invaded the state and occupied the capital. Patriot authorities had granted themselves nearly unlimited punitive powers against anyone they perceived as "inimical" to their cause, imprisoned and banished disaffected inhabitants without charges or trial, mandated oaths of allegiance to their fledgling regime, threatened those who refused to defend their government with economic ruin, and sanctioned the wholesale destruction of untold quantities of private property and the summary execution of untried civilians suspected of illegally transporting foodstuffs. That the year of the occupation did not devolve into a period of constant bloodshed and unchecked tyranny can be attributed only to the fragility of the nascent regime, the general population's refusal to cooperate with its more radical edicts, and the better angels of some Revolutionary leaders who refrained from fully embracing the immense destructive powers theoretically granted them.

As the occupation neared its end in the summer of 1778 and the British made plans to evacuate the American capital, the Revolutionaries of Pennsylvania faced the choice of how to proceed in the wake of this unexpected victory and their recent alliance with France. Radical Revolutionary elements, most notably in the Pennsylvania state government and the militia companies, saw this as an opportunity to press forward with the established pattern of mounting intolerance against those who refused to offer their support for the Patriot cause. Maintaining their vision of a population cleanly divided between virtuous, consenting citizens and traitorous enemies of the people, they saw the weakening of British power as an unprecedented opportunity to punish, neutralize, or cast out the latter and so purify and protect their new republic.

Yet the British evacuation also witnessed the emergence and promotion of a contrary perspective, one which saw the shifting balance of the war as a reason to alter, rather than embrace, the Revolution's past approach to dissent and disaffection. Powerful elements, both within and without the Revolutionary leadership, began to reevaluate the Patriot-vs.-Loyalist dichotomy which denied the existence of the disaffected; to interpret political silence as a sign of tacit consent rather than antagonism; and to suggest that the unity, rather than the ideological purity, of the population might be the more important objective.

Revenge

The advocates of greater intolerance toward dissent and disaffection achieved a series of key legislative victories in the final weeks before the British withdrawal. In April of 1778 the state assembly revived one of their most notorious and despised tools of enforced conformity: the Test Act. In 1777 the government had established the Test and demanded that all adult white males take an oath renouncing the king, pledging themselves to "be faithful And bear true allegiance to the Commonwealth of Pennsylvania as a free and independent State," and committing to the discovery and exposure of "all treasons or traitorous conspiracies . . . formed against this or any of the United States of America."[2] Despite the severe penalties prescribed for those who refused the oath, many Pennsylvanians rejected it. The act's unpopularity and, more importantly, the subsequent British invasion of the capital, crippled attempts to enforce it. Long after the initial July 1 deadline, only a minority of Pennsylvanians had taken the oath.[3] The Revolutionary leadership hoped for better results this time. A new deadline was set on June 1, new modes of enforcement were devised, and the penalties for refusing the oath were made even more severe. The original act stripped dissenters of the right to vote, to hold elected office, to serve on juries, to transfer property, to sue for unpaid debts, and to bear arms. The revised act retained those punishments but also doubled the taxes laid on dissenters and specifically targeted men connected to education, law, medicine, and trade, subjecting them to an additional fine of £500. To make the act enforceable, the revisions empowered any two justices to summon a citizen and demand that he immediately submit to the act under threat of summary fines or imprisonment. Persistent refusal to submit to the Test could now result not only in banishment, but also in the forfeiture of all of one's personal property to the state.[4] Lutheran reverend Henry Muhlenberg neatly summarized the heart of the law in writing that those who rejected the oath would henceforth simply "be deprived of *all* rights."[5] For a steadily growing number of inhabitants, however, even submission to the Test would not be enough. In May the Supreme Executive Council began issuing proclamations listing traitors who had allegedly "aided and assisted the

Enemies of this State and of the United States of America." The accused were ordered to surrender themselves by a given date to the courts and stand trial for high treason. Should they fail to do so, the government would issue a bill of attainder, declare them guilty by legislative fiat, and have their estates seized and distributed among their debtors and the state. Should the accused surrender after the deadline or later be apprehended, there would be no trial; they were simply to be sentenced to death. The council would eventually issue ten such proclamations containing the names of nearly five hundred individuals. On June 25, the *Pennsylvania Evening Post*'s editor, Benjamin Towne, would be assigned the awkward task of publishing his own name among a list of declared traitors. Such attempts to legislatively declare criminal guilt would later be explicitly banned by the US Constitution.[6]

Patriot anger and bitterness toward Loyalists and the disaffected was greatly bolstered by the damage done to Philadelphia in the final weeks before the British left it. Churches had been desecrated and turned into stables for the British cavalry, their pews taken as firewood, their property destroyed. The streets, public buildings, and even private homes were filled with noxious filth that bred unending swarms of flies. The State House, which had been converted into a hospital, was left in such a "filthy & sordid situation" that Congress could not reconvene there but moved to the College of Philadelphia. Prize orchards, groves, and fences had been converted into firewood or building materials, and personal property within private residences had been vandalized, confiscated, or simply stolen. The total effect was overwhelming.[7]

Much of this damage was the inevitable and expected result of so many humans and animals living in such crowded conditions for so many months. Yet the most offensive acts of destruction and defilement appear to have been committed suddenly, in the closing weeks of the occupation, after the army learned of its impending evacuation. Many of the horrors recorded in late June and July are absent from accounts written in April and May and so disturbing that it seems unlikely that the inhabitants would have long endured them without remark. This may have merely reflected the redcoats' lack of concern for a region they were soon to depart, or it may be that they intentionally fouled their former homes in order to vent their frustration at being forced to withdraw or as an act of spite against the returning Patriots. Lieutenant Loftus Cliffe believed that his fellow soldiers "left Philadelphia extremely dissatisfied that it was not consumed."[8]

Yet whether vindictive or incidental, the damage done to the city and the suffering experienced by the Revolutionary refugees elicited intense hostility toward the British and anyone suspected of having aided them.

The frustration and horror of the returning Revolutionaries soon poured forth in the city newspapers and streets. The more radical and outspoken Patriots demanded an immediate and harsh punishment for those they suspected of having betrayed the new nation and having participated in, or at least having failed to prevent, the looting and desecration of the capital. In the *Evening Post*, an author pen-named "Casca" issued "a HINT to the TRAITORS and TORIES" to "lower your heads, and *not stare down* your betters with *angry faces*" and warned that "the day of trial is close at hand when you shall be called upon, to answer for your *impertinence* to the Whigs, and your *treachery* to this country." An anonymous contributor to the *Pennsylvania Packet* warned that, though the redcoats had departed, "a set of wretches, male and female, remain among us, who, having neither the honor of men nor the virtue of women, are a scandal to themselves. . . . Against such it becomes us to unite." He then reprinted the oath of allegiance to remind those who had taken it that they had sworn to turn all traitors over to the state.[9] Few instances of published invective compared to the long and vitriolic polemic signed by "Astrea de Coelis," which filled the entire first page of the *Evening Post*'s July 18 issue. The author denounced the so-called Tory inhabitants as "apostate citizens . . . murderers, traitors, spies and thieves" and compared them to "flies upon a carcase." For this contributor and those of a similar mindset, there were no neutrals or bystanders, no middle group who wanted only to avoid the conflict. "The line between Whig and Tory is very easy to be ascertained," he declared, and it was the duty of all true, virtuous citizens "to separate the Patriot from the traitor, the man of honor from the villain, and to distribute confiscation, slavery, and death to the latter." Coelis's great fear was that the guilty would, by relying on crocodile tears and the tender hearts of Patriots, somehow evade justice. He scoffed at their "death-bed repentance; flying to the magistrate with a tender of their allegiance and fidelity," and chafed under "the formalities of law," writing "The law says, 'every man is to be deemed honest till convicted by trial, and suspicion of guilt is no proof of facts.' Our greatest difficulty arises from the want of sufficient evidence . . . and the sacred regard we entertain for the liberties of the subject, are such as I am afraid will save many a scoundrel from the gallows." He concluded by calling for "an association of citizens for the purposes of collecting the necessary evidence against traitors," an appeal which harkened back to the ad hoc "courts" that had been set up in taverns before the occupation.[10]

Though Coelis may not have known it, moves were already afoot to answer his call. A group of citizens, calling itself the Patriotic Society and largely dominated by Philadelphia's more radical Revolutionary leaders, formed in the weeks after the occupation. The members devoted themselves to discovering evidence against those "sundry persons, notoriously disaffected to the American cause, and others of suspicious characters" who remained in the city. Like Coelis and others who had contributed to the papers, they appealed to a binary and sharply defined understanding of loyalty, believing that it was their duty "to make a proper discrimination between the friends and enemies of America." They too emphasized how the Test Act's oath pledged one to become an informant against any fellow citizens suspected of having engaged in "traitorous" activities, worrying that the people's "misapprehension of the duty they owe their country, and inattention to their oath of allegiance" may have led them "to suppose their appearing as witnesses against such offenders officious and dishonourable." Nearly two hundred men had joined the society by July 25.[11] That same month the state's chief justice, Thomas McKean, took up a post outside the courthouse in Philadelphia in order to be readily available, both for those who wished to turn themselves in to the court and "to hear the charges against Tories accused of joining and assisting the British army."[12]

As had been the case in the summer and fall of 1777, when the Council of Safety had been granted nearly limitless authority to summarily punish and even execute dissenters, the stage appeared to be set for an extensive and bloody wave of Revolutionary vengeance. Hundreds stood already accused of treason and hundreds more were doubtless guilty of dealing with the British army during the months of the occupation. Many would be assigned guilt without the benefit of trial, demagogues in the press cried out for blood, and dozens of men declared themselves ready to discover and finger the "traitors" in their midst.

Though the vast majority of treason charges were made against men, Philadelphia's dissenting and disaffected women faced their own peculiar sorts of condemnation. This was especially true for those young women who had embraced and been embraced by the exuberant social scenes of the occupied city.[13] In 1774, the Continental Association had summoned forth committees to "encourage Frugality, Economy, and Industry" and to "discountenance and discourage every species of extravagance and dissipation." Radical Revolutionaries called for a republican simplicity that would free American consumers from a dependence on British trade and free American souls from the iniquities of profligacy, vanity, and wastefulness. Extravagant and luxurious dress was deemed particularly offensive, as were the evils of "all horse-racing, and all kinds of gaming, cock-fighting, exhibitions of plays, shews, and other expensive diversions and entertainments."[14] In the first half of 1778, as the occupied city was flooded with luxurious imports from Britain and crowded with idle military officers, Philadelphia played host to each and every extravagant vice the radicals decried. When the Revolutionaries reclaimed their capital, they came prepared to chastise those who had so brazenly flouted their moral proscriptions. Of the many sins against simplicity, women's fashion was often the most vociferously attacked symbol of excess. In particular, the "high roll" style in which a woman's hair was, through an expensive and time-consuming process, twisted and carded together with various supporting materials and decorations until it towered a foot or more over the top of her head, was taken as a badge of dissipation.

One returning Patriot denounced this fashion as "absurd, ridiculous and preposterous . . . their hair is dressed, with the assistance of wool, &c. in such a manner as to appear to[o] heavy to be supported by their necks." He grimly proclaimed that "the morals of the inhabitants have suffered vastly. The enemy introduced new fashions and made old vices more common."[15] Countless other Philadelphians vented their rage at such ornaments and the women who wore them through a popular demonstration in the city streets. Celebration of independence on July 4, 1778, was marked by a grand parade thrown by a sizable crowd of Revolutionary radicals, composed primarily of those from the lower economic strata. The centerpiece of this demonstration was what Elizabeth Drinker described as "a viry dirty Woman." Though barefoot and dressed in rags, her hair was styled "with the Monstrous head-dress of the Tory Ladies . . . elegantly and expensively dressed . . . about three feet high and of proportional width, with a profusion of curls, &c &c &c." The display was an unambiguous critique of the women who had remained in Philadelphia during the occupation, embraced British fashion, and consorted with British officers. As an act of intimidation, it had some success.[16]

Women were targeted in more explicit ways as well. Ladies who had remained in the occupied city at times found themselves pointedly excluded from the balls, dinners, and other celebrations hosted by the returning Patriots, including a fete thrown in honor of Martha Washington in December.[17] Conrad Alexandre Gérard de Rayneval, the first French minister sent to the United States following the treaty of alliance, encountered such an attitude when he proposed arranging a dinner and ball in August. He reported back to France that American Patriots "wanted to draw an absolute line of separation between Whigs and Tories, especially among the ladies." The French diplomat's plans for a festive evening were consequently called off, much to his chagrin. "I regard this as treating matters rather seriously," he confided to his superiors.[18] On multiple occasions this social isolation threatened to become true banishment from the city as Revolutionary leaders fretted that "the wives of so many of the most notorious of the British emissaries remain among us" and that, through correspondence with their spouses, they were "receiving and propagating their poisonous, erroneous, wicked falsehoods here; which pernicious practice we conceive ought immediately to be inquired into and remedied." The state government repeatedly considered ordering the wives of all Loyalist refugees out of the city and radical elements of the Pennsylvania militia declared their willingness to unilaterally arrest and exile "the wives and children of those men who had gone with the British, or were within the British lines."[19]

Leniency

The American reoccupation of Philadelphia following the British withdrawal marked what was, perhaps, the single greatest opportunity the Revolutionary radicals would have to coerce consent from the inhabitants, permanently silence their opponents, and otherwise ideologically purify the population. The Patriot regime was, at long last, uncontested in its control of the state and possessed the only remaining military forces; thousands of hitherto overlooked dissenting or disaffected individuals had revealed themselves by aiding, trading with, or at least peacefully tolerating, the British army while it held Philadelphia; legislation in the form of the newly revised Test Act and the first bills of attainder seemed to pave the way for a swift and uncontested execution of Patriot wrath; and the deplorable state of the city upon the British evacuation raised passions to a fevered pitch, leaving at least some outspoken segments of the population poised to strike against the perceived enemies of liberty.

Yet the weeks and months following the British occupation saw, not the political purges and enforced intolerance that some hoped for and many might have expected, but rather a sudden surge of official leniency, a widespread hesitancy to actually enact the harsher elements of Revolutionary law and rhetoric, and a general breakdown of the Patriot-vs.-Traitor dichotomy which had hitherto allowed no room for disaffection or neutrality. In spite of the rhetoric of revenge carried in the papers and the harsh language of the laws, the penalties actually imposed by the state were astonishingly limited. With a few noteworthy exceptions, state authorities and the people generally refused to carry out the program of retribution allowed by the law and demanded by the radicals. The dozens who surrendered themselves to Chief Justice McKean in the weeks after the withdrawal were almost all promptly released. Of the approximately 640 individuals accused of high treason, the majority of whom were charged by proclamation during or immediately after the British occupation, the state executed only six. Well over a hundred, Benjamin Towne among them, were simply discharged and sent home. Dozens were released when grand juries refused to indict them. Others were acquitted, pardoned, or had their charges reduced to misdemeanor offenses, and some eluded the custody of the state by fleeing the region. Of the twenty-six proclaimed persons who surrendered or were captured after the deadline set by their proclamations and who, according to the law, were to be sentenced to death without trial, only one was actually executed and he was killed by the army rather than by civilian authorities.[20]

To the great frustration of citizens like Casca and Coelis, the people repeatedly refused to testify against their neighbors and acquaintances who might have had intercourse with the British military. After nine months of occupation, during which the overcrowded city witnessed constant examples of exchange and interaction between the British and the inhabitants, there should have been no shortage of evidence regarding who had aided or comforted the occupying forces. Yet, as McKean noticed, most of the inhabitants were remarkably reserved when it came to describing each other's actions while the redcoats were in the city. When radicals petitioned the executive council to take more drastic action against the "concealed enemies" remaining in Philadelphia, the council reported encountering "very great difficulties" because "there is a great unwillingness on the part of the people of the city to give the necessary information against the disaffected." The Patriotic Society declared that the traitors within Philadelphia were "intimidating and discouraging the good people of this State from appearing against them." How these traitorous persons were capable of such widespread intimidation at a moment of Revolutionary triumph was left unspecified.[21]

The people exhibited the same leniency when serving as jurors and often doubted that what the state deemed "traitorous" activity truly made one deserving of death. In cases where the sentence upon conviction was likely to be extreme, and particularly in cases of mandatory execution, juries tended to acquit and grand juries refused to indict. This was often true even where the evidence against the accused was overwhelming and, in some cases, juries acquitted defendants who openly confessed to working for the British army.[22] Despite the vengeful rage of a vocal minority, the silent majority of citizens seemingly preferred to put the bloodshed and divisiveness of the war behind them; some simply desired peace after months of living in the seat of war; others were eager to direct their energies toward new, domestic, political conflicts that would determine how the independent nation would be governed. The same factors that had made Pennsylvania so slow to embrace revolution now made it quick to abandon Revolutionary violence.

Similar sentiments stayed the hands of the Revolutionary leadership. Even those who had helped pass the harsh laws against dissent and disaffection often proved hesitant to enforce them in the months and years following the occupation. The assembly granted the state attorney general permission to reduce treason charges to misdemeanors, extended deadlines for some of those charged via proclamation, and occasionally exempted specific individuals from punishment altogether.[23] Convicted offenders were pardoned, saw their fines remitted, and their sentences reduced. Such mercy was not distributed universally, but few men experienced the full weight of the law unless they had committed some particularly heinous offense against persons or property. General John Armstrong, of the Pennsylvania militia, expressed approval for this approach, writing that he was "for the general line of lenity & forgiveness" toward those who "differed only in mere political sentiment." He acknowledged "that a few examples ought to be made of the more atrocious," but made a point of emphasizing "that in the highest degree they ought to be but few."[24]

This leniency in enforcement also extended to that great cudgel of mandated consent: the Test Act. In April, as the Revolutionaries braced themselves for an expected British offensive into the heart of Pennsylvania, the penalties for refusing the Test had increased in severity and new mechanisms had been put in place to simplify enforcement. By late May, however, reassured by knowledge of the impending evacuation of Philadelphia and an American alliance with France, several Revolutionary leaders began reconsidering the wisdom of imposing these penalties on the disaffected population. As early as May 22, Vice President George Bryan began warning state officials that, when it came to those who did not actively pose a threat to the state, "it is the wish of government not to distress them by any unequal fines, or by calling them, without special occasion happens, to take the oath at all."[25] A few days later Bryan again called for a relaxed approach to enforcement, suggesting that the revised act's power to force individuals to immediately take the oath before a justice of the peace "be reserved for persons whose character & conduct shall threaten active mischief against the State." As for those who simply wanted to maintain their neutrality and be left alone, he pointed to the impending British withdrawal and explained that "if the enemy remove out of the State, & these ignorant people become better satisfied of the establishment of our cause, it may be expected that their objections will gradually wear away." The vice president went on to urge "prudent persons . . . to soften the harsh councils of some well meaning but over-zealous & imprudent men."[26] Timothy Matlack requested that officials charged with seizing the estates of those who had refused the Test take a leisurely approach to their duties and, in particular, that they hold off on selling the seized property. As secretary to the Supreme Executive Council, Matlack was well positioned to recognize that body's declining enthusiasm for the act and cautiously warned his correspondent that "applications may be made to Council for lenity, and the possibility of this ought not to be foreclosed."[27]

In December the assembly went further and once again revised the Test Act legislation. Eight months before, in the midst of the occupation, the act had been made more severe; now, with the British army back in New York and the independent government securely in place, it was made even more forgiving than at its inception. Refusal to take the Test still prevented one from political participation in the state, but the threats of imprisonment, banishment, and the loss of property were removed. True citizenship remained a privilege of those who pledged their loyalty to the state, but now dissenters could hope to continue as peaceful and economically viable inhabitants. The council followed the assembly's lead by issuing pardons to those who had previously been imprisoned for refusing the Test.[28]

Such reversals in policy did not escape the notice of groups like the Patriotic Society and their more vengeful allies. No less a figure than Joseph Reed, who was elected president of Pennsylvania's Supreme Executive Council in 1778 and remained fiercely intolerant of dissent and disaffection, complained "that too easy an Ear has been given by the Ministeres [sic] of Justice to the Applications of those who are disaffected to their Country & that from a Fear of the Imputation of Rigour or giving Offence, the contrary Error of extreme Compassion & a Desire to avoid Offence has taken Place." Reed cautioned that such toleration of dissent and disaffection "had a Tendency to weaken Governmt, & encourage the political Sinners of this State."[29] Disregarding appeals to mercy, Reed at one point went so far as to conflate compassion itself with treason, warning the council "that popular Humanity (tho not ment[ioned] in our Treason Laws) is a species of Treason & not the least dangerous Kind."[30]

Reed soon found that his views were increasingly in the minority. Confronted by members of the Patriotic Society and others who, in the wake of the British withdrawal, demanded the creation of a government body formally charged with identifying and seizing any lingering inhabitants of questionable loyalties, the Supreme Executive Council determined such a plan to be outside the scope of its authority. In astonishing contradiction to its actions only a year earlier when it had created a Council of Safety with powers to summarily arrest, imprison, or execute anyone whose "general conduct or conversation may be deemed inimical," the Supreme Executive Council now declared that any such measure would "be opposed by the best Friends of liberty as a most arbitrary exercise of assumed authority; or, if submitted to, would establish a precedent which would have the most dangerous tendency to set up in the executive branch of Government an arbitrary power destructive of the liberty and safety of the people; therefore the Council cannot think of appointing such persons or pretend to give such powers."[31] The council's drastic actions immediately before the occupation seem to have been forgotten.

A similar forgetfulness would eventually ensue with regard to the bills of attainder the state had issued so freely during and after the occupation. By the 1780s, the council would express concern that the practice of declaring guilt by legislation might "greatly affect the lives, liberties, and fortunes, of the Freemen of this Commonwealth," worrying that "to take away the life of a man without a fair and open trial, upon an implication of guilt" would set a dangerous precedent for the future. Among their many queries to the courts was this: "Is such a mode of attainder compatible with the letter and spirit of the Constitution of this State, which establishes, with such strong sanctions, the right of trial by jury?"[32] It was an obvious question, yet one the authorities had previously managed to entirely overlook.

Patriot leaders soon found a slew of practical justifications for their newfound preference for leniency. Men like Bryan, Matlack, and McKean now pointed to the various political benefits of tolerating disaffection and, at times, even overlooking treason. At this transitional moment, as Pennsylvania's Revolutionaries increasingly shifted their attention from achieving independence to governing the independent state, they recognized that an opportunity still existed to incorporate disengaged and dissenting inhabitants and unite the people behind the new government. Thus, General Armstrong believed that only a few harsh examples should be made with regard to "the Torie affair in Philada," not only because he supported "lenity & forgiveness," but also because he recognized "that the eyes of many will be upon Government respecting it." Bryan warned the sheriffs away from pursuing confiscations and sales because he thought such actions "may be termed rigor by people in general" and alienate them from the state. Like the extreme powers of the 1777 Council of Safety and the bills of attainder, the mass confiscations that had marked the period of the occupation and lost the political affections of so many in southeast Pennsylvania were something the government eventually hoped would be left behind and forgotten. There was little to be gained by provoking fresh outrage and new accusations of tyranny. "On these grounds, we wish it to be understood," Bryan explained, "that Council and Assembly desires to avoid any noise from the people." Having survived the British invasion and firmly secured their control of the government, the Revolutionary regime was slowly moving toward the point at which silence could be seen as acquiescence rather than dissent.[33]

Chief Justice McKean suggested additional political benefits that could be derived from leniency. If the government showed itself willing to grant clemency to the accused and to pardon the convicted, the friends and relatives of those men would be encouraged to submit pleas and applications on their behalf, a process which would not only "create respect to the Rulers," as McKean put it, but necessarily force those applicants to at least nominally acknowledge the authority of the state. Furthermore, when the state granted such applications for mercy, it would "reconcile & endear men to the Government."[34] A handful of dedicated dissenters, like Quaker

Samuel Rowland Fisher, might go so far as to remain imprisoned rather than accept the new state's authority to pardon them, but they proved to be the exception rather than the rule and their stubbornness tended to annoy, rather than inspire, their allies.[35]

Disaffected and Loyalist women who had been subject to severe rhetoric and threats of reprisal or social isolation from radicals also benefited from growing tendencies toward tolerance and leniency. After a brief and sporadic period of shaming, most of the elite young women who had remained in the occupied city were reabsorbed into polite society where they mingled with their more ardent Revolutionary counterparts, continental officers, and even members of Congress. The soldiers garrisoning the reclaimed capital proved especially willing to overlook past political affiliations in the interest of securing a livelier social scene. As Mary Morris, Robert Morris's wife, observed, "our military gentlemen are too liberal to make any distinction between Whig and Tory ladies. If they make any, it is in favor of the latter." The *Pennsylvania Packet* reported in August that some delegates to Congress were to be found at balls which were "graced with Mischianza ladies equally noted for their Tory principles and their late fondness for British debauchees and macaronies." Even so outspoken a Loyalist as Rebecca Franks, who did nothing to hide her preference for the empire, was soon to be found socializing, laughing, and trading barbs and witticisms with generals of the Continental Army.[36]

Though Revolutionary radicals demanded clear, discrete, visible separation between friends and foes even in the realm of women's fashion, the reality of Revolutionary America was a complex hodgepodge of interwoven interests and motivations in which visible action only imperfectly corresponded to political affection.[37] As Timothy Pickering noted in a letter to his wife, the "high hair" which had been so publicly mocked on July 4 did not necessarily signal political allegiance and "the Whig ladies seem as fond of them ['enormous head-dresses'] as others." At the same time, shared criticism of ostentatious dress may have helped to heal the breach between the radical Patriots and their oft-derided enemies, the neutral and disaffected Quakers. Both groups frowned upon the high headdresses, which Elizabeth Drinker dismissed as "that very foolish fashion," and for at least some Revolutionaries, the Quakers now became models of virtuous republican simplicity.[38]

With a few exceptions, attempts to expel the wives of Loyalist refugees also met with great resistance. The government refused to enforce its own demands on this front and even radical leaders like Charles Willson Peale worked to prevent separate groups, such as the city militia, from taking matters into their own hands. Echoing the public and political sensitivities of other Revolutionary leaders, Peale worried that any large-scale roundup of Tory women and children "would cause much affliction and grief" and quickly generate widespread opposition among the people. Though some wives did depart and others, like Grace Galloway, suffered the pains and humiliation of seeing their family property confiscated, most disaffected and Loyalist women were able to make their peace with the Revolutionary regime and continue their lives in Philadelphia if they so chose.[39]

One particularly noteworthy, though perhaps self-serving, proponent of leniency toward dissenters and tolerance of the disaffected was Major General Benedict Arnold. Washington had sent Arnold to Philadelphia with orders "to preserve tranquility and order in the city, and give security to individuals of every class and description; restraining as far as possible, 'till the restoration of civil government, every species of persecution, insult, or abuse, either from the soldiery to the inhabitants, or among each other." Beyond simply protecting the inhabitants from harm, the Patriot leadership had a strong interest in assessing and securing any munitions, provisions, or other stores the British army might have abandoned in the city. Congress wanted immediate action taken to prevent any property which might, potentially, be subject to confiscation transported out of Philadelphia.[40] Washington appears to have been particularly sensitive to the possible "abuse" that might follow the sudden intermingling of Continental soldiers, returning Revolutionaries, and the remaining disaffected and dissenting civilians. Arnold, whose health in 1778 made him ineligible for a battlefield command, may have been chosen, in part, based on his success at preserving "tranquility and order" among prisoners, military men, and civilians at Lake Champlain in 1775. The inhabitants there had praised Arnold for the "humanity and benevolence" he demonstrated toward them as well as the "tenderness and polite treatment" he granted to captured enemy soldiers.[41]

Arnold immediately and continually ran afoul of Pennsylvania's more radical leaders, particularly council president Joseph Reed. Tasked with maintaining the peace and more committed to his own social and economic advancement than to the ideological agendas of the state's new regime, Arnold had little interest in harassing dissenting inhabitants or purifying the city's politics. Demonstrating a general disdain for the radicals' binary distinction between Patriots and traitors, he soon aligned himself with politically suspect business partners, such as Joseph Stansbury, and began his romantic pursuit of the decidedly un-Patriotic Margaret Shippen. Arnold generally waved away all suggestions that he should be more discriminating.[42]

The general also played a prominent role in welcoming disaffected and dissenting Philadelphians back into American society. This was especially apparent with regard to the elite women whose association with the British army during the occupation might, if the radicals had had their way, have led to their social ostracism. While still courting her, the Revolutionary general informed his Loyalist bride-to-be that "our difference in political sentiments will, I hope, be no bar to my happiness." He doubted the war would continue much longer and assured Peggy Shippen it was high time that "peace and domestic happiness be restored to every one," regardless of which side they had chosen in the conflict.[43] Arnold had no time for the radicals whose political rigor challenged his pursuit of tranquility and peace. "Some gentlemen . . . were offended by my paying a polite attention to the ladies of this city without first discovering if they were Whigs at bottom," he informed fellow general Nathanael Greene. "Those gentlemen who avow such illiberal sentiments I shall treat with the contempt which I think they deserve by taking no notice of them."[44] Despite the urgings of both Congress and Pennsylvania's more stringent Revolutionaries, Arnold arranged for lavish entertainments in the newly liberated city and freely invited guests with connections from across the political spectrum. "Will you not think it extraordinary," seethed Reed in November, "that General Arnold made a public entertainment the night before last, of which not only common Tory ladies, but the wives and daughters of persons proscribed by the State, and now with the enemy at New York, formed a very considerable number."[45] Arnold's disregard for the past and present political affections, if any, of his business partners, romantic pursuits, and the guests doubtless provided some social cover for others who were eager to promote unity and tranquility among their friends and neighbors in the aftermath of the occupation.

"If things proceed in the same train much longer," warned Pennsylvania's president, "I would advise every Continental officer to leave his uniform at the last stage, and procure a scarlet coat, as the only mode of insuring respect and notice."[46] Reed, among others, fought fiercely to bring Arnold down. While financial misdealing and abuse of power would ultimately become the dominant themes in attacks against the general, his failure to suitably distinguish between those the radicals saw as true, virtuous

Patriots and those they deemed disloyal and undeserving also became a point of public contention and hardened the resolve of his enemies. In January of 1779, Pennsylvania's executive council publicly denounced Arnold's behavior as "highly discouraging to those who have manifested attachment to the liberties and interests of America." They also indicted him for being "disrespectful to the supreme executive authority," which is to say, to themselves.[47] To substantiate these claims, the council provided a long list of Arnold's alleged misdeeds. The final item accused Arnold of demonstrating "discouragement and neglect" to those "who have adhered to the cause of their country," while showing favor "towards those of another character": Loyalists, dissenters, and the disaffected. The council saw his behavior in this regard as "too notorious to need proof or illustration." The same charges would be read out in the opening of Arnold's court-martial later that year.[48]

The mounting pressure for leniency and reconciliation was sometimes most apparent when the state *did* follow through in officially executing alleged traitors. The trials and executions of Abraham Carlisle and John Roberts, both elderly Quakers who confessed to collaborating with the British, laid bare the tension between, on the one hand, lingering radical pressure to unflinchingly apply the full might of the new government against those who failed to support it and, on the other, a growing desire to show leniency to all but the most virulent Loyalists. The attempt to save Carlisle and Roberts also revealed how, in the minds of thousands of Pennsylvanians, the British occupation and withdrawal signaled a new phase in the Revolution which necessitated a different approach to dissent and disaffection.

Neither of the two accused men claimed to be wholly innocent of the treasonous charges brought against them. Carlisle, a carpenter who lived in Bladen's Court off Elfreth's Alley, was employed by the British to grant or deny permits to civilians which would allow them to pass safely through British lines. Roberts, a miller from outside the city, performed duties as a civilian scout and was accused of encouraging others to enlist and of plotting, though never carrying out, the armed rescue of Henry Drinker and his fellow exiles. Both men were included in the Proclamation of Attainder issued by the Supreme Executive Council on May 8, 1778, remained in Philadelphia after the British departed, duly surrendered themselves to state authorities, were tried and convicted in late September, and executed on November 4. Of the one hundred and twenty-nine men who were charged with treason by proclamation and voluntarily handed themselves over to the authorities, only these two were put to death.[49] It remains unclear precisely why they were singled out. They were not unique in being convicted and sentenced to death, nor was their treason unusually heinous, nor did they persist in refusing their allegiance to the state after the British departed. That they were Quakers certainly counted against them in the eyes of some radical leaders. Joseph Reed suggested that if the government granted clemency to these wealthy Quakers, who had arguably betrayed not only their country but their religious pacifism by serving the British, it could hardly prosecute the many less affluent and hypocritical individuals accused of treason.[50]

Opposition to the executions was breathtaking in its extent. Some seven thousand citizens, approximately a quarter of Philadelphia's total population, signed petitions calling for clemency for one or both men. The signers included every juror who had convicted Carlisle and ten of those who had convicted Roberts, as well as McKean and the other justices of the supreme court and those of the city and county courts of Oyer and Terminer. The outcry stretched across boundaries of politics, religion, and class. Carlisle was defended by conservative icons like James Wilson, and anti-Constitutionalist leaders like Benjamin Rush and David Clymer signed the petitions, but so too did numerous members of the Patriotic Society and the militia's radical Committee of Privates. More than a dozen men who had been held prisoner in Philadelphia while Roberts and Carlisle worked for the British army spoke out on their behalf.[51]

Though they failed to prevent Carlisle's and Roberts's untimely demise, the petitions did reveal how the people's perceptions of the Revolution, and those who refused to join it, had begun to change following the British evacuation. Few of the petitioners protested the convictions themselves. The jurors who decided the verdict, the judges who determined the sentence, and the people at large generally admitted "that the unfortunate John Roberts and Abraham Carlisle, most justly merit the Sentence which the Law has lately pronounced against them." Nor was compassion the sole, or even the primary, justification offered for clemency, though Christian forgiveness and charity were certainly invoked. Rather, the petitions incorporate practical and political reasons for sparing the lives of the condemned traitors, and a key component of this reasoning was the belief that the British withdrawal signaled the beginning of a new, and permanent, period of security for the independent government. As one set of petitioners explained, "from all human Probability the British Enemy will never again visit this State, and the intestine Enemies thereof be for ever prevented doing that Mischief which a rooted and fixed Enmity to their Country would instigate them to perform."[52] With the military question settled, at least for Pennsylvania, there was no longer a need to fear the secret machinations of those who showed less than total allegiance to the Revolution. Another petition echoed this sentiment, arguing that "the only ground upon which the taking of the life of an Offender can be Justified, is the necessity of making examples to prevent the Commission of like Crimes," but since "there is no probability that the Enemy will again invade this State. . . . Examples in the present case are not absolutely Necessary." Though in the midst of an invasion and occupation, it might have been justifiable to make examples of a few foes in order to terrify the rest into submission, a tactic Washington had repeatedly embraced in trying to stop trade with the occupied city, now that the military threat had passed, presumably for good, such acts of brutality could be set aside.[53]

In light of this new Revolutionary context, the petitioners appealed to the same political logic that spurred private calls for leniency from leaders like Bryan, Armstrong, and McKean. One petition argued that "the Power and Vigour of Government" was displayed at least as much in showing mercy as in inflicting punishment and, just as Armstrong had warned that the eyes of the people would be on the government as it responded to incidents of treason, so these petitioners hoped that granting these men a pardon would convince "the World that the Conduct of these States has not proceeded from Resentment, but from the purest Principles of Liberty and Lenity." Another petition countered the calls for harsh examples to be made of offenders by asserting that a pardon would furnish "an Example to be pointed to on future Occasions" of the government's humanity, which might be of more value than an example of its unyielding commitment to the law.[54]

Other petitions displayed a growing sensitivity to the difference between, as Bryan put it, those who "threaten active mischief against the State" and the "ignorant people" whose "objections will gradually wear away"; in short, between true loyalism and disaffection. Carlisle's treason, claimed the petitioners, "was the Effect rather of an undue Attachment to his own Safety and Interest . . . than of a Malicious and deliberate Intention to aid and assist the Enemies of the United States," and Roberts had acted "under the influence of fear," rather than animosity against the nation and had since "renounced his former Connections & Attachments, and . . . will hereafter exert his many good Qualities in favor of the cause he has now adopted." Though of dubious accuracy with regard to the men's political affections toward Britain, such appeals suggest a weakening of the strict binary between friends and foes, of the belief that all opposition is essentially the same, which placed the disaffected in such an untenable position during much of the war.[55]

The Revolutionaries' slowly expanding willingness to accept leniency and reconciliation with the disaffected came at a time when new political battle lines were being drawn across the state, or rather, when the relative importance of preexisting divisions was shifting. The Revolutionaries had always been conscious of divisions within their own ranks, but so long as the future of American independence itself remained uncertain and the government unstable, and particularly while the British maintained an army within the state capital, these internal disputes were often seen as secondary to the perceived passive threat of dissenters and the active threat of the redcoats. With the British withdrawn and the new regime firmly in command, the Revolutionaries increasingly shifted their attention away from the battle for home rule and toward how their new, independent nation would be governed. The growing prominence of the struggle between the radicals and those who might, with some irony, be referred to as "Revolutionary conservatives" dramatically changed the political landscape for the disaffected in the years after the occupation.

As had been the case since the first days of the Revolution, economic choices continued to be integral facets of allegiance and division. Pennsylvania's long year as the seat of war had a devastating effect on the local economy. The prior occupations of Boston and New York had increased Philadelphia's prominence as an Atlantic port and turned the city into a key site of military industry, creating jobs and pouring money into the region. The British invasion and occupation brought those benefits to an end. The city and county of Philadelphia suffered the loss of hundreds of thousands of pounds at the hands of the redcoats, to say nothing of the damage and destruction wrought by the Patriot forces. Though the process of rebuilding created a temporary surge of new jobs in the immediate aftermath of the withdrawal, much of the wartime employment that fled the city in 1777 never returned.[56] Continental inflation worsened as Congress continued to print ever greater quantities of money. Though the economic chaos sometimes encouraged the Patriots to lash out at the disaffected, assuming that they must somehow be behind anything which harmed the nation, it also served to separate Revolutionaries into competing camps which increasingly saw each other as more important enemies.

In 1779, two organizations emerged in Philadelphia that became symbolic of the defining political fault line in Pennsylvania. In January, conservative opponents of the state constitution formed the Republican Society and denounced the existing government as tyrannical. A few months later, their radical opponents responded by creating the Constitutional Society. The two societies differed in a host of ways. The Republicans, led by men such as Robert Morris, James Wilson, Benjamin Rush, and Thomas Mifflin, tended to be wealthier than their opponents. Quakers, Anglicans, Lutherans, and followers of various neutral and pacifist sects all found a home among them. The Constitutional Society, which included Thomas Paine, Charles Willson Peale, and Timothy Matlack, was primarily composed of middling sort radicals, such as shopkeepers and the less affluent artisans, and largely dominated by Presbyterians. Pre-Revolutionary leaders, both political and economic, tended to join with the Republicans while those who had previously struggled to find a voice in colonial Pennsylvania filled the ranks of the Constitutionalists.[57] Yet both societies shared a commitment to American independence and were led by staunch Revolutionaries. As these emerging parties clashed on the political battlefield and ever more Philadelphians joined their ranks, the binary distinction between "Whig and Tory," which had trapped the disaffected in an intolerable no-man's-land, was often replaced by the division between "Republican and Constitutionalist." Observing the new parties take shape, Silas Deane lamented that the Revolutionaries in Philadelphia were "quarrelling among ourselves, and can scarcely be constrained from plunging our swords in each other's bosoms" while their "common enemy" carried on the war elsewhere. Alexander Graydon acknowledged the distracting nature of this new struggle, contrasting "the greater contest with the mother country" with what he dismissed as "domestic broils."[58]

This rising political system eased the plight of the disaffected in ways beyond simply dividing their potential oppressors against one another. The Constitutionalists were more likely to retain the strict political dichotomy which pitted the virtuous, proconstitution, "People" against a corrupt and muddled combination of moderates, neutrals, and Loyalists, though, as seen above, even devout Constitutionalist leaders like Bryan and Matlack became more open to leniency in the wake of the occupation. For their part, the Republicans soon came to see the disaffected as a potential source of political power and actively courted them. While the Constitutionalists sought to strengthen the Test Act and strip dissenters of their rights, the Republicans attempted to protect the interests of pacifists and mild dissenters in the hopes of gaining their support at the ballot box.[59] Republican Benjamin Rush expressed hope that, since the British had failed to offer them any relief, those "men who once appeared neutral, or lukewarm in the cause" might join his party in resisting the Constitutionalists, seeing it as their "only means of defending and securing themselves."[60] Graydon unambiguously recorded that "to counteract the constitutionalists, the disaffected to the revolution were invited to fall into the republican ranks." He was also invited to join but declined, in part because he "did not fully relish the policy of courting the disaffected, and those who had played a safe and calculating game."[61]

The disaffected were also aided by the emergence and growth of further divisions among the defenders of the radical state constitution, most notably around issues of militia service and economic policy. The economic instability following the occupation, and particularly the collapse of the Continental currency, repeatedly put radicals from the lower economic strata, often led by the militia, at odds with the middling sort radicals who dominated groups like the Constitutional Society. The militia and their allies often bore the brunt of runaway inflation and believed that neutral nonparticipants and those wealthy enough to hire substitutes to serve in their stead were treating them "with Indignity and Contempt." In response, they demanded more immediate and drastic interventions than the Constitutionalist leadership, which was increasingly concerned with public perception and social stability, was willing to countenance. The failure of price controls on essential goods and the weakness of the militia laws planted a wedge between the radical leadership and their political base. The government's unexpected leniency toward the disaffected and its refusal to wield the full retributive weight of the law also enraged many militiamen, who suspected that dissenters and pacifists were somehow behind the economic collapse.[62]

Consequently, Constitutionalist leaders often found themselves unable to control their supporters in the streets, to the detriment of their own political aspirations and Revolutionary unity more generally. This problem notoriously came to a head little more than a year after the British withdrawal in the infamous "Fort Wilson Riot," an incident that highlighted both the Constitutionalists' inability to sway the city militia and the growing significance of internal divides among the Revolutionaries. Though the militia's stated intent on October 4, 1779, was "that of sending away the wives and children of those men who had gone with the British," an objective which implies a continued focus on the division between Revolutionaries and supposed Loyalists, the events of the day suggest more complicated motivations. The militia did not in fact arrest any women or children. Instead, they apprehended a small group of men, most of whom were quite wealthy, including Henry Drinker's brother John Drinker, whose recent offenses involved violating price controls, not service to the British. Their most significant target became Republican stalwart James Wilson. Wilson had defended accused traitors in the courts but was himself unquestionably a Revolutionary, having signed the Declaration of Independence and served as a member of the Continental Congress. Though it's entirely possible that capturing Wilson was not their original intention, the militiamen quickly warmed to the idea, going so far as to release all their earlier targets before reaching his home.[63]

Charles Willson Peale, a prominent Constitutionalist, repeatedly, if futilely, attempted to obstruct the series of events that led to the violent clash at Wilson's home, joining with fellow radical leaders to "use every argument in their power to prevent any proceedings in that vain and dangerous undertaking." Joseph Reed himself, aided by Timothy Matlack, led the city's light cavalry in forcibly bringing the riot to an end, killing several militiamen in the process. Benedict Arnold made an attempt to assist, but Reed refused his help, knowing that the radical elements among the militia would only be further incensed by the general's presence.[64] Wilson was only one of many active and noteworthy Revolutionaries who found themselves in open conflict with groups of radicals. Robert Morris, Whitehead Humphreys, and Arnold himself, all of whom, at that point, were regarded as strong advocates of independence, were subjected to the sorts of attacks, both political and physical, once more closely associated with so-called "Tories" and Loyalists.[65] Only days after the attack on Wilson, Arnold requested a new personal guard made up of Continental soldiers; he no longer trusted the militia of Pennsylvania to protect him.[66]

Incidents like the Fort Wilson Riot and the radical government's general inability to stabilize the economy alienated the electorate and enervated support for the Constitutionalists among the lower sort radicals. As a result, beginning in 1780, the tides of political power in Pennsylvania shifted decisively toward the Republicans and continued to do so through what remained of the war.[67] The lower sort radicals who maintained the grandest democratic goals for the government and who were most willing to actively pursue and persecute political dissenters often found themselves isolated and abandoned, rejected by more lenient conservatives and disavowed by more cautious and affluent Constitutionalists. Left out of the new regime's emerging political divide, they marked the emergence of a new class of disaffected, defined by domestic politics and economic position rather than loyalty toward Britain.[68]

EPILOGUE

Elizabeth and Henry Drinker remained in Philadelphia. They and their children were eventually accepted by the American republic, though the process was a slow one. Henry Drinker maintained his refusal to serve in the state militia and the family steadfastly rejected taxes which they saw as financing the war. For these violations they were repeatedly fined by the state and Continental governments. As the Drinkers also refused to voluntarily pay these fines, their property was regularly subject to seizure by various officials. Over the course of one year Elizabeth recorded the loss of eleven pewter dishes of various sizes, five tables, two mirrors, a dozen chairs, a pair of brass andirons, and two brass kettles.[1] Though the fines were a regular inconvenience, such hardships paled in comparison to the forced exile and threats of violence which were now behind them. The family lost more property to riotous Revolutionaries following Cornwallis's surrender at Yorktown in 1781. Many Quaker homes were assaulted by Patriot crowds on October 24 for failing to celebrate the American victory. For nearly three hours men in the street hurled insults and stones against the Drinker house. The family "had near 70 panes of Glass broken [and] the sash lights and two panels of the front parlor broke in pieces." Unsatisfied with mere exterior damage, the crowd eventually smashed through the front door and threw yet more stones into the house but, thankfully, did not attempt to enter.

Elizabeth maintained some degree of contact with the British major who had lived in her home for the latter half of the occupation. Her diary mentions receiving letters from him at the end of 1778 and early in 1781. She leaves no record of what the letters contained, if there had been others, or if she ever replied. In the fall of 1781 Elizabeth received news that Crammond had died of disease in British-occupied New York. She recorded then that the major had "behav'd so in our Family as to gain our esteem." Then, in 1795, a curious young man arrived on Elizabeth's doorstep. His name was Henry Sibble. His mother, Jane, had been a servant in the Drinker home in the 1770s and during the occupation had, perhaps unbeknownst to the rest of the household, formed a bond with Philip George Sibble, one of Major Crammond's Hessian orderlies. When the redcoats departed for New York, Philip Sibble deserted the army and set off to peacefully make his fortune in America with Jane by his side. He eventually became a physician, had a son, and settled in Easton, Pennsylvania, where, according to Elizabeth, he "sells medicine, and makes money fast, German like." In visiting the Drinker home, young Henry Sibble came to see the place where his own story had begun, seventeen years earlier, during the British occupation of Philadelphia.[2]

The Drinker family was spared from the horrors of the yellow fever epidemic which ravaged Philadelphia in 1793, killing roughly 10 percent of the population. Having fled to a country home outside the city, they waited out the disease in relative safety. Elizabeth marveled at the seemingly endless reports of death and dislocation that came to her almost daily: a neighbor in Chestnut Street who had tended, lost, and buried five members of his own family before the disease took him too; "40 odd burials in the Lutherine burying ground and upwards of 30 in the Potters-field, on third day last"; "since second day, morning, 390 or upwards have been bury'd"; "upwards of 20,000 had left their dwellings, and retired into the Country." She recorded name after name in her diary, friends, neighbors, persons of interest, and strangers, but never a name from her own family; "may we be humble, and thankful for favours received."[3]

Elizabeth continued her diary, on and off, for most of her life, though rarely with the regularity and detail which marked the months of the British occupation. She was a voracious reader at times in her later years, consuming books of all sorts and making use of Philadelphia's libraries. "I read a little of most things," she declared, and she often recorded her impressions in her diary. In the first half of 1803, along with biographies of Milton and Louis XVI, the Canterbury Tales, and numerous other works, she read Rousseau's *Letters of an Italian Nun* ("a flowery writer, but a man of bad principles"), William Godwin's *Things as They Are* ("The Story is very interesting—but I like not the Author nor his principles"), and *The Life, Adventures, and Opinions of Col. George Hanger, Written by Himself* ("very proper to light a fire with"). She wrote that, in many ways, Mary Wollstonecraft's *The Rights of Women* "speaks my mind," though she was "not for quite so much independence."[4]

Elizabeth Drinker died on November 24, 1807, at the age of 73. She left five living children and nineteen grandchildren. Henry Drinker passed away two years later at the age of 76.[5]

James Allen's story ended far sooner. The events of the occupation had broken him in more ways than one. Being charged with treason was among the least of his worries, and indeed, nothing came of it. His immediate concerns were more personal than political. "Our family," he wrote, "is totally unhinged." His brother Andrew was preparing to travel to England; William remained an officer with the British army; John was dead. One sister had fled with the redcoats to New York; another was just returned to Philadelphia from exile in New Jersey. James himself hoped to put both the conflict and continent behind him by traveling to France, but illness made this impractical. He complained of "a collection of wind in the upper part of the Chest, accompanied with a shortness of breath, & a weariness." "I am so reduced that my acquaintance do not readily recognize me," he wrote in July, and blamed the illness on "the uneasiness of my mind at the state of public affairs & the distress of my family." Unable to cross the Atlantic, he planned to return to the countryside and recover there, but soon became too sick for even that short journey. He died, in Philadelphia, on September 19, 1778, at the age of 37.[6]

Individuals like the Drinkers and Allen proved to be historically awkward for those, like John Adams, who preferred to remember the Americans of the Revolution as being neatly divided into mutually exclusive political camps and, within those camps, wholly unified in their objectives. Adams liked to discuss "the people" of Revolutionary America in broad terms. "The Revolution was in the minds and hearts of the people," he wrote to Hezekiah Niles in 1818. It was a "radical change in the principles, opinions, sentiments, and affections of the people," a change which was "common to all." In Adams's mind the transformation was "perhaps a singular example in the history of mankind," remarkable both for its totality and the way it simultaneously affected nearly all of the vastly different peoples of America. "Thirteen clocks were made to strike together," he declared, "a perfection of mechanism, which no artist had ever before effected."[7]

Doubtless Adams's soaring vision of the Revolution was shared by many of "the people" who lived through it. Their conception of their "duties and obligations," of their material interests, of the British Empire, and their place in it changed, and that change in understanding led them to change the world. They fought, in various ways and for a variety of objectives: liberty (both political and economic), independence, wealth, power, religion, and an empire of their own in the New World. For these goals, among others, many of "the people" of America rose up and, at great cost, broke the chains which bound them to Great Britain and established a new nation. Their story has become the traditional narrative of the nation's founding.

Yet the Drinkers, the Allens, and many others remind us that theirs was not the only story; they were not the only "people." Adams's miraculous moment has been complicated in many ways over the years as we have come to realize what a diverse and divided group "the people" really were. Alongside the Patriots, who strove for independence, were the Loyalists, who resisted it, whose conception of their "duties and obligations" had not changed. Interwoven with and apart from these two sides were also the women and slaves of America, on whom society imposed duties and obligations of a much more immediate and intimate nature than those that bound the colonies to Great Britain. Around about them all dwelt peoples whose ancestors lived in America long before the age of British colonization. Certainly they did not all experience the same mental revolution. Rather, these so-called minorities often carried out revolutions of their own, changes in their hearts and minds, in their understandings of their duties and obligations, and, in some cases, in their material circumstances. Their stories are entwined with, but still distinct from, the traditional Patriot narrative of national independence.[8]

Yet perhaps the story of the Patriots, of those who sacrificed to secure American liberty from the empire, is itself a minority story. And perhaps it is the story of a smaller minority than we often imagine. For aside from the substantial portion of Americans, like the Drinkers, who were openly neutral, there were some whose apparent commitment to the Revolution was only nominal, made in response to pressure or persecution. Others, like Allen, stood with the Patriots in 1765 or 1774, when the goal of the Revolution was liberty *within* the empire, but abandoned their ranks in 1776 and after, in the midst of a long war for freedom *from* the empire.

Pennsylvania certainly held many such people, though it took an invasion by the British army for the full scope of their disaffection to become apparent. Before the invasion, the Patriots of Pennsylvania faced constant difficulties in creating a militia, in conforming commercial transactions to the virtuous model of republicanism, in guaranteeing politically responsible speech and writing, and even in securing a vote for independence itself. The months of the invasion and occupation proved that much of the unity and consent they had assembled was a sham. Put forward out of fear, convenience, or avarice, it melted away along with the Revolutionaries' ability to forcibly control the region: the militia collapsed, the countryside rushed to trade with the enemy, and wherever the British could reach it seemed that the Patriots had no friends left.

Those months are revealing of more than just the extent of disaffection in Pennsylvania. Boycotts and militias could theoretically demonstrate the unity of the people, giving ordinary Americans ways to express their dedication to the cause in languages everyone could understand. For the Revolutionaries, such displays of unity helped to justify the Revolution and the new, independent governments it established on the basis of popular consent. Yet, where commitment to the cause was shallow or primarily the result of external pressures, the desire to see loyalty and commitment manifested through visible, tangible actions proved to be a double-edged sword. Because the Patriots believed they needed a united, virtuous people to legitimate their Revolution, they placed tremendous and sometimes coercive pressure on their fellow colonists to join them. In so doing they inadvertently set themselves up to suffer sudden and catastrophic reversals when that pressure was removed and the people were freed to abandon the cause they had never wholeheartedly embraced. Such was the case following the British capture of Philadelphia.

The brutality of the Revolutionary response, mixed as it was with accusations of high treason, demonstrates how threatening these reversals could seem to a new nation that claimed to rule in accordance with the will of the people. In the attempt to preserve their vision of liberty, the Patriots at times imbued individuals and committees with tyrannical powers. Disaffection was most dangerous to the Revolution, and thus most likely to be persecuted without mercy, when the Revolutionary regimes lost their monopolies on coercive force and so strove, in Washington's words, "to make examples" out of the few dissenters over whom they could exercise power. The British evacuation of Philadelphia, perceived as a signal that the Revolutionary governments in Pennsylvania were finally secure in their control of the state, opened the door for an eventual integration of dissent and disaffection. Government by "the people" could be tolerant once the people were less threatening. The passage of time and the absence of a competing political power made the explicit and expressed consent of the populace less important to the legitimacy of the regime and so freed the people from the worst of the pressures to consent.

The lens of disaffection also shows the awkward and at times contradictory position the British found themselves in while occupying Philadelphia. Because the region was disaffected from the Revolution, rather than truly loyal to the empire, the British were able to purchase considerable material support but unable to inspire declarations of allegiance or secure much-needed enlistments in the army. Choices which won the affections of the surrounding countryside, and so threatened the Continentals at Valley Forge, could alienate inhabitants within the occupied city itself. Such was the case in Howe's refusal to reestablish the colonial paper currency and his hesitancy to launch a more forceful campaign in 1778. The local farmers benefited from the flow of specie and were freed from the worst rigors of war, while the people within Philadelphia faced bankruptcy and found themselves trapped in a besieged city with thousands of idle soldiers. Loyalists demanded a more rigorous enforcement of the oaths of allegiance, yet the Revolutionaries' experience suggests that this was precisely the course of action that would have further alienated the disaffected. Though the people's indifference and antipathy severely undercut the Revolutionaries' position in the state, it did surprisingly little to further the aims of the empire. The incessant plundering, burning, and brutality of the army while in the city certainly did nothing to help its situation.

Southeastern Pennsylvania, with its fragmented society and long history of pacifism, was a particularly rich site for this study. Further research is needed to determine to what extent the role of disaffection there was typical or exceptional for Revolutionary America as a whole. Evidence from New York suggests it was not unique.[9] The war in the South, complicated as it was by the ubiquity of slavery, a greater history of violence, and the full intervention of other European powers, may be a particularly challenging and rewarding place for an analysis of disaffection.[10] The understudied occupation of Charleston and Britain's experience in attempting to restore civil government in Georgia are promising points of comparison. There too one finds environments where neither the Patriots nor the British could exercise complete control and times when authority, and hence the benefits of allegiance, shifted suddenly from one side to the other. This study suggests that those are the times and places where disaffection is most visible.[11]

Ironically, the degree of uniformity that the Patriots so dearly desired, that their acts of coercion were meant to create, and that Adams would later fondly, if falsely, imagine to have existed, proved to be wholly unnecessary in the end. The success of the Revolution and the longevity of the nation that eventually arose from it demonstrate that new nations, even new republics, can in fact be secured and established without the unified, expressed consent of the people. Loyalism and disaffection can be overcome, or at least overlooked. Some hearts and minds were altered of their own accord in the fifteen years before Lexington and Concord; others were made to yield, were conquered, through social pressure, fines, threats, or outright coercion; and still others were simply forgotten, their discordant notes and suspicious silences lost amid the historic echoes of Adams's thirteen perfectly synchronized clocks. We would do well to restore that disharmony to our memory of the Revolution.[12]

NOTES

Introduction

Note to epigraph: Henry Melchior Muhlenberg, *The Journals of Henry Melchior Muhlenberg* (Philadelphia: Evangelical Lutheran Ministerium of Pennsylvania and Adjacent States, 1942), 1:107.

1. For the full text of the law, see "An Act to Empower the Supreme Executive Council of This Commonwealth to Provide for the Security Thereof in Special Cases Where no Provision is Already Made by Law," *The Statutes at Large of Pennsylvania from 1682 to 1801* (Harrisburg, PA: Wm. Stanley Ray, 1903), 9:139.

2. This vignette is based on a number of sources, including Elizabeth Sandwith Drinker, *The Diary of Elizabeth Drinker*, ed. Elaine Forman Crane (Boston: Northeastern University Press, 1991), 1:227–229; Nicholas B. Wainwright and Sarah Logan Fisher, "'A Diary of Trifling Occurrences': Philadelphia, 1776–1778," *Pennsylvania Magazine of History and Biography* 82, no. 4 (October 1958): 444–447 (hereafter cited in notes as *PMHB*); James Donald Anderson, "Thomas Wharton, Exile in Virginia, 1777–1778," *Virginia Magazine of History and Biography* 89, no. 4 (October 1981), 427–428; John Pemberton, *The Life and Travels of John Pemberton, a Minister of the Gospel of Christ* (London: Charles Gilpin, 1844), 72–74; "An Act to Empower the Supreme Executive Council," 9:139; Thomas Gilpin, *Exiles in Virginia: With Observations on the Conduct of the Society of Friends During the Revolutionary War, Comprising the Official Papers of the Government Relating to That Period, 1777–1778* (Philadelphia, 1848), 65; *Colonial Records of Pennsylvania or Minutes of the Supreme Executive Council of Pennsylvania, from Its Organization to the Termination of the Revolution* (Harrisburg, PA: Theo. Fenn, 1852), 11:287–289; *Journals of the Continental Congress, 1774–1789* (hereafter cited as *JCC*), ed. Worthington C. Ford et al. (Washington, DC: US Government Printing Office, 1904–1937), 8:694–695. The descriptions of the flowering trees in Drinker's garden come from her descriptions of that space in the 1790s, and so are meant to offer a general sense of the aesthetics rather than a specific depiction of the colors in 1777. On the house and garden see Elizabeth Sandwith Drinker, *The Diary of Elizabeth Drinker: The Life Cycle of an Eighteenth-Century Woman*, ed. Elaine Forman Crane, abridged ed. (Philadelphia: University of Pennsylvania Press, 2010), 162; Elizabeth Sandwith Drinker, *Extracts from the Journal of Elizabeth Drinker, from 1759 to 1807, A.D.*, ed. Henry D. Biddle (Philadelphia: J. B. Lippincott, 1889), 27; and Elizabeth Evans, *Weathering the Storm: Women of the American Revolution* (New York: Charles Scribner's Sons, 1975), 152–153.

3. Some recent examples include Maya Jasanoff, *Liberty's Exiles: American Loyalists in the Revolutionary World* (New York: Knopf, 2011); Thomas B. Allen, *Tories: Fighting for the King in*

America's First Civil War (New York: Harper, 2010); Joseph S. Tiedemann, *The Other Loyalists: Ordinary People, Royalism, and the Revolution in the Middle Colonies, 1763–1787* (Albany: State University of New York Press, 2009); Ruma Chopra, *Unnatural Rebellion: Loyalists in New York City During the Revolution* (Charlottesville: University of Virginia Press, 2011); Douglas MacGregor, "Double Dishonor: Loyalists on the Middle Frontier," and William Pencak, "Out of Many, One: Pennsylvania's Loyalist Clergy in the American Revolution," both in *Pennsylvania's Revolution*, ed. William Pencak (University Park: Pennsylvania State University Press, 2010); Robert M. Calhoon et al., *Tory Insurgents: The Loyalist Perception and Other Essays*, rev. and expanded ed. (Columbia: University of South Carolina Press, 2010). Older works of particular relevance here include Paul Hubert Smith, *Loyalists and Redcoats: A Study in British Revolutionary Policy* (Chapel Hill: University of North Carolina Press, 1964); Wallace Brown, *The King's Friends: The Composition and Motives of the American Loyalist Claimants* (Providence, RI: Brown University Press, 1965); Wilbur Henry Siebert, *The Loyalists of Pennsylvania* (Boston: Gregg Press, 1972).

4. Donald Johnson argues that American histories have often obscured all but the most infamous opponents of the Revolution, preferring to depict a "total break with Britain" rather than the ambiguous, complex reality of the situation during the 1760s and 1770s. See Donald F. Johnson, "Forgiving and Forgetting in Postrevolutionary America," in *Experiencing Empire: Power, People, and Revolution in Early America*, ed. Patrick Griffin (Charlottesville: University of Virginia Press, 2017), 171–173.

5. John W. Shy, *A People Numerous and Armed: Reflections on the Military Struggle for American Independence* (New York: Oxford University Press, 1976), 236.

6. Anne M. Ousterhout makes a compelling case for the utility of the term "disaffected" over "loyalist" in describing much of the opposition to the Revolution in Pennsylvania: see Anne M. Ousterhout, *A State Divided: Opposition in Pennsylvania to the American Revolution* (New York: Greenwood Press, 1987), 5. However, while Ousterhout tends to portray loyalism as one subcategory of disaffection, I use the words to describe related but distinct political sentiments and affections. A vast number of disengaged and disinterested Americans were not, by any meaningful definition of the term, "Revolutionary," but that does not mean they were Loyalist or felt any significant obligation, duty, or attachment to Great Britain. Setting the category of the disaffected not just in between but *apart from* both the Revolutionaries and the Loyalists is essential if we are to engage in the worthwhile efforts of identifying their part in the Revolution and seeing the Revolution through their eyes.

Sung Bok Kim presents a compelling depiction of the plight and perspective of the disaffected in one county in New York. See Sung Bok Kim, "The Limits of Politicization in the American Revolution: The Experience of Westchester County, New York," *Journal of American History* 80 (December 1, 1993): 868–889. Ron Hoffman makes similar use of the term in wrestling with the manifold complexities of the war in the American South, defining the "disaffected" or "disinterested" as those "people who clearly opposed making an appreciable sacrifice for either belligerent." See Ronald Hoffman, "The 'Disaffected' in the Revolutionary South," in *The American Revolution*, ed. Alfred F. Young (DeKalb: Northern Illinois University Press, 1976), 273–316.

Holger Hoock, in his work on violence in the Revolution, recognizes these people by noting the Revolutionaries' antipathy toward the "as-yet-uncommitted" and persecution of anyone who was "not explicitly a Patriot." The following pages affirm Hoock's assertions about the ubiquity and political importance of Revolutionary violence. Holger Hoock, *Scars of Independence: America's Violent Birth* (New York: Crown, 2017), 18.

7. On Americans' strong and long-lived attachment to the king see Brendan McConville, *The King's Three Faces: The Rise and Fall of Royal America, 1688–1776* (Chapel Hill: University of North Carolina Press, 2006).

8. James Allen, "Diary of James Allen, Esq., of Philadelphia, Counsellor-at-Law, 1770–1778," *PMHB* 9, no. 2 (July 1885): 186.

9. James Allen, "Diary of James Allen, Esq., of Philadelphia, Counsellor-at-Law, 1770–1778 (concluded)," *PMHB* 9, no. 4 (January 1886): 427.

10. "John Adams to Thomas Jefferson," August 24, 1815, in John Adams, Thomas Jefferson, and Abigail Adams, *The Adams-Jefferson Letters: The Complete Correspondence Between Thomas Jefferson and Abigail and John Adams*, ed. Lester J. Cappon (Chapel Hill: University of North Carolina Press, 1959), 2:455.

11. Shy, *A People Numerous and Armed*, 2. For a long time, historians of the Revolution seemed content to follow Adams's suggestion and limit their explorations of the meaning and nature of the Revolution to the years before the war. Consider T. H. Breen's invaluable association between the marketplace and politics or, more recently, his depiction of American patriots as violent "insurgents." Both themes play important roles in the story of the occupation, a period when market exchanges with the city were granted extreme political significance and when the Patriots' ability to deploy coercive violence rose and fell wildly. Yet Breen closes out both *The Marketplace of Revolution* (Oxford: Oxford University Press, 2004) and *American Insurgents, American Patriots* (New York: Hill and Wang, 2010) just as the war opens.

Studies of Pennsylvania's fractured political nature, and of Revolutionary cities across the colonies, all too often did the same. Richard Ryerson's *The Revolution Is Now Begun: The Radical Committees of Philadelphia, 1765–1776* (Philadelphia: University of Pennsylvania Press, 1978); David Hawke's *In the Midst of a Revolution* (Philadelphia: University of Pennsylvania Press, 1961); Gary Nash's seminal *The Urban Crucible: The Northern Seaports and the Origins of the American Revolution* (Cambridge, MA: Harvard University Press, 1979); and Benjamin Carp's more recent *Rebels Rising: Cities and the American Revolution* (New York: Oxford University Press, 2007) all set out frameworks and insights without which this book would have been impossible and which, I hope, it carries forward. Yet all brought their analyses to a close around 1776.

The general, though by no means universal, tendency to see the Declaration of Independence or, in studies of Pennsylvania, the 1776 state constitution as a definitive endpoint for analysis risks portraying the War for Independence as a qualitatively distinct period of the Revolution, one not subject to the same transformative forces which had been working on society up to that point. Thankfully, the war itself has garnered greater attention from social and political historians of late, and it is hoped that the pages which follow will join with other new examinations of how the armed struggle changed, and was changed by, society. Of particular note is Robert G. Parkinson's study of how the war years shaped what the "common cause" of the Revolution was and how Americans described and understood it. See Parkinson, *The Common Cause: Creating Race and Nation in the American Revolution* (Chapel Hill: University of North Carolina Press, 2016). While Parkinson argues that studying the experiences of the war is crucial for recognizing the ways racial understandings shaped the "common cause" for white Patriots, this book points to the same period to argue that, even among white Americans, the cause was often less "common" than our traditional narratives suggest.

12. Gordon Wood, *The Creation of the American Republic, 1776–1787* (Chapel Hill: University of North Carolina Press, 1969), 53, 57–58, 61–63; John Adams, "Novanglus," in *The Works of John*

Adams, Second President of the United States: With a Life of the Author, Notes and Illustrations, ed. Charles Francis Adams, 10 vols. (Boston: Charles C. Little and James Brown, 1851), 4:79.

13. The nation's recent military ventures in the Middle East have prompted renewed focus on the revolutionary conflict both by members of the military and historians who look for modern-day lessons or comparisons to America's founding war. For example see Breen, *American Insurgents, American Patriots*; Paul D. Montanus, "A Failed Counterinsurgency Strategy: The British Southern Campaign, 1780–1781: Are There Lessons for Today?" in *USAWC Strategy Research Project* (Carlisle, PA: US Army War College, 2005); William R. Polk, *Violent Politics: A History of Insurgency, Terrorism, and Guerrilla War, from the American Revolution to Iraq* (New York: Harper, 2007); Michael Rose, *Washington's War: Insurgency Warfare from the American Revolution to Iraq* (New York: Pegasus, 2009).

14. Eyal Benvenisti succinctly summarizes the modern consensus on the meaning of "occupation" in defining it as "the effective control of a power (be it one or more states or an international organization, such as the United Nations) over a territory to which that power has no sovereign title, without the volition of the sovereign of that territory," noting that "the foundation upon which the entire law of occupation is based is the principle of inalienability of sovereignty through the actual or threatened use of force." Eyal Benvenisti, *The International Law of Occupation* (Princeton, NJ: Princeton University Press, 2004), 4–5. See also Gerhard von Glahn, *The Occupation of Enemy Territory: A Commentary on the Law and Practice of Belligerent Occupation* (Minneapolis: University Of Minnesota Press, 1957); and Peter M. R. Stirk, *The Politics of Military Occupation* (Edinburgh: Edinburgh University Press, 2009).

15. As the modern language of "occupation" was not available to them, contemporaries generally said that the British "took possession" of Philadelphia. For example, Joseph Stansbury rhymed "when the British Troops first took Possession / It [colonial currency] pass'd as formerly by your Concession" in a poem to General Howe; and one of John Watson's American subjects recalled the time "When our own troops took possession of the city." See Joseph Stansbury and Jonathan Odell, "The Petition of Philadelphia to Sir William Howe," in *The Loyal Verses of Joseph Stansbury and Doctor Jonathan Odell Relating to the American Revolution*, ed. Winthrop Sargent (Albany, NY: J. Munsell, 1860), 17; "Recollections of the Occupation of Philadelphia by the British Forces in 1777 and 78," in John F. Watson, Historical Collections (Am 3013), 1823, 402, Historical Society of Pennsylvania (hereafter HSP). See also "A State of the Circumstances of Philadelphia When the British Troops Took Possession, &ca," George Sackville Germain Papers, William L. Clements Library, University of Michigan (hereafter WCL).

16. "An Elector," *Pennsylvania Gazette*, May 15, 1776.

17. Hawke, *In the Midst of a Revolution*, 44–45; Joseph S. Tiedemann provides a similar description of New York in *Reluctant Revolutionaries: New York City and the Road to Independence, 1763–1776* (Ithaca, NY: Cornell University Press, 2008).

18. "Remarks on the Instructions," *American Archives*, ed. Peter Force and M. St. Clair Clarke, 4th ser. (Washington, DC: M. St. Clair Clarke and Peter Force, 1840), 3:1793.

19. Hawke, *In the Midst of a Revolution*, 33; Ousterhout, *A State Divided*, 130–131.

20. J. Allen, "Diary of James Allen," 187.

21. Hawke, *In the Midst of a Revolution*, 59–61.

22. *Journals of the American Congress: From 1774 to 1788* (Washington, DC: Way and Gideon, 1823), 1:839; Hawke, *In the Midst of a Revolution*, 93–94; Ryerson, *The Revolution Is Now Begun*, 238–239.

23. Ousterhout, *A State Divided*, 134.

24. Ousterhout, *A State Divided*, 153; Robert Brunhouse, *Counter-Revolution in Pennsylvania* (Harrisburg: Pennsylvania Historical Commission, 1942), 21; Ryerson, *The Revolution Is Now Begun*, 234n149.

25. Ousterhout, *A State Divided*, 153–154.

Chapter 1. Consent

Note to epigraph: "An Act to Empower the Supreme Executive Council of This Commonwealth to Provide for the Security Thereof in Special Cases Where no Provision is Already Made by Law," *The Statutes at Large of Pennsylvania from 1682 to 1801*, 9:139.

1. J. Allen, "Diary of James Allen," 179, 185–186; "James Allen," in *Lawmaking and Legislators in Pennsylvania: A Biographical Dictionary*, vol. 3, *Lawmaking and Legislators in Pennsylvania: 1757–1775*, ed. Craig W. Horle, Joseph S. Foster, and Laurie M. Wolfe (Philadelphia: University of Pennsylvania Press, 1991), 225.

2. J. Allen, "Diary of James Allen," 186.

3. Hawke, *In the Midst of a Revolution*, 33, 59–61; Ousterhout, *A State Divided*, 130–131, 153–154; Ryerson, *The Revolution Is Now Begun*, 146–147, 234n149; Brunhouse, *Counter-Revolution in Pennsylvania*, 21; "Votes of the Assembly," *Pennsylvania Archives*, 8th ser., 8:7586 (September 26, 1776).

4. "To Samuel Washington," in *The Papers of George Washington, Revolutionary War Series*, ed. Philander D. Chase, 21 vols. (Charlottesville: University of Virginia Press, 1997), 7:369–370 (hereafter *PGW*).

5. Wallace Brown, *The King's Friends: The Composition and Motives of the American Loyalist Claimants* (Providence, RI: Brown University Press, 1965), 131, 138, 145–146, 137. Brown notes that a mere .07 percent of the population of Pennsylvania appear as claimants, one of the smallest percentages of any colony, whereas claims from neighboring New York and New Jersey represent .54 percent and .19 percent of their populations, respectively.

6. Wood, *Creation of the American Republic*, 55.

7. *Pennsylvania Journal*, August 5 and 20, 1774.

8. Drinker's observations were eventually published, with a note from the printer, in the *Pennsylvania Journal*. He subsequently had them printed as a separate pamphlet: John Drinker, *Observations on the Late Popular Measures, Offered to the Serious Consideration of the Sober Inhabitants of Pennsylvania* (Philadelphia: Printed for "A Tradesman," 1774), 3, 5, 20; also see the *Pennsylvania Journal*, August 5 and 20, 1774. For an example of the sort of "scandalous handbills" Drinker was referring to, see Committee for Tarring and Feathering, *To the Delaware Pilots* (Philadelphia, 1773), Early American Imprints, ser. 1.

9. *Rivington's New-York Gazetteer*, July 7 and 14, 1774. Also see Anne M. Ousterhout's analysis of the state of the press in Philadelphia in 1774: Ousterhout, *A State Divided*, 67.

10. *Pennsylvania Evening Post*, November 16, 1776.

11. On Benjamin Towne, the politically flexible printer of the *Evening Post*, see Dwight L. Teeter, "Benjamin Towne: The Precarious Career of a Persistent Printer," *PMHB* 89, no. 3 (July 1965): 318, 322; Ousterhout, *A State Divided*, 60 and 96n12.

12. "An Anxious By-Stander" also devoted a few lines to carefully questioning Congress's timing with regard to the boycott, suggesting that since it would punish merchants who had

placed orders prior to the legislation going into effect, it amounted to an ex post facto law that punished the innocent along with the guilty. An Anxious By-Stander, *Pennsylvania Gazette*, January 4, 1775.

13. Philadelphus, *Pennsylvania Gazette*, January 11, 1775.

14. "An Ordinance for punishing persons guilty of certain offences therein mentioned against the United States Of America," *American Archives*, 5th ser., 2:37–38 (September 12, 1776).

15. Anne M. Ousterhout, "Controlling the Opposition in Pennsylvania During the American Revolution," *PMHB* 105, no. 1 (January 1981): 9.

16. "Votes of the Assembly," *Pennsylvania Archives*, 8th ser., 8:7586 (September 26, 1776); Ousterhout, "Controlling the Opposition," 9.

17. "Minutes of a Meeting at the Indian Queen, 1776," *Pennsylvania Archives*, 1st ser., 5:73–75; Ousterhout, *A State Divided*, 280.

18. *Pennsylvania Archives*, 1st ser., 5:94–95, 98–99, 106, and 145.

19. Christopher Marshall, *Passages from the Remembrancer of Christopher Marshall*, ed. William Duane Jr. (Philadelphia: James Crissy, 1839), 24 (May 2, 1775).

20. Ibid., 35 (July 17, 1775).

21. Ibid., 86–87 (June 10, 1776).

22. Christopher Marshall, Diaries, January 9, 1776, Christopher Marshall Papers (hereafter Marshall Diaries), HSP.

23. James Allen, "Diary of James Allen (continued)," *PMHB* 9, no. 3 (October 1885): 281.

24. For example, see Muhlenberg, *Journals*, 3:5, 28, 55, 101–104 (January 9, April 3, July 1, 1777, and November 12, 1777).

25. *Pennsylvania Archives*, 2nd ser., 14:543.

26. The full oath reads "I _____ _____ do declare that I do not hold myself bound to bear allegiance to George the Third, King of Great Britain, &c., and that I will not, by any means, directly or indirectly, oppose the establishment of a free Government in this Province by the Convention now to be chosen, nor the measures adopted by the Congress against the tyranny attempted to be established in these Colonies by the Court of Great Britain." *American Archives*, 4th ser., 6:953–954 (June 20, 1776).

27. Francis Jennings, *The Creation of America: Through Revolution to Empire* (New York: Cambridge University Press, 2000), 181.

28. The full oath reads "I _____ _____ do profess faith in God the Father and in Jesus Christ, his Eternal Son, the true God, and in the Holy Spirit, one God, blessed for evermore; and do acknowledge the Holy Scriptures of the Old and New Testament to be given by Divine Inspiration." Christopher Marshall, *Extracts from the Diary of Christopher Marshall: Kept in Philadelphia and Lancaster, During the American Revolution, 1774–1781*, ed. William Duane Jr. (Albany, NY: Joel Munsell, 1877), 79n2.

29. The full oath required of assemblymen reads "I do believe in one God, the creator and governor of the universe, the rewarder of the good and the punisher of the wicked. And I do acknowledge the Scriptures of the Old and New Testament to be given by Divine inspiration," Section 10 of the 1776 Constitution of Pennsylvania; Brunhouse, *Counter-Revolution in Pennsylvania*, 16.

30. Steven Rosswurm, *Arms, Country, and Class: The Philadelphia Militia and the "Lower Sort" During the American Revolution, 1775–1783* (New Brunswick, NJ: Rutgers University Press, 1987), 123.

31. *Pennsylvania Archives*, 2nd ser., 3:6.
32. Brunhouse, *Counter-Revolution in Pennsylvania*, 40–41.
33. Ousterhout, *A State Divided*, 161.
34. *Pennsylvania Archives*, 2nd ser., 3:6.
35. Muhlenberg, *Journals*, 3:55 (July 1, 1777).
36. Bringing such intentions to fruition, however, proved extremely difficult. Unwilling to accept the people's general refusal of the Test, the Patriots would repeatedly revise and reinstitute the oath as the months passed. Ousterhout, *A State Divided*, 162–163, 191–194; "Proclamation of Pardon to Prisoners Under Test Laws, 1778," *Pennsylvania Archives*, 1st ser., 7:130–131; Brunhouse, *Counter-Revolution in Pennsylvania*, 40–41; Ousterhout, *A State Divided*, 161.
37. J. Anderson, "Thomas Wharton, Exile in Virginia," 431, 427; Ousterhout, "Controlling the Opposition," 14; "An Act to Empower the Supreme Executive Council of This Commonwealth to Provide for the Security Thereof in Special Cases Where no Provision is Already Made by Law," *The Statutes at Large of Pennsylvania from 1682 to 1801*, 9:139; J. Anderson, "Thomas Wharton, Exile in Virginia," 431. Additional information on the prisoners can be found in Robert F. Oaks, "Philadelphians in Exile: The Problem of Loyalty During the American Revolution," *PMHB* 96, no. 3 (July 1972): 298–325.
38. E. Drinker, *Diary of Elizabeth Drinker*, 1:227–229.
39. Women, in particular, found themselves endowed with an expanded political role as a result of the politicization of commerce. Charged with acquiring many of the day-to-day luxuries and necessities colonial families consumed, they often had the power to make or break the nonconsumption movement. Breen, *Marketplace of Revolution*, xv–xvii, 229–234, and 279–289, 309, 327; Linda Kerber, *Women of the Republic: Intellect and Ideology in Revolutionary America* (Chapel Hill: University of North Carolina Press, 1980), 38–41; Jan Lewis, "The Republican Wife: Virtue and Seduction in the Early Republic," *William and Mary Quarterly* 44, no. 4 (October 1, 1987): 689–721; T. H. Breen, "'Baubles of Britain': The American and Consumer Revolutions of the Eighteenth Century," *Past and Present* 119 (May 1988): 103; "James Madison to William Bradford," January 20, 1775, in *The Papers of James Madison*, ed. W. T. Hutchinson and William M. E. Rachal, 3 vols. (Chicago: University of Chicago Press, 1962), 1:135.
40. Alexander Robertson, *To the Public* (New York, 1769), Early American Imprints, ser. 1.
41. *Connecticut Courant*, April 3, 1775; Breen, *Marketplace of Revolution*, 327–329.
42. *Massachusetts Spy*, January 13, 1774; Breen, *Marketplace of Revolution*, 294–296. For other examples of "ignorance" and "accident" being invoked as excuses in Massachusetts, see the account of a man from Montague who somehow "inadvertently purchased" tea from a peddler and of the men of Truro in the *Massachusetts Spy*, February 17 and March 31, 1774, and recounted by Breen in "Baubles of Britain," 99, and *Marketplace of Revolution*, 314–316, respectively.
43. Thomas B. Taylor, "The Philadelphia Counterpart of the Boston Tea Party (As Shown by the Correspondence of James & Drinker), Conclusion," *Bulletin of Friends' Historical Society of Philadelphia* 3, no. 1 (1909): 29; E. Drinker, *Diary of Elizabeth Drinker*, 1:196.
44. "To the Delaware Pilots" and "To Capt. Ayres," in Taylor, "Philadelphia Counterpart of the Boston Tea Party," 48–49.
45. Taylor, "Philadelphia Counterpart of the Boston Tea Party," 29; Evans, *Weathering the Storm*, 153–154.
46. Article 11, see "The Association" in Henry Steele Commager, ed., *Documents of American History* (New York: F. S. Crofts, 1941), 84–87.

47. Breen, *American Insurgents, American Patriots,* 186, quoting the *North Carolina Gazette,* April 14, 1775.

48. Ousterhout, *A State Divided,* 103–104.

49. Ousterhout, *A State Divided,* 103–104; Francis S. Fox, "Pennsylvania's Revolutionary Militia Law: The Statute That Transformed the State," *Pennsylvania History* 80, no. 2 (Spring 2014): 204.

50. The Revolutionaries used the term "Associators" to describe various different groups at different times. A company of men who joined together in 1747 to serve as a voluntary militia before the passage of the militia laws called themselves the Pennsylvania Associators. Individuals who subscribed to the Continental Association of 1774 were also known as Associators. When Pennsylvanians finally implemented mandatory militia service in 1775, they used the term "Associator" to refer to a participating member of the militia, describing those who refused to show up for practices or turn out for service as "Non-Associators." In the pages that follow, including quotations, "Non-Associators" refers to those who refused to serve with the militia. For additional information on the original Pennsylvania Associators, see Joseph Seymour, *The Pennsylvania Associators, 1747–1777* (Yardley, PA: Westholme, 2012).

51. "Resolutions directing the Mode of Levying Taxes on Non-Associators in Pennsylvania," *Pennsylvania Archives,* 8th ser., 8:7380–7384 (November 25, 1775).

52. "Resolutions directing the Mode of Levying Taxes on Non-Associators," *Pennsylvania Archives,* 8th ser., 8:7485–7490 (March 29, 1776).

53. "An Ordinance for rendering the burthen of Associators and NonAssociators in the defence of this State as nearly equal as may be," *American Archives,* 5th ser., 2:42–45 (September 14, 1776).

54. "Votes of the Assembly," *Pennsylvania Archives,* 8th ser., 8:7586 (September 26, 1776).

55. Rosswurm, *Arms, Country, and Class,* 136; Ryerson, *The Revolution Is Now Begun,* 231–234; "Proceedings of the Provincial Conference," *American Archives,* 4th ser., 6:953.

56. "Votes of the Assembly," *Pennsylvania Archives,* 8th ser., 8:7259–7260 (September 29, 1775).

57. "Votes of the Assembly," *Pennsylvania Archives,* 8th ser., 8:7261–7262 (September 29, 1775).

58. See the address from the Committee of Privates copied in the *Pennsylvania Gazette,* October 11, 1775.

59. "An Ordinance for rendering the burthen of Associators and NonAssociators in the defence of this State as nearly equal as may be," *American Archives,* 5th ser., 2:42–45 (September 14, 1776).

60. J. Allen, "Diary of James Allen," 186, 191.

61. Ibid., 191, 194–195.

62. Ibid., 191, 195–196.

63. Ibid., 191, 196.

64. Wood, *Creation of the American Republic,* 57–58. Wood's entire section on "The Public Good" provides an overview of this assumption, 53–65.

65. Barbara Clark Smith makes a similar argument, although her tone is significantly different from Wood's. See Barbara Clark Smith, *The Freedoms We Lost: Consent and Resistance in Revolutionary America* (New York: New Press, 2010).

66. Wood, *Creation of the American Republic,* 63, quoting *Charleston S. C. Gazette,* September 26, 1775.

67. Muhlenberg, *Journals*, 3:55 (July 1, 1777).

68. Ousterhout, *A State Divided*, 130.

69. "Votes of the Assembly," *Pennsylvania Archives*, 8th ser., 8:7505–7507 (April 6, 1776); "Ordinance for disarming Non-Associators," *American Archives*, 5th ser., 2:6 (July 19, 1776).

70. A complete breakdown of offenses and punishments may be found in the appendix in Ousterhout, *A State Divided*, 319–323.

71. It was not at all unusual for the crowds or militias to carry enforcement to harsher extremes than the Revolutionary governments and committees officially authorized. This was true in Pennsylvania and in other colonies as well. See for example Michael A. McDonnell, "Popular Mobilization and Political Culture in Revolutionary Virginia: The Failure of the Minutemen and the Revolution from Below," *Journal of American History* 85, no. 3 (December 1, 1998): 959; Breen, *American Insurgents, American Patriots*, 186–197, 202.

72. Breen, *American Insurgents, American Patriots*, 201; Shy, *A People Numerous and Armed*, 237.

Interlude. The Brothers Allen

1. The following narrative of the Allen brothers is composed from the following sources: J. Allen, "Diary of James Allen," 176–177; Edward F. DeLancy, "Chief Justice William Allen," *PMHB* 1 (1877): 207–211; Charles P. Keith, "Andrew Allen," *PMHB* 10, no. 4 (1887): 361–365.

2. "William Allen," in Horle, Foster, and Wolfe, *Lawmaking and Legislators in Pennsylvania: 1757–1775*, 260–268. Chief Justice Allen would ultimately flee to England. Like most of his sons, he supported resistance, even violent resistance, to perceived parliamentary overreach but saw independence on the Revolutionaries' terms as a greater evil.

3. William Howe, *The Narrative of Lieut. Gen. Sir William Howe* (London: H. Baldwin, 1781), 17–18; Howe to Germain, December 20, 1776, Germain Papers, vol. 5, WCL.

4. Robert Middlekauff, *The Glorious Cause: The American Revolution, 1763–1789* (New York: Oxford University Press, 2007), 370–377; John Jackson, *With the British Army in Philadelphia, 1777–1778* (San Rafael, CA: Presidio Press, 1979), 2–5.

5. Howe, *Narrative of Howe*, 17–18; Howe to Germain, December 20, 1776, Germain Papers, vol. 5, WCL.

6. Ambrose Serle, *The American Journal of Ambrose Serle, Secretary to Lord Howe, 1776–1778*, ed. Edward H. Tatum Jr. (San Marino, CA: Huntington Library, 1940), 163–165, 200.

7. Ira D. Gruber, *The Howe Brothers and the American Revolution* (Chapel Hill: University of North Carolina Press, 2011), 222–223.

8. Stephen Conway, "To Subdue America: British Army Officers and the Conduct of the Revolutionary War," *William and Mary Quarterly* 43 (July 1986): 384–385. Conway demonstrates that many officers of lower rank held similar conciliatory sentiments, though there also existed a strong contingent of "hard-liners" who believed a harsh response was needed in order to bring rebellious America to its knees. Regrettably for the conciliators, the latter group tended to leave the deepest and most lasting impressions in the minds of American civilians.

9. Howe would receive some support for this plan even from Lord Germain, who rarely agreed with Howe or deigned to support him. In response to one of Howe's early proposals to invade Pennsylvania, Germain replied, "If we may credit the accounts which arrive from all quarters relative to the good inclinations of the inhabitants, there is every reason to expect that

your success in Pennsylvania will enable you to raise from among them such a force as may be sufficient for the interior defense of the province and leave the army at liberty to proceed to offensive operations." Germain to Howe, May 18, 1777, Germain Papers, vol. 6, WCL; Andrew Jackson O'Shaughnessy, *The Men Who Lost America: British Leadership, the American Revolution, and the Fate of the Empire* (New Haven, CT: Yale University Press, 2013), 90, 98, 105.

10. Serle, *American Journal*, 164, 165, 166–167, 190, 192.

Chapter 2. Invasion

Note to epigraph: "Remonstrance of Council and Assembly to Congress, 1777," *Pennsylvania Archives*, 1st ser., 6:104–105.

1. John Peebles, Journal, August 25–26, 1777, in John Peebles, Journal, 1776–1782, David Library of the American Revolution (hereafter DLAR), Washington Crossing, PA, microfilm; Serle, *American Journal*, 241, 245.

2. Serle, *American Journal*, 246.

3. Carl Leopold Baurmeister, *Revolution in America: Confidential Letters and Journals, 1776–1784* (New Brunswick, NJ: Rutgers University Press, 1957), 99.

4. Serle, *American Journal*, 244–245, 249–250. Emphasis in the original.

5. "To John Augustine Washington," October 18, 1777, *PGW*, 11:551; Wayne K. Bodle, *The Valley Forge Winter: Civilians and Soldiers in War* (University Park: Pennsylvania State University Press, 2002), 51; "Anthony Wayne to Thomas Wharton," November 22, 1777, *Pennsylvania Archives*, 1st ser., 6:25.

6. "To John Augustine Washington," October 18, 1777, *PGW*, 11:551; William Howe to George Germain, Head of Elk, August 30, 1777, Germain Papers, 6:13, WCL.

7. "From Joseph Jones," September 30, 1777, *PGW*, 11:353–354; Jackson, *With the British Army in Philadelphia*, 14.

8. John Adams, *Diary and Autobiography of John Adams*, ed. L. H. Butterfield (Cambridge, MA: Belknap Press, 1961), 2:263.

9. James Grant, October 20, 1777, Letterbook 4, James Grant Papers, Army Career Series, Film 687, Reel 28, DLAR.

10. "Richard M'Allister to President Wharton," June 16, 1777, *Pennsylvania Archives*, 1st ser., 5:369.

11. "Richard M'Allister to President Wharton," July 4, 1777, *Pennsylvania Archives*, 1st ser., 5:412.

12. Percentages exclude those who, because of their role in government, work in a war-related trade, or other reason, were able to secure an exemption from the state. See Table A.3 in Rosswurm, *Arms, Country, and Class*, 262, 143.

13. Josiah Parker to John Page, August 5, 1777, Schoff Revolutionary War Collection, Box 2, WCL.

14. Fox, "Pennsylvania's Revolutionary Militia Law," 205; *PGW*, 11:54n1; *JCC*, 8:666–667; "Hancock to Certain States," August 23, 1777, in *Letters of Delegates to Congress, 1774–1789*, ed. Paul Hubert Smith et al. (Washington, DC: Library of Congress, 1976–2000), 7:536; Mordecai Gist of Maryland placed the number of "enrolled" militia in Pennsylvania at some 62,000 men: Bodle, *Valley Forge Winter*, 50.

15. "Return Of the militia belonging to the state of pennsylvania, September 6, 1777," *Pennsylvania Archives*, 1st ser., 5:595; "From John Hancock," September 6, 1777, *PGW*, 11:159.

16. See Table A.3 in Rosswurm, *Arms, Country, and Class*, 262, 143.

17. "R. Macalester to President of Council," August 28, 1777, *Pennsylvania Archives*, 1st ser., 5:558–561.

18. Rosswurm, *Arms, Country, and Class*, 143–144, 145.

19. George Adams Boyd, *Elias Boudinot: Patriot and Statesman, 1740–1821* (Princeton, NJ: Princeton University Press, 1952), 43.

20. John Armstrong to Thomas Wharton, October 2, 1777, Joseph Reed Papers, Film 266, DLAR.

21. See *PGW*, 11:315n2.

22. Ibid.

23. John E. Ferling, *Almost a Miracle: The American Victory in the War of Independence* (Oxford: Oxford University Press, 2007), 233.

24. Bodle, *Valley Forge Winter*, 46.

25. "To Thomas Wharton Jr.," October 17–18, 1777, *PGW*, 11:539–540.

26. Bodle, *Valley Forge Winter*, 104.

27. Grant, October 20, 1777, Letterbook 4, James Grant Papers, DLAR.

28. Friedrich von Muenchhausen, *At General Howe's Side, 1776–1778: The Diary of General William Howe's Aide de Camp* (Monmouth Beach, NJ: Philip Freneau Press, 1974), 24; "Baurmeister to von Jungkenn," in Carl Leopold Baurmeister, *Letters from Major Baurmeister to Colonel von Jungkenn Written During the Philadelphia Campaign, 1777–1778* (Philadelphia: Historical Society of Pennsylvania, 1937), 3–4; Peebles, Journal, August 25 and 28, 1777, microfilm, n.d., DLAR.

29. "A State of the Circumstances of Philadelphia when the British Troops took Possession, &ca.," cataloged as 1777, but no more precise date given, Germain Papers, vol. 6, WCL.

30. Loftus Cliffe to Jack Cliffe, October 24, 1777, Folder 12, Loftus Cliffe Papers, WCL; Marshall Diaries, October 16, 1777, HSP.

31. Muenchhausen, *At General Howe's Side*, 30.

32. Ibid., 24; Worthington Ford, *Defences of Philadelphia in 1777* (Brooklyn, NY: Historical Printing Club, 1897), 69–70, 80; "From Thomas McKean," October 18, 1777, *PGW*, 11:442–443.

33. For examples, see Muenchhausen, *At General Howe's Side*, 26; Johann von Ewald, *Diary of the American War: A Hessian Journal* (New Haven, CT: Yale University Press, 1979), 81, 87–88; Peebles, Journal, August 23, 1777, DLAR.

34. For examples see Report of the Loyalist Claims Commission for Gideon Vernon, Great Britain, Audit Office Records (hereafter GB.AO), 12/40/272, 66/37, 109/300, Film 263, DLAR, and George Playter [aka Playton] GB.AO 12/102/211, 13/111/108–123, Film 263–264, DLAR; Marshall Diaries, October 16, 1777, HSP.

35. See the editors' note, *PGW*, 11:189; Stephen R. Taaffe, *The Philadelphia Campaign, 1777–1778* (Lawrence: University Press of Kansas, 2003), 89.

36. Sir William Howe's Defense (Before a Select Committee of the House of Commons) of his Conduct as Command-in-Chief of the British Forces in the War of Independence, Henry Strachey Papers, Box 2, Folder 51, WCL.

37. Ewald, *Diary of the American War*, 76; Baurmeister, *Revolution in America*, 105.

38. Grant, October 20, 1777, Letterbook 4, James Grant Papers, DLAR. Interestingly, Hessian Capt. Johann von Ewald does report that a civilian, possibly Dr. William Smith of the College of

Philadelphia, informed him of the impending attack the night before Washington struck. See Ewald, *Diary of the American War*, 92.

39. Sir William Howe's Defense (Before a Select Committee of the House of Commons) of his Conduct as Command-in-Chief of the British Forces in the War of Independence, Henry Strachey Papers, Box 2, Folder 51, WCL; "To John Hancock," September 23, 1777, *PGW*, 11:301.

40. Jackson, *With the British Army in Philadelphia*, 3.

41. "General Orders," August 23, 24, 1777, *PGW*, 11:49–51; "Henry Marchant to Nicholas Cooke," August 24, 1777, *Letters of Delegates to Congress*, 7:541; Taaffe, *Philadelphia Campaign*, 57–58.

42. Middlekauff, *Glorious Cause*, 392.

43. "To John Hancock," August 23, 1777, *PGW*, 11:52.

44. Alexander Graydon, *Memoirs of His Own Time: With Reminiscences of the Men and Events of the Revolution* (Philadelphia: Lindsay and Blakiston, 1846), 290.

45. "General Orders," August 23, 24, 1777, *PGW*, 11:49–51; Ferling, *Almost a Miracle*, 245.

46. For more on camp followers, male and female, see Holly A. Mayer, *Belonging to the Army: Camp Followers and Community During the American Revolution* (Columbia: University of South Carolina Press, 1996).

47. "Henry Marchant to Nicholas Cooke," August 24, 1777, *Letters of Delegates to Congress*, 7:541; Middlekauff, *Glorious Cause*, 392.

48. Graydon, *Memoirs of His Own Time*, 291.

49. Ibid.

50. Joseph Townsend, *Some Account of the British Army Under the Command of General Howe, and of the Battle of Brandywine on The memorable September 11th, 1777, and the Adventures of that Day, Which Came to the Knowledge and Observation of Joseph Townsend, Late of Baltimore, Md.* (Philadelphia: Historical Society of Pennsylvania, 1846), 18. Townsend's account was later republished as *The Battle of Brandywine* (New York: New York Times, 1969); Taaffe, *Philadelphia Campaign*, 55.

51. Townsend, *Battle of Brandywine*, 21.

52. Ibid., 21–22.

53. Ibid., 24.

54. Ibid., 26–29.

55. E. Drinker, *Diary of Elizabeth Drinker*, 1:229–231.

56. James Allen, "Diary of James Allen, Esq., of Philadelphia, Counsellor-at-Law, 1770–1778 (continued)," *PMHB* 9, no. 3 (October 1885): 290, 293.

57. E. Drinker, *Diary of Elizabeth Drinker*, 1:232; Wainwright and Fisher, "'A Diary of Trifling Occurrences,'" 448; Jackson, *With the British Army in Philadelphia*, 13–15.

58. David W. Maxey, *Treason on Trial in Revolutionary Pennsylvania: The Case of John Roberts, Miller* (Philadelphia: American Philosophical Society, 2011), 54–55.

59. E. Drinker, *Diary of Elizabeth Drinker*, 1:232–236; J. Allen, "Diary of James Allen, (continued)," 286.

60. E. Drinker, *Diary of Elizabeth Drinker*, 1:235.

61. John Fanning Watson, *Annals of Philadelphia and Pennsylvania* (Philadelphia: Leary, Stuart, 1927), 2:284.

62. Ibid., 2:287.

63. Robert Morton, "Diary of Robert Morton," *PMHB* 1, no. 1 (1877): 7–8.

64. Francis Downman, *The Services of Lieut.-Colonel Francis Downman, R.A., in France, North America, and the West Indies, Between the Years 1758 and 1784*, ed. F. A. Whinyates (Woolwich: Royal Artillery Institution, 1898), 35–36.

65. John Montrésor and G. D. Scull, "Journal of Captain John Montrésor, July 1, 1777, to July 1, 1778, Chief Engineer of the British Army (continued)," *PMHB* 6 (1882): 41.

66. Peebles, Journal, September 26, 1777, DLAR.

67. E. Drinker, *Diary of Elizabeth Drinker*, 1:235.

68. "Nathanael Greene to Jacob Greene," June 4, 1777, in *The Papers of General Nathanael Greene* (hereafter *PNG*), ed. Richard K. Showman (Chapel Hill: University of North Carolina Press for the Rhode Island Historical Society, 1976), 2:104; E. Drinker, *Diary of Elizabeth Drinker*, 1:227–236.

69. Ferling, *Almost a Miracle*, 247–252; Middlekauff, *Glorious Cause*, 392–396.

70. "From John Hancock," October 9, 1777, *PGW*, 11:461.

71. *JCC*, 8:751–752.

72. Ibid.

73. *JCC*, 9:784–785.

74. "To John Hancock," October 10, 1777, *PGW*, 11:473–475; "From John Hancock," October 14, 1777, *PGW*, 11:504.

75. Samuel Hazard, ed., *The Register of Pennsylvania: Devoted to the Preservation of Every Kind of Useful Information Respecting the State*, 7 vols. (Philadelphia: W. F. Geddes, 1828–1831), 3:200. Note that, though these "evil-minded persons" are so numerous as to require the creation of such a council to control them, the British are still held to be the "common" enemy of the people.

76. Hazard, *Register of Pennsylvania*, 3:200.

77. Ibid.

78. Constitution of the Commonwealth of Pennsylvania (1776), Declaration of Rights, art. IX, X, and XII.

79. J. Allen, "Diary of James Allen (continued)," 289.

80. Anne M. Ousterhout has tabulated, to the extent possible from extant records, the punishments inflicted on those accused of disloyal acts in Pennsylvania during the revolution. See Ousterhout, "Controlling the Opposition," 18–23. Francis Jennings provides a scathing indictment of Pennsylvania's radical government, its violation of its own Declaration of Rights, and the potentially tyrannical powers of the Council of Safety, see Jennings, *Creation of America*, 180–192.

81. Ousterhout, *A State Divided*, 297.

82. Editors' notes in *PGW*, 12:444–445.

83. For the best description of Washington's choice of winter quarters, including a detailed analysis of the political implications, see Bodle, *Valley Forge Winter*, 55–73. The brief overview here owes a tremendous debt to Bodle's narrative and analysis.

84. Bodle, *Valley Forge Winter*, 57.

85. "To Johann Kalb," December 1, 1777, *PGW*, 12:464.

86. "From Henry Knox," December 1, 1777, *PGW*, 12:465.

87. "From Major General Lafayette," December 1, 1777, *PGW*, 12:466–468.

88. Bodle, *Valley Forge Winter*, 255–256.

89. "From Joseph Reed," December 4, 1777, *PGW*, 12:548–552.

90. Ibid.

91. "From James Irvine," December 1, 1777, *PGW*, 12:463–464.

92. "From John Cadwalader," December 3, 1777, *PGW*, 12:507–510.

93. Ibid. Cadwalader goes on to list a host of ills that will befall the Revolution in Pennsylvania should Washington fail to adequately support it with his army. Also see "From John Armstrong," December 1, 1777, *PGW*, 12:455.

94. *JCC*, 9:972.

95. Bodle, *Valley Forge Winter*, 57, 63–64. Notably, the five officers who joined Congress in advocating a winter campaign were all Pennsylvanians and four of them were from the militia, see Bodle, *Valley Forge Winter*, 60–61.

96. "Remonstrance of Council and Assembly to Congress," 1777, *Pennsylvania Archives*, 1st ser., 6:104–105. Though the Remonstrance is undated, Bodle suggests it was written on December 15 and no later than December 17. See *Valley Forge Winter*, 281n36.

97. Bodle, *Valley Forge Winter*, 70, 71.

98. Bodle, *Valley Forge Winter*, 64, 67.

99. John Adams went so far as to list the various advantages the Revolutionaries would reap from having their capital occupied by the British. John Adams to Abigail Adams, August 1, 1777, Adams Family Papers: An Electronic Archive, Boston: Massachusetts Historical Society, http://www.masshist.org/digitaladams/; "Nathanael Greene to George Washington," April 25, 1778, *PNG*, 355–361. Greene was less worried about the military significance of the city than the impact of its loss on the people's morale. "The real injury by the loss of Philadelphia," he wrote, "bears but a small proportion to the effect it had from the imaginary estimation given it by the public." James Allen had voiced similar sentiments in early October, noting that "the minds of people are much changed by the loss of Philadelphia." J. Allen, "Diary of James Allen (continued)," 294.

100. Breen, *Marketplace of Revolution*, xv–xvi.

Interlude. The Road to Virginia

1. Oaks, "Philadelphians in Exile," 307; J. Anderson, "Thomas Wharton, Exile in Virginia," 434.

2. Henry Drinker to Elizabeth Drinker, September 12, 1777, Henry and Elizabeth Drinker Letters (MC 854), Special Collections, Haverford College, Haverford, PA (hereafter Drinker Letters); J. Anderson, "Thomas Wharton, Exile in Virginia," 434.

3. J. Anderson, "Thomas Wharton, Exile in Virginia," 434; Oaks, "Philadelphians in Exile," 307.

4. Henry Drinker to Elizabeth Drinker, September 13, 1777, Drinker Letters.

5. At his treason trial in September 1778, Roberts's defense did its best to suggest that this meeting with Galloway never took place, despite the prosecution producing multiple witnesses who claimed to have heard Roberts describe it in detail. Notably, even the Quaker Meeting for Suffering in Philadelphia, which eventually concluded that Roberts had been unjustly convicted and executed, accepted that he did indeed make this rescue attempt and did not doubt the narrative of the prosecution in this respect. Maxey, *Treason on Trial in Revolutionary Pennsylvania*, 21, 165–166.

6. Gilpin, *Exiles in Virginia*, 135–136; J. Anderson, "Thomas Wharton, Exile in Virginia," 435.

7. Gilpin, *Exiles in Virginia*, 136; J. Anderson, "Thomas Wharton, Exile in Virginia," 435.

8. Gilpin, *Exiles in Virginia*, 136.
9. Gilpin, *Exiles in Virginia*, 136–142; Oaks, "Philadelphians in Exile," 307; J. Anderson, "Thomas Wharton, Exile in Virginia," 435.
10. Henry Drinker to Elizabeth Drinker, September 18, 1777, Drinker Letters.
11. Henry Drinker to Elizabeth Drinker, September 16 and 20, 1777, Drinker Letters.
12. Henry Drinker to Elizabeth Drinker, September 20, 1777, Drinker Letters; E. Drinker, *Diary of Elizabeth Drinker*, 1:233.
13. Henry Drinker to Elizabeth Drinker, September 16, 18–19, 1777, Drinker Letters; Gilpin, *Exiles in Virginia*, 138. Underlining in the original.
14. Gilpin, *Exiles in Virginia*, 143–158; Oaks, "Philadelphians in Exile," 309; J. Anderson, "Thomas Wharton, Exile in Virginia," 436–437.

Chapter 3. Siege

Note to epigraph: Ewald, *Diary of the American War*, xxvi, 122.
1. Ewald, *Diary of the American War*, xxv–xxvi.
2. "William Smith (1727–1803)," Penn Biographies, University of Pennsylvania, University Archives and Record Center, http://www.archives.upenn.edu/people/1700s/smith_wm.html.
3. Ewald, *Diary of the American War*, 92–93.
4. Grant, October 20, 1777, Letterbook 4, James Grant Papers, DLAR. It seems that neither Lieutenant General James Grant nor Sir William Howe, the British commander in chief in America, was informed of Smith's revelations before the attack.
5. Hamilton B. Tompkins, "Contemporary Account of the Battle of Germantown," *PMHB* 11, no. 3 (October 1, 1887): 330; E. Drinker, *Diary of Elizabeth Drinker*, 1:239.
6. J. Allen, "Diary of James Allen (continued)," 294.
7. Tompkins, "Contemporary Account of the Battle of Germantown," 331.
8. Jackson, *With the British Army in Philadelphia*, 29–51.
9. Historian John Jackson described Philadelphia as "Howe's self-imposed prison for himself and for nearly fifty thousand civilian and military personnel." Jackson, *With the British Army in Philadelphia*, 53.
10. "John Adams to Abigail Adams," August 29, 1777, in John and Abigail Adams, *The Letters of John and Abigail Adams*, ed. Frank Shuffelton (New York: Penguin, 2003), 206.
11. "George Walton to Benjamin Franklin," December 20, 1777, *The Papers of Benjamin Franklin*, vol. 25, ed. William B. Willcox (New Haven, CT: Yale University Press, 1986), 327–329.
12. "To John Hancock," September 23, 1777, *PGW*, 11:301–302.
13. Grant, November 30, 1777, Letterbook 4, James Grant Papers, DLAR.
14. *Papers of Benjamin Franklin*, 25:328; Jackson, *With the British Army in Philadelphia*, 14–15; Robert Proud, "Letters of Robert Proud," *PMHB* 34, no. 1 (1910): 62–63, 72–73; E. Drinker, *Diary of Elizabeth Drinker*, 1:231–232, September 18–19, 1777.
15. Bodle, *Valley Forge Winter*, 47–48; Grant, November 30, 1777, Letterbook 4, James Grant Papers, DLAR.
16. Jackson, *With the British Army in Philadelphia*, 275–277.
17. *JCC*, 9:784–785.
18. Pennsylvania Council of Safety, "In Council of Safety. Lancaster, 21st October, 1777," (Lancaster, PA: Printed by Francis Bailey, 1777), Early American Imprints, ser. 1.

19. Bodle, *Valley Forge Winter*, 133, 136–137.
20. "From Colonel Joseph Ellis," January 15, 1778, *PGW*, 13:247; Bodle, *Valley Forge Winter*, 186–187.
21. Ewald, *Diary of the American War*, 104.
22. E. Drinker, *Diary of Elizabeth Drinker*, 1:245–246.
23. Serle, *American Journal*, 265.
24. See the example of Chester County in From Joseph Reed to unknown, October 27, 1777, Joseph Reed Papers, Film 266, DLAR.
25. Muhlenberg, *Journals*, 3:92, October 25, 1777.
26. J. Allen, "Diary of James Allen (concluded)," 424; Wainwright and Fisher, "'A Diary of Trifling Occurrences,'" 454; Proud, "Letters of Robert Proud," 62–63.
27. Taaffe, *Philadelphia Campaign*, 125; Jackson, *With the British Army in Philadelphia*, 89. Muenchhausen reports that four sloops attempted the run under cover of darkness one night in November; three of the four made it through unscathed. Muenchhausen, *At General Howe's Side*, 43.
28. Wainwright and Fisher, "'A Diary of Trifling Occurrences,'" 454–456.
29. Jackson, *With the British Army in Philadelphia*, 89.
30. Alms House Managers, Minutes, 1766–1778, Record Group 35-2.3, Philadelphia City Archives. The full text of the petition the managers sent to General Howe is copied under the entry for December 16, 1777.
31. Taaffe, *Philadelphia Campaign*, 108–144; Jackson, *With the British Army in Philadelphia*, 53–80.
32. John André, November 20, 1777, John André Manuscript, Schoff Revolutionary War Collection, WCL.
33. Wainwright and Fisher, "'A Diary of Trifling Occurrences,'" 458.
34. William Loage made it past the American troops with flour, butter, and other goods, though "as his prises were high and hard money demanded," Drinker chose not to do business with him. E. Drinker, *Diary of Elizabeth Drinker*, 1:263–264.
35. Elizabeth Drinker to Henry Drinker, December 18, 1777, Drinker Letters.
36. Morton, "Diary of Robert Morton," 62–63.
37. Baurmeister, *Revolution in America*, 120–121.
38. John Clark Jr., "Letters from Major John Clark Jr. to General Washington Written During the Occupation of Philadelphia by the British Army," *Bulletin of the Historical Society of Pennsylvania* 1 (1847): 25.
39. "From Major John Jameson," December 31, 1777, *PGW*, 13:81–82.
40. Marshall Diaries, January 6, 1778, in Christopher Marshall Papers, HSP.
41. "From Brigadier General James Potter," January 11, 1778, *PGW*, 12:202–203.
42. "From Colonel Walter Stewart," January 18, 1778, *PGW*, 13:276–277.
43. "To Colonel Walter Stewart," January 22, 1778, *PGW*, 13:317.
44. "From Colonel Joseph Ellis," February 8, 1778, *PGW*, 13:476–478; Bodle, *Valley Forge Winter*, 187.
45. "To Thomas Wharton Jr.," October 17–18, 1777, *PGW*, 11:539–540.
46. "From Major General John Armstrong," December 30, 1777, *PGW*, 13:57–58; "To Thomas Wharton Jr.," January 1, 1778, *PGW*, 13:108–109; "From Thomas Wharton Jr.," January 3, 1778, *PGW*, 13:136–137; *PGW*, 11:54n1; *JCC*, 8:666–667; "Hancock to Certain States," August 23, 1777, *Letters of Delegates*, ed. P. Smith et al., 7:536.

47. "Thomas Wharton Jr. to Brigadier General John Lacey," January 9, 1778, in Hazard, *Register of Pennsylvania*, 3:297; "From Thomas Wharton Jr.," January 3, 1778, *PGW*, 13:137.

48. "From Thomas Wharton Jr.," February 17, 1778, *PGW*, 13:574.

49. "General Lacey to Council," January 24, February 2, and February 15, 1778, Hazard, *Register of Pennsylvania*, 3:298, 305.

50. "From Colonel Walter Stewart," January 28, 1778, *PGW*, 13:371–372.

51. "To Brigadier General John Lacey," February 8, 1778, *PGW*, 13:477–478; "Lacey to Thomas Wharton Jr.," *Pennsylvania Archives*, 1st ser., 6:226.

52. "From Major Francis Murray," February 13, 1778, *PGW*, 13:522–523.

53. "From Brigadier General John Lacey Jr.," February 19, 1778, *PGW*, 13:392.

54. Bodle, *Valley Forge Winter*, 50.

55. Baurmeister, *Revolution in America*, 134.

56. McAllister told Thomas Wharton Jr. that the primary explanation provided by the people who would not serve was that the militia were not being paid, though he himself felt that this only "afoards to those Called an Excuse." "R. M'Calester to President Wharton," York Town, January 22, 1778, *Pennsylvania Archives*, 1st ser., 6:196. The Reverend Muhlenberg inadvertently helped to provide other men with excuses. Immediately following the state's effort to raise a larger force in early January, Muhlenberg was confronted by a number of parents who desired him to look up their sons' baptismal records and thus confirm their birthdates. These boys were generally just slightly too young to qualify for militia service, and it seems likely that their parents wanted proof of their ineligibility. Muhlenberg, *Journals*, 3:119.

57. "From Brigadier General John Lacey Jr.," February 20, 1778, *PGW*, 13:611.

58. "From Brigadier General Anthony Wayne," February 26, 1778, *PGW*, 13:677–678.

59. "To Thomas Wharton Jr.," February 12, 1778, *PGW*, 13:519.

60. "From Thomas Wharton Jr.," February 17, 1778, *PGW*, 13:574.

61. "Lacey to Armstrong," April 28, 1778, Hazard, *Register of Pennsylvania*, 3:342; "General Lacey to Council," March 11, 1778, Hazard, *Register of Pennsylvania*, 3:307–308.

62. *Pennsylvania Archives*, 1st ser., 6:390–391; "From Brigadier General John Lacey Jr.," April 20, 1778, *PGW*, 14:569; "Lacey to Armstrong," April 28, 1778, Hazard, *Register of Pennsylvania*, 3:342.

63. *Pennsylvania Archives*, 1st ser., 6:399.

64. "To Henry Laurens," April 10, 1778, *PGW*, 14:459.

65. "To Thomas Wharton Jr.," April 11, 1778, *PGW*, 14:482; "From Thomas Wharton Jr.," April 13, 1778, *PGW*, 14:506.

66. "From Brigadier General Anthony Wayne," February 26 and March 5, 1778, *PGW*, 13:677–678 and 14:73; "From Col. Joseph Ellis," February 8, 1778, *PGW*, 13:476–478; "To Col. Joseph Ellis," February 24, 1778, *PGW*, 13:653–654.

67. "Col. Joseph Ellis to Governor William Livingston," March 23, 1778, *PGW*, 14:283n1.

68. "General Lacey to General Armstrong," May 7, 1778, Hazard, *Register of Pennsylvania*, 3:343; "General Lacey to General Washington," May 2, 1778, Hazard, *Register of Pennsylvania*, 3:342–343; Montrésor and Scull, "Journal of Captain John Montrésor," 202–203; Baurmeister, *Revolution in America*, 168–169; Jackson, *With the British Army in Philadelphia*, 223–225; Taaffe, *Philadelphia Campaign*, 188; John Graves Simcoe, *Simcoe's Military Journal?: A History of the Operations of a Partisan Corps, Called the Queen's Rangers* (New York: Bartlett and Welford, 1844), 56–60.

69. "To President Thomas Wharton Jr.," May 11, 1778, and "To Brigadier General William Maxwell," May 7, 1778, *The Writings of George Washington from the Original Manuscript Sources, 1745–1799*, ed. George Fitzpatrick, vol. 11 (Washington, DC: US Government Printing Office, 1934), 357–358, 369–370; Bodle, *Valley Forge Winter*, 232–233.

70. The distinction suggested here, between economic motivations and political ones, was held loosely by contemporaries, a fact that was especially apparent earlier in the Revolution, as the Revolutionaries struggled to justify their resistance to and eventual departure from the British Empire. Economic motivations could be rebranded as political in order to present a stronger argument for independence or, in this case, to legitimate a harsher response to disaffection. For many, however, at a time when the concept of liberty was closely tied to the possession of property and *in*dependence was cast as the opposite of material *dependence*, the line between material interest and political or constitutional legitimacy could be fuzzy. For a recent exploration of the economic foundations of the Revolution and how they were presented/interpreted by the Revolutionaries and others, see the roundtable in the October 2011 issue of the *William and Mary Quarterly*, particularly Staughton Lynd and David Waldstreicher, "Free Trade, Sovereignty, and Slavery: Toward an Economic Interpretation of American Independence," *William and Mary Quarterly* 68, no. 4 (October 1, 2011): 597–630; and Barbara Clark Smith, "Beyond the 'Economic,'" *William and Mary Quarterly* 68, no. 4 (October 1, 2011): 639–643.

71. Muenchhausen, *At General Howe's Side*, 49; Ewald, *Diary of the American War*, 121.

72. "Memorandum sent with a letter from Major General Stirling to Washington," December 26, 1777, *PGW*, 12:10–11; see also "From Brigadier General James Potter," January 11, 1778, *PGW*, 13:202–203. Major John Clark wrote to Nathanael Greene that even the Quakers could be persuaded to supply information to the Continental Army if they would only be released from militia requirements and allowed to return to their practices of trading produce with the markets in Philadelphia. "From Major John Clark Jr.," January 10, 1778, *PNG*, 2:249.

73. Richard Buel, *In Irons: Britain's Naval Supremacy and the American Revolutionary Economy* (New Haven, CT: Yale University Press, 1998), 12, 107–113.

74. Baurmeister, *Revolution in America*, 150.

75. Israel Angell, *The Diary of Colonel Israel Angell Commanding Officer, 2nd Rhode Island Regiment, Continental Army*, transcribed by Edward Field (Providence, RI: Preston and Rounds, 1899), digitized by Norman Desmarais, Digital Commons, Providence College, http://digitalcommons.providence.edu/primary/2.

76. The problem of illicit trade across the lines also plagued the longer British occupation of New York City where, as Judith Van Buskirk notes, "a number of citizens put the profit motive or family survival above civic virtue." Many of the same factors that drove Americans to trade with occupied Philadelphia, including the depreciation of Continental money, the traditional system of trade between city and country, disaffection toward the patriot regime, and the desire to take advantage of imported goods also pushed inhabitants toward the markets of British-held New York. Judith L. Van Buskirk, *Generous Enemies: Patriots and Loyalists in Revolutionary New York* (Philadelphia: University of Pennsylvania Press, 2002), 105–128 (quote from 108); Kim, "Limits of Politicization in the American Revolution," 883.

77. As Robert Morris noted early in 1777, disheartening events, such as Congress being forced to flee the capital to avoid capture by the British, had an inflationary effect. The actual occupation of the city did not bode well for Congress's ability to repay its debts. Anne Bezanson, *Prices and Inflation During the American Revolution: Pennsylvania, 1770–1790* (Philadelphia: University of Pennsylvania Press, 1951), 18, 35–37, 64. While Bezanson's work represents one of the, if

not the, most thorough investigations of depreciation during the war, estimates vary from source to source. Nonetheless, sources agree that a precipitous collapse in the value of the currency was underway. For one alternative tally kept by a contemporary merchant, see Watson, *Annals of Philadelphia*, 2:299.

78. Joseph Reed Papers, January 7 and February 1, 1778, DLAR.
79. Marshall Diaries, January 22, 1778, in Christopher Marshall Papers, HSP.
80. Bezanson, *Prices and Inflation During the American Revolution*, 35–37.
81. Elias Boudinot, Elias Boudinot Letterbook, 1777–1778, State Historical Society of Wisconsin, microfilm ed., 1978, film 567, DLAR; Boyd, *Elias Boudinot*, 49.
82. "Memorandum sent with a letter from Major General Stirling to Washington," Genl. Potter's Qrs [Radnor, PA], December 12, 1777, *PGW*, 12:10–11.
83. "From Colonel Walter Stewart," January 18, 1778, *PGW*, 13: 276–277.
84. One of Watson's interviewees recalled that farmers from Chester County, who had had goods taken from them while the British were advancing up from Maryland, came to the city to present their certificates and were duly paid in full. They then spent much of their new wealth in the city's stores before leaving. Such exchanges eased some of the suffering in the city by promoting the local circulation of hard currency. Watson, *Annals of Philadelphia*, 2:285.
85. Bodle, *Valley Forge Winter*, 111.
86. *JCC*, 9:784–785; Angell, *Diary of Colonel Israel Angell*, January 31, 1778.
87. Women also featured prominently among those who illegally traded with British-occupied New York City. See Van Buskirk, *Generous Enemies*, 121.
88. "From Brigadier General John Lacey Jr.," January 26, 1778, *PGW*, 13:351–352; Major John Jameson (*PGW*, 13:351–352) reported that the people caught going to the Philadelphia markets were "mostly women." Somewhat later, Capt. Stephen Chambers (*PGW*, 14:279–281) declared that "most of the people taken now are old Men & Women."
89. For a few examples, see Muhlenberg, *Journals*, 3:121, 134, 147, 151–152; and Marshall Diaries, November 6, 1777 and January 6, 1778, in Christopher Marshall Papers, HSP.
90. J. Allen, "Diary of James Allen (continued)," 296; J. Allen, "Diary of James Allen (concluded)," 427.
91. "General Orders," February 4, 1778, *PGW*, 13:455, 455–456n1.
92. "From Major John Jameson," February 1, 1778, *PGW*, 13:437; "From Major General John Armstrong," December 26, 1777, *PGW*, 13:2–3.
93. Angell, *Diary of Colonel Israel Angell*, January 31, 1778.
94. Joseph Reed to [not addressed], February 1, 1778, Joseph Reed Papers, DLAR.
95. Clark, "Letters from Major John Clark Jr. to General Washington," 23–24. It's unknown what, if any, punishment was issued in response to this indecent proposal.
96. Baurmeister, *Revolution in America*, 134.
97. "From Colonel Walter Stewart," January 28, 1778, *PGW*, 13:371–372.
98. Ewald, *Diary of the American War*, 119.
99. This is one of the "Revolutionary Exploits of Colonel Allen McLane," recorded in Watson's *Annals of Philadelphia*, 2:322.
100. *JCC*, 9:751, 784, 1013–1015; "From Brigadier General James Mitchell Varnum," December 22, 1777, *PGW*, 12:675.
101. *JCC*, 9:1068.
102. "From Brigadier General James Potter," January 11, 1778, *PGW*, 13:202. There also appears to have been confusion over precisely which goods were to be confiscated and who was

entitled to keep them. See "General Armstrong to General Lacey," April 21 and May 5, 1778, in Hazard, *Register of Pennsylvania*, 3:341, 343.

103. John A. Nagy, *Spies in the Continental Capital: Espionage Across Pennsylvania During the American Revolution* (Yardley, PA: Westholme, 2011), 104.

104. "To Brigadier General James Potter," January 12, 1778, *PGW*, 13:209.

105. "To Brigadier General John Lacey Jr.," January 23, 1778, *PGW*, 13:323–324.

106. "To Colonel Walter Stewart," January 22, 1778, *PGW*, 13:317; "To Brigadier General John Lacey Jr.," January 23, 1778, *PGW*, 13:323–324; "To Brigadier General John Lacey Jr.," January 23, 1778, *PGW*, 13:323–324; "To Israel Angell," February 1, 1778, *PGW*, 13:433–434; "To Major John Jameson," February 1, 1778, *PGW*, 13:437. George Walton, congressional delegate from Georgia, left Pennsylvania in the fall of 1777 under the impression that "it was declared death to be caught in carrying any thing into the City." "George Walton to Benjamin Franklin," December 20, 1777, *Papers of Benjamin Franklin*, 25:327–329.

107. Lacey was told to make certain his powers were "known to the people that they may again have warning." See "To Brigadier General John Lacey Jr.," January 23, 1778, *PGW*, 13:23–24; see also "To John Hancock," October 10, 1777, *PGW*, 11:473–475; "From John Hancock," October 14, 1777, *PGW*, 11:504.

108. For example, see "From Brigadier General John Lacey Jr.," January 26, 1778, *PGW*, 13:351; and "To Brigadier General John Lacey Jr.," March 2, 1778, *PGW*, 14:32–33.

109. Philip Kirk was found guilty of supplying the British with cattle and, in addition to being imprisoned while the enemy remained in the state, was to have all his property, both real and personal, taken from him. Though he approved everything else the court had done, Washington exercised his authority to suspend this last punishment, expressing his continued discomfort with the powers he had been granted and his opinion that such "confiscation of property is a matter not cognizable by martial Law." The court-martial of civilians appears in the General Orders of February 8, March 1, April 13, and April 18, 1778. *PGW*, 13:475, 14:1–3, 491–493, 544. Also see "From Brigadier General John Lacey Jr.," April 9, 1778, *PGW*, 14:435.

110. "To Brigadier General John Lacey Jr.," March 2, 1778, *PGW*, 14:32–33.

111. Muenchhausen, *At General Howe's Side*, 47; Peebles also reported on the destruction of the mills at Frankford, see Peebles, Journal, February 14, 1778, microfilm, n.d., DLAR.

112. "To Major John Jameson," February 1, 1778, *PGW*, 13:437.

113. "From Major John Jameson," February 2, 1778, *PGW*, 13:440. Beginning on February 8, Jameson and Lacey began destroying the mills. By the eleventh, their task was complete. "From Brigadier General John Lacey Jr.," February 11, 1778, *PGW*, 13:510–511.

114. "To Brigadier General John Lacey Jr.," February 8, 1778, *PGW*, 13:477–478; "To Capt. Stephen Chambers," February 27, 1778, *PGW*, 13:679–680; "General Orders," March 7, 1778, *PGW*, 14:81.

115. "General Armstrong to General Lacey," May 5, 1778, Hazard, *Register of Pennsylvania*, 3:343; Joseph Reed to [not addressed], Joseph Reed Papers, DLAR.

116. "To George Washington," February 15, 1778, *PNG*, 285.

117. André, November 20, 1777, John André Manuscript, Schoff Revolutionary War Collection, WCL; Jackson also records the occasional killing of farmers by American pickets. Jackson, *With the British Army in Philadelphia*, 163.

118. "To Brigadier General John Lacey Jr.," February 8, 1778, *PGW*, 13:477–478.

119. "General Lacey's Orders to His Scouting Party," March 19, 1778, Hazard, *Register of Pennsylvania*, 3:308.

120. "General Orders," January 20, 1778, *PGW*, 13:286–287; "Proclamation on Market at Valley Forge," January 30, 1778, *PGW*, 13:415. I owe a debt to Wayne Bodle for highlighting the significance of the specific wording of this proclamation. See Bodle, *Valley Forge Winter*, 165.

121. "Proclamation on Market at Valley Forge," January 30, 1778, *PGW*, 13:415.

122. "General Orders," February 8, 1778, *PGW*, 13:476.

123. "To William Buchanan," February 7, 1778, *PGW*, 13:465.

124. Bodle, *Valley Forge Winter*, 165.

125. "To Major General Nathanael Greene," February 12, 1778, *PGW*, 13:514.

126. "To George Washington," February 15, 1778, *PNG*, 285.

127. "From Major General Nathanael Greene," February 16, 1778, *PGW*, 13:557–558. The severity of Greene's measures caught the attention of at least one officer in Philadelphia. Major Baurmeister recorded that "the rebels are devastating the land and carrying off everything," so that "the whole country around Valley Forge is devastated," and that Revolutionaries were "always looking for [those bringing goods to Philadelphia] and maltreat those they catch." Baurmeister, *Revolution in America*, 157.

128. "From Major General Nathanael Greene," February 17, 1778, *PGW*, 13:569–570.

129. "To George Washington," February 15, 1778, *PNG*, 285; "To Major General Nathanael Greene," February 16, 1778, *PGW*, 13:556–557; "To George Washington," February 16, 1778, *PNG* 2:286–287.

130. "To Brigadier General Anthony Wayne," February 28, 1778, *PGW*, 13:517n2; "From Capt. John Barry," February 26, 1778, *PGW*, 13:672; "From Brigadier Gen. Anthony Wayne," February 25, 1778, *PGW*, 13:668; "Brigadier Gen. Anthony Wayne to Col. Joseph Ellis," *PGW*, 13:669n2; "From Brigadier Gen. Anthony Wayne," March 14, 1778, *PGW*, 14:180.

131. "To Gov. William Livingston," April 14, 1778, *PGW*, 14:513–514; "From Brigadier Gen. Anthony Wayne," February 26, 1778, *PGW*, 13:677–678; Bodle, *Valley Forge Winter*, 216–219.

132. Ewald, *Diary of the American War*, 117.

133. Ewald, *Diary of the American War*, 121. Ewald doesn't provide a source for this report, but in terms of influencing trade with the city, the perception that it *could* be accurate matters more than whether it really was. Muenchhausen and Baurmeister also recorded the danger faced by the local populace in the late winter and early spring. See Muenchhausen, *At General Howe's Side*, 49; and Baurmeister, *Revolution in America*, 157. Robert Proud also described how "the Vigilance of the Rebel Party by Means of the Country Militia, supported by Washington's Army has on every Side distressed the Inhabitants of this City to a high Degree, by preventing Provisions coming in from the Country." Proud, "Letters of Robert Proud," 70–71.

134. Eliza Farmar, "Letters of Eliza Farmar to Her Nephew," *PMHB* 40 (1916): 207.

135. Ewald, *Diary of the American War*, 117; "From Colonel Walter Stewart," January 18, 1778, *PGW*, 13:276–277; Muenchhausen, *At General Howe's Side*, 49; Bodle, *Valley Forge Winter*, 175; Simcoe, *Simcoe's Military Journal*, 27–28, 34–36.

136. Simcoe, *Simcoe's Military Journal*, 34–37.

137. "From Brigadier General John Lacey Jr.," February 27, 1778, *PGW*, 13:683; "To Brigadier General John Lacey Jr.," April 11, 1778, *PGW*, 14:476; "Lacey to Pres. Thomas Wharton Jr.," Hazard, *Register of Pennsylvania*, 3:307.

138. "To Brigadier General John Lacey Jr.," April 11, 1778, *PGW*, 14:476.

139. "From Brigadier General John Lacey Jr.," March 29, 1778, *PGW*, 14:352–353.

140. "To Brigadier General John Lacey Jr.," March 31, 1778, *PGW*, 14:638.

141. Joseph Reed to [not addressed], Camp Valley Forge, February 1, 1778, Joseph Reed Papers, DLAR.

142. J. B. Smith[?] to Joseph Reed, February 21, 1778, Joseph Reed Papers, DLAR. Underlining in the original.

143. Grant, January 22, 1778, Letterbook 4, James Grant Papers, DLAR.

144. Sir William Howe's Defense (Before a Select Committee of the House of Commons) of his Conduct as Command-in-Chief of the British Forces in the War of Independence, Henry Strachey Papers, Box 2, Folder 51, WCL. As it was composed to help defend his choices in America, Howe's report on the progress of the war likely contained a self-serving bias. However, the general trend he notes here reflects a common sentiment felt by British and Hessian officers.

145. Unsurprisingly, this same vicious cycle of mandated participation, increased disaffection, and a brutal crackdown was apt to emerge wherever the population's lack of ideological enthusiasm was deemed a threat to the cause. See, for example, Kim, "Limits of Politicization in the American Revolution," 868–889.

146. Wayne Bodle suggests a similar cycle in *Valley Forge Winter*, 164, 177; Captain John André was quick to recognize that the British and Revolutionaries responded to the commercial choices of the populace differently. While the Patriots declared trade with their enemy to be treason and even threatened the traders with death, André noted that "we on our part hold forth no such punishment to offenders against us." He at first believed that this was a mistake and encouraged the British to adopt equally harsh policies so that the populace would be "reduced to the agreeable alternative of choosing by whom they would be hanged." André, Philadelphia Camp, November 20, 1777, John André Manuscript, Box 2, Schoff Revolutionary War Collection, WCL.

147. "General Lacey to Council," March 11, 1778, Hazard, *Register of Pennsylvania*, 3:307–308.

148. "From Brigadier General John Lacey Jr.," March 29, 1778, *PGW*, 14:352–353.

149. Esther de Berdt to [Mary Jarvis?], Norrington, February 23, 1778, Joseph Reed Papers, DLAR.

150. Joseph Galloway, June 17, 1778, "Reason against abandoning Philadelphia & the Province of Pennsylvania," Sir Henry Clinton Papers, 35:46, WCL.

151. "An Account of the number of Persons who have taken the Oath of Allegiance at Philadelphia from the 30th September 1777 to the 17th June 1778, being nearly the time the British Troops were in possession of Philadelphia, with an Account of the number of Deserters from the Rebel Army and Fleet, that came in during that time, properly distinguished, viz.," June 1778, George Germain Papers, WCL; "An account of the number of Deserted Soldiers, Galleymen &c from the Rebel Army and Fleet, who have come in to Philadelphia and taken the Oath of Allegiance—with a particular account of the places in which they were born," George Germain Papers, vol. 7, WCL.

152. Joseph Galloway, "Proposal for covering and reducing the Country as the British Army shall pass through it," Sir Henry Clinton Papers, 35:47, WCL; Howe to Germain, October 21, 1777, George Germain Papers, vol. 6, WCL; P. Smith, *Loyalists and Redcoats*, 47; *Pennsylvania Evening Post*, March 6, 1778.

Interlude. Crossing the Lines

1. J. Allen, "Diary of James Allen," 177; "Historic Sites," Lehigh County Historical Society, http://www.lehighvalleyheritagemuseum.org/HistoricSites.htm.

2. J. Allen, "Diary of James Allen (continued)," 296.

3. J. Allen, "Diary of James Allen (continued)," 296; J. Allen, "Diary of James Allen (concluded)," 429.

4. J. Allen, "Diary of James Allen (continued)," 296.

5. J. Allen, "Diary of James Allen (concluded)," 427.

6. J. Allen, "Diary of James Allen," 192; J. Allen, "Diary of James Allen (concluded)," 430; *Pennsylvania Archives*, 1st ser., 6:407.

7. J. Allen, "Diary of James Allen (concluded)," 425.

8. J. Allen, "Diary of James Allen (concluded)," 430–431.

9. J. Allen, "Diary of James Allen (concluded)," 431–432.

10. J. Allen, "Diary of James Allen (concluded)," 433–434, 440; *Black list a list of those Tories who took part with Great Britain, in the Revolutionary War, and were attainted of high treason, commonly called the Black list ; to which is prefixed the legal opinions of Attorney Generals McKean & Dallas, &c.* (Philadelphia: Printed for the proprietor, 1802), available via Archive.org: https://archive.org/details/blacklistlistoftoophil.

Chapter 4. Occupation

Note to epigraph: Sir William Howe's Defense (Before a Select Committee of the House of Commons) of his Conduct as Command-in-Chief of the British Forces in the War of Independence, Henry Strachey Papers, Box 2, Folder 51, WCL.

1. E. Drinker, *Diary of Elizabeth Drinker*, 1:251. Drinker generally refused to allow either army, British or Continental, to confiscate materials from her family. Her refusals were occasionally honored. In this case, the soldier disregarded her objections but, in taking only a single blanket, seems to have done all he could to limit the distress of the family while still obeying his orders.

2. E. Drinker, *Diary of Elizabeth Drinker*, 1:258, 3:2170.

3. E. Drinker, *Diary of Elizabeth Drinker*, 1:258.

4. Elizabeth Drinker to Henry Drinker, December 3, 1777, Drinker Letters.

5. E. Drinker, *Diary of Elizabeth Drinker*, 1:236, 239–241, 256–257.

6. Henry Drinker to Elizabeth Drinker, September 18, 1777, January 26 and 30, February 7, 1778, Drinker Letters.

7. Joseph Reed to [not addressed], Camp Valley Forge, February 1, 1778, Joseph Reed Papers, Film 266, Reel 2, DLAR.

8. Jackson, *With the British Army in Philadelphia*, 277.

9. A Journal of Sundry Matters happening during the Stay of the Enemy at Germantown, September 25, 1777, in the Joseph Reed Papers, DLAR; Watson, *Annals of Philadelphia*, 2:282–283.

10. Morton, "Diary of Robert Morton," 1, 8.

11. Morton, "Diary of Robert Morton," 7–8.

12. E. Drinker, *Diary of Elizabeth Drinker*, 1:235–237.

13. Proud, "Letters of Robert Proud," 1, 63, 64, 70.

14. Watson, *Annals of Philadelphia*, 2:282–283.

15. Wainwright and Fisher, "'A Diary of Trifling Occurrences,'" 450.

16. The same leniency was even extended to British defectors, provided they voluntarily returned to the service before December 1. These proclamations were issued August 27, September 28, and October 8, 1777. All three were reprinted in the *Pennsylvania Evening Post*, October 11, 1777.

17. Morton, "Diary of Robert Morton," 7.

18. E. Drinker, *Diary of Elizabeth Drinker*, 1:257; John Fanning Watson, Jacob Mordecai, and Whitfield J. Bell Jr., "Addenda to Watson's Annals of Philadelphia: Notes by Jacob Mordecai, 1836," *PMHB* 98, no. 2 (April 1, 1974): 164; Proud, "Letters of Robert Proud," 73.

19. John M. Coleman, "Joseph Galloway and the British Occupation of Philadelphia," *Pennsylvania History* 30 (1963): 286–288, 291.

20. Watson, *Annals of Philadelphia*, 207, 284; Jackson, *With the British Army in Philadelphia*, 25; E. Drinker, *Diary of Elizabeth Drinker*, 1:248, 265–268.

21. Bezanson, *Prices and Inflation During the American Revolution*, 18, 35–37, 64; Watson, *Annals of Philadelphia*, 2:299.

22. *JCC*, 4:49.

23. *Pennsylvania Gazette*, February 14, 1776.

24. *JCC*, 7:36–37.

25. *JCC*, 9:990.

26. *Pennsylvania Evening Post*, November 27, 1777.

27. Morton, "Diary of Robert Morton," 32–33.

28. *Pennsylvania Evening Post*, November 27, 1777.

29. *Pennsylvania Evening Post*, October 11 and November 6, 1777.

30. Joseph Reed to [unaddressed], October 27, 1777, Joseph Reed Papers, DLAR.

31. Runaway advertisement for Mike High, *Pennsylvania Evening Post*, July 25, 1778; Robert Neill, "The Bolton and Dunn Houses," Maryland Historical Trust Site Survey, accessed February 13, 2018, https://mht.maryland.gov/secure/medusa/PDF/Kent/K-22.pdf.; Serle, *American Journal*, 249.

32. "To William Bradford," November 26, 1774, and "From William Bradford," January 4, 1775, *The Papers of James Madison*, 1:129, 132.

33. Virginian slaves had volunteered to fight under Dunmore in exchange for freedom even before the proclamation was issued and their eagerness may have encouraged the governor to take the fatal step. See "Deposition of John Randolph in Regard to the Removal of the Powder," in "Virginia Legislative Papers," *Virginia Magazine of History and Biography* 15 (October 1907): 150. Lieutenant General Thomas Gage, British commander in Boston, had expected such a move from Dunmore since May of 1775. The Virginia House of Burgesses had long expressed concern about "a Scheme, the most diabolical . . . to offer Freedom to our Slaves, and turn them against their Masters." See Benjamin Quarles, *The Negro in the American Revolution* (Chapel Hill: University of North Carolina Press, 1961), 22.

34. *Pennsylvania Evening Post*, December 14, 1775.

35. Muhlenberg, *Journals*, 3:78.

36. *Pennsylvania Evening Post*, July 25, 1778; *Pennsylvania Ledger*, February 11, 1778; *Pennsylvania Gazette*, July 7, 1779, February 24, 1779.

37. Billy G. Smith, "Black Women Who Stole Themselves in Eighteenth-Century America," in *Inequality in Early America*, ed. Carla Gardina Pestana and Sharon V. Salinger (Hanover, NH: University Press of New England, 1999), 142, 146.

38. *Pennsylvania Evening Post*, October 14, 1777.

39. "An Account of the number of Persons who have taken the Oath of Allegiance at Philadelphia from the 30th September 1777 to the 17th June 1778, being nearly the time the British Troops were in possession of Philadelphia, with an Account of the number of Deserters from the Rebel Army and Fleet, that came in during that time, properly distinguished," June 1778, George Germain Papers, WCL. Joseph Casino has suggested that adding the oath requirement may have been Howe's way of justifying the destruction and plunder which he knew the army would inevitably engage in. See Casino, "British Counterinsurgent Policy and Civilian Loyalties, 1776–1777, Part One: Promises and Plunder," Philadelphia Center for Early American Studies Seminar, March 5, 1982.

40. This situation mirrored that in the region around New York City. The British army consistently failed to embrace the restrained and respectful relationship with civilians that its leaders desired. See Gruber, *Howe Brothers*, 145–146; Downman, *Services of Lieut.-Colonel Francis Downman*, 30.

41. Serle, *American Journal*, 245; Baurmeister, *Revolution in America*, 99.

42. William Brooke Rawle, "Plundering by the British Army During the American Revolution," *PMHB* 25 (1901): 114.

43. Stephen Kemble et al., *The Kemble Papers* (New York: New York Historical Society, 1884), 1:504.

44. A Journal of Sundry Matters happening during the Stay of the Enemy at Germantown, Joseph Reed Papers, Film 266, Reel 2, DLAR.

45. *Pennsylvania Evening Post*, November 8, 1777.

46. *Pennsylvania Evening Post*, December 27, and December 30, 1777, January 3, January 6, February 19, March 11, and May 8, 1778.

47. *Pennsylvania Evening Post*, March 23, 1778.

48. *Pennsylvania Evening Post*, March 11 and May 8, 1778; Wainwright and Fisher, "'A Diary of Trifling Occurrences,'" 455–456, 463; Morton, "Diary of Robert Morton," 8, 24.

49. General Orders, Philadelphia, December 18, 1777, quoted in "Lord Mahon and the American War," *Colburn's United Service Magazine and Naval and Military Journal* (London: Colburn, 1852), 338.

50. O'Shaughnessy, *The Men Who Lost America*, 111; "State of the Rank and File fit for Duty &ca," Henry Clinton Papers 35:1, May 20, 1778, WCL.

51. Wainwright and Fisher, "'A Diary of Trifling Occurrences,'" 458–459; E. Drinker, *Diary of Elizabeth Drinker*, 1:261; Morton, "Diary of Robert Morton," 37.

52. "Solomon Bush to Henry Lazarus," Chestnut Hill, November 15, 1777, in Fritz Hirschfeld, *George Washington and the Jews* (Newark: University of Delaware Press, 2005), 115.

53. "Tench Tilghman to Robert Morris," HQ in Whitemarsh, November 29, 1777, in "Letters to Robert Morris," *Collections of the New-York Historical Society for the Year 1878* (New York: Printed for the Society, 1879), 433.

54. Muhlenberg, *Journals*, 3:107; "Facts of the American Revolution by Mrs. D. Logan," in John F. Watson, Historical Collections (Am 3013), 145–148, HSP. Robert Morton secured a clear prospect of the fires by climbing to the top of Christ Church steeple. See Morton, "Diary of Robert Morton," 31; John F. Watson, Historical Collections, Supplement (Am 3013), 1823, HSP; A Journal of Sundry Matters happening during the Stay of the Enemy at Germantown, November 22, 1777, in the Joseph Reed Papers, Film 266, Reel 2, DLAR.

55. "Tench Tilghman to Robert Morris," HQ in Whitemarsh, November 29, 1777, "Letters to Robert Morris," Revolutionary Papers, Vol. 1, *Collections of the New-York Historical Society for the Year 1878* (New York: Printed for the Society, 1879), 433; E. Drinker, *Diary of Elizabeth Drinker*, 1:256–257; Morton, "Diary of Robert Morton," 30; "Facts of the American Revolution by Mrs. D. Logan," 145–148; John F. Watson, Historical Collections, Supplement (Am 3013), 1823, HSP.

56. Muhlenberg, *Journals*, 3:107. In labeling Britain a bad parent, Muhlenberg was tapping into a well-established vein of patriotic rhetoric previously deployed by Franklin, among others. David Waldstreicher, *Runaway America: Benjamin Franklin, Slavery, and the American Revolution* (New York: Hill and Wang, 2004), 140–142.

57. Ewald, *Diary of the American War*, 109.

58. Wainwright and Fisher, "'A Diary of Trifling Occurrences,'" 458–459; Morton, "Diary of Robert Morton," 34–35.

59. E. Drinker, *Diary of Elizabeth Drinker*, 1:256; A Journal of Sundry Matters happening during the Stay of the Enemy at Germantown, November 25 and 26, 1777, in the Joseph Reed Papers, Film 266, Reel 2, DLAR.

60. André, Philadelphia Camp, November 20, 1777, John André Manuscript, Schoff Revolutionary War Collection, WCL.

61. Morton, "Diary of Robert Morton," 15.

62. Charles Stedman, *The History of the Origin, Progress, and Termination of the American War*, 2 vols. (Dublin, 1794), 1:330.

63. For example, Wainwright and Fisher, "'A Diary of Trifling Occurrences,'" 450; Proud, "Letters of Robert Proud," 73; E. Drinker, *Diary of Elizabeth Drinker*, 1:235; Morton, "Diary of Robert Morton," 7.

64. Baurmeister, *Revolution in America*, 139.

65. Thomas Parke to James Pemberton, November 10, 1777, Pemberton Family Papers, 31:16, HSP.

66. "Jedidiah Huntington to Jonathan Trumbull," HQ, sixteen miles from Philadelphia, October 24, 1777, "The Trumbull Papers, Part III," *Collections of the Massachusetts Historical Society*, 7th ser. (Boston: Published by the Society, 1902), 2:171. Solomon Bush made almost exactly the same assessment a short time later. "Solomon Bush to Henry Lazarus," Chestnut Hill, November 15, 1777, in Hirschfeld, *George Washington and the Jews*, 115.

67. Morton, "Diary of Robert Morton," 23–24, 34–35.

68. Thomas Parke to James Pemberton, November 10, 1777, Pemberton Family Papers, 31:16, HSP; Adams, "Diary Entry for September 16, 1777," *Works of John Adams*, 2:437.

69. Morton, "Diary of Robert Morton," 23–24.

70. Jackson, *With the British Army in Philadelphia*, 98; "Joseph Galloway to Gov. McKean," in Ernest Hickok Baldwin, *Joseph Galloway, the Loyalist Politician* (Philadelphia, 1902), 99.

71. Morton, "Diary of Robert Morton," 30.

72. Morton, "The Diary of Robert Morton," 7–8.

73. See Jackson, *With the British Army in Philadelphia*, 189–196; Peebles, Journal, October 1, 1777, Film 440, DLAR.

74. E. Drinker, *Diary of Elizabeth Drinker*, 1:263.

75. Frederick Bernays Wiener, *Civilians Under Military Justice: The British Practice Since 1689, Especially in North America* (Chicago: University of Chicago Press, 1967), 147.

76. See Great Britain, War Office, Judge Advocate General's Office, Court Martial Proceedings and Board of General Officer's Minutes, Film 675, DLAR (hereafter GB.WO).

77. On Brown and Dillion see GB.WO 71/85/203; on Mary Fygis see GB.WO 71/85/442; on Duncan and Buck see GB.WO 71/85/284–285.
78. See the entry for October 29, 1777, in Orderly Book of Sergeant Major Richards, October 26–December 17, 1777 (Orders, Returns, Morning Reports, and Accounts of British Troops, 1776–1781), Film 9, DLAR; Jackson, *With the British Army in Philadelphia*, 173.
79. Morton, *Diary of Robert Morton*, 9–10.
80. Orderly Book of Sergeant Major Richards, October 29 and 31, 1777, DLAR; for McSkimming's court-marital records see GB.WO 71/84/401.
81. Morton, "Diary of Robert Morton," 9–11.
82. Eyre Coote, Orderly Book, March 24, 1778, Eyre Coote Papers, n.d., WCL; Peebles, Journal, March 24, 1778; on Fisher's court-martial see GB.WO 71/85/290.
83. GB.WO 71/86/291.
84. Peebles, Journal, October 19, 1777; Muenchhausen, *At General Howe's Side*, 40.
85. E. Drinker, *Diary of Elizabeth Drinker*, 1:268.
86. E. Drinker, *Diary of Elizabeth Drinker*, 1:265–268.
87. E. Drinker, *Diary of Elizabeth Drinker*, 1:271–272; Elizabeth Drinker to Henry Drinker, December 31, 1777, Drinker Letters.
88. Watson, *Annals of Philadelphia*, 284.
89. E. Drinker, *Diary of Elizabeth Drinker*, 1:266–268. For several other examples of officers taking up residence in the homes of reluctant inhabitants see John F. Watson, "Recollections of the occupation of Philadelphia by the British forces in 1777 and 78," in Historical Collections (Am 3013), 1823, HSP.
90. General Orders, Head Quarters, Philadelphia, December 14, 1777, "Lord Mahon and the American War," *Colburn's United Service Magazine and Naval and Military Journal* (London: Colburn, 1852), 338.
91. Watson, Mordecai, and Bell Jr., "Addenda to Watson's Annals," 164; Proud, "Letters of Robert Proud," 73.
92. Joseph Reed to Thomas Wharton, November 4, 1777, Joseph Reed Papers.
93. Morton, "Diary of Robert Morton," 12; *Pennsylvania Evening Post*, October 11, 1777.
94. *Pennsylvania Evening Post*, November 6, 1777.
95. Stansbury and Odell, *The Loyal Verses of Joseph Stansbury*, 17–19.
96. *Pennsylvania Evening Post*, November 27, 1777.
97. *Pennsylvania Evening Post*, November 27, 1777.
98. *Pennsylvania Evening Post*, November 27, 1777.
99. Stansbury and Odell, *The Loyal Verses of Joseph Stansbury*, 17–19, 128–129.
100. Carl Leopold Baurmeister, Bernhard A. Uhlendorf, and Edna Vosper, "Letters of Major Baurmeister During the Philadelphia Campaign, 1777–1778, II," *PMHB* 60, no. 1 (January 1, 1936): 50.
101. William Howe to George Germain, Philadelphia, October 22, 1777, George Germain Papers, vol. 6, no. 15, WCL.
102. Jackson, *With the British Army in Philadelphia*, 107–115; William Howe to George Germain, Philadelphia, October 30, 1777, George Germain Papers, vol. 6, no. 18.
103. "John Clark Jr. to George Washington," December 3, 1777, Clark, "Letters from Major John Clark Jr. to Gen. Washington," 1–22.
104. Morton, "Diary of Robert Morton," 32–33, 37.

105. See, for example, Wainwright and Fisher, "'A Diary of Trifling Occurrences,'" 458, 460; E. Drinker, *Diary of Elizabeth Drinker*, 1:262–264; Proud, "Letters of Robert Proud," 65; Clark, "Letters from Major John Clark Jr. to Gen. Washington," 22. The campaign to restore the value of colonial paper had some success in early 1778 as local merchants were themselves able to begin importing goods from Britain. Newspaper ads show some traders willing to accept the currency in January, February, and March, but generally only in partial payment. By the end of April, the colonial money had again lost nearly all its value. See, for example, the ads from John and Chamless Hart, Jonas Philips, and Francis Jeyes in *Pennsylvania Evening Post*, January 10 and 20, 1778, and *Pennsylvania Ledger*, January 21, 1778, respectively.

106. Marshall Diaries, November 2, 1777, in Christopher Marshall Papers, HSP.

107. Muhlenberg, *Journals*, 3:108.

108. Proud, "Letters of Robert Proud," 72–73, 70.

109. Clark, "Letters from Major John Clark Jr. to Gen. Washington," 5. Drinker believed that the officers sent out to record the number of inhabitants, houses, and shops were doing so "that in case provisions should be scarce each may draw in proportion with the Army." This was, more likely, simply part of the army's effort to find suitable quarters for its officers. See E. Drinker, *Diary of Elizabeth Drinker*, 1:238.

110. Loftus Cliffe, Journal, November 23, 1777, Loftus Cliffe Papers, WCL. Underlining in the original.

111. Joseph Reed to [unaddressed], Norristown, November 30, 1777, Joseph Reed Papers, DLAR; Clark, "Letters from Major John Clark Jr. to Gen. Washington,"10–11.

112. On the expansive relief network of eighteenth-century Philadelphia, see Carl Bridenbaugh and Jessica Bridenbaugh, *Rebels and Gentlemen: Philadelphia in the Age of Franklin* (New York: Reynal and Hitchcock, 1942). For references to the closing of various philanthropic societies see John K. Alexander, *Render Them Submissive: Responses to Poverty in Philadelphia, 1760–1800* (Amherst: University of Massachusetts Press, 1980), 66, 127–129. The minutes of all the British benevolent societies in Philadelphia also show that they closed during the Revolution. See Society of the Sons of Saint George, Constitution and Meeting Minutes 1772–1949, HSP; Saint Andrew's Society of Philadelphia, Minutes, 1749–1776, 1786–1833, and Treasurer's Accounts, 1759–1843, American Philosophical Society (hereafter APS).

113. Alms House Managers, Minutes, 1766–1778, Record Group 35-2.3, Philadelphia City Archives (hereafter PCA). For the reassembling of the Overseers of the Poor after the occupation see Ground Rents Due the Overseers of the Poor, Minutes, March 1774 to May 1782, Record Group 35-1.1, PCA.

114. Alms House Managers, Minutes, 1766–1778, Record Group 35-2.3, PCA. The full text of the petition sent to General Howe appears in the entry for December 16, 1777.

115. Alms House Managers, Minutes, 1766–1778, Record Group 35-2.3, PCA.

116. Muhlenberg, *Journals*, 3:106 and 108; Clark, "Letters from Major John Clark Jr. to Gen. Washington,"10–11; Joseph Reed to [unaddressed], Norristown, November 30, 1777, Joseph Reed Papers, DLAR.

117. Clark, "Letters from Major John Clark Jr. to Gen. Washington,"16.

118. Sir Henry Strachey, ALS, to Lady Jane Strachey, Philadelphia, December 26, 1777, Henry Strachey Papers, WCL; Baurmeister, *Revolution in America*, 150.

119. Ewald, *Diary of the American War*, 117–118; Loftus Cliffe, ALS, to Bartholomew Cliffe, Philadelphia, January 20, 1778, Folder 14, Loftus Cliffe Papers, WCL; James Grant, Philadelphia,

January 22 and March 25, 1778, James Grant Papers, Army Career Series. Letterbook 4, Film 687, Reel 28, DLAR.

120. Marshall Diaries, January 6, 1778, in Christopher Marshall Papers, HSP; "To Major John Jameson," February 1, 1778, *PGW*, 13:437; Proud, "Letters of Robert Proud," 70.

121. Alms House Managers, Minutes, 1766–1778, Record Group 35–2.3, PCA. In February Galloway publicized the troubled state of public relief in the city and its causes, appointed a number of men to collect charitable donations, and used his prominence and position to direct the better-off inhabitants to them. See the proclamation in the *Pennsylvania Evening Post*, February 12, 1778.

122. Todd Braisted, "The Black Pioneers and Others: The Military Role of Black Loyalists in the American War for Independence," in *Moving On: Black Loyalists in the Afro-Atlantic World*, ed. John W. Pulis (New York: Garland, 1999), 11–12.

123. Braisted, "Black Pioneers and Others," 12; Muhlenberg, *Journals*, 3:78, 104–105.

124. Through much of the war, British policies toward enslaved Americans were ambiguous and uncertain. In the summer of 1779 Sir Henry Clinton, then the commanding British general in America, would issue a new decree from his headquarters in Phillipsburg, New York, firmly declaring that slaves who abandoned *rebel* masters and sought protection from the British army would find freedom and protection there. More than that, Clinton went on to "promise to every NEGROE Who shall desert the Rebel Standard, full Security to follow within these Lines, the Occupation which he shall think proper," thus eliminating the requirement that runaways work for or serve in the army, a prerequisite which had limited some past offers of freedom, such as Dunmore's. When the British took control of Philadelphia in October of 1777, such official promises of "Refuge" and "Security" had yet to be made. See "Proclamation," *Royal Gazette*, February 2, 1780, p. 4.

125. My count of slave ads is limited to those who ran from masters in or immediately around Philadelphia. For the period of the occupation, the *Pennsylvania Evening Post*, *Pennsylvania Ledger*, and *Royal Pennsylvania Gazette* were my sources for ads. For the period before the occupation I searched the *Pennsylvania Evening Post*, *Pennsylvania Ledger*, and *Pennsylvania Packet*. My population estimates come from Billy G. Smith's "Death and Life in a Colonial Immigrant City: A Demographic Analysis of Philadelphia," *Journal of Economic History* 37, no. 4 (December 1977): table 1, p. 865; and Howe's census data as quoted in J. Thomas Scharf and Thompson Westcott, *History of Philadelphia, 1609–1884* (Philadelphia: L. H. Everts, 1884), 1:367.

126. Many of the runaway ads published in Philadelphia, both before and during the occupation, explicitly forbade "masters of vessels" from harboring slaves and threatened legal action against those who did. The details of Tony's attempted escape in the winter of 1777/78 appear in a runaway ad posted in the *Pennsylvania Evening Post* when he attempted another escape after the occupation in September of 1778. See *Pennsylvania Evening Post*, September 4, 1778.

127. Judith Van Buskirk asks similar questions of slaves in occupied New York. See Van Buskirk, *Generous Enemies*, 139; Billy G. Smith and Richard Wojtowicz, *Blacks Who Stole Themselves: Advertisements for Runaways in the Pennsylvania Gazette, 1728–1790* (Philadelphia: University of Pennsylvania Press, 1989), 8–9.

128. Based on a tally of advertisements from the *Pennsylvania Evening Post*, *Pennsylvania Ledger*, and *Royal Pennsylvania Gazette* during the occupation and from *Pennsylvania Evening Post*, *Pennsylvania Ledger*, and *Pennsylvania Packet* before the occupation; Duche's ad appears in the *Pennsylvania Evening Post*, May 20, 1778.

129. *Royal Pennsylvania Gazette*, March 20, 1778.

130. Baurmeister, *Revolution in America*, 131, 171–172.

131. The advertisement for George appeared in the *Pennsylvania Ledger*, May 6, 1778. The advertisement for William appeared in the *Pennsylvania Evening Post*, December 12, 1777.

132. The Black Pioneers raised by Clinton increased its numbers from 172 to 200 during the occupation, though a smaller company also called the Black Pioneers and commanded by Capt. Robert Richard Crowe dissolved or was disbanded in the city. Gary B. Nash, *Forging Freedom: The Formation of Philadelphia's Black Community 1720–1840* (Cambridge, MA: Harvard University Press, 1988), 49; Braisted, "Black Pioneers and Others," 4, 14, and 23. Howe's orders to remove African Americans from provincial units appear in General Orders, 16th March 1777, for his Majesty's Provincial Forces, King's American Regiment Orderly Book, 1776–1777, WCL. Also see Quarles, *The Negro in the American Revolution*, 147.

133. Orders of March 22, 1778, see Braisted, "Black Pioneers and Others," 12; Quarles, *The Negro in the American Revolution*, 135.

134. My count of advertisements in Philadelphia papers seeking to hire servants, and desiring or willing to accept blacks or mulattos, shows only half as many, on average, during the occupation as compared with the same period the year before. Papers searched include *Pennsylvania Evening Post, Pennsylvania Ledger, Pennsylvania Packet* (through August 1777, when it moved to York), and the *Royal Pennsylvania Gazette*.

135. Johann Conrad Döhla, *A Hessian Diary of the American Revolution*, ed. Bruce E. Burgoyne (Norman: University of Oklahoma Press, 1990), 68.

136. Nash, *Forging Freedom*, 56.

137. Ewald, *Diary of the American War*, 305; Van Buskirk, *Generous Enemies*, 136.

138. *Pennsylvania Evening Post*, July 25, 1778.

139. In two proclamations issued on December 4, Galloway was named superintendent general and superintendent of imports and exports, making him the most powerful civilian in the city. See *Pennsylvania Evening Post*, December 4, 1777.

140. J. Allen, "Diary of James Allen (concluded)," 435.

141. Jackson, *With the British Army in Philadelphia*, 47.

142. *Pennsylvania Evening Post*, December 9, 1777, January 10 and February 24, 1778. The surge of clothing in "the newest fashions" during the occupation marked only one point in the larger, ongoing debate over proper attire, and the symbolism behind it, in Revolutionary America. As the largest port city in British America and the political capital of the new nation, Philadelphia was often a pivotal site in this debate. See Kate Haulman, "Fashion and the Culture Wars of Revolutionary Philadelphia," *William and Mary Quarterly* 62, no. 4 (October 1, 2005): 625–662.

143. Rebecca Franks, "A Letter of Miss Rebecca Franks, 1778," *PMHB* 16, no. 2 (July 1892): 217; E. Drinker, *Diary of Elizabeth Drinker*, 1:264–265.

144. Most overviews of the British possession devote a section to this subject. A sample of the literature focused on this topic specifically would include Helen Yalof, "British Military Theatricals in Philadelphia During the Revolutionary War" (PhD diss., New York University, 1972); Darlene Emmert Fisher, "Social Life in Philadelphia During the British Occupation," *Pennsylvania History* 37, no. 3 (July 1970): 237–260; Randall Fuller, "Theaters of the American Revolution: The Valley Forge 'Cato' and the Meschianza in Their Transcultural Contexts," *Early American Literature* 34, no. 2 (1999): 126–146; Meredith H. Lair, "Redcoat Theater: Negotiating Identity in

Occupied Philadelphia, 1777–1778," in *Pennsylvania's Revolution*, ed. William Pencak (University Park: Pennsylvania State University Press, 2010); Fred Lewis Pattee, "The British Theater in Philadelphia in 1778," *American Literature* 6, no. 4 (January 1935): 381–388; Thomas Clark Pollock, "Notes on Professor Pattee's 'The British Theater in Philadelphia in 1778,'" *American Literature* 7, no. 3 (November 1935): 310–314.

145. J. Allen, "Diary of James Allen (concluded)," 436.

146. Sir Henry Strachey to Lady Jane Strachey, March 24, 1778, Henry Strachey Papers, Box 1, WCL.

147. J. Allen, "Diary of James Allen (concluded)," 436; Peebles, Journal, May 18, 1777, microfilm, n.d., DLAR; Stedman, *History of the Origin, Progress, and Termination of the American War*, 1:385–386; Downman, *Services of Lieut.-Colonel Francis Downman*, 60–62.

148. E. Drinker, *Diary of Elizabeth Drinker*, 1:306; Stedman, *History of the Origin, Progress, and Termination of the American War*, 1:385–386.

149. J. Allen, "Diary of James Allen (concluded)," 436.

150. Sir William Howe's Defense (Before a Select Committee of the House of Commons) of his Conduct as Command-in-Chief of the British Forces in the War of Independence, Henry Strachey Papers, Box 2, Folder 51, WCL.

151. "Sir James Murray to Elizabeth Smyth," March 5, 1778, in *Letters from America 1776–1779: Being Letters of Brunswick, Hessian and Waldeck; Officers with the British Armies During the Revolution*, ed. Ray W. Pettengill (Whitefish, MT: Kessinger, 2006), 54.

152. Howe, *Narrative of Howe*, 56.

153. Howe to Germain, October 21, 1777, Germain Papers, vol. 6, WCL; Howe, *Narrative of Howe*, 53–54; Jackson, *With the British Army in Philadelphia*, 99–100. Enlistees were offered 50 to 200 acres of land, free from quitrents for ten years. Gruber, *Howe Brothers*, 244.

Interlude. Elizabeth Drinker Goes to Washington

1. Elizabeth Drinker to Henry Drinker, January 1, 19, and February 26, 1778, Drinker Letters.

2. E. Drinker, *Diary of Elizabeth Drinker*, 1:266; Elizabeth Drinker to Henry Drinker, February 26, 1778, Drinker Letters.

3. Elizabeth Drinker to Henry Drinker, January 5, 8, February 7, 14, 17, and 26, 1778, Drinker Letters.

4. E. Drinker, *Diary of Elizabeth Drinker*, 1:273; Elizabeth Drinker to Henry Drinker, January 25 and February 26, 1778, Drinker Letters.

5. E. Drinker, *Diary of Elizabeth Drinker*, 1:274.

6. Henry Drinker to Elizabeth Drinker, January 26, 30, and February 7, 1778, Drinker Letters.

7. Elizabeth Drinker to Henry Drinker, December 8, 1777, Drinker Letters.

8. E. Drinker, *Diary of Elizabeth Drinker*, 1:280–281, 282, 289.

9. E. Drinker, *Diary of Elizabeth Drinker*, 1:392–395.

10. Maxey, *Treason on Trial in Revolutionary Pennsylvania*, 24.

11. E. Drinker, *Diary of Elizabeth Drinker*, 1:297; "Washington to Council," *Pennsylvania Archives*, 1st ser., 6:401; J. Anderson, "Thomas Wharton, Exile in Virginia," 444; Oaks, "Philadelphians in Exile," 322.

12. E. Drinker, *Diary of Elizabeth Drinker*, 1:298–302.

13. "Minutes of the Supreme Executive Council," April 27, 1778, *Colonial Records of Pennsylvania*, 11:472–474; E. Drinker, *Diary of Elizabeth Drinker*, 1:302–304; J. Anderson, "Thomas Wharton, Exile in Virginia," 445–446; Gilpin, *Exiles in Virginia*, 223.

14. E. Drinker, *Diary of Elizabeth Drinker*, 1:303–305, 308.

Chapter 5. Evacuation

Note to epigraph: Serle, *American Journal*, 295–296.

1. *Pennsylvania Evening Post*, March 6, 1778.
2. E. Drinker, *Diary of Elizabeth Drinker*, 1:238–239; Morton, "Diary of Robert Morton," 16.
3. Wainwright and Fisher, "'A Diary of Trifling Occurrences,'" 451; J. Allen, "Diary of James Allen (continued)," 292.
4. William Howe to George Germain, August 30 and October 22, 1777, George Germain Papers, vol. 6, WCL.
5. James Grant of Ballindalloch Papers, October 20, 1777, Letterbook 4, DLAR.
6. Serle, *American Journal*, 260.
7. Muenchhausen, *At General Howe's Side*, 38.
8. Serle, *American Journal*, 262; Henry Strachey to Jane Strachey, December 2, 1777, fol. 42, Henry Strachey Papers, New Collection, WCL.
9. For example, see Downman, *Services of Lieut.-Colonel Francis Downman*, 46; Gruber, *Howe Brothers*, 255–256.
10. Muenchhausen, *At General Howe's Side*, 42.
11. Grant, November 30, 1777, Letterbook 4, James Grant Papers, DLAR; Henry Strachey to Jane Strachey, December 2, 1777, fol. 42, Henry Strachey Papers; Loftus Cliffe to Bartholomew Cliffe, November 12, 1777, fol. 13, Loftus Cliffe Papers, WCL. Underlining in the original.
12. The *Pennsylvania Ledger* published the same terms on November 5, 1777.
13. *Pennsylvania Evening Post*, January 3, 1778.
14. *Pennsylvania Evening Post*, October 16, and November 1, 1777, and January 6, March 6, April 8 and 10, 1778.
15. Jackson, *With the British Army in Philadelphia*, 231; Muenchhausen, *At General Howe's Side*, 52.
16. J. Allen, "Diary of James Allen (concluded)," 435; Muenchhausen, *At General Howe's Side*, 52; Muhlenberg, *Journals*, 3:149; Bodle, *Valley Forge Winter*, 227.
17. Wainwright and Fisher, "'A Diary of Trifling Occurrences,'" 462.
18. J. Allen, "Diary of James Allen (concluded)," 429–436.
19. Serle, *American Journal*, 287.
20. "Nathanael Greene to George Washington," April 25, 1778, *PNG*, 2:355–357.
21. Jackson, *With the British Army in Philadelphia*, 254.
22. Muenchhausen, *At General Howe's Side*, 54.
23. Baurmeister, *Revolution in America*, 163; Grant, March 25, 1778, Letterbook 4, James Grant Papers, DLAR; Muenchhausen, *At General Howe's Side*, 49.
24. Ewald, *Diary of the American War*, 121; Simcoe, *Simcoe's Military Journal*, 60.
25. Montrésor and Scull, "Journal of Captain John Montrésor," 201; Jackson, *With the British Army in Philadelphia*, 230, 255, 256.
26. E. Drinker, *Diary of Elizabeth Drinker*, 1:307.

27. Serle, *American Journal*, 297–298.
28. Baurmeister, *Revolution in America*, 174, 180.
29. Joseph Reed to "Hetty," June 9, 1778, Joseph Reed Papers, DLAR; Baurmeister, *Revolution in America*, 179.
30. Serle, *American Journal*, 304–307.
31. William Eden to George Germain, June 19, 1778, George Germain to William Eden, July 3, 1778, and Draft of a letter to the Commissioners, July 1778, in George Germain Papers, vol. 7, WCL.
32. J. Allen, "Diary of James Allen (concluded)," 436–438.
33. E. Drinker, *Diary of Elizabeth Drinker*, 309; Joseph Reed to "Hetty," June 9, 1778, Joseph Reed Papers, DLAR.
34. Ewald, *Diary of the American War*, 130–131.
35. Ibid.
36. Joseph Galloway, "Proposal for covering and reducing the Country as the British Army shall pass through it," June 17, 1778, Henry Clinton Papers, 35:47, WCL.
37. Serle, *American Journal*, 299–301.
38. J. Allen, "Diary of James Allen(concluded)," 436–438.
39. Serle, *American Journal*, 295; Ewald, *Diary of the American War*, 130–131.
40. Peter Miller to Henry Clinton, May 26, 1778, Henry Clinton Papers, 35:10, WCL.
41. Ewald, *Diary of the American War*, 131; E. Drinker, *Diary of Elizabeth Drinker*, 1:311; Jackson, *With the British Army in Philadelphia*, 260.
42. By some accounts, no fewer than four thousand refugees sought protection with the British in Philadelphia. "A State of the Circumstances of Philadelphia when the British Troops took Possession, &ca.," George Germain Papers, vol. 6; Baurmeister, *Letters from Major Baurmeister*, 61; Ewald, *Diary of the American War*, 131; Döhla, *A Hessian Diary of the American Revolution*, 74.
43. E. Drinker, *Diary of Elizabeth Drinker*, 1:309–311.
44. Baurmeister, *Revolution in America*, 182; Wainwright and Fisher, "'A Diary of Trifling Occurrences,'" 465; Loftus Cliffe to Charles Tottenham, July 5, 1778, Loftus Cliffe Papers, WCL.
45. Jackson, *With the British Army in Philadelphia*, 266.
46. When the British evacuated New York in 1783, a record was kept of all blacks who left the city. For many of them, their city of origin and status, slave or free, was noted. For a published version of the entire list, see Graham Russell Hodges, ed., *The Black Loyalist Directory: African Americans in Exile After the American Revolution* (New York: Garland, 1996). Debra Newman's examination of this list, also known as the "Inspection Roll of Negroes," finds these seventy-five individuals. It is possible that many more were in Philadelphia and departed at the same time as the British but did not remain in New York long enough to be found on the inspection roll. Debra Newman, "They Left with the British: Black Women in the Evacuation of Philadelphia, 1778," *Pennsylvania Heritage* 4 (1977): 20–23. The course of the Black Pioneers after Philadelphia is followed in Braisted, "Black Pioneers and Others," 14–18.
47. *Pennsylvania Evening Post*, July 25, 1778; *Pennsylvania Gazette*, July 7, 1779; *Pennsylvania Gazette*, February 24, 1779.
48. J. Anderson, "Thomas Wharton, Exile in Virginia," 427; Baurmeister, *Revolution in America*, 174.
49. Muhlenberg, *Journals*, 3:158.

50. Wainwright and Fisher, "'A Diary of Trifling Occurrences,'" 462–463; E. Drinker, *Diary of Elizabeth Drinker*, 1:308–310.

51. Serle, *American Journal*, 295–296.

52. Nesbit Balfour to Henry Strachey, June 17, 1778, Henry Strachey Papers, New Collection, fol. 50, WCL.

53. Serle, *American Journal*, 301–302.

54. Grant, October 12, 1778, Letterbook 4, James Grant of Ballindalloch Papers,DLAR.

55. Henry Clinton to Henry Fiennes Pelham-Clinton, May 28, 1778, Henry Clinton Papers, 35:4, WCL.

56. Memorandum by Sir Henry Clinton, June 6, 1778, Sir Henry Clinton Papers, 35:34, WCL.

57. William Eden to George Germain, June 19, 1778, George Germain Papers, vol. 7, WCL.

58. George Johnstone to Henry Laurens, June 10, 1778, and Henry Laurens to George Johnstone, June 14, 1778, Sir Henry Clinton Papers, 35:45, WCL.

59. "Earl of Carlisle to George Selwyn," June 10, 1778, in William Bradford Reed, *Life and Correspondence of Joseph Reed: Military Secretary of Washington, at Cambridge, Adjutant-General of the Continental Army, Member of the Congress of the United States, and President of the Executive Council of the State of Pennsylvania*, 2 vols. (Philadelphia: Lindsay and Blakiston, 1847), 1:380.

60. E[dward?] Biddle to Joseph Reed, June 6, 1778, Joseph Reed Papers, DLAR.

61. Joseph Reed to "Hetty," June 9, 1778, Joseph Reed Papers, DLAR; Bodle, *Valley Forge Winter*, 242.

62. John Witherspoon, *The Humble Confession, Declaration, Recantation, and Apology of Benjamin Towne, Printer in Philadelphia* (Philadelphia, 1778).

63. J. Allen, "Diary of James Allen (concluded)," 440.

64. Clinton's minutes of conversations with Lord Howe and with Galloway, May 1778, Sir Henry Clinton Papers, 35:18, WCL; Stedman, *History of the Origin, Progress, and Termination of the American War*, 1:380; Serle, *American Journal*, 295.

65. J. Allen, "Diary of James Allen (concluded)," 436–438.

66. Joseph Galloway, "Reason against abandoning Philadelphia & the Province of Pennsylvania," Sir Henry Clinton Papers, 35:46, WCL.

67. Serle, *American Journal*, 302–303.

68. Mark Lender, "The 'Cockpit' Reconsidered: Revolutionary New Jersey as a Military Theater," in *New Jersey in the American Revolution*, ed. Barbara J. Mitnick (New Brunswick, NJ: Rutgers University Press, 2005), 56.

Interlude. Change and Continuity

1. At least two members of the family, Ann's brother John Cooper and her third son Benjamin Whitall, did pick a side in the struggle. John served as a member of the Second Continental Congress; Benjamin was an officer in the Continental Army. Kathryn S. Dodson, *The Whitall Family Day Book: A Look at the American Revolution Through the Eyes of Everyday People* (Woodbury, NJ: Gloucester County Board of Chosen Freeholders, 1989), 2, 15.

2. Job Whitall, *The Diary of Job Whitall, Gloucester County, New Jersey, 1775–1779*, transcribed by Florence DeHuff Friel (Woodbury, NJ: Gloucester County Historical Society, 1992), 21, 29, 56 (February 24, 1776, May 8, 1776, February 4, 1777).

3. Whitall, *Diary of Job Whitall*, 16, 50, 55, 72, 73, 74–75 (January 12, November 29, 1776, January 20, August 15, August 19, September 2, 1777).

4. Whitall, *Diary of Job Whitall*, 19 (February 7, 1776).

5. Whitall, *Diary of Job Whitall*, 61 (April 16, 1777); Dodson, *Whitall Family Day Book*, 2.

6. Jackson, *With the British Army in Philadelphia*, 63–66; Angell, *Diary of Colonel Israel Angell*, October 22, 23, 1777.

7. Whitall, *Diary of Job Whitall*, 80–81 (October 22, 23, 1777).

8. Ann Whitall's encounter with the cannonball was first recorded in 1801 by a historian who claimed to have heard it from James Whitall, her husband. The Whitall house still stands and, by some accounts, the damage caused by the stray shot can still be discerned. Job's diary makes no mention of this brief adventure. Lee Patrick Anderson, *Forty Minutes by the Delaware: The Story of the Whitalls, Red Bank Plantation and the Battle for Fort Mercer* (Parkland, FL: Universal Publishers, 1999), 115–117.

9. Whitall, *Diary of Job Whitall*, 80–81 (October 23, 1777); Richard R. Poots, "Historical Survey of the Ann Cooper Whitall House," May 20, 1968, available at the Gloucester County Historical Society Library.

10. Whitall, *Diary of Job Whitall*, 85 (November 21, 1777).

11. Job's wife and son made one trip to Philadelphia shortly before the occupation officially ended. The boy, David, was ill and the severity of the situation apparently prompted the exceptional and risky journey across the lines to seek medical assistance. Whitall, *Diary of Job Whitall*, 111 (June 2, 1778).

12. Following this event Job's father and several neighbors traveled to Philadelphia in pursuit of the thieves. They found two of the men and, presumably with the assistance of the authorities there, succeeded in recovering at least some of the clothing that had been lost. Whitall, *Diary of Job Whitall*, 113–114 (June 22, 23, 25, 1778).

13. Hannah Whitall Smith, *John M. Whitall: The Story of His Life* (Philadelphia: printed for the family, 1879), 8–9; Frank H. Stewart, comp. and ed., *Notes on Old Gloucester County, New Jersey* (Camden, NJ: New Jersey Society of Pennsylvania, 1937), 3:167. Applications to the Daughters of the American Revolution citing Ann Whitall as an ancestor are collected in the folder labeled "Whitall Family (D.A.R. Applications)" in the Whitall Family Papers held by the Gloucester County Historical Society Library.

Chapter 6. Aftermath

Note to epigraph: E. Drinker, *Diary of Elizabeth Drinker*, 1:361.

1. "T. Matlack to Jona. D. Sergeant," July 9, 1778, *Pennsylvania Archives*, 1st ser., 6:630.

2. *Pennsylvania Archives*, 2nd ser., 3:6.

3. Ousterhout, *A State Divided*, 162–163.

4. Ousterhout, *A State Divided*, 191–192. Ousterhout suggests that the fine specifically targeting those associated with education would have been particularly disastrous for Pennsylvania sects, such as the Quakers, who ran their own schools.

5. Muhlenberg, *Journals*, 3:158.

6. *Pennsylvania Archives*, 3rd ser., 10:519–544; Ousterhout, *A State Divided*, 12–13, 23; *Pennsylvania Evening Post*, June 25, 1778. The governments of New York, South Carolina, and Georgia

would also issue bills of attainder against individuals in British-occupied territory. Johnson, "Forgiving and Forgetting in Postrevolutionary America," 174; Article I, Sections 9 and 10 of the US Constitution forbid the issuing of bills of attainder to both Congress and the states, respectively.

7. Marshall Diaries, June 23–26, 1778, in Christopher Marshall Papers, HSP; Muhlenberg, *Journals*, 3:167–169, 171; Jackson, *With the British Army in Philadelphia*, 263–269; Peter S. Duponceau, "Autobiographical Letters of Peter S. Duponceau," *PMHB* 40, no. 2 (1916): 184–185; "Josiah Bartlett, to Col. Langdon," July 13, 1778, in John W. Jordan and Josiah Bartlett, "Sessions of the Continental Congress Held in the College of Philadelphia in July, 1778," *PMHB* 22, no. 1 (January 1, 1898): 114–115; Nelson Waite Rightmyer, "Churches Under Enemy Occupation: Philadelphia, 1777–8," *Church History* 14, no. 1 (March 1945): 45–46, 48.

8. Wainwright and Fisher, "'A Diary of Trifling Occurrences,'" 464; Loftus Cliffe to Charles Tottenham, July 5, 1778, Loftus Cliffe Papers, WCL.

9. *Pennsylvania Evening Post*, July 16, 1778; *Pennsylvania Packet*, August 18, 1778.

10. *Pennsylvania Evening Post*, July 18, 1778.

11. *Pennsylvania Evening Post*, July 25 and August 6, 1778; Rosswurm, *Arms, Country, and Class*, 154–155. The Patriotic Society would not be the only, or the last, popular committee devoted to hunting down evidence against fellow citizens. See, for example, a similar group assembled approximately a year later "to inquire what persons are now remaining in this city and its environs disaffected to the United States" in the *Pennsylvania Evening Post*, June 5, 1779.

12. *Pennsylvania Evening Post*, July 8, 1778.

13. The conflict over women's fashion during and after the occupation and its hypothetical political implications marks only one example of what Kate Haulman has called a "culture war" in which "the Whig style of politics confronted the Tory politics of style, the former repeatedly and unsuccessfully attempting to destroy the latter." Haulman, "Fashion and the Culture Wars," 629.

14. "The Association read and signed," *American Archives*, 4th ser., 1: 914–915.

15. "From a Late Philadelphia Paper," *Continental Journal* (Boston), July 30, 1778.

16. For the deepest analysis of this incident, see Susan Klepp, "Rough Music on Independence Day, 1778," in *Riot and Revelry in Early America*, ed. William Pencak, Matthew Dennis, and Simon P. Newman (University Park: Pennsylvania State University Press, 2002), 156–176; E. Drinker, *Diary of Elizabeth Drinker*, 1:314; Rosswurm, *Arms, Country, and Class*, 154. Richard Henry Lee recorded that, with a few exceptions, "The Tory women are very much mortified." See "Richard Henry Lee to Francis Lightfoot Lee," July 5, 1778, in Richard Henry Lee, *The Letters of Richard Henry Lee*, ed. James Curtis Ballagh (New York: Macmillan, 1911), 1:421. More than a critique, the procession carried a tacit threat. The "dirty Woman" was escorted through the streets to the sound of music; the beating of drums is specifically recorded. As Klepp notes in her analysis of the incident, "The drummer probably beat the 'Whore's March' or the 'Rogue's March,' which announced the expulsion of 'idle' women from military encampments." If so, the July 4 exhibition was merely the most elaborate of many instances in which Philadelphia radicals called for "Tory" women, and particularly the wives and children of Loyalist refugees, to be expelled from Philadelphia or otherwise punished.

17. Mark Jacob and Stephen H. Case, *Treacherous Beauty: Peggy Shippen, the Woman Behind Benedict Arnold's Plot to Betray America* (Guilford, CT: Lyons Press, 2012), 55–56; Scharf and Westcott, *History of Philadelphia*, 2:899.

18. "Gérard de Rayneval to Count de Vergennes," August 24, 1778, in John Durand, "American History in the French Archives," *New Princeton Review* 4 (1887): 329.

19. *Pennsylvania Evening Post*, June 12, 1779; "Statement of Charles Willson Peale," in Reed, *Life and Correspondence of Joseph Reed*, 423; Ousterhout, *A State Divided*, 210; Samuel Rowland Fisher, "Journal of Samuel Rowland Fisher, of Philadelphia, 1779–1781 (continued)," *PMHB* 41, no. 3 (1917): 293–295.

20. Ousterhout, *A State Divided*, 186; Ousterhout, "Controlling the Opposition," 17, 23; on Benjamin Towne, see *Pennsylvania Archives*, 6th ser., 13:477.

21. Ousterhout, *A State Divided*, 186; *Pennsylvania Archives*, 1st ser., 6:628; *Pennsylvania Evening Post*, July 25, 1778.

22. Ousterhout, "Controlling the Opposition," 27.

23. Ousterhout, "Controlling the Opposition," 27.

24. "General [John] Armstrong to V[ice] P[resident] Bryan, 1778," July 24, 1778, *Pennsylvania Archives*, 1st ser., 6:661–663.

25. "George Bryan to Col. John Weitzel," May 22, 1778, *Pennsylvania Archives*, 1st ser., 6:541.

26. "George Bryan to John Thorne," May 25, 1778, *Pennsylvania Archives*, 2nd ser., 3:169–170.

27. *Pennsylvania Archives*, 1st ser., 6:622.

28. Ousterhout, *A State Divided*, 194; "Proclamation of Pardon to Prisoners Under Test Laws, 1778," *Pennsylvania Archives*, 1st ser., 7:130–131.

29. "Joseph Reed to Thomas McKean," April 20, 1779, *Pennsylvania Archives*, 1st ser., 7:328.

30. "Joseph Reed to Supreme Executive Council," October 23, 1778, quoted in Peter C. Messer, "'A Species of Treason & Not the Least Dangerous Kind': The Treason Trials of Abraham Carlisle and John Roberts," *PMHB* 123, no. 4 (October 1, 1999): 320.

31. *Pennsylvania Archives*, 1st ser., 6:628.

32. Ousterhout, "Controlling the Opposition," 30–31; Respublica v. Doan, 1 U.S. 86 (1784), see: http://supreme.justia.com/cases/federal/us/1/86/.

33. "General [John] Armstrong to V[ice] P[resident] Bryan, 1778," July 24, 1778, *Pennsylvania Archives*, 1st ser., 6:661–663; "V. P. George Bryan to Col. John Weitzel," May 22, 1778, *Pennsylvania Archives*, 1st ser., 6:541.

34. Ousterhout, *A State Divided*, 184–185.

35. Fisher recounts his ordeal in his journal. S. Fisher, "Journal of Samuel Rowland Fisher, of Philadelphia, 1779–1781," *PMHB* 41 (1917): 145–197, 274–333, 399–457; Ousterhout, *A State Divided*, 284–285.

36. Jacob and Case, *Treacherous Beauty*, 55–56; *Pennsylvania Packet*, August 29, 1778; Scharf and Westcott, *History of Philadelphia*, 2:1692, 3:898–899; Carl Van Doren, *Secret History of the American Revolution: An Account of the Conspiracies of Benedict Arnold and Numerous Others, Drawn from the Secret Service Papers* (New York: Viking, 1941), 184; Graydon, *Memoirs of His Own Time*, 469.

37. Haulman, "Fashion and the Culture Wars," 625, 629, 659–660.

38. "Timothy Pickering to his wife," in Scharf and Westcott, *History of Philadelphia*, 2:900; E. Drinker, *Diary of Elizabeth Drinker*, 1:314; Klepp, "Rough Music," 162, 166–167, 171.

39. "Statement of Charles Willson Peale," in Reed, *Life and Correspondence of Joseph Reed*, 423; Judith L. Van Buskirk, "They Didn't Join the Band: Disaffected Women in Revolutionary Philadelphia," *Pennsylvania History* 62 (July 1995): 308, 317, 324; Ousterhout, *A State Divided*, 210.

40. "George Washington to Benedict Arnold," in *The Writings of George Washington*, ed. Jared Sparks (Boston: Russell, Odiorne, and Metcalf, 1834), 5:413 (available via Google Books); "Proclamation of General Arnold, 1778," *Pennsylvania Archives*, 1st ser., 6:606–607.

41. "Address of the principal Inhabitants on Lake Champlain to Benedict Arnold," *American Archives*, 4th ser., 2:1087–1088.

42. Jacob and Case, *Treacherous Beauty*, 79.

43. Van Doren, *Secret History of the American Revolution*, 185.

44. Van Doren, *Secret History of the American Revolution*, 185.

45. "Reed to Greene," November 5, 1778, in Reed, *Life and Correspondence of Joseph Reed*, 2:37–38.

46. "Reed to Greene," November 5, 1778, in Reed, *Life and Correspondence of Joseph Reed*, 2:37–38.

47. Van Doren, *Secret History of the American Revolution*, 189.

48. Van Doren, *Secret History of the American Revolution*, 190n59; "Proceedings of a general court martial of the line, held at Raritan, in the state of New-Jersey, by order of His Excellency George Washington, Esq. general and commander in chief of the Army of the United States of America, for the trial of Major General Arnold, June 1, 1779," published by order of Congress, Early American Imprints.

49. *Pennsylvania Packet*, November 5, 1778; Rosswurm, *Arms, Country, and Class*, 158; Ousterhout, *A State Divided*, 196; Messer, "'A Species of Treason,'" 303–304.

50. Maxey, *Treason on Trial in Revolutionary Pennsylvania*, 95. David W. Maxey provides, by far, the most complete and compelling description of Roberts's trial, including transcripts of witness testimony and a thoughtful analysis of what "treason" can mean in a Revolutionary context.

51. Many of these petitions are collected together. See "Memorials in Favor of John Roberts and Ab'm Carlisle, 1778," *Pennsylvania Archives*, 1st ser., 7:21–44, 52–58; Messer, "'A Species of Treason,'" 304–305; Rosswurm, *Arms, Country, and Class*, 158–159.

52. "Memorials in Favor of John Roberts and Ab'm Carlisle, 1778," *Pennsylvania Archives*, 1st ser., 7:21, 22.

53. "Memorials in Favor of John Roberts and Ab'm Carlisle, 1778," *Pennsylvania Archives*, 1st ser., 7:22.

54. "Memorials in Favor of John Roberts and Ab'm Carlisle, 1778," *Pennsylvania Archives*, 1st ser., 7:55.

55. "Memorials in Favor of John Roberts and Ab'm Carlisle, 1778," *Pennsylvania Archives*, 1st ser., 7:24, 28, 55.

56. Rosswurm, *Arms, Country, and Class*, 164–167; Anthony Cuthbert, "Assessment of Damages Done by the British Troops During the Occupation of Philadelphia, 1777–1778," *PMHB* 25, no. 3 (1901): 323–335; Hugh Jones, "Assessment of Damages Done by the British Troops During the Occupation of Philadelphia, 1777–1778 (concluded)," *PMHB* 25, no. 4 (1901): 544–559. Richard Buel has written a compelling and broad description of the relationship between wartime destruction, military occupation, and the Revolutionary economy. See Buel, *In Irons: Britain's Naval Supremacy and the American Revolutionary Economy* (New Haven, CT: Yale University Press, 1998).

57. Richard Alan Ryerson, "Republican Theory and Partisan Reality in Revolutionary Pennsylvania: Toward a New View of the Constitutionalist Party," in *Sovereign States in an Age of Uncertainty*, ed. Ronald Hoffman and Peter J. Albert (Charlottesville: University Press of Virginia, 1981), 95–133; Rosswurm, *Arms, Country, and Class*, 176–177; Ousterhout, *A State Divided*, 202–203; *Pennsylvania Gazette*, March 24, 1779; Owen S. Ireland, "The Crux of Politics: Religion and

Party in Pennsylvania, 1778–1789," *William and Mary Quarterly*, 3rd ser., 42, no. 4 (October 1985): 454–456; Burton Alva Konkle, *George Bryan and the Constitution of Pennsylvania, 1731–1791* (Philadelphia: William J. Campbell, 1922), 172–174.

58. Ellis Paxson Oberholtzer, *Robert Morris: Patriot and Financier* (New York: Macmillan, 1903), 56; Graydon, *Memoirs of His Own Time*, 332–333.

59. Consider, for example, the mass meeting in May 1779, led by prominent Constitutionalist general Daniel Roberdeau, which seamlessly moved from denunciations of wealthy merchants, including some patriots, to condemnation of those "inimical to the interest and independence of the United States." Roberdeau Buchanan, *Genealogy of the Roberdeau Family, including a Biography of General Daniel Roberdeau of the Revolutionary Army, and the Continental Congress; and Signer of the Articles of Confederation* (Washington, DC: Joseph L. Pearson, 1876), 84–85; Ousterhout, *A State Divided*, 198; Brunhouse, *Counter-Revolution in Pennsylvania*, 16; Ousterhout, *A State Divided*, 190, 202–203.

60. Rosswurm, *Arms, Country, and Class*, 158–159; quoting John Rush to John Dickinson, Wilmington, March 20, 1778, John Dickinson Papers (LCP), no. 18, HSP.

61. Graydon, *Memoirs of His Own Time*, 332–333.

62. Steven Rosswurm traces the causes and course of this breach in the final third of his book on the Philadelphia militia. See Rosswurm, *Arms, Country, and Class*, 201–248.

63. Joseph Reed later had these men arrested, ostensibly solely for their own protection. Thomas Story's father, Enoch Story, had been a noteworthy agent serving the British during the occupation and fled during the withdrawal, but the son was discharged without being tried for treason. "Statement of Charles Willson Peale," in Reed, *Life and Correspondence of Joseph Reed*, 423; Rosswurm, *Arms, Country, and Class*, 182, 212–213; Ousterhout, *A State Divided*, 205–206.

64. "Statement of Charles Willson Peale," in Reed, *Life and Correspondence of Joseph Reed*, 424; S. Fisher, "Journal of Samuel Rowland Fisher," 169–173; John K. Alexander, "The Fort Wilson Incident of 1779: A Case Study of the Revolutionary Crowd," *William and Mary Quarterly* 31, no. 4 (October 1, 1974): 601–602; Rosswurm, *Arms, Country, and Class*, 210–217, 218.

65. On the violent assault on Humphreys's home, carried out in retribution for an anti-Constitutionalist essay which appeared in the *Evening Post*, see Brunhouse, *Counter-Revolution in Pennsylvania*, 74–75; Ousterhout, *A State Divided*, 200–201; *Pennsylvania Evening Post*, August 2, 1779.

66. Rosswurm, *Arms, Country, and Class*, 218.

67. This shift is charted in detail from two strikingly different perspectives in the work of Steven Rosswurm and Robert Brunhouse. Though Rosswurm clearly sympathizes with the radical militia and Brunhouse unambiguously agrees with the conservative perspective of the Republicans, both scholars recognize the same split within the Constitutionalist Party and the rise of the conservatives beginning in 1780. See Rosswurm, *Arms, Country, and Class*, 203–248; and Brunhouse, *Counter-Revolution in Pennsylvania*, 88–155.

68. Rosswurm, *Arms, Country, and Class*, 203.

Epilogue

1. Elizabeth Evans, *Weathering the Storm: Women of the American Revolution* (New York: Charles Scribner's Sons, 1975), 176–177. A display of similar items and an account of the Drinkers' losses due to fines can be seen at the Museum of the American Revolution in Philadelphia.

2. E. Drinker, *Diary of Elizabeth Drinker*, 1:337, 386, 392, 756, 795.

3. E. Drinker, *Diary of Elizabeth Drinker*, 1:500, 507–508, 525; Evans, *Weathering the Storm*, 181; Helena M. Wall, " 'My Constant Attension on My Sick Child': The Fragility of Family Life in the World of Elizabeth Drinker," in *Children in Colonial America*, ed. James Marten (New York: New York University Press, 2007), 158.

4. E. Drinker, *Diary of Elizabeth Drinker*, 1:718–719, lxxiv; Evans, *Weathering the Storm*, 183–184.

5. E. Drinker, *Diary of Elizabeth Drinker*, 1:lxxiv.

6. J. Allen, "Diary of James Allen," 176; J. Allen, "Diary of James Allen (concluded)," 440.

7. "John Adams to Hezekiah Niles," February 13, 1818, *Works of John Adams*, 10:828. Adams's appeal to "the people" as a single, sovereign authority whose will could justify either a government or a revolution flowed from seventeenth-century English conceptions which empowered Parliament to set the sovereignty of the people against the divine right of the king and would, later, empower the federal government in its claims of supremacy over the states. Edmund Morgan artfully follows this long transition. See Morgan, *The Invention of the People: The Rise of Popular Sovereignty in England and America* (New York: W. W. Norton, 1988).

8. Notably, Robert G. Parkinson's work in *The Common Cause* highlights not only how some racial minorities were excluded from the unifying Revolutionary narrative, but how that exclusion was essential in bringing white Patriots together.

9. Sung Bok Kim demonstrates the growth of disaffection in Westchester County and how the Patriot response could deepen it, Joseph S. Tiedemann shows New York to be a similarly fragmented society with similar results for the Revolution, and Judith Van Buskirk's work on occupied New York demonstrates many similarities in the movement of goods across the lines and the eventual assimilation of dissenters, among other things. See Kim, "Limits of Politicization in the American Revolution"; Tiedemann, *Reluctant Revolutionaries*; and Van Buskirk, *Generous Enemies*.

10. Ronald Hoffman's investigation of the Revolutionary South, and particularly of Maryland, suggests the potential of looking more closely at that region with an eye on disaffection and dissention. Maryland's path is particularly intriguing. Though Pennsylvania and Maryland shared many traits and each created a new constitution to accommodate the Revolution, Pennsylvania's governing document became the most radical of all the states, whereas Maryland's was deeply conservative. See Ronald Hoffman, *A Spirit of Dissension: Economics, Politics and Revolution in Maryland* (Baltimore: Johns Hopkins University Press, 1973).

11. Michael A. McDonnell's work on Virginia shows strong similarities with some of my findings of Pennsylvania. See McDonnell, "Popular Mobilization and Political Culture in Revolutionary Virginia," 946–981; Benjamin Carp makes a strong case for the importance of cities in shaping the path toward independence, though he somewhat dismisses their value during the war, and suggests that Americans have long had a tendency to overlook the significance of urban centers in the Revolution. See Carp, *Rebels Rising*, 214–217, 223.

12. Donald Johnson's work suggests that this tendency to forget the disunity of the war years, to prefer tacit forgiveness over vengeance, was to be found throughout the new nation. The "public memory of the Revolution," reflected in some of its earliest histories, underwent a general transformation which took until the early nineteenth century to fully work itself out. See Johnson, "Forgiving and Forgetting in Postrevolutionary America," 178–179.

BIBLIOGRAPHY

Abbreviations

APS: American Philosophical Society
DLAR: David Library of the American Revolution
GB.AO: Great Britain. Audit Office Records
GB.WO: Great Britain. War Office Records, Judge Advocate General's Office
HSP: Historical Society of Pennsylvania, Philadelphia, PA
JCC: *Journals of the Continental Congress, 1774–1789*
PCA: Philadelphia City Archives
PGW: *The Papers of George Washington*
PMHB: *Pennsylvania Magazine of History and Biography*
PNG: *The Papers of General Nathanael Greene*
WCL: William L. Clements Library, University of Michigan, Ann Arbor, MI

Archives

Accounts of theatrical performances for the entertainment of British soldiers during the Revolution, 1775–1780. HSP.
Allen, James. Diary, 1770–1778. HSP.
Alms House Managers. Minutes, 1766–1778. PCA.
André, John. Letter regarding the Battle of Germantown, 1777. APS.
Boudinot, Elias. Letterbook, 1777–1778. Microfilm. DLAR.
Cliffe, Loftus. Papers, 1769–1784. WCL.
Clinton, Henry. Papers, 1736–1850. WCL.
Coote, Eyre. Papers, 1775–1925. WCL.
Dickinson, John. Papers (LCP). HSP.
Dickinson Family Papers, 1676–1885. HSP.
Drinker, Elizabeth Sandwith. Diaries, 1758–1807. HSP.
Drinker, Henry. Papers, 1747–1867. HSP.
Drinker, Henry, and Elizabeth Drinker. Letters (MC 854). Quaker and Special Collections. Haverford College, Haverford, PA.
Drinker Family Papers, 1722–1889 and 1777–1965. HSP.
Feinstone, Sol. Collection of the American Revolution. APS.

Fisher, Sarah Logan. Diaries, 1776–1795. HSP.
Galloway, Grace Growden. Papers, 1778–1781. HSP.
Germain, George Sackville. Papers, 1683–1785. WCL.
Grant, James, of Ballindalloch. Papers, 1740–1819 (bulk 1760–1780). Army Career Series. Microfilm. DLAR.
Great Britain. Audit Office. Records of the American Loyalist Claims Commission, 1776–1831 (AO 12). Microfilm. DLAR.
Great Britain. Audit Office. Records of the American Loyalist Claims Commission, 1780–1835 (AO 13). Microfilm. DLAR.
Great Britain. War Office. American Rebellion Entry Books, 1773–1783. Microfilm. DLAR.
Great Britain. War Office. Judge Advocate General's Office. Court Martial Proceedings and Board of General Officer's Minutes (WO 71/80–97). Microfilm. DLAR.
Great Britain. War Office. Misc. (Headquarters Records). Microfilm. DLAR.
Ground rents due the overseers of the poor. Minutes, March 1774 to May 1782. PCA.
Hillegas, Michael. Papers, 1757–1782. HSP.
Hiltzheimer, Jacob. Diaries, 1765–1798. APS.
Hopkins, Thomas. Journal, 1780. HSP.
Howe, William. Orderly Book, 1776–1778. WCL.
Jones, Robert Strettel. Papers, 1761–1779. APS.
King's American Regiment Orderly Book, 1776–1777. WCL.
Knox, William. Papers, 1757–1811. WCL.
Marshall, Christopher. Papers, 1744–ca. 1971. HSP.
Orderly Book of Sergeant Major Richards, October 26–December 17, 1777 (orders, returns, morning reports, and accounts of British troops, 1776–1781). Microfilm. DLAR.
Peebles, John. Journal, 1776–1782. Microfilm. DLAR.
Pemberton Family Papers, 1641–1880. HSP.
Reed, Joseph. Papers, 1757–1785. Microfilm. DLAR.
Saint Andrew's Society of Philadelphia. Minutes, 1749–1776, 1786–1833. APS.
Schoff Revolutionary War Collection, 1766–1896. WCL.
Shippen, Edward. Letters and Papers, 1727–1781. APS.
Society of the Sons of Saint George. Constitution and meeting minutes, 1772–1949. HSP.
Strachey, Henry. Papers, 1768–1802. WCL.
Sullivan, Sergeant Thomas, H. M. Forty-Ninth Regiment of Foot. Journal, 1775–1778. HSP.
Vaux, George. Papers, 1738–1985. APS.
Watson, John F. Historical Collections (Am 3013), 1823. HSP.
Whitall, Job. Diary, 1775–1779. Gloucester County Historical Society Library.
Whitall Family Papers. Gloucester County Historical Society Library.
Wister, Sarah. Journal, 1777–1778. HSP.

Newspapers

Charleston S. C. Gazette, Charleston, SC
Connecticut Courant, Hartford, CT
Continental Journal, Boston, MA
Massachusetts Spy, Boston, MA

North Carolina Gazette, New Bern, NC
Pennsylvania Evening Post, Philadelphia, PA
Pennsylvania Gazette, Philadelphia, PA
Pennsylvania Journal, Philadelphia, PA
Pennsylvania Ledger, Philadelphia, PA
Pennsylvania Packet, Philadelphia and Lancaster, PA
Rivington's New-York Gazetteer (*Royal Gazette*), New York, NY
Royal Pennsylvania Gazette, Philadelphia, PA

Published Archives; Primary and Secondary Sources

Adams, John. *Diary and Autobiography of John Adams*. Ed. L. H. Butterfield. 4 vols. Cambridge, MA: Belknap Press, 1961.
———. *The Works of John Adams, Second President of the United States: With a Life of the Author, Notes and Illustrations*. Ed. Charles Francis Adams. 10 vols. Boston: Little, Brown, 1850–1856.
Adams, John, and Abigail Adams. *The Letters of John and Abigail Adams*. Ed. Frank Shuffelton. New York: Penguin, 2003.
Adams, John, Thomas Jefferson, and Abigail Adams. *The Adams-Jefferson Letters: The Complete Correspondence Between Thomas Jefferson and Abigail and John Adams*. Ed. Lester J. Cappon. 2 vols. Chapel Hill: University of North Carolina Press, 1959.
Adams Family Papers: An Electronic Archive. Boston: Massachusetts Historical Society, http://www.masshist.org/digitaladams/.
Alexander, John K. "The Fort Wilson Incident of 1779: A Case Study of the Revolutionary Crowd." *William and Mary Quarterly* 31, no. 4 (October 1, 1974): 589–612.
———. *Render Them Submissive: Responses to Poverty in Philadelphia, 1760–1800*. Amherst: University of Massachusetts Press, 1980.
Allen, James. "Diary of James Allen, Esq., of Philadelphia, Counsellor-at-Law, 1770–1778." *Pennsylvania Magazine of History and Biography* 9, no. 2 (July 1885): 176–196.
———. "Diary of James Allen, Esq., of Philadelphia, Counsellor-at-Law, 1770–1778 (continued)." *Pennsylvania Magazine of History and Biography* 9, no. 3 (October 1885): 278–296.
———. "Diary of James Allen, Esq., of Philadelphia, Counsellor-at-Law, 1770–1778 (concluded)." *Pennsylvania Magazine of History and Biography* 9, no. 4 (January 1886): 424–441.
Allen, Thomas B. *Tories: Fighting for the King in America's First Civil War*. New York: Harper, 2010.
American Archives, ed. Peter Force and M. St. Clair Clarke. 4th ser., 6 vols.; 5th ser., 3 vols. Washington, DC: M. St. Clair Clarke and Peter Force, 1837–1853. http://amarch.lib.niu.edu/
Anderson, Benedict. *Imagined Communities: Reflections on the Origin and Spread of Nationalism*. London: Verso, 1983.
Anderson, James Donald. "Thomas Wharton, Exile in Virginia, 1777–1778." *Virginia Magazine of History and Biography* 89, no. 4 (October 1981): 425–447.
Anderson, Lee Patrick. *Forty Minutes by the Delaware: The Story of the Whitalls, Red Bank Plantation and the Battle for Fort Mercer*. Parkland, FL: Universal Publishers, 1999.
Angell, Israel. *The Diary of Colonel Israel Angell Commanding Officer, 2nd Rhode Island Regiment, Continental Army*. Transcribed by Edward Field. Providence, RI: Preston and Rounds, 1899.

Digitized by Norman Desmarais. Digital Commons, Providence College. http://digitalcommons.providence.edu/primary/2.

Appleby, Joyce. *Liberalism and Republicanism in the Historical Imagination.* Cambridge, MA: Harvard University Press, 1992.

Archer, Richard. *As If an Enemy's Country: The British Occupation of Boston and the Origins of Revolution.* New York: Oxford University Press, 2010.

Bailyn, Bernard. *The Ideological Origins of the American Revolution.* Cambridge, MA: Harvard University Press, 1967.

Baldwin, Ernest Hickok. *Joseph Galloway, the Loyalist Politician.* Philadelphia, 1902.

Barck, Oscar Theodore. *New York City During the War for Independence, With Special Reference to the Period of British Occupation.* Port Washington, NY: I. J. Friedman, 1967.

Baurmeister, Carl Leopold. *Letters from Major Baurmeister to Colonel von Jungkenn Written During the Philadelphia Campaign, 1777–1778.* Philadelphia: Historical Society of Pennsylvania, 1937.

———. *Revolution in America: Confidential Letters and Journals, 1776–1784.* New Brunswick, NJ: Rutgers University Press, 1957.

Baurmeister, Carl Leopold, Bernhard A. Uhlendorf, and Edna Vosper. "Letters of Major Baurmeister During the Philadelphia Campaign, 1777–1778." *Pennsylvania Magazine of History and Biography* 59, no. 4 (October 1935): 392–419.

———. "Letters of Major Baurmeister During the Philadelphia Campaign, 1777–1778. II." *Pennsylvania Magazine of History and Biography* 60, no. 1 (January 1, 1936): 34–52.

Benvenisti, Eyal. *The International Law of Occupation.* Princeton, NJ: Princeton University Press, 2004.

Bezanson, Anne. *Prices and Inflation During the American Revolution: Pennsylvania, 1770–1790.* Philadelphia: University of Pennsylvania Press, 1951.

Black list: A list of those Tories who took part with Great Britain, in the Revolutionary War, and were attainted of high treason, commonly called the Black list ; to which is prefixed the legal opinions of Attorney Generals McKean & Dallas, &c. Philadelphia: Printed for the proprietor, 1802. https://archive.org/details/blacklistlistoftoophil.

Bodle, Wayne K. *The Valley Forge Winter: Civilians and Soldiers in War.* University Park: Pennsylvania State University Press, 2002.

Boyd, George Adams. *Elias Boudinot: Patriot and Statesman, 1740–1821.* Princeton, NJ: Princeton University Press, 1952.

Braisted, Todd. "The Black Pioneers and Others: The Military Role of Black Loyalists in the American War for Independence." In *Moving On: Black Loyalists in the Afro-Atlantic World*, ed. John W. Pulis, 3–38. New York: Garland, 1999.

Breen, T. H. *American Insurgents, American Patriots.* New York: Hill and Wang, 2010.

———. "'Baubles of Britain': The American and Consumer Revolutions of the Eighteenth Century." *Past and Present* 119 (May 1988): 73–104.

———. "An Empire of Goods: The Anglicization of Colonial America, 1690–1776." *Journal of British Studies* 25 (October 1986): 467–499.

———. *The Marketplace of Revolution: How Consumer Politics Shaped American Independence.* Oxford: Oxford University Press, 2004.

Bridenbaugh, Carl, and Jessica Bridenbaugh. *Rebels and Gentlemen: Philadelphia in the Age of Franklin.* New York: Reynal and Hitchcock, 1942.

Brown, Wallace. *The King's Friends: The Composition and Motives of the American Loyalist Claimants*. Providence, RI: Brown University Press, 1965.
Brunhouse, Robert. *Counter-Revolution in Pennsylvania*. Harrisburg: Pennsylvania Historical Commission, 1942.
Buchanan, Roberdeau. *Genealogy of the Roberdeau Family, Including a Biography of General Daniel Roberdeau of the Revolutionary Army, and the Continental Congress; and Signer of the Articles of Confederation*. Washington, DC: Joseph L. Pearson, 1876.
Buel, Richard. *In Irons: Britain's Naval Supremacy and the American Revolutionary Economy*. New Haven, CT: Yale University Press, 1998.
Calhoon, Robert M., Timothy M. Barnes, Robert Scott Davis, Donald C. Lord, Janice Potter-MacKinnon, and Robert M. Weir. *Tory Insurgents: The Loyalist Perception and Other Essays*. Rev. and expanded ed. Columbia: University of South Carolina Press, 2010.
Carp, Benjamin. *Rebels Rising: Cities and the American Revolution*. New York: Oxford University Press, 2007.
Carr, Jacqueline Barbara. *After the Siege: A Social History of Boston, 1775–1800*. Boston: Northeastern University Press, 2004.
Casino, Joseph. "British Counterinsurgent Policy and Civilian Loyalties, 1776–1777, Part One: Promises and Plunder." Philadelphia Center for Early American Studies Seminar, March 5, 1982.
Chopra, Ruma. *Unnatural Rebellion: Loyalists in New York City During the Revolution*. Charlottesville: University of Virginia Press, 2011.
Clark, John, Jr. "Letters from Major John Clark Jr. to Gen. Washington Written During the Occupation of Philadelphia by the British Army." *Bulletin of the Historical Society of Pennsylvania* 1 (1847): 3–34.
Colburn's United Service Magazine and Naval and Military Journal. London: Colburn, 1852. http://books.google.com/books?id=A-u208UrjWwC.
Coldham, Peter Wilson. *American Migrations 1765–1799: The Lives, Times, and Families of Colonial Americans*. Baltimore: Genealogical Publishing, 2000.
Coleman, John M. "Joseph Galloway and the British Occupation of Philadelphia." *Pennsylvania History* 30 (1963): 272–300.
Collections of the Massachusetts Historical Society. 7th ser. Boston: Published by the Society, 1902. http://books.google.com/books?id=vO9BAAAAYAAJ.
Collections of the New-York Historical Society for the Year 1878. New York: Printed for the Society, 1879. http://books.google.com/books?id=XFcOAAAAIAAJ.
Colonial Records of Pennsylvania or Minutes of the Supreme Executive Council of Pennsylvania, from Its Organization to the Termination of the Revolution. Vol. 11. Harrisburg, PA: Theo. Fenn, 1852.
Commager, Henry Steele, ed. *Documents of American History*. New York: F. S. Crofts, 1941.
Committee for Tarring and Feathering. *To the Delaware Pilots*. Philadelphia, 1773. Early American Imprints, ser. 1: Evans, 1639–1800, no. 12941. https://www.readex.com/content/early-american-imprints-series-i-evans-1639-1800.
Conway, Stephen. "To Subdue America: British Army Officers and the Conduct of the Revolutionary War." *William and Mary Quarterly* 43 (July 1986): 381–407.
Cuthbert, Anthony. "Assessment of Damages Done by the British Troops During the Occupation of Philadelphia, 1777–1778." *Pennsylvania Magazine of History and Biography* 25, no. 3 (1901): 323–335.

DeLancy, Edward F. "Chief Justice William Allen," *Pennsylvania Magazine of History and Biography* 1 (1877): 202–211.

Dodson, Kathryn S. *The Whitall Family Day Book: A Look at the American Revolution Through the Eyes of Everyday People.* Woodbury, NJ: Gloucester County Board of Chosen Freeholders, 1989.

Doerflinger, Thomas M. "Philadelphia Merchants and the Logic of Moderation, 1760–1775." *William and Mary Quarterly* 40 (April 1983): 197–226.

———. *A Vigorous Spirit of Enterprise: Merchants and Economic Development in Revolutionary Philadelphia.* Chapel Hill: University of North Carolina Press, 1986.

Döhla, Johann Conrad. *A Hessian Diary of the American Revolution.* Ed. Bruce E. Burgoyne. Norman: University of Oklahoma Press, 1990.

Downman, Francis. *The Services of Lieut.-Colonel Francis Downman, R.A., in France, North America, and the West Indies, Between the Years 1758 and 1784.* Ed. F. A. Whinyates. Woolwich: Royal Artillery Institution, 1898.

Drinker, Elizabeth Sandwith. *The Diary of Elizabeth Drinker.* Ed. Elaine Forman Crane. 3 vols. Boston: Northeastern University Press, 1991.

———. *The Diary of Elizabeth Drinker: The Life Cycle of an Eighteenth-Century Woman.* Ed. Elaine Forman Crane. Abridged ed. Philadelphia: University of Pennsylvania Press, 2010.

———. *Extracts from the Journal of Elizabeth Drinker, from 1759 to 1807, A.D.* Ed. Henry D. Biddle. Philadelphia: J. B. Lippincott, 1889.

Drinker, John. *Observations on the Late Popular Measures, Offered to the Serious Consideration of the Sober Inhabitants of Pennsylvania.* Philadelphia: Printed for "A Tradesman," 1774.

Duponceau, Peter S. "Autobiographical Letters of Peter S. Duponceau." *Pennsylvania Magazine of History and Biography* 40, no. 2 (1916): 172–186.

Durand, John. "American History in the French Archives." *New Princeton Review* 4 (1887): 328–342.

Egnal, Marc, and Joseph A. Ernst. "An Economic Interpretation of the American Revolution." *William and Mary Quarterly* 29 (January 1972): 4–32.

Evans, Elizabeth. *Weathering the Storm: Women of the American Revolution.* New York: Charles Scribner's Sons, 1975.

Ewald, Johann von. *Diary of the American War: A Hessian Journal.* New Haven, CT: Yale University Press, 1979.

Farmar, Eliza. "Letters of Eliza Farmar to Her Nephew." *Pennsylvania Magazine of History and Biography* 40 (1916): 199–207.

Ferling, John E. *Almost a Miracle: The American Victory in the War of Independence.* Oxford: Oxford University Press, 2007.

Fisher, Darlene Emmert. "Social Life in Philadelphia During the British Occupation." *Pennsylvania History* 37, no. 3 (July 1970): 237–260.

Fisher, Samuel Rowland. "Journal of Samuel Rowland Fisher, of Philadelphia, 1779–1781." *Pennsylvania Magazine of History and Biography* 41 (1917): 145–197, 274–333, 399–457.

Ford, Worthington. *Defences of Philadelphia in 1777.* Brooklyn, NY: Historical Printing Club, 1897.

Fox, Francis S. "Pennsylvania's Revolutionary Militia Law: The Statute That Transformed the State." *Pennsylvania History* 80, no. 2 (Spring 2014): 204–214.

———. *Sweet Land of Liberty: The Ordeal of the American Revolution in Northampton County, Pennsylvania.* University Park: Pennsylvania State University Press, 2000.

Franklin, Benjamin. *The Papers of Benjamin Franklin.* Ed. William B. Willcox, Leonard W. Labaree, and Barbara Oberg. Vol. 25. New Haven, CT: Yale University Press, 1986.

Franks, Rebecca. "A Letter of Miss Rebecca Franks, 1778." *Pennsylvania Magazine of History and Biography* 16, no. 2 (July 1892): 216–218.

———. "Letter of Miss Rebecca Franks." *Pennsylvania Magazine of History and Biography* 23, no. 3 (January 1, 1899): 303–309.

Fuller, Randall. "Theaters of the American Revolution: The Valley Forge 'Cato' and the Meschianza in Their Transcultural Contexts." *Early American Literature* 34, no. 2 (1999): 126–146.

Furstenberg, Francois. *In the Name of the Father: Washington's Legacy, Slavery, and the Making of a Nation.* New York: Penguin, 2006.

Geib, George Winthrop. "A History of Philadelphia, 1776–1789." PhD diss., University of Wisconsin, 1969.

Gilpin, Thomas. *Exiles in Virginia: With Observations on the Conduct of the Society of Friends During the Revolutionary War, Comprising the Official Papers of the Government Relating to That Period, 1777–1778.* Philadelphia, 1848.

Glahn, Gerhard von. *The Occupation of Enemy Territory: A Commentary on the Law and Practice of Belligerent Occupation.* Minneapolis: University Of Minnesota Press, 1957.

Graydon, Alexander. *Memoirs of His Own Time: With Reminiscences of the Men and Events of the Revolution.* Philadelphia: Lindsay and Blakiston, 1846.

Greene, Nathanael. *The Papers of General Nathanael Greene.* Ed. Richard K. Showman. 2 vols. Chapel Hill: University of North Carolina Press for the Rhode Island Historical Society, 1976.

Gruber, Ira D. *The Howe Brothers and the American Revolution.* Chapel Hill: University of North Carolina Press, 2011.

Haulman, Kate. "Fashion and the Culture Wars of Revolutionary Philadelphia." *William and Mary Quarterly* 62, no. 4 (October 1, 2005): 625–662. doi:10.2307/3491443.

———. *The Politics of Fashion in Eighteenth-Century America.* Chapel Hill: University of North Carolina Press, 2011.

Hawke, David. *In the Midst of a Revolution.* Philadelphia: University of Pennsylvania Press, 1961.

Hazard, Samuel, ed. *The Register of Pennsylvania: Devoted to the Preservation of Every Kind of Useful Information Respecting the State.* 7 vols. Philadelphia: W. F. Geddes, 1828–1831. Available via the Hathi Trust Digital Library: http://catalog.hathitrust.org/Record/004253165.

Higginbotham, Don. *The War of American Independence: Military Attitudes, Policies, and Practice, 1763–1789.* Boston: Northeastern University Press, 1983.

Hirschfeld, Fritz. *George Washington and the Jews.* Newark: University of Delaware Press, 2005.

"Historic Sites." Lehigh County Historical Society. http://www.lehighvalleyheritagemuseum.org/HistoricSites.htm.

Hodges, Graham Russell, ed. *The Black Loyalist Directory: African Americans in Exile After the American Revolution.* New York: Garland, 1996.

Hoffman, Ronald. "The 'Disaffected' in the Revolutionary South." In *The American Revolution*, ed. Alfred Young, 273–316. DeKalb: Northern Illinois University Press, 1976.

———. *A Spirit of Dissension: Economics, Politics and Revolution in Maryland.* Baltimore: Johns Hopkins University Press, 1973.

Hoock, Holger. *Scars of Independence: America's Violent Birth.* New York: Crown, 2017.

Horle, Craig W., Joseph S. Foster, and Laurie M. Wolfe, eds. *Lawmaking and Legislators in Pennsylvania:1757–1775.* Vol. 3 of *Lawmaking and Legislators in Pennsylvania: A Biographical Dictionary.* Philadelphia: University of Pennsylvania Press, 2005.

Howe, William. *The Narrative of Lieut. Gen. Sir William Howe.* London: H. Baldwin, 1781.
Inman, George. "George Inman's Narrative of the American Revolution." *Pennsylvania Magazine of History and Biography* 7 (1883): 237–248.
Ireland, Owen S. "The Crux of Politics: Religion and Party in Pennsylvania, 1778–1789." *William and Mary Quarterly*, 3rd ser., 42, no. 4 (October 1985): 453–475.
Jackson, John. *With the British Army in Philadelphia, 1777–1778.* San Rafael, CA: Presidio Press, 1979.
Jacob, Mark, and Stephen H. Case. *Treacherous Beauty: Peggy Shippen, the Woman Behind Benedict Arnold's Plot to Betray America.* Guilford, CT: Lyons Press, 2012.
Jasanoff, Maya. *Liberty's Exiles: American Loyalists in the Revolutionary World.* New York: Knopf, 2011.
Jennings, Francis. *The Creation of America: Through Revolution to Empire.* New York: Cambridge University Press, 2000.
Johnson, Donald F. "Forgiving and Forgetting in Postrevolutionary America." In *Experiencing Empire: Power, People, and Revolution in Early America*, ed. Patrick Griffin, 171–188. Charlottesville: University of Virginia Press, 2017.
Jones, Hugh. "Assessment of Damages Done by the British Troops During the Occupation of Philadelphia, 1777–1778 (concluded)." *Pennsylvania Magazine of History and Biography* 25, no. 4 (1901): 544–559.
Jordan, John W., and Josiah Bartlett. "Sessions of the Continental Congress Held in the College of Philadelphia in July, 1778." *Pennsylvania Magazine of History and Biography* 22, no. 1 (January 1, 1898): 114–115.
Journals of the American Congress: From 1774 to 1788. Vol. 1. Washington, DC: Way and Gideon, 1823.
Journals of the Continental Congress, 1774–1789. Ed. Worthington C. Ford, Gaillard Hunt, John Clement Fitzpatrick, Roscoe R. Hill, Kenneth E. Harris, and Steven D. Tilley. 34 vols. Washington, DC: US Government Printing Office, 1904–1937.
Keith, Charles P. "Andrew Allen." *Pennsylvania Magazine of History and Biography* 10, no. 4 (1887): 361–365.
Kemble, Stephen, Henry Clinton, Daniel Jones, and William Howe Howe. *The Kemble Papers.* 2 vols. New York: New York Historical Society, 1884.
Kerber, Linda. *Women of the Republic: Intellect and Ideology in Revolutionary America.* Chapel Hill: University of North Carolina Press, 1980.
Kim, Sung Bok. "The Limits of Politicization in the American Revolution: The Experience of Westchester County, New York." *Journal of American History* 80 (December 1, 1993): 868–889.
Klepp, Susan E. "Rough Music on Independence Day, 1778." In *Riot and Revelry in Early America*, ed. William Pencak, Matthew Dennis, and Simon P. Newman, 156–178. University Park: Pennsylvania State University Press, 2002.
Klepp, Susan E., Farley Ward Grubb, and Anne Pfaelzer De Ortiz, eds. *Souls for Sale: Two German Redemptioners Come to Revolutionary America: The Life Stories of John Frederick Whitehead and Johann Carl Büttner.* University Park: Pennsylvania State University Press, 2006.
Konkle, Burton Alva. *George Bryan and the Constitution of Pennsylvania, 1731–1791.* Philadelphia: William J. Campbell, 1922.
Lair, Meredith H. "Redcoat Theater: Negotiating Identity in Occupied Philadelphia, 1777–1778." In *Pennsylvania's Revolution*, ed. William Pencak, 192–210. University Park: Pennsylvania State University Press, 2010.

Lee, Richard Henry. *The Letters of Richard Henry Lee*. Ed. James Curtis Ballagh. 2 vols. New York: Macmillan, 1911.

Lender, Mark. "The 'Cockpit' Reconsidered: Revolutionary New Jersey as a Military Theater." In *New Jersey in the American Revolution*, ed. Barbara J. Mitnick, 79–104. New Brunswick, NJ: Rutgers University Press, 2005.

Letters of Delegates to Congress, 1774–1789. Ed. Paul Hubert Smith and Ronald M Gephart. 25 vols. Washington, DC: Library of Congress, 1976–2000.

Lewis, Jan. "The Republican Wife: Virtue and Seduction in the Early Republic." *William and Mary Quarterly* 44, no. 4 (October 1, 1987): 689–721.

Lynd, Staughton, and David Waldstreicher. "Free Trade, Sovereignty, and Slavery: Toward an Economic Interpretation of American Independence." *William and Mary Quarterly* 68, no. 4 (October 1, 2011): 597–630.

———. "Reflections on Economic Interpretation, Slavery, the People Out of Doors, and Top Down Versus Bottom Up." *William and Mary Quarterly* 68, no. 4 (October 1, 2011): 649–656.

MacGregor, Douglas. "Double Dishonor: Loyalists on the Middle Frontier." In *Pennsylvania's Revolution*, ed. William Pencak, 144–167. University Park: Pennsylvania State University Press, 2010.

Madison, James. *The Papers of James Madison*. Ed. W. T. Hutchinson and William M. E. Rachal. 3 vols. Chicago: University of Chicago Press, 1962.

Maier, Pauline. *From Resistance to Revolution: Colonial Radicals and the Development of American Opposition to Britain, 1765–1776*. New York: Knopf, 1972.

Major, Emma. "Serle, Ambrose." *Oxford Dictionary of National Biography*. Online ed. Oxford University Press.

Marshall, Christopher. *Extracts from the Diary of Christopher Marshall: Kept in Philadelphia and Lancaster, During the American Revolution, 1774–1781*. Ed. William Duane Jr. Albany, NY: Joel Munsell, 1877.

———. *Passages from the Remembrancer of Christopher Marshall*. Ed. William Duane Jr. Philadelphia: James Crissy, 1839.

Maxey, David W. *Treason on Trial in Revolutionary Pennsylvania: The Case of John Roberts, Miller*. Philadelphia: American Philosophical Society, 2011.

Mayer, Holly A. *Belonging to the Army: Camp Followers and Community During the American Revolution*. Columbia: University of South Carolina Press, 1996.

McConville, Brendan. *The King's Three Faces: The Rise and Fall of Royal America, 1688–1776*. Chapel Hill: University of North Carolina Press, 2006.

McCowen, George Smith. *The British Occupation of Charleston, 1780–82*. Columbia: University of South Carolina Press, 1972.

McDonnell, Michael A. "Popular Mobilization and Political Culture in Revolutionary Virginia: The Failure of the Minutemen and the Revolution from Below." *Journal of American History* 85, no. 3 (December 1, 1998): 946–981.

Messer, Peter C. "'A Species of Treason & Not the Least Dangerous Kind': The Treason Trials of Abraham Carlisle and John Roberts." *Pennsylvania Magazine of History and Biography* 123, no. 4 (October 1, 1999): 303–332.

Middlekauff, Robert. *The Glorious Cause: The American Revolution, 1763–1789*. New York: Oxford University Press, 2007.

Miller, John C. *Origins of the American Revolution*. Stanford, CA: Stanford University Press, 1957.

Mishoff, Willard O. "Business in Philadelphia During the British Occupation, 1777–1778." *Pennsylvania Magazine of History and Biography* 61 (April 1937): 165–181.

Montanus, Paul D. "A Failed Counterinsurgency Strategy: The British Southern Campaign, 1780–1781: Are There Lessons for Today?" In *USAWC Strategy Research Project*. Carlisle, PA: US Army War College, 2005.

Montrésor, John, and G. D. Scull. "Journal of Captain John Montrésor, July 1, 1777, to July 1, 1778, Chief Engineer of the British Army." *Pennsylvania Magazine of History and Biography* 6 (1882): 34–57, 189–206, 284–299.

Morgan, Edmund. *The Invention of the People: The Rise of Popular Sovereignty in England and America*. New York: W. W. Norton, 1988.

Morton, Robert. "The Diary of Robert Morton." *Pennsylvania Magazine of History and Biography* 1, no. 1 (1877): 1–39.

Muenchhausen, Friedrich von. *At General Howe's Side, 1776–1778: The Diary of General William Howe's Aide de Camp*. Monmouth Beach, NJ: Philip Freneau Press, 1974.

Muhlenberg, Henry Melchior. *The Journals of Henry Melchior Muhlenberg*. 3 vols. Philadelphia: Evangelical Lutheran Ministerium of Pennsylvania and Adjacent States, 1942.

Nagy, John A. *Spies in the Continental Capital: Espionage Across Pennsylvania During the American Revolution*. Yardley, PA: Westholme, 2011.

Nash, Gary B. *Forging Freedom: The Formation of Philadelphia's Black Community, 1720–1840*. Cambridge, MA: Harvard University Press, 1988.

———. "Slaves and Slave Owners in Colonial Philadelphia." *William and Mary Quarterly* 30, no. 2 (April 1973): 223–256.

———. *The Urban Crucible: The Northern Seaports and the Origins of the American Revolution*. Cambridge, MA: Harvard University Press, 1979.

Neill, Robert. "The Bolton and Dunn Houses." Maryland Historical Trust Site Survey. Accessed February 13, 2018. https://mht.maryland.gov/secure/medusa/PDF/Kent/K-22.pdf.

Nelson, William, ed. *The Plain-Dealer: The First Newspaper in New Jersey*. Priv. print, 1894.

Newman, Debra. "They Left with the British: Black Women in the Evacuation of Philadelphia, 1778." *Pennsylvania Heritage* 4 (1977): 20–23.

Oaks, Robert F. "Philadelphia Merchants and the First Continental Congress." *Pennsylvania History* 40, no. 2 (April 1, 1973): 148–166.

———. "Philadelphians in Exile: The Problem of Loyalty During the American Revolution." *Pennsylvania Magazine of History and Biography* 96, no. 3 (July 1972): 298–325.

Oberholtzer, Ellis Paxson. *Robert Morris: Patriot and Financier*. New York: Macmillan, 1903.

O'Shaughnessy, Andrew Jackson. *The Men Who Lost America: British Leadership, the American Revolution, and the Fate of the Empire*. New Haven, CT: Yale University Press, 2013.

Ousterhout, Anne M. "Controlling the Opposition in Pennsylvania During the American Revolution." *Pennsylvania Magazine of History and Biography* 105, no. 1 (January 1981): 3–34.

———. *A State Divided: Opposition in Pennsylvania to the American Revolution*. New York: Greenwood Press, 1987.

Parkinson, Robert G. *The Common Cause: Creating Race and Nation in the American Revolution*. Chapel Hill: University of North Carolina Press, 2016.

Parliamentary Register; or, History of the Proceedings and Debates of the House of Commons. London, 1775–1804. Eighteenth Century Collections Online. Gale. Temple University Libraries.

Pattee, Fred Lewis. "The British Theater in Philadelphia in 1778." *American Literature* 6, no. 4 (January 1935): 381–388.

Peebles, John. *John Peebles' American War: The Diary of a Scottish Grenadier, 1776–1782*. Mechanicsburg, PA: Stackpole Books, 1998.
Pemberton, John. *The Life and Travels of John Pemberton, a Minister of the Gospel of Christ*. London: Charles Gilpin, 1844.
Pencak, William. "Out of Many, One: Pennsylvania's Loyalist Clergy in the American Revolution." In *Pennsylvania's Revolution*, ed. William Pencak, 97–120. University Park: Pennsylvania State University Press, 2010.
Penn Biographies. University of Pennsylvania. University Archives and Record Center. http://www.archives.upenn.edu/people/bioa.html.
Pennsylvania Archives, 1st ser. 12 vols.; 2nd ser. 19 vols.; 8th ser. 8 vols. Philadelphia: Joseph Severns, 1852–1935.
Pennsylvania Council of Safety. "In Council of Safety. Lancaster, October 21, 1777." Lancaster, PA: Printed by Francis Bailey, 1777. Early American Imprints, ser. 1: Evans, 1639–1800, no. 15529. https://www.readex.com/content/early-american-imprints-series-i-evans-1639-1800.
Pettengill, Ray W. *Letters from America, 1776–1779: Being Letters of Brunswick, Hessian and Waldeck; Officers with the British Armies During the Revolution*. Whitefish, MT: Kessinger, 2006.
Polf, William A. *Garrison Town: The British Occupation of New York City, 1776–1783*. Albany: New York State American Revolution Bicentennial Commission, 1976.
Polk, William R. *Violent Politics: A History of Insurgency, Terrorism, and Guerrilla War, from the American Revolution to Iraq*. New York: Harper, 2007.
Pollock, Thomas Clark. "Notes on Professor Pattee's 'The British Theater in Philadelphia in 1778.'" *American Literature* 7, no. 3 (November 1935): 310–314.
Poots, Richard R. "Historical Survey of the Ann Cooper Whitall House." May 20, 1968. Available at the Gloucester County Historical Society Library.
"Proceedings of a general court martial of the line, held at Raritan, in the state of New-Jersey, by order of His Excellency George Washington, Esq. general and commander in chief of the Army of the United States of America, for the trial of Major General Arnold, June 1, 1779." Published by order of Congress. Early American Imprints. ser. 1: Evans, 1639–1800. https://www.readex.com/content/early-american-imprints-series-i-evans-1639-1800.
Proud, Robert. "Letter of Robert Proud, the Historian, 1778." *Pennsylvania Magazine of History and Biography* 29, no. 2 (1905): 229–231.
———. "Letters of Robert Proud." *Pennsylvania Magazine of History and Biography* 34, no. 1 (1910): 62–73.
Quarles, Benjamin. *The Negro in the American Revolution*. Chapel Hill: University of North Carolina Press, 1961.
Rawle, William Brooke. "Plundering by the British Army During the American Revolution." *Pennsylvania Magazine of History and Biography* 25 (1901): 114–117.
Reed, William Bradford. *Life and Correspondence of Joseph Reed: Military Secretary of Washington, at Cambridge, Adjutant-General of the Continental Army, Member of the Congress of the United States, and President of the Executive Council of the State of Pennsylvania*. 2 vols. Philadelphia: Lindsay and Blakiston, 1847.
Resch, John Phillips, and Walter Sargent. *War and Society in the American Revolution: Mobilization and Home Fronts*. DeKalb: Northern Illinois University Press, 2007.
Respublica v. Doan. 1 U.S. 86 (1784). http://supreme.justia.com/cases/federal/us/1/86/.
Rightmyer, Nelson Waite. "Churches Under Enemy Occupation: Philadelphia, 1777–8." *Church History* 14, no. 1 (March 1945): 33–60.

Robertson, Alexander. *To the Public.* New York, 1769. Early American Imprints, ser. 1: Evans, 1639–1800, no. 11445. https://www.readex.com/content/early-american-imprints-series-i-evans-1639-1800.

Rose, Michael. *Washington's War: Insurgency Warfare from the American Revolution to Iraq.* New York: Pegasus, 2009.

Rosswurm, Steven. *Arms, Country, and Class: The Philadelphia Militia and the "Lower Sort" During the American Revolution, 1775–1783.* New Brunswick, NJ: Rutgers University Press, 1987.

Ryerson, Richard Alan. "Republican Theory and Partisan Reality in Revolutionary Pennsylvania: Toward a New View of the Constitutionalist Party." In *Sovereign States in an Age of Uncertainty,* ed. Ronald Hoffman and Peter J. Albert, 95–133. Charlottesville: University Press of Virginia, 1981.

———. *The Revolution Is Now Begun: The Radical Committees of Philadelphia, 1765–1776.* Philadelphia: University of Pennsylvania Press, 1978.

Scharf, J. Thomas, and Thompson Westcott. *History of Philadelphia, 1609–1884.* 3 vols. Philadelphia: L. H. Everts, 1884.

Seabury, Samuel. *Free Thoughts on the Proceedings of the Continental Congress, &c.* New York, 1774.

Serle, Ambrose. *The American Journal of Ambrose Serle, Secretary to Lord Howe, 1776–1778.* Ed. Edward H. Tatum Jr. San Marino, CA: Huntington Library, 1940.

Seybolt, Robert Francis. *A Contemporary British Account of General Sir William Howe's Military Operations in 1777.* Worcester, MA: American Antiquarian Society, 1931.

Seymour, Joseph. *The Pennsylvania Associators, 1747–1777.* Yardley, PA: Westholme, 2012.

Shy, John W. *A People Numerous and Armed: Reflections on the Military Struggle for American Independence.* New York: Oxford University Press, 1976.

Siebert, Wilbur Henry. *The Loyalists of Pennsylvania.* Boston: Gregg Press, 1972.

Simcoe, John Graves. *Simcoe's Military Journal: A History of the Operations of a Partisan Corps, Called the Queen's Rangers.* New York: Bartlett and Welford, 1844.

Slaymaker, Samuel R. "Mrs. Frazer's Philadelphia Campaign." *Journal of the Lancaster County Historical Society* 73 (1969): 185–209.

Smith, Barbara Clark. "Beyond the 'Economic.'" *William and Mary Quarterly* 68, no. 4 (October 1, 2011): 639–643.

———. *The Freedoms We Lost: Consent and Resistance in Revolutionary America.* New York: New Press, 2010.

Smith, Billy G. "Black Women Who Stole Themselves in Eighteenth-Century America." In *Inequality in Early America,* ed. Carla Gardina Pestana and Sharon V. Salinger, 134–159. Hanover, NH: University Press of New England, 1999.

———. "Death and Life in a Colonial Immigrant City: A Demographic Analysis of Philadelphia." *Journal of Economic History* 37, no. 4 (December 1977): 863–889.

———. *The "Lower Sort": Philadelphia's Laboring People, 1750–1800.* Ithaca, NY: Cornell University Press, 1990.

Smith, Billy G., and Richard Wojtowicz. *Blacks Who Stole Themselves: Advertisements for Runaways in the Pennsylvania Gazette, 1728–1790.* Philadelphia: University of Pennsylvania Press, 1989.

Smith, Hannah Whitall. *John M. Whitall: The Story of His Life.* Philadelphia: Printed for the family, 1879.

Smith, Paul Hubert. *Loyalists and Redcoats: A Study in British Revolutionary Policy.* Chapel Hill: University of North Carolina Press, 1964.

Stansbury, Joseph, and Jonathan Odell. *The Loyal Verses of Joseph Stansbury and Doctor Jonathan Odell Relating to the American Revolution.* Ed. Winthrop Sargent. Albany, NY: J. Munsell, 1860.

The Statutes at Large of Pennsylvania from 1682 to 1801. Vol. 9. Harrisburg, PA: Wm. Stanley Ray, 1903.

Stedman, Charles. *The History of the Origin, Progress, and Termination of the American War.* 2 vols. Dublin, 1794.

Stein, Roslyn. "The British Occupation of Philadelphia, September 1777–June 1778." PhD diss., Columbia University, 1937.

Stewart, Frank H., comp. and ed. *Notes on Old Gloucester County, New Jersey.* Vol. 3. Camden, NJ: New Jersey Society of Pennsylvania, 1937.

Stirk, Peter M. R. *The Politics of Military Occupation.* Edinburgh: Edinburgh University Press, 2009.

Taaffe, Stephen R. *The Philadelphia Campaign, 1777–1778.* Lawrence: University Press of Kansas, 2003.

Tatum, Edward H. "Ambrose Serle, Secretary to Lord Howe, 1776–1778." *Huntington Library Quarterly* 2 (April 1938): 265–284.

Taylor, Thomas B. "The Philadelphia Counterpart of the Boston Tea Party (As Shown by the Correspondence of James & Drinker), Conclusion." *Bulletin of Friends' Historical Society of Philadelphia* 3, no. 1 (1909): 21–49.

Teeter, Dwight L. "Benjamin Towne: The Precarious Career of a Persistent Printer." *Pennsylvania Magazine of History and Biography* 89, no. 3 (July 1965): 316–330.

Tiedemann, Joseph S. *The Other Loyalists: Ordinary People, Royalism, and the Revolution in the Middle Colonies, 1763–1787.* Albany: State University of New York Press, 2009.

———. *Reluctant Revolutionaries: New York City and the Road to Independence, 1763–1776.* Ithaca, NY: Cornell University Press, 2008.

Tompkins, Hamilton B. "Contemporary Account of the Battle of Germantown." *Pennsylvania Magazine of History and Biography* 11, no. 3 (October 1, 1887): 330–332.

To the Several Battalions of Military Associators in the Province of Pennsylvania. Printed in Philadelphia, 1776. Early American Imprints, ser. 1: Evans, 1639–1800, no. 15115. https://www.readex.com/content/early-american-imprints-series-i-evans-1639-1800.

Townsend, Joseph. *The Battle of Brandywine.* New York: New York Times, 1969.

———. *Some Account of the British Army Under the Command of General Howe, and of the Battle of Brandywine on The memorable September 11th, 1777, and the Adventures of that Day, Which Came to the Knowledge and Observation of Joseph Townsend, Late of Baltimore, Md.* Philadelphia: Historical Society of Pennsylvania, 1846.

Van Buskirk, Judith L. *Generous Enemies: Patriots and Loyalists in Revolutionary New York.* Philadelphia: University of Pennsylvania Press, 2002.

———. "They Didn't Join the Band: Disaffected Women in Revolutionary Philadelphia." *Pennsylvania History* 62 (July 1995): 306–329.

Van Doren, Carl. *Secret History of the American Revolution: An Account of the Conspiracies of Benedict Arnold and Numerous Others, Drawn from the Secret Service Papers.* New York: Viking, 1941.

"Virginia Legislative Papers." *Virginia Magazine of History and Biography* 15 (October 1907): 148–165.

Wainwright, Nicholas B., and Sarah Logan Fisher. "'A Diary of Trifling Occurrences': Philadelphia, 1776–1778." *Pennsylvania Magazine of History and Biography* 82, no. 4 (October 1958): 411–465.

Waldstreicher, David. *Runaway America: Benjamin Franklin, Slavery, and the American Revolution.* New York: Hill and Wang, 2004.

Wall, Helena M. "'My Constant Attension on My Sick Child': The Fragility of Family Life in the World of Elizabeth Drinker." In *Children in Colonial America*, ed. James Marten, 155–167. New York: New York University Press, 2007.

Washington, George. *The Papers of George Washington, Revolutionary War Series.* Ed. Philander D. Chase, Dorothy Twohig, Frank E Grizzard, David R Hoth, William M Ferraro, Edward G Lengel, and Benjamin L Huggins. 25 vols. Charlottesville: University of Virginia Press, 1985–.

———. *The Writings of George Washington: Being His Correspondence, Addresses, Messages, and Other Papers, Official and Private.* Vol. 5. Ed. Jared Sparks. Boston: Russell, Odiorne, and Metcalf, 1834.

———. *The Writings of George Washington from the Original Manuscript Sources, 1745–1799.* Ed. George Fitzpatrick. 39 vols. Washington, DC: US Government Printing Office, 1931–1944.

Watson, John Fanning. *Annals of Philadelphia and Pennsylvania.* 3 vols. Philadelphia: Leary, Stuart, 1927.

Watson, John Fanning, Jacob Mordecai, and Whitfield J. Bell Jr. "Addenda to Watson's Annals of Philadelphia: Notes by Jacob Mordecai, 1836." *Pennsylvania Magazine of History and Biography* 98, no. 2 (April 1, 1974): 131–170.

Weigley, Russel F., ed. *Philadelphia: A 300-Year History.* New York: W. W. Norton, 1982.

Whitall, Job. *The Diary of Job Whitall, Gloucester County, New Jersey, 1775–1779.* Transcribed by Florence DeHuff Friel. Woodbury, NJ: Gloucester County Historical Society, 1992.

Wiener, Frederick Bernays. *Civilians Under Military Justice: The British Practice Since 1689, Especially in North America.* Chicago: University of Chicago Press, 1967.

Willing, Thomas. *Willing Letters and Papers: Edited with a Biographical Essay of Thomas Willing of Philadelphia.* Ed. Thomas Willing Balch. Philadelphia: Allen, Lane and Scott, 1922.

Witherspoon, John. *The Humble Confession, Declaration, Recantation, and Apology of Benjamin Towne, Printer in Philadelphia.* Philadelphia, 1778. Early American Imprints, ser. 1: Evans, 1639–1800, no. 16173. https://www.readex.com/content/early-american-imprints-series-i-evans-1639-1800.

Wood, Gordon. *The Creation of the American Republic, 1776–1787.* Chapel Hill: University of North Carolina Press, 1969.

Yalof, Helen. "British Military Theatricals in Philadelphia During the Revolutionary War." PhD diss., New York University, 1972.

INDEX

Page numbers in italics refer to figures.

"An Act to Empower the Supreme Executive Council" (Pennsylvania, 1777), 19
Adams, John: on Continental Army's march through Philadelphia, 61; and disaffected in Pennsylvania, 52; on plundering by British army, 141; on Revolutionary leaders and tyranny, 10; Revolution in hearts and minds, 9; on trapping Howe in Philadelphia, 86; vision of the Revolution, 225, 270n7
advertisements: for goods, 160, 258n105; for runaway slaves, 156, 157, 259nn125–26
alienation: and confiscations, 115; and courts-martial, 142–44; and Germantown fires, 141–42; and Philadelphia elite, 162; and plundering, 140–41
allegiance, oaths of: to the British king, 117–18, 135–36, 255n39; to Patriot regime, 29, 190–91, 194, 201, 236n26. See also religious tests; Test Act
Allen, Andrew, 45–46, 47–49, 122, 183, 225
Allen, Elizabeth, 121–22
Allen, James: on alliance with France, 177, 178; on arrival of peace commission, 181; on Battle of Germantown, 85; on conditions in occupied Philadelphia, 162; death of, 225; and depreciation of income, 120; distancing from Revolution, 8, 16, 19–20; entering Philadelphia, 123; on entertainments in occupied Philadelphia, 161; on exodus from Philadelphia, 64; on freedom of speech in occupied Philadelphia, 160; on intelligence from women, 103; militia experience of, 19–20, 40–41, 119–20; oath of allegiance to Revolutionaries by, 191; occupation of Philadelphia's effect on morale, 244n99; on oppression by Revolutionaries, 70; on Philadelphia embargo, 89; on Revolutionary arsonists, 65; on rumors of Burgoyne's victory, 175; on suppression of dissent, 28; on sympathy with Loyalists, 183; and Trout Hall, 119, 122–23
Allen, John, 45, 46, 47–49, 122, 123, 225
Allen, William, 45, 225, 239n2
Allen, William, Jr., 46, 47–49, 122
Allentown, Pennsylvania, 119
Alms House, 152–53, 154–55
American Revolution, narratives of, 193, 225–27, 270nn7–8
American South, British assault on, 189
André, John, 90, 139, 252n146
Angell, Israel, 100, 104
Armstrong, John, 95, 104, 108, 208, 211
Arnold, Benedict, 174, 213–15, 221
Arping, Joel, 27
arson. See fires
Articles of Association (Congress, 1774), 37
"Astrea de Coelis," 203–4
Ayres, Samuel, 36

Balfour, Nesbit, 139, 187
Baurmeister, Carl Leopold: buying of slaves by, 157, 158; on condition of British army, 179; on Continental foraging expeditions, 251n127; on decline of Pennsylvania militia, 95; on departure of Philadelphians with British army, 184; on effect of plundering, 140; on flow of goods into occupied Philadelphia, 91, 251n133; on intelligence from women, 104; on uncertainty of evacuation of Philadelphia, 180–81
Beggarstown, Pennsylvania, 138–39
Benezet, Joyce, 169
Bettering House, 90
bills of attainder, 202, 206, 210–11, 265n6 (chap. 6)

286   Index

Black Pioneers, 155, 157–58, 185, 260n132
boarders, military, 131, 144–46, 165–68, 171
Bolton, John, 133
Bond, Thomas, 121
Boston Tea Party, 7
Boudinot, Elias, 55, 102
boycott of British goods, 34–35, 45, 204–5. *See also* commerce, political language of
Bradford, William, 2, 3
Brandywine Creek, Battle of, 57, 61–63
Brattle, James, 28
British army: ambivalence to allegiances, 162; as armed escorts for civilian traders, 113–14; cut off from waterborne supplies, 87–88, 89; damage to Philadelphia by, 202–3; desertion from, 144; evacuation of Philadelphia, 173–74, 178–80, 184, 187–89, 216–17; familiarity with, 127–28; foraging expeditions by, 140; hope for renewed military action, 178–80; as liberators, 129–30; living conditions of, 154–55, 179–80; march through Philadelphia, 65–66; numbers of, 179; and plundering, 130, 140–41; as protectors from foraging, 117; quartering officers in Philadelphia, 131; setting fires, 138–40; and slaves, 134, 157, 158–59, 259n124; and trade with civilians, 67, 92–93. *See also* Howe, William; Royal Navy
Brown, Robert, 142
Bryan, George, 209, 211, 217
Buck, Thomas, 142–43
Burgoyne, John, 46–47, 55, 173, 174–76
Bush, Solomon, 137

Cadwalader, John, 72
Caldwell, Samuel, 76, 77, 78
Carlisle, 5th Earl of (Frederick Howard), 188
Carlisle, Abraham, 215–16, 217
Casino, Joseph, 255n39
certificates for confiscated items, 102, 111, 249n84
Chambers, Stephen, 249n88
Chew, Benjamin, 60
citizen associations against traitors, 203–4, 266n11
Clarke, John, 92
Cliffe, Loftus, 152, 154, 176, 202
Clinton, Henry, 155, 158, 183, 188, 191, 259n124, 260n132
Clymer, David, 216

coercive force: Continental Army as, 58–61, 70; militias as, 67; and Revolutionaries, 41–42, 44, 58, 70, 116–17
College of Philadelphia, 83, 84
colonial currency. *See* currency, colonial
commerce, political language of, 33–37, 149–50, 237n39
"Committee for Tarring and Feathering," 24, 36
Committee of Inspection and Observation, Philadelphia, 45, 132
Committee of Privates, 216
Committee of Safety, 46
Committee of the City of Philadelphia, 16
confiscations, 102, 111, 115, 197, 249n84, 250n109. *See also* foraging expeditions; plundering
consent, expressions of: mandating of by Patriots, 28–32; militia service as, 37–41; and Revolution ideology, 10, 190; silence as sign of, 200, 211; through threats of violence, 43
constitution, Pennsylvania, 5
Constitutional Society, 219–22, 269n59
Continental Army: as alienating civilians, 115; as coercive force, 58–61, 70; desertions from, 177; foraging expeditions by, 113, 251n127; march through Philadelphia, 59–61; occupation of Whitall house, 196; opening of market for, 110–11; plundering by, 108, 119; punishments for trading with British, 108–10; strength of, 60–61, 179; winter campaign of, 72; winter quarters of, 70–73; women in, 60–61
Continental Association, 204–5
Continental Congress: disarming of disaffected by, 42–43; and perception of militia, 96–97; price fixing by, 101–2; waiving of personal rights by, 67–68
Continental currency. *See* currency, Continental
Cooper, John, 264n1
Cornwallis, Charles, Second Earl Cornwallis, 65, 129, 131, 136
Council of Safety, Pennsylvania: abolishment of, 70; and freedom of press, 24; and militia, 40–41; powers of, 26, 27, 69–70; on trade with occupied Philadelphia, 88
courts-martial as alienating, 142–44
Cowles, Solomon, 34
Crammond, J. C., 145–46, 165–68, 171, 180, 184, 223

Crane, David, 185
Cresheim, Pennsylvania, 138–39
Crooked Billet raid, 98, 99
Crowe, Robert Richard, 260n132
currency, colonial, 132–33, 146–51, *149*, 183, 258n105
currency, Continental: counterfeiting of, *149*; decline of, 101, 120, 131–32, 218, 248n77; and Job Whitall, 194, 197; refusal to accept, 132, 133
currency, hard, 102, 116, 147, 249n84. *See also* specie

Daughters of the American Revolution, 198
Deane, Silas, 219
Declaration of Independence, 195
de Kalb, Johann, 71
desertion: from British army, 144; from Continental Army, 177; from militias, 54–56
Deshler, David, 41
Dickinson, John, 17
Dillion, John, 142
Döhla, Johann, 158
Donop, Carl von, 195, 196
Downman, Francis, 65–66
Drinker, Elizabeth Sandwith: on arrival of British in Philadelphia, 65, 66; on banishment of disaffected, 199; on British army as liberators, 129; on British plundering, 137; on calm in Philadelphia, 130–31; on chaos in Philadelphia before invasion, 63–64; correspondence with Crammond, 184, 223; death of, 225; diary of, 224; as disaffected, 1, 6; on end of British occupation of Philadelphia, 186; on exile of H. Drinker, 4, 32; on fires near Philadelphia, 139; on hairstyles, 161, 205; home invasion of, 124, 126, 167; on the Meschianza, 162; and military boarders, 131, 144–46, 165–68; and petition to free Quaker exiles, 168–70; on Philadelphia embargo, 89, 91; residence of, 3; on rumors of Burgoyne's victory, 175; silhouette of, *166*; on uncertainty of British evacuation, 180–81
Drinker, Henry: after British occupation of Philadelphia, 223–24; death of, 225; as disaffected, 1; exiled to Virginia, 4, 76–77, 78, 82; health of, 169; letters home, 80–81, 127; and military boarders, 167–68, 171; plot to rescue, 215; residence of, 3; return from exile, 170;

171; silhouette of, *77*; and Tea Act, 35–37; and Test Act, 31–32
Drinker, Henry, Jr., 3, 65, 81
Drinker, John, 23, 25, 132, 199, 221
drunkeness, 144
Duane, James, 28
Duche, Andrew, 157
Duche, Mary, 144
Duncan, James, 142
Dunmore, Lord (John Murray, 4th Earl of Dunmore), 134, 254n33, 259n124

East India Company, 35, 36
Eddy, Mary, 146
Eden, William, 184, 188
Ellis, Joseph, 93, 97, 98
embargo on Philadelphia. *See* trade with British forces
Emlen, Samuel, 2
entertainments, 205, 214
Erskine, William, 187
Ewald, Johann: on attack of Valley Forge, 180; on departure of Philadelphians with British army, 184; on fires set by British army, 139; on illicit trade, 100; intelligence from William Smith, 83, 84–85; on Philadelphia embargo, 89, 91, 113, 251n133; on runaway slaves, 159; on sympathy with Loyalists, 182, 183
execution: and courts-martial, 143–44; and leniency, 208; opposition to, 216–18; for trading with British Army, 88, 107, 109; for treason, 215–18, 244n5
exiled Quakers: journey to Virginia, 76–82; petition to Washington, 168–70; plot to rescue, 78, 215, 244n5; return of, 170–71; and Supreme Executive Council, 4; and Test Act, 32
exodus from Philadelphia before British invasion, 64
exodus from Philadelphia of poor people, 153
expression, limits to freedom of, 23–27

Faden, William, *125*
Fairhill, destruction of, 138
Farmar, Eliza, 114
farmers, 91, 99–100, 102–3, 112–14, 117, 177, 228, 249n84
fashion, women's, 160–61, 205, 212, 260n142

fines: imposed by Patriots, 194, 265n4 (chap. 6); for refusing militia service, 38–39
fires: in Germantown, 138–40, 141–42, 255n54; by Revolutionaries, 65, 139
Fisher, John, 143–44
Fisher, Samuel Rowland, 132, 212
Fisher, Sarah Logan: on calm in Philadelphia, 130; on chaos in Philadelphia before invasion, 64; on end of British occupation of Philadelphia, 186; on fires set by British army, 139; on Philadelphia embargo, 89, 91; on plundering by British army, 137; on rumors of Burgoyne's victory, 175
Fisher, Thomas, 3
Fitzpatrick, Nathanial, 144
flour, 100, 102, 107–8, 114
foraging expeditions: by British army, 140; by Continental Army, 111–12, 113, 117, 251n127
Fort Mercer, 87–88, 89, 90, 147, 195–96, 198
Fort Mifflin, 87–88, 89, 90, 147
"Fort Wilson Riot," 220–21, 269n63
France, alliance with United States, 172, 173–74, 176–77
Franklin, Benjamin, 74, 172–73, 177
Franks, Rebecca, 143, 160–61, 212
Frazer, Persifor, 185
Fygis, Mary, 142

Galloway, Grace, 185, 213
Galloway, Joseph: and Colonial currency, 147; creation of civil police force, 141; and Howe's decision to capture Philadelphia, 47–48; loss of faith in Britain, 191–92; and Loyalists in Philadelphia, 117–18; as most powerful civilian, 260n139; and poor relief, 155, 259n121; proposed rescue of Quaker exiles, 78, 244n5; and renewed military action, 178, 182–83; and Serle, 49; tasked with calming Philadelphia residents, 131
Gates, Horatio, 55, 173, 174, 175
General Assembly, Pennsylvania, 16
George (Captain Smyth's slave), 157
Germain, Lord George, 239n9
Germantown, Battle of, 84–86
Germantown, Pennsylvania: British army in, 83; fires in, 138–40, 139, 141–42, 255n54; plundering in, 136, 137–38
Gerry, Elbridge, 72
Gilpin, Thomas, 169
Gist, Mordecai, 240n14

Grant, James: on abandonment of Philadelphia, 87; on Burgoyne's surrender, 175, 176; on condition of British army, 154; on disaffected in Pennsylvania, 52, 116; on evacuation of Philadelphia, 187–88; on lack of intelligence, 57–58; on supply of provisions, 56
Graydon, Alexander, 60, 61, 219
Greene, Nathanael, 66, 74, 111–12, 170, 178–79, 244n99
Grey, Charles, 187

hairstyles, 160–61, 205, 212
Hamilton, Alexander, 64
Hamilton, James, 121
Hancock, John, 53, 67, 68
Harcourt, William, 143
Harris, John, 82
Hessians, 128, 158
High, Mike, 133–34, 159, 185
HMS *Fanny*, 50
HMS *Porcupine*, 177
HMS *Zebra*, 142
horses, 56
Howe, Richard, 47
Howe, William: and Black Pioneers, 158; and colonial currency, 133, 150–51; concern for Philadelphia poor, 153; on decision to capture Philadelphia, 46–49; destruction of Forts Mercer and Mifflin, 90; failure of Loyalists to join army, 52, 163, 183, 239n9; foraging expedition in New Jersey, 112; need for geographic intelligence, 57; on oaths of allegiance to British king, 135–36; and plundering, 50–51, 137, 140–41; and pro-British propaganda, 175; proposal to rescue exiled Quakers by, 78; as protector of Philadelphia inhabitants, 124, 127, 130; trade with civilians in New Jersey, 92–93; uncertainty of evacuation of Philadelphia, 180–81
Howell, Joshua, 126
Humphreys, Whitehead, 221
Humphries, James, Jr., 24
Hunt, John, 2, 3, 169
Hunt, Rachel, 169
Huntington, Jedidiah, 140

independence, rejection of, 46
Indian Queen Tavern, 26–27

intelligence networks, civilian, 57–58, 63, 84–85, 98, 112, 131, 248n72; women in, 103, 104–5
Irvine, James, 72

James (David Crane's slave), 185
James, Abel, 35–37, 126, 129
James, Chalkley, 124, 126
Jameson, John, 92, 102, 108, 249n88, 250n113
Jane (Drinker servant), 224
Johnstone, George, 188
Jones, Joseph, 52, 72
Jones, Owen, 168
Jones, Susanna, 168, 169
juries, leniency of, 208
justices of the peace, 25–26, 31

Kelly, Ann, 124, 126
Kern, Samuel, 62
Kirk, Philip, 250n109
Knox, Henry, 71
Kunze, Margaretta, 151

Lacey, John, Jr., 93–94, 96, 99, 109, 114, 117, 250n113
Lafayette, Marquis de, 71
Lee, Charles, 170
leniency, 207–18; and Arnold, 213–15; and beginnings of independent government, 216–17; and Constitutional Society, 220; of juries, 208; political benefits of, 211–12; and women, 212–13
Levan, Daniel, 81
livestock, 56, 197, 250n109
Loyalists: and British evacuation, 182, 183–84; in narrative of the Revolution, 226; in Pennsylvania, 21–22; promise of in Pennsylvania, 48, 49, 52, 163, 183, 239n9

Madison, James, 33
Marchant, Henry, 61
Marshall, Christopher: on condition of British army, 154; and Continental currency, 101; investigation of Brattle by, 27–28; and religious test, 30; and starvation in occupied Philadelphia, 151; on trade with occupied Philadelphia, 92; and women as conveyors of provisions, 103
martial law, 68, 88, 106, 250n109
Maryland, 51, 56

Matlack, Timothy, 199, 209, 219, 221
Maxwell, William, 98
McAllister, Richard, 52–53, 54, 95, 247n56
McKean, Thomas, 78, 80, 204, 207, 211, 216
McSkimming, William, 143
"merchant-strangers," 147–48, 150
Meschianza, 161, 162, 212
Mifflin, Thomas, 219
militia, Maryland, 85
militia, New Jersey, 85, 88, 93, 97–98, 112, 192
militia, Pennsylvania: as alienating civilians, 115; at Battle of Germantown, 85; vs. Constitutional Society, 220–21; decline in numbers, 54–56, 93–97, 98, 99, 247n56; and James Allen, 20, 40–41, 119–20; and Philadelphia embargo, 88; plundering by, 41; service in, 37–41; strength of, 52–56, 240n14; Washington on lack of support by, 55–56; in York County, 52–53, 54
militias: at Battle of Germantown, 85; coercive force of, 67; Continental Congress's perception of, 96–97; disarming of Non-Associators by, 43; punishments for civilian traders with British by, 108–10
militias, New England, 55
militia service: as expression of consent, 37–41; as mandatory, 38–39, 54; and voting privileges, 39
Miller, Peter, 183–84
mills, destruction of, 107–8, 250n113
money: as loyalty, 149–50. See also currency
Monmouth, Battle of, 192
Montrésor, John, 66
Mordecai, Jacob, 131
Morris, Mary, 212
Morris, Robert, 17, 72, 219, 221, 248n77
Morris, Samuel, 79
Morton, Robert: on British invasion of Philadelphia, 128–29, 130, 142; on British plundering, 137, 140, 141; and colonial currency, 151; and Continental currency, 131; and executions, 143; on fires in Germantown, 138, 139, 255n54; on Philadelphia embargo, 91; on rumors of Burgoyne's victory, 175
Muenchhausen, Friedrich von, 57, 175, 176, 177, 179, 251n133
Muhlenberg, Henry Melchoir: and Black Pioneers, 155; on coercive force, 42; conversion to Revolutionary will, 28–29; on

Muhlenberg, Henry Melchoir (*continued*) disaffected, 1; on fate of Quakers after evacuation, 186; and fires in Germantown, 138; on liberation of slaves by British, 134; and militia service, 247n56; on refusal to swear allegiance, 31, 201; on starvation in occupied Philadelphia, 89; on women as conveyors of provisions, 103
Murray, Francis, 94–95, 144
Murray, James, 162

Nesbit, Alexander, 76, 77, 78
New Jersey: foraging expeditions in, 112; militia in, 85, 88, 93, 97–98, 112, 192; trade with British army in, 92–93
Newport, Rhode Island, 189
newspapers: ads for goods in, 160; and freedom of press, 23–25; hostility toward traitors in, 202–3; misinformation about Franklin, 177; pro-British propaganda in, 174–76; publication of boycott violators, 34–35; runaway slave ads in, 156, 157, 259nn125–26
New York, 24, 159, 173
New York City, New York, 189, 248n76, 249n87, 255n40
Nicholls, Maria, 143
Non-Associators, 38–40, 43, 120, 238n50
Norris, J. P., 65
Norris, Mrs., 131, 146

"occupation," 12, 234n14–15
Overseers of the Poor, 152
Owings, Robert, 29

Paine, Thomas, 219
Paoli, Battle of, 57, 66–67
Parke, Thomas, 140
Parker, Josiah, 53
Patriotic Society, 204, 207–8, 210, 216, 266n11
Patriots. *See* Revolutionaries, Pennsylvania
peace commission, British, 181–82, 188
Peale, Charles Willson, 213, 219, 221
Peebles, John, 66
Peg (Persifor Frazer's slave), 185
Pemberton, James, 129, 170, 171
Pemberton, John, 2–3
Pemberton, Mary, 143, 169
Pemberton, Phebe, 143, 169
Penn, John, 191

Pennsylvania: disaffected in, 52; as a fragmented society, 15; as last to declare independence, 15; new government of, 17; Patriot government after British evacuation, 190; promise of Loyalists in, 48, 49, 52, 163, 183, 239n9. *See also* militia, Pennsylvania; Philadelphia, Pennsylvania
Pennsylvania Evening Post: and former slaves in Philadelphia, 134; on French alliance, 176–77; hostility toward traitors in, 202; listings of traitors in, 202; and occupation of Philadelphia, 24, 160; pro-British propaganda in, 174, 176; rumors of Franklin's death, 172; and slave sales, 157
Pennsylvania Gazette, 24–25
Pennsylvania government: Continental Army's winter quarters, 72–73; as immune from judicial interference, 80; increasing power of, 68–70. *See also* Patriots; Revolutionaries, Pennsylvania
Pennsylvania Ledger, 24, 157
Pennsylvania Mercury, 24
Pennsylvania Packet, 202, 212
perjury, 142
Philadelphia, Pennsylvania: armed escorts for civilian traders to, 113–14; breaches in embargo of, 90–93; British army numbers in, 179; British capture of, 11–12, 49, 195; British evacuation of, 173–74, 178–80; capture of as a trap, 86–87; chaos in before British capture, 63–64; comparison to modern city, 12–15; Continental money in, 101, 131–32, 248n77; crime in, 142; damage to, 202–3; departure of citizens from, 128; E. Allen's permission to enter, 121–22; effect of occupation on morale, 244n99; elite in, 160–62; encouragement for Howe to capture, 46–49; end of British occupation, 184; evacuation of as sign of British loss, 187–89; evacuation of people from near, 114–15; fires by Revolutionaries, 65, 139; and flour, 107–8; hearts and minds won to Revolutionary ideology, 199; Howe as protector of, 124; James Allen entering, 123; lessons learned from British occupation, 189–90; limits to freedom of expression in, 23–27; living conditions of British in, 179–80; Loyalists after British evacuation of, 183–84, 185; maps of, 14, 125; march of British army through, 65–66; march of Continental Army

through, 59–61; military boarders in, 131, 144–46, 165–68, 171; misinformation about Franklin, 177; new military projects in, 180–81; newspapers in, 23–25; occupation as mild government, 162; plundering in, 136–37; poor relief in, 153, 259n121; population of, 137; pro-British propaganda in, 174–76; Quaker population after British occupation, 186; reemergence of trade in, 100, 248n76; rejection of independence, 16–17; reluctance to serve in militia, 53, 240n12; reoccupation by Revolutionary radicals, 206; residents fleeing with British army from, 184, 263n42; runaway slaves in, 259nn125–26; slaves after British evacuation, 185–86, 263n46; slave sales in, 156–57; starvation in, 86, 89, 151–53, 251n133; stripping of area around, 105–7; uncertainty of evacuation, 180–81; war's effect on economy, 218; women in, 103–5, 249n88, 266n16; yellow fever epidemic in, 224
Philadelphia City Cavalry, First Troop of, 46
Pickering, Timothy, 55, 212
Pleasants, Mary, 169
Pleasants, Samuel, 170
plundering: as alienating, 140–41; by British army, 50–51, 130, 136–37, 255n39; and civil police force, 141; by Continental Army, 108, 119; as indiscriminate, 137–38; of Job Whitall, 197–98, 265n12; and militias, 41
police force, civil, 141, 142
Polly (ship), 35–36
poor relief, sources of, 152–53, 155, 259n121
Potter, James, 16, 92
poverty, 152
press, freedom of, 23–24
Proclamation of Attainder, 215–16
propaganda, pro-British, 174–76
prostitution, 134
Proud, Robert: on British army as liberators, 129; on calm in Philadelphia, 131; and economic hardship, 154, 155; on Philadelphia embargo, 91, 251n133; on starvation in Philadelphia, 151
Provincial Conference, 29
provisions, 103–4
punishments, corporal, 107
punishments of civilians, 142–43

Quakers: after British occupation, 186, 265n4 (chap. 6); assault on homes by Revolutionaries, 223; and courts-martial, 143–44; and religious tests, 29–30; as source of intelligence, 248n72. *See also* exiled Quakers
quartering of officers. *See* boarders, military
Queen's Rangers, 114, 144

Rankin, James, 16
rape, 142, 143
Rawle, William, 136
Rayneval, Conrad Alexandre Gérard de, 206
Reading, Pennsylvania, 78–79
Red Bank Battlefield Park, 193
Reed, Esther de Berdt, 117
Reed, Joseph: and Arnold, 213, 214; and Continental currency, 101; and execution, 216; on familiarity with the British, 115, 127; and Fort Wilson Riot, 221, 269n63; intolerance of dissent by, 210; on oaths of allegiance, 191; on penalties for illicit trade, 104, 108; on placement of winter quarters, 71–72; and uncertainty of British evacuation, 181
religious tests, 29–30, 236nn28–29
"Remonstrance of Council and Assembly to Congress," 73
Republican Society, 219–22
Revolutionaries, Pennsylvania: assault on Quaker homes by, 223; and British evacuation, 182; creation of own government, 20–21; declining confidence in, 115–16; enforcement of militia laws, 54; establishment of government after British evacuation, 190; expressions of consent to, 190; fines and military taxes imposed by, 194, 265n4 (chap. 6); freedom from British trade, 204–5; limits to freedom of expression by, 23–27; mandating expressions of consent, 28–32; and militia attendance, 38–39; oaths of allegiance to, 190–91; reoccupation of Philadelphia, 206; Republican vs. Constitutional Societies, 219–22; suppression of dissent, 28; threats of personal violence by, 194; use of coercive force, 44
Revolutionary ideology: and coercive force, 41–42, 116–17; consequences of, 10–11; conversion of opponents, 28–29; as dependent on consent, 26; disaffected as threat to, 22–23, 227; intolerance toward neutrality, 200; Non-Associators as threat to, 39–40; winning of Philadelphia hearts and minds, 199

rights, waiving of, 67–68
Rittenhouse, David, 2
Rivington's New-York Gazetteer, 24
Roberdeau, Daniel, 269n59
Roberts, John, 65, 78, 170, 215–16, 217–18, 244n5
Robertson, Alexander, 34
Royal Navy, 49, 56–57, 87–88, 89, 90
Rush, Benjamin, 216, 219

Sandwith, Mary, 124, 126
Saratoga, Battles of, 11, 55, 173
Sergeant, Jonathan D., 199
Serle, Ambrose: disaffection in Maryland, 51; at Elk River, 50; influence of Allen brothers on, 49; Loyalists after British evacuation, 172, 183, 191, 192; and Philadelphia embargo, 89; and pro-British propaganda, 175; and promises of Loyalist support, 47, 48, 183; and uncertainty of British evacuation, 181; on uncertainty of British evacuation, 180
shaming, public, 142
Shippen, Margaret, 214
Shippen, William, 121
Sibble, Henry, 224
Sibble, Philip George, 224
Simcoe, John Graves, 180
slaves: ads for runaways, 157, 259nn125–26; after end of British occupation, 185–86, 263n46; in the Black Pioneers, 155, 157–58, 185, 260n132; British as liberators, 133–34, 254n33, 259n124; British policies toward, 155–59; as entertainment, 158–59; in narrative of the Revolution, 226; sales of, 156–57; and Serle, 51
slaves, female, 134
Smith, J. B., 115
Smith, Thomas, 16
Smith, William, 83–85
social ostracism, 206, 214
specie, 150, 154. *See also* currency, hard
Stamp Act protests, 19, 33
Stansbury, Joseph, 27, 147, 150, 214
starvation: in Philadelphia, 89, 151–53; at Valley Forge, 86, 112
Stedman, Charles, 161
Stewart, Walter, 92, 102, 104–5
Stirling, Lord (William Alexander), 100, 102
Strachey, Henry, 161, 175–76
Supreme Executive Council: authority to imprison, 4, 19; and Council of Safety, 69–70; James Allen for treason for entering Philadelphia, 123; and leniency, 210; and Pennsylvania militia, 96, 97; Proclamation of Attainder by, 215–16; proclamations of traitors by, 201–2; return of Quaker exiles, 170, 171; search for enemies of the state, 1–5

Tea Act, 33, 34–37
Test Act: and citizenship, 209; and Constitutional Society, 220; institution of, 30; and James Allen, 120; leniency of, 208–9; and Quaker exiles, 31–32, 80; revival of, 201, 206, 265n4 (chap. 6). *See also* allegiance, oaths of
tests, religious, 29–30, 236nn28–29
theft, 142
Thomas, Arthur, 27, 132
Tony (Samuel Hudson's slave), 156, 259n126
Towne, Benjamin, 160, 191, 202, 207
Townsend, Joseph, 61–63
Townshend boycotts, 34
Townshend Duties, 33
trade with British forces: armed escorts for, 113–14; economic cause of, 99–100, 248n70; embargo against, 89, 90–93, 251n133; and execution, 88, 107, 252n146; military punishments for, 108–10; reemergence of in Philadelphia, 100, 248n76; between Royal Navy and civilians, 56–57; as threat to Revolution, 67; and women, 103, 249n87
traitors: and citizen associations, 203–4, 266n11; departure from Philadelphia, 183–84, 185; proclamations of by Supreme Executive Council, 201–2; refusal of neighbors to testify against, 207–8; seizure of property from, 88
treason: executions for, 207, 215–18; and James Allen, 123; and martial law, 68; and Test Act, 31
trials, disregard for, 70
Trout Hall, 119, 121, 122, 123
Tryon, William, 28
tyranny, Revolutionary ideology and, 10–11
Tyson, Matthias, 106

United States, alliance with France, 172, 173–74, 176–77

Valley Forge: as Continental Army's winter quarters, 73; creation of market near, 110–11; starvation at, 86, 112, 179

Varnum, James Mitchell, 106
venereal disease, 144
vengeance, Revolutionary, 204
violence, threats of, 43, 194. *See also* coercive force
voting privileges: and militiamen, 39; religious tests for, 29–30, 236n26

Walker, Nathanial, 80
Walton, George, 86–87
Washington, George: appointment of Arnold, 213; attempt to reclaim Philadelphia, 84–86; breaches in embargo of Philadelphia, 90–93; complete freedom, 88; on conditions of British army, 154–55; creation of market, 110–11; on disaffected in Pennsylvania, 21, 51, 52; and foraging expeditions, 111–12; increasing powers given to, 67–68, 250n109; on lack of intelligence, 58, 63; on lack of militia support, 55–56; march through Philadelphia, 59–61; on Pennsylvania militia's numbers, 93–97; permission for E. Allen to enter Philadelphia, 121; on Philadelphia as a trap, 87; and Quaker exiles, 168–70; on strength of Continental Army, 179; to strip country around Philadelphia, 105–7; winter quarters of, 70–73; on women as conveyors of provisions, 103
Washington, Martha, 170
Watson, John Fanning, 65
Wayne, Anthony, 51–52, 66, 95, 97, 112

West Indies, 174
Wharton, Thomas, 76
Wharton, Thomas, Jr., 94, 96, 97, 171
Whitall, Ann, 193, 194–95, 196, 265n8, 265n13
Whitall, Benjamin, 264n1
Whitall, David, 265n11
Whitall, James, 193, 194–95, 196, 198
Whitall, Job: and battle at Fort Mercer, 195–96; diary of, 193–98; intrusion of war in daily life, 195; signs of war in diary of, 196–97, 265n11
William (runaway slave), 157
Willing, Thomas, 130
Wilson, James, 216, 219, 221
Winchester, Virginia, exiled Quakers' journey to, 77–82
Witherspoon, John, 191
Withington, Ebenezer, 34–35
women: and the Continental Army, 60–61; leniency toward, 212–13; in narrative of the Revolution, 226; and politicization of commerce, 237n39, 249n87; as primary conveyors of provisions and intelligence, 103–5, 249n88; social ostracism of, 206, 214, 266n16; as traitors, 204–6
writs of habeas corpus, 78

yellow fever epidemic, 198, 224
York County, Pennsylvania, militia in, 52–53, 54
Yorktown, surrender at, 223

ACKNOWLEDGMENTS

We historians have an advantage over the novelists in that we are, almost by definition, always aided by a cadre of coauthors from the past, men and women whose lives laid out the twists and turns of our narratives long before we began to compose them. More people than I can ever know have had a hand in preserving the documents and artifacts which are the foundation for all my storytelling and analysis, but two have provided special inspiration along the way. Their perspectives and experiences, their frankness and emotion, and (crucially) their choice to record so much of their lives and thoughts, brought particular meaning and enjoyment to the work. My sincere thanks to Elizabeth Sandwith Drinker (1735–1807) and James Allen (1742–1778).

Among the living I am indebted, first, to David Waldstreicher, who has supported my pursuit of history from its very beginning. Over the years he has been a dedicated adviser, an insightful critic of my research, an advocate for my writing, and my friend. My work on the British occupation of Philadelphia would never have begun without him. The greatest appreciation is also due to Gregory Urwin, Susan E. Klepp, Judith L. Van Buskirk, Michael McDonnell, Daniel Ritcher, Michael Zuckerman, Brenna O'Rourke Holland, Susan Brandt, and many others, who have all improved the preceding pages through their insights, criticisms, suggestions, and encouragement. They have been an unending source of enthusiasm even when my own passion wavered.

This project would have been impossible without the assistance provided by the good people of the Historical Society of Pennsylvania, the David Library of the American Revolution, the William L. Clements Library, Fort Ticonderoga, and the McNeil Center for Early American Studies. I also wish to gratefully acknowledge the immense generosity of the American Council of Learned Societies and the Pennsylvania State Society Daughters of the American Colonists, who expressed their belief in the value of my research with many kind words and much practical aid. I am grateful to the University of Pennsylvania Press for publishing this book and particularly to Robert Lockart, who could not have been more supportive and has shown me far more patience than I deserve.

Finally, I cannot sufficiently thank the people who took countless hours out of their own busy lives to maintain my home, family, and sanity while I buried myself in old books or tapped endlessly at the keyboard. Sarah Sullivan and Jackie Clifton deserve far more appreciation than I can possibly express here and I hope they know that I am ever mindful and grateful for their labors and love. Thank you.

www.ingramcontent.com/pod-product-compliance
Lightning Source LLC
Chambersburg PA
CBHW021850230426
43671CB00006B/338